The Emergence of a Tradition: Essays in Honor of Jesús Huerta de Soto, Volume I

David Howden • Philipp Bagus
Editors

The Emergence of a Tradition: Essays in Honor of Jesús Huerta de Soto, Volume I

Money and the Market Process

palgrave
macmillan

Editors
David Howden
Department of Business
Saint Louis University –
Madrid Campus
Madrid, Spain

Philipp Bagus
Department of Applied Economics I
and History of Economic Institutions
(and Moral Philosophy)
Universidad Rey Juan Carlos
Madrid, Spain

ISBN 978-3-031-17416-2 ISBN 978-3-031-17414-8 (eBook)
https://doi.org/10.1007/978-3-031-17414-8

This Palgrave Macmillan imprint is published by the registered company Springer Nature Switzerland AG.
The registered company address is: Gewerbestrasse 11, 6330 Cham, Switzerland

Contents

List of Contributors

Anton Afanasiev Central Economic and Mathematics Institute of Russian Academy of Sciences, Moscow, Russia

Romain Baeriswyl Swiss National Bank, Zurich, Switzerland

Philipp Bagus Department of Applied Economics I and History of Economic Institutions (and Moral Philosophy), Universidad Rey Juan Carlos, Madrid, Spain

Toby Baxendale London, UK

Peter J. Boettke George Mason University, Fairfax, VA, USA

Francisco Cabrillo Complutense University of Madrid, Madrid, Spain

Óscar R. Carreiro Universidad Rey Juan Carlos, Madrid, Spain

Leef H. Dierks Lübeck University of Applied Sciences, Lübeck, Germany

Richard M. Ebeling The Citadel: Military College of South Carolina, Charleston, SC, USA

Carmelo Ferlito Center for Market Education, Kuala Lumpur, Malaysia

Eduardo Fernández Luiña Universidad Francisco Marroquín, Guatemala City, Guatemala

Bernardo Ferrero Ciencias Sociales y Juridicas, Universidad Rey Juan Carlos, Madrid, Spain

Santiago García Echevarría Universidad de Alcalá, Alcalá de Henares, Spain

David Howden Department of Business, Saint Louis University – Madrid Campus, Madrid, Spain

Juan Huerta de Soto Huarte Cobas Asset Management, Madrid, Spain

Jörg Guido Hülsmann University of Angers, Angers, France

Massimiliano Neri Universidad Francisco Marroquín, Guatemala City, Guatemala

Thorsten Polleit University of Bayreuth, Bayreuth, Germany

Shawn Ritenour Grove City College, Grove City, PA, USA

Carlos Rodríguez Braun Complutense University of Madrid (Retired), Madrid, Spain

Joseph T. Salerno Mises Institute, Auburn, AL, USA

Gunther Schnabl Leipzig University, Leipzig, Germany

Pedro Schwartz Universidad Camilo José Cela, Madrid, Spain

Josef Šíma Metropolitan University Prague, Prague, Czech Republic

Mark Skousen Chapman University, Orange, CA, USA

Juan Torras Instituto von Mises Barcelona, Barcelona, Spain

Leonidas Zelmanovitz Liberty Fund, Indianapolis, IN, USA

List of Figures

Hayek's Overinvestment Theory and the Stability of the Euro Area

The Greatest Economist Who Ever Lived

The Entrepreneur and Entrepreneurship: A Practical Framework for Firm Analysis

List of Tables

The Austrian Theory of Consumption Period Planning: Some Neglected Contributions from the Interwar Period

Jesús Huerta de Soto: A Biographical Sketch

David Howden and Philipp Bagus

Thousands of leaflets rained down on the theater goers. The Spanish civil war had just ended and there was as much uncertainty as to Spain's future as ever. The military dictatorship of *El Generalissimo* Francisco Franco had held strong power over the country since the war's end in 1939. Dissenters existed, quietly for the most part, biding their time until the country would be prepared for another change of power. Among these dissenters were the communists and their sympathizers. But other claims to the Spanish government also existed. For Jesús Huerta Ballester the obvious and rightful claimant was Don Juan, the count of Barcelona: King in exile and claimant to the Spanish throne as Juan III.

Jesús Huerta threw these leaflets helter-skelter in the crowded theater before running for the exit. Yelling "fire" in a crowded theater was more

D. Howden (✉)
Department of Business, Saint Louis University – Madrid Campus, Madrid, Spain
e-mail: david.howden@slu.edu

P. Bagus
Department of Applied Economics I and History of Economic Institutions (and Moral Philosophy), Universidad Rey Juan Carlos, Madrid, Spain
e-mail: philipp.bagus@urjc.es

D. Howden, P. Bagus (eds.), *The Emergence of a Tradition: Essays in Honor of Jesús Huerta de Soto, Volume I*,
https://doi.org/10.1007/978-3-031-17414-8_1

than enough reason to be paid a visit by the police. This act of political subversion, small as it was, was all the more so.

As the leaflets rained down the curious theater going could read for himself the simple message:

> Ni comunismo.
> Ni enchufes políticos.
> Monarquía.
> Viva Juan III.
>
> Neither communism.
> Nor corrupt politicians.
> Monarchy.
> Long live Juan III.

The brief message was clear. There was no future to be found in the politicians in power, nor in the communist pretenders. The country's best hope laid in the restoration of the Bourbon monarchy.[1]

Jesús Huerta de Soto Ballester, known today chiefly as an economist and political theorist, was born to this Jesús Huerta Ballester. If Jesús the younger is known as one of the loudest liberal voices in the Spanish-speaking world, it was from his father, Jesús the elder, that this quality emerged.

A lieutenant in the Spanish Marine Corps, Jesús Huerta Ballester was proudly Spanish but not deceived by the peace the fascists carved out after the civil war. A classical liberal, he kept a well-stocked library in the family's home at 38 Príncipe de Vergara street in Madrid. Milton Friedman's 1962 classic *Capitalism and Freedom* lay hidden among the broken spines. When a young Jesús Huerta de Soto stumbled on the book at the age of fourteen, he was immediately drawn to the premises. Primed as he was from his father, he quickly absorbed the message of freedom. Capitalism was necessary for a liberal society. Not the liberal society emerging on the West coast of the United States in Universities like Berkeley, but in the European tradition stemming from the Scholastics and the Enlightenment. Spain was in the midst of a dictatorship that had sealed the country off from the new cultural and intellectual currents gaining traction in the Western world. From his home in Madrid, Jesús was well-positioned to

[1] For his subversive actions, Jesús the father was jailed, fined 50,000 pesetas, and had his passport revoked.

understand Friedman's new message in the context of an intellectual climate of a time long past.

It wasn't what Friedman wrote that hooked young Jesús, though it certainly didn't hurt. It was the words that Friedman did not write. It was the "radicals," mentioned but not developed in detail, that captured his attention. According to Friedman, "Recognizing the implicit threat to individualism, the intellectual descendants of the Philosophical Radicals—Dicey, Mises, Hayek, and Simons, to mention only a few—feared that a continued movement toward centralized control of economic activity would prove *The Road to Serfdom*, as Hayek entitled his penetrating analysis of the process." The "road to serfdom" surely described what the young Huerta de Soto saw before his eyes. Who were these thinkers that presciently warned of its arrival?

If there was a message to take away from Friedman's tome, it was that the free society required capitalism to flourish. The teenage Huerta de Soto was sold. He would dedicate his life to studying economics in a bid to help freedom prevail.

Of course, University would get in the way of these plans. Enrolling in October 1973 in the Universidad CEU San Pablo, then a branch campus of the venerable Complutense University of Madrid, the seventeen-year-old Jesús chose to study law, economics, and actuarial science.[2] Richard Lipsey's introductory textbook, *An Introduction to Positive Economics*, was how Jesús cut his teeth learning economics in a formal setting. Here that name, Mises, popped up again. This time there was a book associated with it: *Human Action*. Finally, something tangible for Huerta de Soto to latch on to. The only problem was that such books, much less English language books, were not just found in any bookstore on the streets of Madrid in the early 1970s. Still, the lead was revealed and now Jesús knew where to look to find this alluded to but never fully revealed Mises character.

But then, God reveals himself in mysterious ways. Joaquín Reig Albiol, the son of a Spanish liberal politician from Valencia, stumbled upon Henry Hazlitt's Newsweek review of *Human Action* some decades earlier. Ordering the book from the United States, Reig was entranced by the beauty and clarity of the analysis. Completing his doctoral studies on the works of Ludwig von Mises, it was Reig who translated the treatise into

[2] Decades earlier, Huerta de Soto's grandfather, Jesús Huerta Peña, would become the first actuary in Spain.

Spanish. And it was this Reig translation that Jesús Huerta de Soto would stumble upon accidentally, though as if he were directed by a greater power, in a quiet Madrid bookstore.

Armed with what would have to suffice for the embodiment of Mises, Jesús devoured the work. If his mind was open to the ideas, his eyes were closed to the intellectual community that emerged after the Spanish civil war, and especially after the 1960 Spanish language translation of *Human Action*. This absence would change following a serendipitous late-night meeting with an old friend of his father.

At home in the Príncipe de Vergara apartment, the same apartment he was born in and below which he would work as president of the life insurance company to this day, Jesús studied *Human Action*. The hour was late, even by Madrid standards. Jesús's father returned home with José Ramón Canosa, friends since their time together in the Spanish Marine Corps. If the food was plentiful while the two friends caught up, the drinks were more copious. Tipsy, but no worse for the wear, José Ramón captured the student reading this single text at his desk—his lone insight into the liberalism of Mises.

"Do you like the book?" José Ramón asked. "I have a friend who runs a seminar. They discuss Mises. Maybe you would like to attend?"

The seminar in question was organized by the Reig brothers—Joaquín, the Spanish translator of *Human Action*, and his brother Luis. The members of the group read like a "who's who" list of the Spanish liberal community of the early 1970s. Lucas Beltrán Flórez, professor of economics at the Complutense University of Madrid and Huerta de Soto's future doctoral advisor, was there. Also present was Julio Pascual Vicente, chief economist of the Union of Spanish Entrepreneurs. Alfonso Enrique de Salamanca and the two Reig brothers were stalwart attendees. And a young Pedro Schwartz, rightly proud of his recently completed studies under Karl Popper at the London School of Economics, figured large.

Young Jesús became a consistent figure at the gathering. So too did his father, at least for the first two years. Still younger than the driving age of eighteen, the elder Huerta Ballester dutifully drove his son to the meetings and the two immersed themselves in the intellectual climate together.

The publication of Rothbard's *For a New Liberty* was a turning point for many classical liberals. Coming in the midst of the Vietnam War, the book was a controversial reader for the average conservative. But it carved out a niche and a way forward for the determined libertarian. Instead of being a response to socialism, libertarianism emerged, in Rothbard's view, as a response to conservatism. A faithful application of the doctrines of self-ownership and homesteading results in a bold anarcho-capitalist view of the world.

The book was controversial within broader circles, but also within the Reig seminar. Joaquín was a classical liberal, similar to Mises. His brother Luis took the anarcho-capitalist stance, following Rothbard. Indeed, as the death of Franco neared the seminar's focus would sometimes turn to the political future of Spain and what the best way forward would be. After reading *For a New Liberty* Jesús Huerta de Soto could see no other option: anything less than full anarcho-capitalism would be a failure. Many others take the route of getting "softer" and more forgiving as they age. With Jesús one gets the opposite impression: he seems to become more "radical" with each passing day.

The library in the family home was soon inundated with a flood of new books. Hundreds of books, as Jesús ordered primers and tomes alike to augment his formal studies at university. This autodidactic intellectual fulfillment rivaled his degree as the foundation for what would come later. In class, Jesús would come to be known as a gadfly, always questioning his professors and demanding clarifications. If he was persistent with his questioning, they were not the demands of an ill-informed student. Jesús would frequently pass his classes with the *matricula de honor*, the highest grade in the class. At seventeen, Jesús passed his *Bachiller Superior*—pre-University studies necessary for admission to the Spanish University system until 1977—with the highest grade in his class. His undergraduate degree (a five-year *licenciado* in the Spanish system at the time) in law was conferred on September 23, 1978, *cum laude*. His accreditation as an actuary followed soon after, also *cum laude*. His *licenciatura* in business and economics (with specializations in economics and finance) followed on December 4, 1981, also *cum laude*.

With his formal studies done, Jesús was bound by his name to start work at the company his grandfather founded. He would be the third Jesús Huerta to run the company. Not surprisingly, his own son, aptly named Jesús Huerta de Soto works alongside him and is the only employee to leave the office later than his father. And this Jesús Huerta de Soto's son, not surprisingly also named Jesús Huerta de Soto, will someday be the fifth of his name to run the company. On September 1, 1978, at the age of twenty-two, Jesús started working in the professional capacity his name fated to him.

But through this all, the itch to study, to understand the world, kept gnawing at him. The seed that Friedman sowed—that capitalism was necessary for a liberal society—was being germinated all these years. It just needed space to flourish. Not content to terminate his studies and enter the working world fulltime, Huerta de Soto applied to study in the United States. Being the recipient of a prestigious scholarship offered by the Central Bank of Spain, the University of Pennsylvania, Berkeley, and Stanford all offered Jesús a spot in their MBA programs. The wealth of options created a new and obvious problem: which to choose?

In the end the choice was easy. Jesús's future wife, Sonsoles, had recently moved to California for postgraduate studies in the psychology of education at UCLA. During her sophomore year she transferred to Stanford. With his future happiness on the line, the decision of which MBA program to attend required no further thought.

If the decision was swift and sure, its ramifications were long-lived. Sonsoles and Jesús would go on to have six children (and, at present, eighteen grandchildren). If Huerta de Soto has had a particularly productive career, like most men he points first to his wife when asked how. It was Sonsoles's care of the family and household that gave him the time to study and write. He is the first to admit that his academic and professional achievements are as much her achievements as they are his.

In hindsight, although the decision to study at Stanford was based on reasons only the heart knows, it had important repercussions also on his intellectual development.

The next two years saw the couple living a sinful life together in Stanford. Jesús graduated with his MBA in 1983. But before returning to Spain, he had the opportunity to meet many of the key figures of not just the American libertarian cognoscenti, but also those who came to define the Austrian School of Economics following the death of Ludwig von Mises in 1973. Chief among these were Friedrich Hayek, Murray Rothbard and, later on, Israel Kirzner.

The depth and erudition of the young Huerta de Soto was immediately apparent to all three scholars. Hayek was impressed by the degree to which Jesús marked up without prejudice the copies of his works. At times it seemed as though the Austrian was speaking to one of the few men who actually read *The Pure Theory of Capital*. Even more impressive, this young Spaniard, perhaps a distant relative from a Habsburg Empire long past, seemed to understand the rehabilitation of capital theory that Hayek struggled with. Rothbard was caught off guard by the foreigner. He was funny and seemed to have read and absorbed everything that Rothbard wrote—like a silent observer from thousands of miles away.

Although he would not have the opportunity to meet Kirzner until later, it was this scholar that most affected Huerta de Soto's general approach to economics. The publication of *Competition and Entrepreneurship* in 1973 was a watershed moment. It exposed the degree to which Austrian ideas could be bridged with those prevailing in the mainstream, but without the neoclassical baggage that normally marked the synthesis. Rothbard had pioneered a similar approach earlier in *Man, Economy, and State*, but had been bogged down by the standard use of supply and demand curves. In Kirzner the baggage was shed, and the analysis was freed of its neoclassical shackles. Austrian economics was given another pure revival, similar to that which followed Mises's publication of *Human Action*.[3]

By 1982, Hayek proposed to the Mont Pelerin Society to admit Huerta de Soto as a member. At that year's meeting in Berlin he became, at age twenty-six, the Society's youngest member.

Returning to Spain to resume his position at the helm of the family business and start his family, his attention once again turned to his formal studies. At the direction of Lucas Beltrán Flórez of the Reig seminar, Huerta de Soto completed his doctoral studies in law at the Complutense University of Madrid in 1982.[4] Graduating *cum laude*, his thesis on private pension plans went on to win in 1983 the *International King Juan Carlos Prize for Economic Studies.* (To this date he is still the youngest recipient of the honor.) At a ceremony the award was bestowed on Jesús by the King of Spain himself, Juan Carlos I. The man Huerta de Soto's father backed to be King, Juan III, never ended up on the throne. But the elder Huerta could take some pride in seeing his son awarded this prize by the would-be monarch's son. For his part, the young Huerta de Soto gladly used the prize money to make sure his father would not have to chauffeur him any longer; he bought his first BMW.

[3] When pressed on the mistakes that his intellectual heirs have made, Huerta de Soto is forthcoming. Mises advocated subsidies for the opera. Kirzner believed that some evolved outcomes could be suboptimal even in the absence of government interventions. Hayek, despite his great contributions, took many missteps that set his theories down dead ends. Rothbard is the only economist that Huerta de Soto sees as having completed his life's work without making a single mistake.

[4] Beltrán Flórez spent 1931 and 1932 at the London School of Economics where he studied under Lionel Robbins and Friedrich Hayek.

A second doctoral degree in economics followed in 1992, also at the Complutense University. Here Pedro Schwartz, yet another colleague from the Reig seminars, served as his thesis director. The topic now turned to the controversy surrounding economic calculation under socialism.

The financial independence the family insurance company endowed him with gave Huerta de Soto intellectual freedom. In the wrong hands such freedom can turn to bedlam. History if full of such wasted opportunities. Karl Marx famously used Engel's financial support to rail against the capitalist class. In doing so he harmed no one more than the proletariat—those downtrodden he aimed to embolden.

Huerta de Soto would not fall into the same trap. He persevered to not compromise his beliefs, or to suffer any intellectual infidelities. But above all, he never turned silent when truth needed to be defended. The problem with defending one's principles is that it can be costly. As a consequence of debating with the tribunal for their neoclassical views, he was failed twice during the appointment procedures to become *catedrático*, the highest class of professor in the Spanish University system.

It was only on his third attempt in the year 2000 that he secured his chair at the Rey Juan Carlos University.[5] With this position in hand he gained personal prestige.

His new position as catedrático also brought with it some degree of political power within the University. It would have been easy to use this power to elevate himself further. A lesser man might use his might to punish those who held him back previously. For Huerta de Soto, the accomplishment was an opportunity to give back positively, and build something so that young scholars would not have to suffer as he had.

The first officially accredited postgraduate program in Austrian Economics world-wide opened its doors in 2007. Students flocked from around the globe to be guided by the master himself. At Huerta de Soto's weekly seminar, the observer who closes his eyes will focus his ears on two things. Most obvious is Jesús voice, simultaneously shouting theories and assuaging the listener's doubts. Like any good Southern European, Huerta de Soto uses not just his voice to be understood. His fists pound each other, and his knuckles rap the wooden table to bring the listener to a

[5] Three universities have conferred on him, at present time, honorary doctorate degrees: Universidad Francisco Marroquín, Guatemala (2009); University Alexandru Ioan Cuza de Iasi, Romania (2010); and the Financial University under the Government of the Russian Federation (2011).

higher level of consciousness. More importantly, in the background, a noise hardly louder than a church mouse, fills the air. This is not the sound of knowledge being imparted, but of being received. The scratching and scrawling of dozens of student's pens on paper. Scribbling furiously to not miss a word. Writing on their knees as they sit in an overcrowded room, sweating in the sun of the early Spanish evening.

It is from this room that these students spring their careers forward. To date several hundred well-trained Austrian economists have passed through Huerta de Soto's seminar. Many of these have gone on to obtain their doctoral degrees. Huerta de Soto has directed a staggering forty-one doctoral dissertations over the past two decades, building a school which will flourish and grow for years to come. Through these disciples, Jesús Huerta de Soto Ballester lives on.

These students, under the watchful eyes of Huerta de Soto, will go on to evangelize the world. For the visitor the feeling is that something very special transpires each Thursday evening at Huerta de Soto's main postgraduate seminar. Like clockwork, the weekly enlightenment resumes with a renewed intensity, picking up from that exact point where it left the week prior. Huerta de Soto arrives promptly, never late to class. His aide parks the golden Bentley in the choicest of parking spots. (There is no name to reserve it, but it stands empty, seemingly all week, until Huerta de Soto's arrival.) The bronze bust of Mises, omnipresent at all events associated with the postgraduate program, is moved ceremoniously from his office to the head of the seminar table. An Aquarius, lightly chilled, sits to the right of his seat. His lecture notes, in the middle.

And then enters the man. Taking his seat at the head of the table, he sets his keys beside the soft drink. His key chain, a gold 50 peso Mexican Libertad coin, shines beside the pale blue can, sweating in the afternoon heat.[6] The lecture begins. Students and visitors are in the presence of something new, for the seminar takes a life of its own each week. A feeling pervades that those present are in unchartered territory, that area of economics that cartographers from centuries prior would have marked with a dragon. But for Huerta de Soto, banging the desk as he preaches Austrian economics, Misesian classical liberalism, Rothbardian anarcho-capitalism,

[6] Although normally thought of as a standard one ounce gold coin, the Libertad contains 1.2 troy ounces of gold. This makes it the largest of the standard ounce denomination coins. Like many an advocate for sound money, Huerta de Soto also never leaves home without a trusty gold American Eagle in his pocket.

Hayekian evolution, and the Kirznerian synthesis, there is a profound familiarity to the whole scene.

Sitting beside him through the whole experience is the bust of Mises. It too was at the Reig seminars some fifty years prior. Luis gifted it to Huerta de Soto, two copies of it actually. These two replicas of Mises cast their gaze where Huerta de Soto needs the inspiration most: those spaces where he works. One rests in his academic office at the University where he does his professorial work. The other in the office on Príncipe de Vergara Street where he does his professional work.

The weekly graduate seminar is the culmination of a journey decades in the making. For the observer it's a chance to absorb the fruits of that sometimes perilous trek. But for Jesús Huerta de Soto, it's just another step along the way.

Jesús first met Murray Rothbard (here with Sonsoles) while studying at Stanford in 1980. Rothbard's ethical foundations of libertarianism, ultimately rooted in an evolutionary legal system, proved influential to the young Jesús. The importance of the legal system to the economic sphere was a broad consideration that stuck with Jesús since his undergraduate years. He would extend Rothbard's codification of many nascent ideas more fully in his *Money, Bank Credit, and Economic Cycles.* To his credit, Rothbard is the only economist whose works Jesús can find no quibble with.

With Israel Kirzner in New York in 2006. The 1973 publication of *Competition and Entrepreneurship* introduced a seventeen-year-old Jesús Huerta de Soto to an economic analysis fully detached from any neoclassical roots. It would also spark his life's work in reconciling any differences between Mises and Hayek. Besides entrepreneurship as the focal point of their academic work, the two economists share an additional affinity. Neither uses a computer in his daily life, preferring to write articles, books, and personal correspondence on paper and have it transcribed to a computer only later.

Rocking; always rocking. Whether in his office or relaxing at sea, Jesús is never far from the rocking chair. Beside his office desk (devoid of any forms of technology other than a fountain pen), many a visitor will recall the squeak of his rocking chair vying for the listener's attention against the background din of the radio. The ferocious pace of rocking illustrates the unbridled enthusiasm for life the man has within.

With Nobel laureate James Buchanan at the 1993 Mont Pelerin Society meeting in Rio de Janeiro. Introducing his legal-economic analysis of banking to a large crowd for the first time, Huerta de Soto faced heavy resistance from his panel chair and, to his humiliation, had his speech cut short. Buchanan emerged as an unexpected defender with the Mont Pelerin Society, sparking a friendship that continued until his 2013 death.

The Origins of Austrian Economics in the Treaties of the Theologians of Salamanca

Anton Afanasiev

The works of Professor Jesús Huerta de Soto are well known to the Russian reader. Four of his books have been translated into Russian:

1. *The Austrian School: Market Order and Entrepreneurial Creativity*
2. *Money, Bank Credit, and Economic Cycles*

My acquaintance with Professor Jesús Huerta de Soto began with my fascination with the economic thought of the Spanish School of Salamanca of the sixteenth century in the early 2000s. The fact is that at that time in Russia very little was known about the School of Salamanca and the contribution of its representatives to economic science. Jesús is one of those academic scholars researching the economic heritage of Salamanca. Here are two anecdotal cases of my personal meetings with Jesús.

A. Afanasiev (✉)
Central Economic and Mathematics Institute of Russian Academy of Sciences, Moscow, Russia
e-mail: aanton@cemi.rssi.ru

D. Howden, P. Bagus (eds.), *The Emergence of a Tradition: Essays in Honor of Jesús Huerta de Soto, Volume I*,
https://doi.org/10.1007/978-3-031-17414-8_2

3. *Socialism, Economic Calculation and Entrepreneurship*
4. *The Theory of Dynamic Efficiency*

In addition, in 2013 the journal *Economics and Mathematical Methods* published a Russian translation of his lecture dedicated to the memory of Professor F. A. Hayek's "Economic Recession, Banking Reform and the Future of Capitalism," read in 2010 at the London School of Economics and Political Science (Уэрта де Сото, 2013).

One of the fields of scientific interest of Professor Jesús Huerta de Soto and myself is the history of economic thought and the great Spanish School of Salamanca in the sixteenth to seventeenth centuries.

Thanks to the efforts of historians of Spanish economic thought, we know today that many fundamental economic doctrines and theories were presented and justified by the professors of the School of Salamanca in the sixteenth to seventeenth centuries (Афанасьев, 2004; Afanasiev, 2016).

The first case occurred at Jesús' firm. As you know, Professor Jesús Huerta de Soto, along with other prominent representatives of the neo-Austrian school, does not consider the use of mathematical methods in economics useful. However, the first thing that I saw upon entering Jesús' office was monitors with graphs of the dynamics of securities prices, built on the basis of mathematical models. I stopped to look at these graphs. Jesús said: "Look, Anton. We sometimes use mathematical models in practice for analysis and forecasting. It can be useful."

The second happened at Jesús' house during lunch. His wife, Sonsoles, prepared a delicious meal and invited us to the table. At lunch, Jesús asked which hotel I was staying at in Madrid. I replied that I was not staying in a hotel at all, but in an ordinary hostel near the national library of Spain, because the hostel is cheaper. "Poor Antonio," Jesús said with a sigh. But then Sonsoles came to the rescue. "What's wrong with that, Jesús? Don't you remember: I also often stayed in hostels, especially when I was a student."

I would like to cordially congratulate my great colleague and friend Jesús on this milestone year, wish him good health, and great success in all areas of his activities as a scientist, professor, and businessman.

I. In monetary theory, some of these relevant doctrines and their founding dates are:
  (a) The quantity theory of money (1556).
  (b) The theory of purchasing power parity of money (1535–1594).
  (c) The theory of the marginal value (utility) of money (1583, 1642).
  (d) The doctrine of the demand for money (1601).
  (e) A broad interpretation of the money supply (1601).
  (f) The doctrine of monetary mercantilism (1569) and mercantilism of the favorable trade balance (1600).

II. Regarding price theory, the following are significant:
  (g) The theory and mechanisms of competition between sellers and buyers (1597).
  (h) The justification for the sale with free prices in luxury products (1535) and in articles of first necessity (1552).
  (i) The idea of the impossibility of man knowing the exact value of the fair price of the product (1546, 1617).
  (j) The doctrine of the three main market players based on which the right price can be known (1546).
  (k) Two ways of distinguishing between price formation (one based on the expenses and another based on market forces) based on the number of market participants (1535).

One important scientific contribution of Professor Jesús Huerta de Soto is the study of the origins of the ideas of the neo-Austrian school in the works of Salamancan theologians of the sixteenth and seventeenth centuries. In particular, Huerta de Soto pointed out that in the books of Professor Juan de Salas and Cardinal Juan de Lugo, the idea of the impossibility of human cognition and strictly mathematical calculation of the fair price of a product was expressed.

Thus, the Jesuit Cardinal Juan de Lugo, wondering what the price of equilibrium was, as early as 1643 reached the conclusion that the equilibrium depended on such a large number of specific circumstances that only God was able to know it ("Pretium iustum mathematicum licet soli Deo notum"). Another Jesuit, Juan de Salas, referring to the possibilities of knowing specific market information, reached the very Hayekian conclusion that it was so complex that "quas exacte comprehendere et ponderare Dei est non hominum," in English, "only God, not men, can understand it exactly" that is, only God, and not men, can understand and weigh exactly the information and knowledge that a free market handles with all its particular circumstances of time and place (Huerta de Soto, [2000] 2013, p. 38).

For my part (Афанасьев, 2004, p. 52 and Afanasiev, 2016, pp. 11–12), I found this idea of the impossibility of knowing the value of a fair price by the sovereign and the state in the earlier work of the eminent Spanish theologian Juan de Medina *Codex de Restutitione et Contractibus*: "Let us briefly consider these proofs: if they are sufficient to know the right price and if with them the consciences of the merchants are assured when selling their merchandise. ... Then, as a public authority, the prince or the city that imposes the prices of things, they can lack or exceed in the fixing of the price in many ways, by the rejection or favor of those who sell them, by the requests or requests with which sellers offer them; and for many other causes or ways there is no doubt that the principals and rulers of the public can be corrupted" (Medina, 1546, quaestio 31, f. xcvii, author's translation).

Another important contribution of the Salamanca school, pointed out by Professor Jesús Huerta de Soto and other researchers, is the discovery of the dynamic concept of competition between buyers (Luis de Molina, 1597) and between sellers (Jerónimo Castillo de Bobadilla, 1597). "Furthermore, the Spanish scholastics were the first ones to introduce the dynamic concept of competition (in Latin concurrentium) understood as a process of rivalry among entrepreneurs. For instance, Jerónimo Castillo de Bovadilla (1597) wrote that 'prices will go down as a result of the abundance, rivalry (emulación) and competition (concurrencia) among the sellers'. And this same idea is closely followed by Luis de Molina" (Huerta de Soto, [2000] 2013, p. 38).

Meanwhile, as I showed in my articles (Афанасьев, 2004, p. 52 and Afanasiev, 2016, p. 13), the idea of dynamic competition between sellers was expressed somewhat earlier (1546) by the same Juan de Medina: "On the other hand, goods increase in value for some reason, such as if money is spent on other goods, or if many buyers compete, or if the common need of men increases; then it will be lawful to demand a higher price for them, as a stipend, which otherwise could not be fairly assigned (author's translation).

In this regard, we would like to recall two greats Catholic theologists, the Portuguese Franciscan Rodrigo do Porto and the Spanish doctor Martin de Azpilcueta Navarro. As I have pointed out (Afanasiev, 2016, p. 15–17), in the second Portuguese edition of the *Manual de Confessores e Penitentes*, they, using wheat as an example, gave a moral justification for selling basic necessities at prices higher than state prices (*tasas*) which, in their opinion, could be unfair:

> We said 'fair tax' because the unfair tax does not oblige everyone's opinion. And if it is unfair or not, for giving to one all the wheat and grain, bad, good and very good, new or old, healthy or corrupt, that of a land in which there is much and that of another in which there is little, the one that is sold where it is produced and the one that is brought from afar, even if it is brought from the kingdom without giving anything more for the rents, allowing what is outside the kingdom to be sold as much as possible and much more expensive than that of the own kingdom, being much worse. And if this unequal tax gives the occasion to sin and the occasion of many mortal sins, if we hold that its transgression obliges mortal sin—as the aforementioned doctors say—we refer this to the legislators and to what we have said elsewhere; for now it seems to us (from the above) that the intention of the legislator, who imposes a penalty against whoever sells more than so much, is not to compel mortal sin. Although the transgressor of it would sin mortally if he sold it for remarkably more than is fair, even if he sold it at less than the tax, as some usually sell corrupted bread or wine that is worth little more than nothing: because they break the natural law and the divine. Otherwise, they would not sin mortally if they sold it at the price that was fair before God, even if the rate was exceeded as much as natural justice allows. (Porto, R. d. and Azpilcueta, M. d, 1552, chap. xxiii, pp. 559–560, author's translation)

An important contribution was made by the professors of the Salamanca School to monetary theory, which Professor Jesús Huerta de Soto emphasizes in his works (Huerta de Soto, [2000] 2013, pp. 42–43). In particular, these are the essential economic facts that bank deposits are part of the money supply (first discovered by Luis de Molina and Juan de Lugo) and the negative economic effects produced or generated by fractional-reserve banking (Luis Saravia de la Calle and Martin de Azpilcueta).

Of course, the Scholastic roots of the quantity theory of money are well known. Thanks to Marjorie Grice-Hutchinson, Dr. Martin de Azpilcueta Navarro is known as the discoverer of the quantity theory of money (Grice-Hutchinson, 1952, pp. 53, 62). de Azpilcueta Navarro formulated this theory in his "Comentario resolutorio de cambios" (1556). Who could have been a significant influence on the formation of the quantity theory of Dr. de Azpilcueta Navarro? In my opinion, this is primarily his co-author, Fr. Rodrigo do Porto, whose work *Manual de Confessores e Penitentes* before publication in Coimbra in 1549 was reviewed and approved by Azpilcueta as a reviewer. Indeed, Fr. Rodrigo highlighted two important factors in determining the fair price of a product: the quantity of that product and the money with which it can be bought (Афанасьев, 2004, pp. 44–45 and Afanasiev, 2016, p. 18). Fr. Rodrigo noted:

> For the statement of the aforementioned things, in this matter of buying and selling, it should be noted that the price must be in accordance with the value of the thing being sold or bought, which is not always in one being but changes, according to the times, and the scarcity or abundance of that commodity and of the money with which to buy as it seems in times of barrenness, or fortune, or death. And so when the price is fixed by those who govern the city and place, this will be guarded without fail. (Porto, R. do, 1549, chap. xxiii, p. 393, author's translation)

In conclusion, I would like to point out that the works of Professor Jesús Huerta de Soto establish a very clear connection between the doctrines of the Salamanca professors of the Golden Age and modern economics, free market theory and monetary theory.

References

Афанасьев, А. А. (2004). Экономическая мысль в Испании XVI века—саламанкская школа. *Экономика и математические методы, 40*(4), 26–58.

Уэрта де Сото, Х. (2013). 'Экономическая рецессия, банковская реформа и будущее капитализма' (Перевод с английского Д. Ёжикова). *Экономика и математические методы, 49*(1), 19–32.

Afanasiev, A. A. (2016). La Escuela de Salamanca del siglo XVI: algunas contribuciones a la ciencia económica. *Revista de Empresa y Humanismo, 19*(1), 7–30.

Grice-Hutchinson, M. (1952). *The School of Salamanca: Readings in Spanish Monetary Theory, 1544–1605*. Clarendon Press.

Huerta de Soto, J. (2013). Juan de Mariana y los escolásticos españoles. *Revista de Humanidades, 12*(1), 32–45.

Medina, J. d. (1546). M.D.XL.VI (calendis Martij).

Porto, R. d. (1549). *Manual de Confessores e Penitentes*, M.D.XLIX (27 July).

Porto, R. d., & Azpilcueta, M. d. (1552). *Manual de Confessores & Penitentes*. M.D.LII (13 December).

Would a Retail Central Bank Digital Currency Achieve Its Intended Purpose?

Romain Baeriswyl

National central banks and international financial institutions such as the Bank for International Settlements (BIS) and International Monetary Fund (IMF) have been exploring the pros and cons of central bank digital

---

There is a funny scene in *Delusions of Grandeur*, a film inspired by Victor Hugo's *Ruy Blas*, where Don Salluste, a grandee of Spain, notices by the mere clinking of his gold coins that one is missing. Beyond the humour lies a deeper insight that has stayed with me—good money has a sound. Later, I would learn from another Madrid man that the sound of money also shapes human destiny. It is as if Victor Hugo's choice of setting the scene in Madrid had something of a happy promise. Money has become silent. From the melodic clink of metal to the rustle of fresh, new bills, the sound of money has faded over the centuries. Money may soon be silenced by the monotonous purring of computer fans—sad tones that do not bode well. But let us embrace the great enthusiasm of Jesús Huerta de Soto to face today's challenges with strength and hope.

R. Baeriswyl (✉)
Swiss National Bank, Zurich, Switzerland
e-mail: romain.baeriswyl@snb.ch

D. Howden, P. Bagus (eds.), *The Emergence of a Tradition: Essays in Honor of Jesús Huerta de Soto, Volume I*,
https://doi.org/10.1007/978-3-031-17414-8_3

currency available to the public (retail CBDC, henceforth) over the last few years.[1] The growing interest in retail CBDC has been driven by a combination of several factors.

First, the decline in the use of cash in several jurisdictions suggests that another form of central bank money should be made available to the public. Second, the growing dependence of the economy on electronic payment systems calls for improving their resilience, perhaps through the establishment of a back-up system based on CBDC. Third, advances in new technologies, such as distributed ledger technology (DLT), big data or artificial intelligence, tend to foster concentration in payment systems. By providing a generally accessible alternative medium of exchange, CBDC would increase the diversity and national sovereignty of payment systems.

According to the BIS (2020) and several economists, such as Barrdear and Kumhof (2016), Bindseil (2020), and Bordo and Levin (2017), the issuance of retail CBDC could potentially provide a solution to these challenges. Others, by contrast—for example, Agur et al. (2019), Bech and Garratt (2017), Jordan (2018) or Stevens (2017)—have expressed skepticism about a broadly available CBDC, highlighting the risks to the stability of the banking system posed by such a scheme.

The substitution of risk-free CBDC for risky bank deposits entails some risk transfer from commercial banks to the central bank. To limit the demand for and supply of CBDC, and the related transfer of risk, the literature proposes two mechanisms: the central bank could apply an unattractive interest rate to CBDC, or set an individual quantity ceiling for CBDC holdings.

This chapter analyses how these mechanisms are likely to affect the demand for CBDC as a medium of exchange and store of value and thus the achievement of the intended purposes for issuing retail CBDC.[2]

[1] For information on central bank attitudes towards CBDC and pilot studies, see, for instance, Mancini-Griffoli et al. (2018), CPMI (2018), Barontini and Holden (2019), Niepelt (2018) and the references therein.

[2] The views expressed in this chapter are those of the author and do not necessarily reflect those of the Swiss National Bank. This chapter provides a summary of Baeriswyl et al. (2021).

Definition, Purposes, and Characteristics of Retail CBDC

Economic and financial writings encompass various monetary proposals under the label "CBDC." As a starting point, we define the concept of retail CBDC and review the main purposes and characteristics proposed in the literature.

Broadly speaking, "CBDC, at the most basic level, is simply monetary value stored electronically (digitally, or as an electronic token) that represents a liability of the central bank and can be used to make payments" (Engert & Fung, 2017). According to this broad definition, CBDC can take very different forms. One of them is sight deposits currently held by commercial banks at the central bank, that is, banks' reserves. However, other forms of CBDC may differ from these reserves in a number of characteristics.

The main distinction to be made is between wholesale CBDC, which is accessible only to financial intermediaries, and retail CBDC, which is accessible to the public. Wholesale CBDC already exists in the form of sight deposits held by commercial banks at the central bank; issuing it in another form or through another technological medium would likely have only minor economic consequences. In contrast, issuing retail CBDC could fundamentally change the monetary system. For the sake of simplicity, CBDC in this chapter refers to retail CBDC.

CBDC does not require any particular technology and can be issued just as well with current technology as it can with distributed leger technology (DLT). Nevertheless, the belief that advances in IT and DLT provide the technology required for CBDC underlies many of the proposals for its issuance. Depending on the desired functionalities of CBDC, one technology may be more efficient and attractive than another. We do not address the choice of technology in this chapter and instead focus on the economic implications of CBDC.

An array of arguments has been made for CBDC issuance (BIS, 2020). The main purposes can be regrouped under three headings: (1) providing the public with a digital central bank money as the use of cash is declining; (2) improving the resilience of payments by providing a back-up system; and (3) promoting diversity and sovereignty in payment systems.

Ingves (2018) made the case for an e-krona in Sweden as a way to provide the general public with central bank money, as the use of cash, is in decline. Since a bank deposit is a claim on the bank payable in central bank money, public access to central bank money is a prerequisite for the enforcement of the deposit claim. Without public access to central bank money, the bank's contractual obligation to redeem deposits in central bank money is impossible to fulfil. Thus, if the use of cash declines, CBDC could substitute for cash in this role of providing public access to central bank money.

The issuance of CBDC may improve the resilience of the payment system. CBDC could serve as a back-up emergency medium of exchange in the event of a disruption to the current electronic banking system. Such a back-up would be superior to cash in terms of speed, convenience, and ease of emergency distribution. To the extent that CBDC is provided on a decentralized distributed ledger, it may also be resilient to the risk of single point failure. [3]

The diversity and sovereignty argument for CBDC relies on its potential to mitigate the anti-competitive effects of some financial innovations. The economies of scale and network effects that could arise with the adoption of new technologies (DLT, big data, and artificial intelligence among them) would tend to foster concentration and work against competitive provision of financial services and of payment systems in particular. As a result, payment systems today are highly concentrated in a few large companies that dominate electronic payment networks, and the importance of electronic payments will further grow with the rise of online commerce. By providing a generally accessible alternative medium of exchange, CBDC would make for increased contestability and diversity in payment systems.

Moreover, if an economy depends heavily on payment systems that are in the hands of foreign companies and regulated by foreign authorities, its sovereignty is at stake. A country without its own sovereign payment system depends on foreign providers. As it is issued by the domestic central bank, CBDC would be a means of ensuring the sovereignty of at least one electronic payment system.

[3] A single point of failure is a part of a system that, if it fails, will stop the entire system from working.

Implications for the Conduct of Monetary Policy and the Related Risk Transfer

Since the issuance of CBDC provides a new form of money available to the public, it influences monetary policy. The exact impact of CBDC on the conduct of monetary policy depends largely on the issuance model and potential changes to the monetary system.

We assume in the following that the monetary and banking system remains unchanged, apart from the issuance of CBDC itself. Thus, commercial banks continue to operate under a fractional-reserve system and to issue deposits when granting credit. Money held by non-bank entities therefore enters circulation first as deposits at commercial banks, which can then be converted into central bank money, that is, cash or CBDC. Moreover, to fulfil its mandate of price stability, the central bank continues to influence the expansion of money and credit by steering a short-term interest rate through the issuance of reserves. Finally, we also assume that cash continues to exist.

One of the challenges of issuing CBDC in the current monetary system stems from the transfer of credit risk from commercial banks to the central bank. This risk transfer comes from the coexistence of two kinds of money, that is, central bank money and bank deposits.

As its name suggests, central bank money is issued by the central bank and consists of cash (banknotes), sight deposits that commercial banks hold at the central bank (reserves), and potentially CBDC. Importantly, central bank money is an economic good free of credit risk, as it embodies no credit claim against anyone. It is unredeemable because the holder of central bank money can insist only on the redemption of a given amount of one form of central bank money into another form of the same central bank money. Of course, central bank money is not free of valuation risk with respect to domestic goods (i.e., through inflation) or foreign currencies (i.e., exchange rate depreciation).

In contrast, bank deposits are claims issued by commercial banks redeemable on demand in central bank money. Redemption can be made in cash, possibly in CBDC, or by transferring the funds to another bank. Because their redemption depends on the solvency of the issuing bank, deposits carry a credit risk. They are, however, not (or less) subject to the risk of loss or theft and are more convenient to make payments than cash. Depositors accept deposits as a means of payment in place of central bank money only insofar as they are reasonably confident in the issuing bank's ability to fulfil its contractual obligation to redeem its risky deposits into credit risk-free central bank money.

Although the central bank may not be legally obliged to accommodate the demand for central bank money, it is induced to do so to fulfil its mandate of price stability. If the central bank does not meet rising demand for central bank money, scarcity leads to an increase in money market rates, which slows down the credit-expansion process of banks and causes inflation to fall below target.

When non-banks request redemption of their deposits in cash or in CBDC, the reserves held by banks with the central bank decrease, which affects money market conditions differently depending on whether excess reserves are small or large. The amount of reserves that banks hold in excess of what is legally required (minimum reserve requirement) or of what banks voluntarily demand for their liquidity management determines the impact of reserve fluctuations on the money market.

When excess reserves are small, the decline in banks' reserves following an increase in the demand for cash or CBDC by the public leads to tighter money market conditions and higher short-term interest rates. To prevent an undesired tightening of monetary conditions, the central bank needs to accommodate this demand with a corresponding increase in bank reserves. This accommodation implies an expansion of the central bank's balance sheet and, thereby, a transfer of risk to the central bank.

When excess reserves are large, the decline in bank reserves does not lead to tighter money market conditions and higher short-term interest rates. Thus, the central bank does not have to accommodate the demand for cash or CBDC by non-banks to maintain its monetary policy stance. However, because banks' excess reserves decline, the central bank loses its ability to reduce subsequently its balance sheet and the risk associated with it in case this becomes necessary. Large excess reserves are the result of previous increases in the central bank's balance sheet. By reducing excess reserves, the redemption of deposits into cash or CBDC "locks in" the risk on the central bank's balance sheet.

Does Limiting Risk Transfer Hinder the Achievement of CBDC Purposes?

The previous section has shown that the issuance of CBDC leads to a transfer of risk from commercial banks to the central bank. The risk transferred depends on the quantity of CBDC issued, that is, the size of the central bank's balance sheet, and on the quality of the assets held by the central bank or taken as collateral in lending operations.

One way to limit the transfer of risk is therefore to define a conservative portfolio of eligible collateral or to apply significant haircuts to collateral assets. Although these measures mitigate the materialization of risk for the central bank, they raise at least two issues, which are particularly acute when the demand for CBDC is large and fully accommodated.

First, the choice of the portfolio of eligible collateral by the central bank shapes the allocation of bank lending in the economy. In turn, the central bank would be indirectly involved in the credit allocation process. For example, if the portfolio of eligible collateral consists of government bonds only, banks will have to lend to the government—rather than to households or companies—to obtain the collateral needed to meet CBDC demand. If the portfolio of eligible collateral includes mortgages to households but not loans to businesses, banks will lend more to households and less to businesses. Second, the application of haircuts to collateral assets does not fully eliminate their risk, particularly if the central bank lends massively to commercial banks, leaving the challenge of risk transfer fundamentally unsolved. Moreover, increasing the required haircut increases the volume of eligible collateral needed to meet CBDC demand and thus amplifies the undesirable effect on lending allocation described above.

It is technically possible to leave the supply of CBDC demand-determined and to mitigate the materialization of risk for the central bank with conservative collateral requirements and haircuts, as Brunnermeier and Niepelt (2019) point out. The banking system could then gradually slide—de facto if not de jure—toward a 100%-reserve (i.e., full-reserve or sovereign) monetary system. Nevertheless, most authors, such as Bindseil (2020), Kumhof and Noone (2018), or Panetta (2018), believe that it is desirable to contain the amount of CBDC to avoid sliding toward a 100%-reserve monetary system and to guarantee the competence of commercial banks to grant credit to the economy.

At least two mechanisms can be imagined to limit the amount of CBDC demanded by the public and issued by the central bank: unattractive interest rate and a quantity ceiling.

The transfer of risk can be limited by charging interest on CBDC holdings, much like negative interest rates have been applied in recent years to bank reserves in the euro area or in Switzerland. Digital money is more convenient than cash because of the lower risk of loss or theft and ease of payment; making CBDC more expensive to hold than cash would limit its demand. In normal times, a moderately negative interest rate might limit the demand for CBDC and, thereby, the risk transfer. During crises, interest on CBDC would probably need to be lowered sharply, which would yield uncertain results because even a very negative annual interest entails only small costs over a short period.

Another way to limit the risk transfer is to set a maximum amount of CBDC that each person or firm can hold. A quantity ceiling can be strictly enforced so that any surplus above an individual threshold is automatically transferred into another account at a commercial bank (related to the CBDC account). Alternatively, it can be implemented in a more flexible way by applying an unattractive interest rate to any surplus above a specific threshold, which would induce the holders to rapidly reduce their CBDC holdings. Bindseil (2020) suggests, for example, applying an attractive interest rate up to a ceiling and an unattractive rate on the amount above that ceiling to encourage the use of CBDC as a medium of exchange but not as a store of value.

We now assess the implications of these mechanisms for achieving the various purposes put forward for issuing a retail CBDC. One criterion for evaluating a CBDC's fitness to purpose is to ask whether it is the only and best means for achieving the desired purpose. Moreover, the CBDC design that is fit for one purpose may have unwanted side effects on another of the listed purposes.

Providing the public with central bank money: The disappearance of cash is not a universal phenomenon. With the possible exception of some Scandinavian countries (Sveriges Riksbank, 2018), cash continues to be widely demanded across the world. Even in countries where the use of cash to settle transactions is declining, such as Switzerland (SNB, 2018), the demand for cash as a store of value is increasing, driving up the amount of cash in circulation per capita. As long as the public has access to cash, the issuance of CBDC does not seem necessary to provide it with central bank money.

The mechanisms to limit the demand for CBDC have differentiated effects on the role of CBDC as central bank money. First, if the central bank applies an unattractive interest rate to CBDC, CBDC will be an effective provision of central bank money because the deposit claim against the bank will be fully payable in CBDC (as well as in cash). Although the demand for the redemption of deposits in CBDC may be low due to unattractive remuneration, such a CBDC would enable the bank to fulfil its legal obligation to the depositor. Second, if the central bank applies a quantity ceiling to CBDC holdings, the deposit claim against the bank will be payable in CBDC only up to the ceiling. This naturally hampers the role that CBDC would be intended to play.

In summary, if the purpose for issuing CBDC is to provide the public with central bank money, then applying an unattractive interest rate to CBDC is the most appropriate way to limit its demand.

Improving the resilience of the payment system: The mechanisms to limit the demand for CBDC also have differentiated effects on the achievement of a CBDC-based back-up payment system. To be effective, a back-up payment system must be usable by a large part of the population at all times. This requires that the vast majority of people permanently hold a certain amount of CBDC.

First, if the central bank charges an unattractive interest rate on CBDC, then most people will probably not hold CBDC permanently, thereby making a CBDC-based payment system ineffective as a back-up.

Second, if the central bank applies a quantity ceiling to CBDC holdings, then most people will probably hold CBDC permanently, provided that no unattractive interest rate is charged on those deposits. In this way, CBDC could be used as a means of payment if the current electronic system fails.

In summary, if the purpose of issuing CBDC is to improve the resilience of the payment system, then applying a quantity ceiling to CBDC is the most appropriate way to limit its demand.

Promoting diversity and sovereignty in payments: Mechanisms to limit the issuance of CBDC greatly reduce the chances of widespread use of a CBDC-based payment system for everyday transactions. First, if CBDC earns an unattractive interest rate, one wonders why anyone would make a payment in such a CBDC in the first place. The comparison with cash is useful because it pays no interest, which is, in normal times, unattractive compared to the interest rate on bank deposits. However, cash has the advantages of being free of credit risk and of offering a different technology from the electronic banking payment system, which guarantees anonymity. Those who value the absence of credit risk demand cash typically as a store of value, while those who value cash technology demand cash as a medium of exchange. In contrast, a CBDC-based payment system does not offer a fundamentally different technology to its users than the current electronic banking payment system. Therefore, the main reason why people would hold CBDC with an unattractive interest rate is the absence of credit risk, which is valuable for money hoarded, not for money spent in daily transactions.

Second, if a quantity ceiling applies to CBDC, one may question why people would use CBDC rather than bank deposits to settle transactions. Since CBDC is, unlike bank deposits, free of credit risk, Gresham's law teaches us that people will hoard CBDC (i.e., the "good" money) as a store of value and get rid of bank deposits (i.e., the "bad" money) by making payments with them. This is true regardless of the interest rate applied up to the CBDC ceiling. If CBDC earns an attractive interest rate (compared to bank deposits) up to the ceiling, people would maximize their profits by continuously hoarding their CBDC holdings at the ceiling. In contrast, if CBDC earns an unattractive interest rate (compared to bank deposits) up to the ceiling, we are back to the considerations made in the previous paragraph.

In summary, both mechanisms limiting its issuance will make CBDC unlikely to increase the diversity and sovereignty of payment systems because CBDC will not be used widely as a medium of exchange.

Conclusion

This chapter started by presenting various purposes that would justify the issuance of a retail CBDC. It has pointed out that mechanisms to limit the risk transfers make the use of CBDC as a medium of exchange unlikely. There is thus a trade-off between limiting the risk transfer to central banks and achieving certain CBDC purposes.

If the purpose for issuing CBDC is to provide the public with central bank money, its holding should not be subject to quantity ceilings. Applying an unattractive interest rate to CBDC may then contain its demand in normal times; an unattractive interest rate, however, is likely to contain demand much less in times of financial crisis.

If the purpose of CBDC is to improve the resilience of the payment system as a back-up, the vast majority of people need to hold a certain amount of CBDC at all times. This requires CBDC to be attractively (or at least not unattractively) remunerated up to a certain quantity ceiling. By applying an attractive interest rate up to a ceiling and an unattractive interest rate above that ceiling, CBDC would be able to fulfil its roles as central bank money and as a back-up payment system but may facilitate massive runs in times of financial crisis.

However, mechanisms limiting the demand for CBDC seem to undermine its widespread use as a medium of exchange for everyday transactions. As Gresham's law teaches us, people will hoard their credit risk-free CBDC and spend their risky bank deposits instead. A CBDC-based payment system is therefore unlikely to promote the diversity and sovereignty of payment systems. This purpose would be more easily achieved with a system based on privately issued bank deposits rather than on central bank money.

Overall, the implications of issuing a retail CBDC would depend on its precise design. At worst, if its demand were not limited, it would lead to substantial risk transfers from commercial banks to the central bank. At best, limiting its demand would severely hamper its intended purposes.

References

Agur, I., Ari, A., & Dell'Ariccia, G. (2019). *Designing Central Bank Digital Currencies.* IMF Working Paper, No. 19/252.

Baeriswyl, R., Reynard, S., & Swoboda, A. (2021). *Retail CBDC Purposes and Risk Transfers to the Central Bank.* SNB Working Paper, No. 19/2021.

Barontini, C., & Holden, H. (2019). *Proceeding with Caution—A Survey on Central Bank Digital Currency.* BIS Paper, No. 101.

Barrdear, J., & Kumhof, M. (2016). *The Macroeconomics of Central Bank Issued Digital Currencies.* Bank of England Staff Working Paper, No. 605.

Bech, M., & Garratt, R. (2017). Central Bank Cryptocurrencies. *BIS Quarterly Review*, 55–70.

Bindseil, U. (2020). *Tiered CBDC and the Financial System.* ECB Working Paper Series, No. 2351.

BIS. (2020). *Central Bank Digital Currencies: Foundational Principles and Core Features.* Report no 1 in a series of collaborations from a group of central bank.

Bordo, M., & Levin, A. (2017). Central Bank Digital Currency and the Future of Monetary Policy. *mimeo.*

Brunnermeier, M. K., & Niepelt, D. (2019). On the Equivalence of Private and Public Money. *Journal of Monetary Economics, 106*, 27–41.

Committee on Payments and Market Infrastructures (CPMI). (2018). *Central Bank Digital Currencies.* CPMI Report 174, Basel.

Engert, W., & Fung, B. S. C. (2017). *Central Bank Digital Currency: Motivations and Implications.* Banque of Canada Staff Discussion Paper, No. 2017-16.

Ingves, S. (2018). *The e-krona and the Payments of the Future.* Speech. Retrieved November 6, 2018, from https://www.riksbank.se/globalassets/media/tal/engelska/ingves/2018/the-e-krona-and-the-payments-of-the-future.pdf

Jordan, T. (2018). *How Money is Created by the Central Bank and the Banking System.* Speech at the Zuercher Volkswirtschaftliche Gesellschaft.

Kumhof, M., & Noone, C. (2018). *Central Bank Digital Currencies—Design Principles and Balance Sheet Implications.* Bank of England Staff Working Paper, No. 725.

Mancini-Griffoli, T., Peria, M. S. M., Agur, I., Ari, A., Kiff, J., Popescu, A., & Rochon, C. (2018). *Casting Light on Central Bank Digital Currency.* IMF Staff Discussion Note, SDN/18/08.

Niepelt, D. (2018). *Reserves for All? Central Bank Digital Currency, Deposits, and their (Non)-equivalence.* Discussion Paper 13065, CEPR.

Panetta, F. (2018). 21st Century Cash: Central Banking, Technological Innovation and Digital Currency. In E. Gnan & D. Masciandaro (Eds.), *Do We Need Central Bank Digital Currency?* (pp. 23–33).

SNB (2018). *Survey on payment methods 2017.* Swiss National Bank, May 2018.

Stevens, A. (2017). Digital Currencies: Threats and Opportunities for Monetary Policy. *National Bank of Belgium Economic Review*, 79–92.

Sveriges Riksbank. (2018). *The Riksbank's e-krona Project Report 2.* Sveriges Riksbank.

The Disinterventionist Spiral

Philipp Bagus

Ludwig von Mises' theory of interventionism can be employed fruitfully to the COVID-19 crisis. Interventionism gained a strong foothold in the public health sector and spiraled during the COVID-19 crisis into other areas such as monetary policy, fiscal policy, regulation of transportation, and social gatherings. The health interventionist spiral has been burying civil liberties in the wake of the COVID-19 mass hysteria (Bagus et al., 2021). While the functioning of the interventionist spiral is well known to the Austrian economist, the opposite way is less well studied. Therefore, in this chapter I want to employ Mises' theory of interventionism to develop

Huerta de Soto is the most generous mentor imaginable. His support goes from helping me with publications, promoting my academic career, paid projects such as translations of his works to first-class opera tickets and praising me over the moon. (He likes to tell people that at our first meeting I said I wanted to be the best professor in Europe. I had only said that I wanted to be a professor of economics). Thank you very much for everything, Herr Professor.

P. Bagus (✉)
Department of Applied Economics I and History of Economic Institutions (and Moral Philosophy), Universidad Rey Juan Carlos, Madrid, Spain
e-mail: philipp.bagus@urjc.es

D. Howden, P. Bagus (eds.), *The Emergence of a Tradition: Essays in Honor of Jesús Huerta de Soto, Volume I*,
https://doi.org/10.1007/978-3-031-17414-8_4

a theory of de-interventionism, a theory of de-spiraling. First, I portray Mises' theory of interventionism and how Mises modified it over time. Second, I outline a theory of de-interventionism. Third, I illustrate this theory with the specific example of the reform of a pension system. Lastly, I conclude with some implications for libertarian reformers.

Mises' Theory of Interventionism

Ludwig von Mises pointed already in his 1929 book *Critique of Interventionism* to the unviability of a third way of interventionism: "Either capitalism or socialism, there is no middle of the road." ([1929] 1996, p. 8). Interventionism is unstable because interventions lead to effects that are contrary to the intentions of the advocates of them. The politicians that advocated the intervention then have the option either to get rid of the new intervention or to follow up with another intervention. However, a second intervention will cause other unwelcome side effects that are bad from the point of view of the interventionists ([1929] 1996, p. 8). Thus, pressure amounts to continue the interventionist path adding further interventions, until the interventionist avalanche buries the market economy which turns into a planned economy or socialism, in which production is directed by the state as the de facto owner of the means of production.

Mises illustrates his analysis with the example of price controls. If the government sets maximum prices below market prices in order to benefit consumers, there will be a shortage because production becomes unprofitable at the regulated price and demand increases. The reduction of production and the unsatisfied consumer demand can be considered to be an adverse effect from the point of view of the interventionists themselves. In order to stimulate production by making it profitable again, the government may then regulate the input prices of the good in question. These additional price ceilings constitute the next step in the cumulative interventionist process. As a further consequence, the production of the input factors becomes unprofitable, and the next interventionist step is to impose of price ceiling on the inputs' input factors and so on until all prices in the economy are regulated. As Mises points out, "[i]f government is not inclined to alleviate the situation through removing its limited interventions and lifting its price control its first step must be followed by others." ([1929] 1996, p. 8; Mises comes to the same conclusion in *Human Action* [1949] 1998, p. 857).

His disciple Murray Rothbard argues in the same manner "that every coercive intervention in human affairs brings about further problems that call for the choice; repeal the initial intervention or add another one. It is the feature that makes any 'mixed economy' inherently unstable, tending always toward one or the other polar opposite—pure freedom or total statism" (1976, p. 264).

The end of the interventionist spiral is socialism (Mises [1940] 1998, p. 88). Three comments on Mises' theory of interventionism are in order.

The first comment is that Mises claims that the effects of the interventions are undesirable from the point of view of the advocates of the interventions which creates pressure to introduce follow-up interventions: "[consequences]...which after all are contrary to its [the government's] own intention." (Mises [1929] (1996), p. 8). However, this is not necessarily so for four main reasons.

First, when referring to the point of view of the interventionists Mises deals with subjective valuations which cannot be known with certainty by an outside observer. It is perfectly conceivable that a statist welcomes the effects of the intervention because they give him a justification for further interventions. He may be perfectly aware that he starts rolling an interventionist spiral leading to socialism being his ultimate goal. In this case, the effects of the initial interventions are not undesired but very much desired. Sometimes, for instance, in the European debt crisis, the COVID-19 crisis or in the cases of causing unemployment or mass immigration that increases votes to a certain party or power to the state, this possibility does not seem too far-fetched. Mises could have improved his argument by slightly changing his wording to say that the effects of the intervention are detrimental from the point of view that the interventionists officially defend or pretend to defend.

Second, the side effects of the intervention may not be strong enough to cause an overwhelming pressure toward more interventions such as occurs with minimum wage laws that cause only insignificant or no unemployment when set very low.

Third, the "adverse" effects could just be accepted by the interventionists as a necessary evil without leading to follow-up interventions. For instance, government redistribution reduces capital accumulation and consequently leads to wages that are lower than they otherwise would have been. Politicians may accept a somewhat lower living standard as long as they believe their egalitarian ends are met. In this case, they may resist the pressure to take away the intervention or follow up with another one.

Fourth, simultaneous to the intervention there may occur overlapping effects that compensate or alleviate the "adverse" side effects. For instance, progress in the international division of labor, capital accumulation or innovations may increase productivity so that minimum wage hikes do not cause unemployment or so that the productivity losses caused by some interventionist measures are compensated for. Consequently, there is no visible pressure for follow-up interventions.

The second comment on Mises's theory of intervention is that the interventionist spiral in the case of price controls may be broken by fiscal means. In the case of the shortage of a good whose price has been controlled, the state could subsidize the production of the good or start to produce it. After this intervention, the pressure to regulate other prices is alleviated. Naturally, higher taxes to finance the subsidies or state production will reduce the willingness to produce, and capital accumulation will be below the amount otherwise attained. Yet, these adverse consequences, as pointed out above, could easily be regarded as acceptable so that the cumulative process comes to a halt at this point or is, at least, slowed down considerably.

The third comment we must make is that Mises slightly modified his theory of interventionism from his first account in 1929 to his treatment in *Human Action* in 1949. In 1929 his definition of interventionism is narrower than in *Human Action*. In his first account he states that an "[i]ntervention is a limited order by a social authority forcing owners of the means of production and entrepreneurs to employ their means in a different manner than they otherwise would." ([1929] 1996, p. 4) In his later treatment of 1940 (1998, p. 6) we find a similar definition. He emphasizes the difference to his definition of socialism: "Interventionism seeks to retain private property in the means of production, but authoritative commands, especially prohibitions, are to restrict the action of private owners." ([1929] 1996, p. 1; see also Mises [1940] 1998, p. 10).

Mises ([1929] 1996, p. 5) maintains that there are two types of commands, namely those that directly reduce or prevent production and those that regulate prices. However, in 1929 he does not consider nationalizations or the constitution of public enterprises as interventions. Moreover, fiscal measures such as subsidies are not included in interventionism as it is narrowly defined ([1929] 1996, p. 5). Taxation is excluded also because it does not, according to Mises, redirect production itself ([1929] 1996, p. 30, n. 3).

Thus, Mises restricts his definition of interventionism to cases of price controls and prohibition of production which seems somewhat narrow. Subsidies, taxation, government purchases and sales, as well as public companies also lead to an employment of the factors of production different to the one that otherwise would occur.

Later, in *Human Action* Mises employs a broader view of interventionism. First, he offers a familiar definition of intervention by stating:

> The intervention is a decree issues, directly or indirectly by the authority in charge of the administrative apparatus of coercion and compulsion which forces the entrepreneurs and capitalists to employ some of the factors of production in a way different from what would have resulted if they were only obeying the dictates of the market. [1949] (1998, pp. 714–15)

However, later on, Mises broadens the meaning of interventionism in chapter 36, *The Crisis of Interventionism.* In this chapter he includes as interventionist measures such as taxation, fiscal spending, and the action of state enterprises [Mises, 1949] (1998, pp. 851–54). Mises argues that the interventionist logic also applies to these areas leading to more and more socialization of resources with the consequence of capital consumption. To finance the interventionist measures and its own growth, the government is obliged to tax away more and more fortunes. However, private funds are limited [1949] (1998, p. 852).

Mises concludes his analysis of interventionism:

> The interventionist interlude must come to an end because interventionism cannot lead to a permanent system of social organization...All varieties of interference with the market phenomena not only fail to achieve the ends aimed at by their authors and supporters but bring about a state of affairs which—from the point of view of their authors' and advocates' valuations—is less desirable than the previous state of affairs which they were designed to alter. If one wants to correct their unsuitableness and preposterousness by supplementing the first acts of intervention with more and more of such acts, one must go farther and farther until the market economy has been entirely destroyed and socialism has been substituted for it. [1949] (1998, p. 854)

Two De-interventionist Implications in Mises' Theory of Interventionism

The kernel of Mises' argument is that interventionism is not stable. The interventionist regime will always wander from fewer to more interventions. Sometimes the regime may also wander the opposite direction from more to fewer interventions, though Mises does not emphasize this direction. There always remains the question if an intervention shall be abolished due to its "unintended" side effects or rather be complemented by additional interventions to combat these side effects.

In the same way that interventions lead to pressure toward more interventions, an abolishment of interventions also leads to pressure to abolish further interventions or to reinstitute them. This is so because the abolishment of an intervention eliminates its side effects but makes more noticeable the "negative" consequences of the interventions still in place. The crux of free-market reforms is that they produce pressures to abolish them. This implies that de-interventionism or piecemeal free-market reform is a complicated, daring, and risky endeavor. The endeavor is unstable, fragile, and difficult from a political point of view.

Let us go back to Mises' example of maximum prices. In his account, maximum price caps by way of ceilings lead to the additional intervention of regulating the prices of the input factors in order to make the production of the good profitable again. This additional regulation in turn has the "adverse" effect of making the production of these input factor unprofitable, causing a shortage of the input factors. If there is deregulation and the price regulation of the input factor is abolished, we are back at the point where the production of the good with the maximum price is unprofitable, resulting in a shortage. As this shortage is "undesirable" there is pressure to also abolish the initial regulation of the maximum price. In other words, in the same way that interventions may cause an interventionist spiral, reforms or the abolishment of interventions may lead to a reform spiral. Both can at any point be broken by either removing interventions in the former case or initiating the interventionist process again in the latter case.

This insight derived from the theory of interventionism has implications for free-market reforms. Isolated or piecemeal reforms lead to problems in execution and sustainability resulting from the remaining state interventions. These problems can be exploited by statists as a main argument against the reform and in favor of its abolishment.

The crux of the spiral of de-interventionism is that a reform may lead to adverse side effects or problems from the point of view of the very advocates of the reform (and their opponents, of course). The advocates are then confronted with three choices. First, they can abolish the reform as demanded by its opponents. Second, advocates may introduce complementary interventions to deal with the undesired effects kicking off a new spiral. An example is the Hartz-IV reforms in Germany during the early 2000s that deregulated the labor market. These labor-market reforms culminated with the introduction of a minimum wage in 2015. Third, they may follow through with the dynamics of de-interventionism abolishing further interventions, which in turn may cause additional "undesired" consequences. Free-market reform proposals, therefore, suffer from the problem that they themselves are unstable because they are only partial liberalizations. Successful reforms should be accompanied with deregulations in other fields. A famous example of such an endeavor is the successful monetary and economic reform in Germany in 1948. At the time the price controls of the national socialist regime were still in place. The national socialist regime used inflation to finance the war effort. As a consequence, many goods were only available on the black market. The monetary reform aimed to eliminate the excess money supply created during the war.

However, the monetary reform alone, that is, without the end of price controls, would not have established a functioning market economy dependent on free prices. Similarly, the end of price controls without a monetary reform that eliminated the excess money supply could have caused hyperinflation and the loss of confidence in the new currency.

Hence, Ludwig Erhard, director of economics of the Bizonal Economic Council, later minister of economics and German chancellor, accompanied the monetary reform with a successive and encompassing abolishment of price controls. The combined reforms were a stunning success and the foundation of the post-war German economic miracle.

One can deduce from Mises' standpoint that only a complete abolition of the interferences or interventions in the market economy at one stroke ("immediate abolition," according to Mises [1929] 1996, p. 15) would avoid these problems and establish a free-market economy which is a stable and viable alternative of social cooperation. "I'd push the button," as Leonard Read would say (1946).

Here we see another radical implication of Mises' theory. It should be noted the implications of Mises' theory sometimes are more radical than he seems to be aware of. A similar case is Mises' defense of the minimum state and of the unlimited right of secession up to the individual level (1985, pp. 109–110). As Hans-Hermann Hoppe (2020) has pointed out, unlimited secession makes the membership within a state voluntary and allows for anarcho-capitalism. Mises does not seem to be aware of the radical implications of his defense of unlimited secession.

Similar to the case of secession, there is a radical idea implied in Mises' theory of interventionism which puts Mises close to Murray Rothbard's view on state interventions. Following Leonard Read, Rothbard maintains that a libertarian should be in favor of abolishing all government interferences at one stroke. Rothbard's argument, however, is based not only on economic and political theory but also on natural law ethics. Rothbard argues that if there would be a button that would abolish the state altogether, the libertarian should press it (1998, p. 259). Mises' theory of interventionism seems to give support to this approach from the point of view of economic theory. The Misesian, who is asked to establish a stable and viable form of social cooperation to evade the chaos of socialism, would follow his libertarian companion and press Read's and Rothbard's button—at least so it seems.

Reform of the Pension System as an Illustration of a De-interventionist Spiral

An example of such a de-interventionist spiral is a reform of the public pay-as-you-go pension system and a transition toward a capital-based pension system as defended by Huerta de Soto (2007). A transition toward a capital-based free-market system comes with the problem that people close to or at the age of retirement may not have saved sufficiently in the past and must rely on the public pay-as-you-go system. In the transition period, the young working population would have to pay public pensions for the retired and save for their own retirement. Of course, the retired could simply be supported directly by their children during the transition making the pay-as-you-go payments voluntary. Yet, not every retiree has children willing to do so and birth rates have fallen. So, there is an "undesired" consequence of the reform, namely that the life of the retired during the transition period may become more difficult. Note that this is essentially the situation following the market reforms in the Soviet Union in the 1990s and the reason why nostalgic elderly wanted to return to socialism.

There are several ways that further deregulation may help to make pension reform a (political) success. One way to support the retired are private donations; private charities may fill the gap. In order to increase the willingness for private donations, a tax cut would be helpful. The tax cut is a reversion or abolition of a state interference as a response to problems caused by the initial reform.

Another revision to alleviate the "adverse" effects of the reform is to make the labor market more flexible and facilitate the creation of jobs specifically for the elderly, for instance, by reducing social security contributions or by permitting workers to continue working past retirement age. Of course, this implies also the abolition or reduction of further interventions.

The transition to and acceptance of a capital-based pension system is also exacerbated by other interventions, most notably in the monetary field. In times of financial repression, savings end up financing the state. Insurance, pensions funds, or banks are forced to invest part of the savings in low or even negative yielding government bonds. The yield of short-term savings is artificially reduced. Financial interventions make it more difficult to get a positive real yield on savings to provide for retirement. A capital-based private pension system is further threatened by the possibility and uncertainty of future state interventions in the monetary field.

Thus, the end of a negative interest rate policy, financial deregulation or monetary reform could facilitate the acceptance and success of a reform of the pension system. Yet, these further reforms and de-interventions would cause other consequences that some people would consider to be detrimental. One direct consequence of a less interventionist monetary policy, or even a complete monetary reform, would be that the financing of the state would be reduced. Real government spending would fall. The state's role in the economy would be reduced thereby leading to problems for those that depend on the state. Further deregulation would facilitate the reincorporation of these people into productive activities.

Moreover, a deregulation of financial markets, for instance, by way of the abolishment of the Basel regulations, would make further monetary reforms necessary, because some of these regulations restrict the capacity of banks to create new money through credit expansion. A fully backed commodity money as defended by Huerta de Soto (2020) and others would solve this problem. The introduction of a fully backed commodity money such as a pure gold standard is a form of de-intervention because the privilege of banks to hold fractional reserves is eliminated and the grant of this privilege was an intervention. A monetary system that complies with the principles of private law, that is, that obliges them to hold 100 percent reserves on demand deposits, would have the additional advantage of establishing an economy where there would be a tendency of the purchasing power of money to increase when productivity increases outstrip gold production. The increase in the purchasing power of money facilitates procuring capital for retirement. Hence, the introduction of a full commodity money would alleviate the problems stemming from the pension reform and facilitate the transition.

Yet, further problems amount from such a monetary reform following the logic of the de-interventionist spiral. Such a reform would require downward price flexibility as the purchasing power of money would likely increase in the long run. In order to prevent the unemployment of resources, regulations that cause price rigidities should be abolished. Labor market deregulations are especially important in this regard, as privileges for labor unions and minimum wage laws make wages rigid.

Another problem with such a monetary reform would be the possible default of companies that have adjusted their business model to today's inflationary environment and depend on its ongoing existence by relying on high levels of debt. Thus, the tendency toward an increase in the purchasing power of money stemming from the new monetary system poses problems to these companies. Flexibility of other markets (a de-intervention) becomes even more pertinent. Increases in flexibility facilitate the transfer of factors of production from the overindebted failed companies into new, more profitable projects and reduces the length of unemployment.

Conclusion

As we can observe, there is not only an interventionist spiral but there is also an analogous de-interventionist spiral. Reforms collide with still existing interventions leading to problems from the (official) point of view of reformers and non-reformers alike. There is pressure to abolish further interventions and reduce the role of the state. When further interferences are abolished, there arise new tensions with still existing ones. The reform path is unstable. Either the path is followed through toward anarcho-capitalism or reforms are eventually undone by accumulating interventions anew. There is no third way.

References

Bagus, P., Peña-Ramos, J. S., & Sánchez-Bayón, A. (2021). COVID-19 and the Political Economy of Mass Hysteria. *International Journal of Environmental Research and Public Health, 18*(4), 1376.

Hoppe, H.-H. (2020). Mises on Secession. *Mises Daily Articles, June 7*. https://mises.org/library/mises-secession

Huerta de Soto, J. ([1998] 2020). *Money, Bank Credit and Economic Cycles*. 4th revised ed. Ludwig von Mises Institute.

Huerta de Soto, J. (2007). *Ahorro y previsión en el seguro de vida*. Unión Editorial.

Mises, L. v. ([1927] 1985). *Liberalism: In the Classic Tradition*. Foundation for Economic Education.

Mises, L. v. ([1929] 1996). *Critique of Interventionism*. 2nd revised ed. Foundation for Economic Education.

Mises, L. v. ([1940] 1998). *Interventionism: An Economic Analysis*. Foundation for Economic Education.

Mises, L. v. ([1949] 1998). *Human Action*. Scholar's Edition. Ludwig von Mises Institute.

Read, L. (1946). *I'd Push the Button*. Foundation for Economic Education.

Rothbard, M. N. (1976). *Power and Market Government and the Economy*. Sheed Andrews and McMeel.

Rothbard, M.N. ([1982] 1998). *The Ethics of Liberty*. New York University Press.

The Spontaneous Issue of Lancashire Bills of Exchange as Money

Toby Baxendale

This is an exploration into an episode in British industrial history where banks did not exist, at least not in their present form. Although their modern formation had just started, the payment and credit mechanism for trade flourished. Lancashire bills are a great example of spontaneous money. More importantly for the greatest industrial city of the world at that time, they were preferred over any other type of money. They would still also exist today except tragic state interference.

Professor Jesús Huerta de Soto inspired me to look at money, credit and banking in a different way. For that I am grateful. It is a privilege to learn under one of the great teachers of the world.

T. Baxendale (✉)
London, UK
e-mail: mail@tobybaxendale.com

D. Howden, P. Bagus (eds.), *The Emergence of a Tradition: Essays in Honor of Jesús Huerta de Soto, Volume I*,
https://doi.org/10.1007/978-3-031-17414-8_5

Early Banking in Manchester

The first Manchester Bank, was called Byrom, Sedgwick, Allen and Place. It opened in 1771. It was not the only Manchester banking business. In Liverpool, at this time, merchants were also establishing banks. The majority of trade was conducted via the medium of bill discounting. Due to Liverpool being a port, marine insurance was also allied to banking (Redford, 1934, p. 248). The first banks in the UK's main industrial area were nearly one hundred years behind the establishment of the Bank of England and the Scottish banks.

Crick and Wadsworth (1936, pp. 142–43) note the significance of Manchester and the close by City of Liverpool, by observing that the more agricultural the area, the more likely small circulation note issued by banks were to be established. The theory is that the industrialists have more developed capital structures, need money for longer, and sell things less frequently. For the farmers the opposite was true. Farmers produce fresh product all the time; selling to many different people in small and regular quantities which made a note an easier method to facilitate trade than gold, silver, or bills. However, Crick and Wadsworth also suggest bills in Lancashire issued in smaller quantities performed the same role. Lancashire was attracting produce from around the Empire to process into finished goods and sending it out to the four corners of the world. This would mean it would have counterparties with no knowledge whether a small county bank in region X or region Y of the world was commercially sound or not. Therefore, either credit granted to receive money upon the sale of the goods at their final sale to the consumer, supported by a bill, or money received (gold or silver) from a bill discounter, who may have better local knowledge, taking the counterparty risk, would be one way they choose bills over notes as a medium of exchange. Confidence in the fellow industrialist, supplier or customer was higher than that of the local bank.

As the industrial revolution was maturing we can see that bills were used as the primary medium of exchange across the whole country as the preferred facilitator of exchange. This part of our country's history is one of the UK's finest, as banking approximated a free system. Money, especially bills of exchange circulating as money, had arisen from the market to solve the problem of exchange, and was doing a good job.

Ashton (1934) picks up the story of the Lancashire bills and asserts that two papers written by Henry Baker of the Manchester and Salford Bank infer that (1) agricultural areas had more residents and more banks and (2) the industrialists were less thrifty than farmers.

We note the inference that the Lancastrian industrialist was less thrifty than his agricultural counterpart. However, leaving aside the issue of who was or was not thrifty, to build these great pioneering enterprises, you needed savings, [1] or other people's savings, in substantial amounts. So, I think it is more an issue that they saved and invested all they could and needed more! To deepen and lengthen their capital structure to produce more, they needed to save to invest. We must also remember that the industrialist's inventory of surplus goods is his savings, as that is what he, in the future, will part with for other goods and services via the medium of money. Bills not yet matured and inventory will also be savings. Aston (1934, p. 104) overlooked this point. However, promisingly, he develops the point that bills by their nature were more conducive to international trade than notes issued via a county bank. As bills were issued, backed by physical items of manufactured goods, in international trade, they were deemed better security than a promissory note issued by a local county bank. Ashton also gives us clues as to why they have almost vanished today from the commercial realm as the stamp duty applied to them was less advantageous than that on notes or a cheque, as the latter provided quicker redemption in money.

Digging a bit further into the historical record, we see that these bills arose spontaneously to fulfill a need to be able to facilitate the smooth transmission of trade. A perceptive book written by Wadsworth and Mann (1931) documents this history. They explain (pp. 37–38) how in the early 1600s cotton production was used to spin into working men's garments in the first industrial processes. This was facilitated by bills which made sure the cotton was paid for, by raising a "bonde" or bill obligatorily "payable at four months." As a result, bonds and bills facilitated the early start of the industrial revolution. They helped fill the time gap between having to have the cotton and then manufacturing into a garment and selling it for cash. A bill signed over for discounting to cash would give the owner of that bill the right to that eventual produce should the producer not pay (pp. 91–92). Credit was granted and discounted bills accepted and paid with *specie*, not with notes or other such fiduciary credit. The Crown

[1] Pressnell and Orbell (1985, p. xix) write that "The historic role of the bill broker was to facilitate the movement of bills from area where industry was developing rapidly, and which consequently was short of cash, to agricultural areas which had a large surplus of savings."

accepted these bills for tax purposes, leading them to function broadly as money.

How the Lancashire Industrialist Understood Money

It would seem that the industrialists knew the distinction instinctively between a claim and credit transaction. They only dealt in *specie* and bills of exchange. Specie always gave ability to the owner to make actual claim transactions with money *on other goods and services* until paid, as opposed to a credit transaction where you only have a right to get the *loaned money back at a certain time* in the future. A discounted bill could then function like a credit transaction as the owner who provided the specie to pay for the original goods now waits until the final goods are sold and paid back in specie with a premium, but they always had recourse, in the eventuality of non-payment, to assert their ownership right over the goods. With bank runs being reasonably frequent, they viewed it better to own a right to the final payment of goods and services, from people they knew and conducted business with, than hope that the notes they owned could be redeemed in specie at a county bank.

These Lancashire bills were money. We can see that Ashton (1939, p. 104) looked at the activities of a number of bills and noted *that bills passed from person to person*, in exchange for goods and services *prior to* the ultimate payment of the goods when the original goods that were discounted against were sold. This is how a good proportion of bills functioned at the time.

What Happened in Manchester? Why Did These Lancashire Bills Decline?

Samuel Oldknow and the Arkwrights (Unwin et al. 1924) is a most spectacular historical investigation into one of the pioneering mill owners of the day. It points out that even after the 1793 panic and collapse of many businesses and then moving on to the outbreak of the Napoleonic War, while other parts of the nation were allowing notes to be issued, Manchester was having nothing to do with this: A meeting at Manchester resolved that *during* the emergency it could not be considered disreputable for houses to make payments in their own notes, payable in three months with interest. (Unwin et al. 1924, pp. 179–80).

In the absence of banks, they continued to issue their own bills against goods sold. In general, the industrialists remained deeply suspicious of anything to do with county banks and note issuers. The authors (Unwin et al. 1924, p. 190) note that the bills that the Oldknow company issued started to decline in value as there was a general inflation in the late 1790s. Holding bills of a fixed nominal sum while inflation increasing decreased the real value of the bills. This general inflation was not helped by the suspension of specie payments in 1797, brought about by the Napoleonic War. Therefore, it would be more sensible to move to holding notes which could circulate more quickly as the merchant deleveraged from any inflationary effect on trade.

Another reason for their demise what the imposition of a stamp tax (1815) on bills. Wright (1913, pp. 69–70) notes:

> On May 27th, 1815, a petition was signed for the presentation to the " Rt. Hon. Nicholas Vansittart, Chancellor of the Exchequer, etc., etc., etc.," in which it was stated that the Directors of the Chamber felt much alarm and uneasiness at the proposed increase of the taxes on stamps and inland bills of exchange and promissory notes, and at the multiplication of the classes thereof."

The stamps on bills were unusually large which encouraged people to issue them for long periods rather than short periods, generally making them less attractive vis-a-vis notes and slowing trade considerably.

We can see the problem as section XIV of the Stamp Act 1815 allowed notes, once the tax had been paid, to circulate and be reissued with no extra tax paid, unlike bills that needed to pay the tax each time. Conversely in Section XX, the Bank of England exempted itself and its notes from anything so inconvenient as tax except for one modest annual payment (see also section XXI of the Stamp Act). No bill issuer could compete with the Bank of England under such conditions.

It would seem that this Act coupled with inflationary forces allow us to understand why the Lancashire Bills of Exchange—indeed all bills at the time—entered a rapid period of decline, allowing us to enter into the age of the note issuing banks.

Thornton (1939, p. 214) commenting on the demise of bills in favor of notes, also supports this view, as does Redford (1934, p. 209). The final blow seems to have come when in 1825 the Bank of England expanded its operations to the Lancashire area. Hitherto its notes were, in the main, limited to London and its immediate neighborhood. Now it could press its paper into Lancashire and crowd out the bill system.

What Lessons Can Be Learned Concerning the Manchester Bill Period?

During the dawn of the Industrial Revolution, there is little evidence in Manchester of booms and busts. As the banking system elsewhere becomes established, there is more evidence of boom and busts. In Checkland (1975) we can see in the Scottish banking system busts in 1760s, 1772, 1778, 1793, 1797, 1802–03, 1809–10, 1810–11, 1818–19, 1825–26, 1836–37, 1839, and 1845–47. During these periods, the Scottish banks were free and more innovative in contrast to their English counterparts. However, as Sechrest (2008, p. 83–84) points out, critiquing White's interpretation of Pressnell and Orbell's (1985) data, the English and the Scottish systems had nearly identical failure rates, at 14.90% and 14.88%. In other words, they were equally unstable. This contrasts with the relatively tranquil non-bank credit system in the most industrialized city in the world: Manchester.

When businessmen were settling their accounts via the use of bills against the sale of these goods with *specie* being advanced, the people and businesses of Manchester could save without having their money intermediated by the banking system creating more notes and liabilities of the system. This ensured that only those savings put forth to go into investment for industry and more productive activity were made. This, in Lancashire, naturally helped create a much more stable and prosperous community, indeed, the most industrial in the world at the time. What is more, it was done largely without bank credit with its ability to over issue notes in relation to specie. Capitalist savings in Manchester was done via the bill system. This period in history shows us how a non-bank generated credit system could work to the satisfaction of the most industrious citizens of the world at the time. This contrasts with the county bank system, which was credit driven and more prone to boom and bust. The Lancashire traders were clearly weary of stepping into the county bank note issuing environment due to the potential instability in them manifested by periods of bank runs and banks going bust. With regard to the current advocates of fractional-reserve free banking, I urge them to consider the theoretical implications of this, based on the supporting empirical evidence of Manchester and its bill system: that full-reserve banking was a success in the first industrial city of the world. This would set free banking on a much more stable financial system, as we have seen in Manchester.

With the invention of the blockchain and the various coins that exist on the blockchain, while none are the final good for which all goods and services exchange, that is, money, some of those coin products may well achieve that status in the coming years. As we approach this next stage of the technology revolution, like those Lancashire industrialists, we may well see the birth of spontaneously issued money to facilitate the ongoing decentralized finance boom. We have started to witness the emergence of 100% reserved banks in the State of Wyoming, called Special Purpose Depository Institutes (which are the only banks I am aware of) that can hold cryptographic assets, which, by their nature are unique code that can't be co-mingled as fiat money can be in a conventional fiat banking system. We may come full circle to the start of the Industrial Revolution where the full-reserve bank was the preferred banking system, at least in the greatest city of the Industrial Revolution.

References

Ashton, T. S. (1934). *Economic and Social Investigations in Manchester: 1833–1933*. P. S: King and Sons.

Ashton, T. S. (1939). *An Eighteenth Century Industrialist*. Manchester University Press.

Checkland, S. G. (1975). *Scottish Banking, A History, 1695–1973*. Collins.

Crick, W. T., & Wadsworth, J. E. W. (1936). *A Hundred Years of Joint Stock Banking*. Hodder and Stoughton.

Huerta de Soto, J. (2006). *Money, Bank Credit and Economic Cycles*. Ludwig von Mises Institute.

Pressnell, L. S., & Orbell, J. (1985). *A Guide to the Historical Records of British Banking*. Palgrave Macmillan.

Redford, A. (1934). *Manchester Merchants and Foreign Trade, 1794–1838*. Manchester University Press.

Sechrest, L. J. (2008). *Free Banking Theory, History, and a Laissez-Faire Model*. Ludwig von Mises Institute.

Smith, A. (1784). *Wealth of Nations* (3rd ed.). W. Strahan and T. Cadell.

Thornton, H. (1939). *Enquiry into the Paper Credit of Great Britain*. George Allen & Unwin Ltd.
Unwin, G., Hulme, A., & Taylor, T. (1924). *Samuel Oldknow and the Arkwrights: The Industrial Revolution at Stockport and Marple*. Manchester University Press.
Wadsworth, A. P., & Mann, J. D. L. (1931). *The Cotton Trade and Industrial Lancashire, 1600–1780*. Manchester University Press.
Wright, G. H. (1913). *Chronicles of the Birmingham Chamber of Commerce, 1813–1913*. Birmingham Chamber of Commerce.

Jesús Huerta de Soto as Scholar, Teacher, and Academic Entrepreneur: A View from the US

Peter J. Boettke

The Austrian School of Economics has throughout its history had many variants—almost as many as practitioners. Of course, many times the emphasis on differences was highlighted for reasons other than scholarly pursuits, but there are substantive issues that produce the variations as well. Even in the differences, though, there are also points of common

I consider it a great honor to write an appreciation of Professor Jesús Huerta de Soto. He is, to put it simply, a force of nature. I first became aware of Professor de Soto when I began working at New York University in 1990. Professor Kirzner, in one of our first meetings after I joined the faculty, asked me if I knew Jesús Huerta de Soto of Spain. I said I wasn't sure, if my memory is correct, to which Professor Kirzner informed that I should because he was the leading representative of the Austrian School in the Spanish speaking world.

P. J. Boettke (✉)
George Mason University, Fairfax, VA, USA
e-mail: pboettke@gmu.edu

D. Howden, P. Bagus (eds.), *The Emergence of a Tradition: Essays in Honor of Jesús Huerta de Soto, Volume I*,
https://doi.org/10.1007/978-3-031-17414-8_6

ground which are ignored at the risk of great interpretative peril. There is much more common ground, for example, between Mises and Hayek, then there are fundamental disagreements. And, their shared research program is to be contrasted with that of say Keynes-Samuelson or Friedman-Lucas. Still, there are differences that are fruitfully explored by scholars. In the end, a lot turns on the temperament of the scholar and the emphasis that they place in their own set of teaching and scholarly pursuits.

Professor Huerta de Soto is part of the tradition of the Austrian School that emphasizes the ethical, judicial, and economic principles of a free society. In this, he is part of a Natural Law tradition. In the modern Austrian School of Economics this was best represented by the work of Murray Rothbard. Mises and Hayek operated out of a different intellectual tradition, though their work was obviously critical to informing this Rothbardian wing of the school. Kirzner sits in-between in a unique way, but his ethical system does not derive from utilitarian calculus as it does for Mises and Hayek.

I don't want to get weighed down in this note of appreciation with the subtle substantive differences between ethical individualism, rule utilitarianism, and natural law doctrine and how they relate to the various strands of the Austrian School, my point is merely to point out that Professor Huerta de Soto's work as a teacher and scholar is clearly placed within one of those strands. As his monumental work on *Money, Bank Credit and Economic Cycles* (2006) demonstrates, Huerta de Soto brings the ethical and judicial perspective to his economic analysis. But the economic analysis is grounded in the subjectivism of Menger, the capital analytics of Bohm-Bawerk, the monetary calculation arguments of Mises, the knowledge and discovery arguments of Hayek and the entrepreneurial theory of the market process of Kirzner. In short, he synthesizes, just as Rothbard did before him, a variety of perspectives to create his own unique voice (as any reader of the treasure trove of footnotes in *Man, Economy and State* would discover).

Some of the best work demonstrating Professor Huerta de Soto's synthesis of the various contributions of Austrian economists is in his work on socialist calculation and the debate with the market socialists. In his contribution of *The Oxford Handbook of Austrian Economics*, Huerta de Soto addresses the various market socialist proposals and demonstrates their shortcomings as revealed by the Austrian School of Economics. Socialism, by its nature, "obstructs, impedes, or prevents the entrepreneurial creation of precisely that information authorities would need to truly coordinate society with their commands" (2015, 96). As he goes on, "Not even the kindest person on earth, with the best of intentions and greatest of knowledge, could organize society based on the coercive socialist framework." The essence of the problem with socialism is not a computational complexity problem, nor is it an incentive alignment issue—no doubt socialist planners would have to confront both—but the foundational problem is that absent of the entrepreneurial market process itself, the requisite informational inputs would be absent. The information, or knowledge, of the market is contextual in nature and doesn't exist outside of that context. Economic calculation of alternative uses of scarce resources emerges within this context. It is in this context that economic decision makers using the tools provided by the price system can begin to sort from the array of technologically feasible projects to those that are economically viable. The market is a process of creative discovery of new and better ways, and it is a process of selection where previous less effective ways are discarded and more effective alternative paths are pursued. The market, as Mises stressed, is a process continually unfolding through time.

This process takes place within an ethical and judicial framework, and thus economic *science* cannot proceed as if exchange and production take place within an institutional vacuum. Professor Huerta de Soto's work as a scholar makes sure we never commit that error.

Two other aspects of Professor de Soto's academic activities must be stressed. He is an outstanding teacher, and his doctoral students developed outstanding careers as scholars, policy analysts, public intellectuals, and academic entrepreneurs. The Spanish speaking world is vast, and within that vast world there is a constant presence of the Austrian School of Economics, and that constant presence in contemporary times is due to Professor Huerta de Soto. Not only has he been the teacher of teachers in Europe, in Latin America, and even in China, but he has through his work as a publisher ensured a steady supply of translations on all the classic works in Austrian economics as well as many contemporary works. His work has indeed been tireless in championing the writings of the Austrian economists.

In the end, Professor Kirzner was right. Professor Jesús Huerta de Soto is a name anyone working within the Austrian School of Economics must know and respect. He has an impressive record as a scholar developing an ethical, judicial, and economic system of thought that addresses the foundational issues of a free and prosperous society. He has been a passionate and committed teacher of the Austrian School of Economics that has produced scores of teachers and thinkers throughout the globe. And, he has worked tirelessly to make sure generations of students in the Spanish speaking world will have available for them the classic and modern writings of representatives of the Austrian School.

That is some career, and there is still much for him to do. Professor Kirzner alerted me to the wonderful opportunity to learn from this great scholar, teacher, and entrepreneur some thirty years ago, and it is my sincere hope that we will all continue to learn from him for another thirty plus years and that legions more will follow in his footsteps as a scholar, teacher, and academic entrepreneur.

References

Huerta de Soto, J. (2006). *Money, Bank Credit and Economic Cycles.* Ludwig von Mises Institute.

Huerta de Soto, J. (2015). Austrians Versus Market Socialists. In P. Boettke & C. Coyne (Eds.), *Oxford Handbook of Austrian Economics.* Oxford University Press.

Rehabilitation of the Bankrupt Firm: Property Rights and Entrepreneurship

Francisco Cabrillo

In this chapter I present some reflections on the dilemma of liquidation–reorganization in bankruptcy proceedings, leading to the conclusion that the idea of rehabilitating at high-cost those companies that are not able to stay in the market on their own can be inefficient and collides with some

It was not easy to stand for the principles of a free market economy in Spain in the early 1980s. The socialist party won the general election of 1982 with a program prone to higher taxes, higher public expenditure and even the nationalization of some basic sectors of the Spanish economy. Fortunately, the most radical proposals of its manifesto were never put into practice. But the mood was certainly favorable to liberal ideas, neither in politics nor in the universities.

There were however some small groups of businessmen and academics going against the current ideas. In the Complutense University of Madrid Professors Lucas Beltrán and Pedro Schwartz were members of the Mont Pelerin Society. Beltrán was a former student and friend of Friedrich Hayek and Schwartz

F. Cabrillo (✉)
Complutense University of Madrid, Madrid, Spain

D. Howden, P. Bagus (eds.), *The Emergence of a Tradition: Essays in Honor of Jesús Huerta de Soto, Volume I*,
https://doi.org/10.1007/978-3-031-17414-8_7

of the basic principles of business economics and the role that the entrepreneur should play in the firm.

Bankruptcy plays an important role in market economies. Although bankruptcy procedures are usually very complex, due to the conflicting interests of different groups—debtors, creditors, workers, and the government—and to the many regulations by which they are affected, their economic rationality is clear: bankruptcy is a collective action procedure whose goal is to get a better allocation of resources and move capital and labor to areas in which social productivity is higher (Jackson, 1986). When collecting their credit from of a bankruptcy procedure, creditors play a non-cooperative game, in which each individual maximizing strategy produces an inefficient outcome. Social costs increase when each creditor tries to get the highest possible amount of money from debtor's assets. These strategies reduce the net value of the debtor's estate and generate the inefficient outcome characteristic of a prisoner's dilemma. Bankruptcy law prohibits such strategies and incentives cooperation of creditors to avoid such unwanted effects.

The foundations of bankruptcy law were established within an economic framework which was characterized by a prevalence of private law contracts freely undertaken by both parties and by a low level of government control of the economic activity. This is the way that this institution is still designed in most countries. However, it would be tantamount to closing one's eyes to real life to not accept that important changes have taken place in the framework in which bankruptcy law is currently developed, with a higher level of government control and a greater relevance of the role played by the stakeholders.

The efficiency of bankruptcy procedures has been widely discussed in recent years. And the present COVID crisis puts in the foreground the

had studied in London with Lionel Robbins and Karl Popper. In 1978 a free market think tank was formed, the Instituto de Economía de Mercado. Jesús Huerta de Soto, as an undergraduate, was already involved in the group of businessmen and publishers that was trying to spread the principles of Austrian economics in Spain. He joined soon the Complutense group and wrote his two PhD dissertations under Beltrán and Schwartz. I met him for the first time in those years. I remember being a member of his dissertation committee and to have shared with him a graduate seminar for PhD candidates. And there began a friendship that lives on forty years later.

debate between liquidation and reorganization of the bankrupt firm. Advocates of reorganization present it as a socially efficient procedure that reduces the high social costs of liquidation. Principles like "social welfare" or "public interest" are often used to advocate for a greater use of rehabilitation procedures. And in the present crisis higher rates of unemployment may be used as a strong argument to try to avoid liquidations. Critics argue, however, that rehabilitation is a procedure that breaks down the basic principles of bankruptcy and may be, in the long run, more expensive than liquidation.

Debates about this topic have been common in the last few years due to the pandemic, since governments have to make decisions on granting aid to some companies to keep them alive and, at the same time, on refusing such aid to many other companies that are considered not strong enough to stay in the market. But the reform of bankruptcy law has been widely discussed in Europe and the United States for many years, and one of the outcomes of these debates has been the substantial development of the reorganization procedures for bankrupt companies.

Reorganization basically consists of the implementation of a rehabilitation plan in order to allow a firm to stay in business. Although the best-known bankruptcy provisions for reorganization are those contained in the chapter "History and Economic Theorizing" of the American Bankruptcy Code, similar provisions can be found in many other countries. Each reorganization procedure has its own peculiarities. Some bankruptcy codes (the American Bankruptcy Code, for instance) allow the original management to stay in charge of the firm in most cases. Others, for example, the British Insolvency Act of 1986, appoint an administrator to lead the company during the bankruptcy proceedings. The role of creditors in the proceedings may also differ. Some procedures require the conversion of debt into stock, while others offer diverse alternatives to the creditors. Credit priorities do not always receive the same treatment. Differences also exist between the voting systems on asset sales or postponement grants to the debtor. Employees play a relevant role in some reorganization proceedings, and almost none in others. But in every case, the main objective of the procedure is to put the company on a solid base and to try to guarantee its survival.

Should liquidation or reorganization be the main concern of courts and judges in bankruptcy cases? Some codes consider liquidation and reorganization of the firm as alternatives, without showing any special preference for one or the other. Other codes, however, favor the rehabilitation of the firm.

In any bankruptcy procedure it is essential to evaluate the firm's assets and liabilities in the most accurate possible way since the decision between liquidation and reorganization usually depends on this valuation. Most bankruptcy codes are, however, very vague when dealing with the value of a company. Judges have therefore significant discretionary powers in a subject they usually know little about. For instance, there is substantial evidence to suggest that, in the United States, the valuation of bankrupt firms by judges in order to consider its possibilities for rehabilitation is systematically overstated (Jackson, 1986, p. 220). This concern has led a number of scholars to seek alternative procedures that provide market-based estimates of a firm's value.

There are two main methods to evaluate an insolvent firm: the balance method and the feasibility method. The balance method is static. It uses the market value of assets and liabilities in order to determine whether the company has a positive or negative net worth. A negative net worth would imply liquidation, while a positive net worth would pave the way for reorganization. This method has two inherent problems: first, there is the usual problem with the valuation of equipment and inventories when they may have to be sold in the short run. This possibility requires that these evaluations should be made as cautiously as possible. For instance, if inventories can be valued at the original cost or at the present market value, the lowest one should be used. Second, the fact that there is a net worth does not guarantee the future survival of the firm in the market. A company whose net worth is positive because it owns expensive equipment or valuable buildings should be liquidated if there is no demand for its product in the market.

The feasibility method is dynamic. It does not focus on the static value of the firm's assets and liabilities but rather on the probability of survival that a reorganized company would have in a specific market. According to this method a firm should be rehabilitated if the discounted value of its future cash flows is expected to be positive. This is a strong argument from an economic perspective. But this method poses a major problem: the subjective judgements, unavoidable in these evaluations, permit different interest groups to seek rents and try to get a court decision convenient to their own interests, as will be discussed in the following section of this chapter.

Property Rights in a Bankruptcy Procedure

American data show that as many as nine out of ten small- and middle-sized firms fail after going into a Chapter 11 (American Bankruptcy Code) reorganization procedure. In this context, Franks and Torous (1989) present historical data on firms under reorganization. In Italy and France, rehabilitation procedures have been criticized as a useless and expensive prologue to liquidation or even as procedures that anaesthetize creditors. And in Britain, where the reorganization procedure has been considered a possible improvement of the old bankruptcy law, its relative success has been due to a most efficient system of liquidation that allows the new managers to sell the profitable divisions of the bankrupt firm for good prices. And many bankruptcy scholars claim that reorganization is time-consuming, that it involves high administrative costs and often reduces the company's value. For instance, Bradley (1992) and Baird (1986) are good examples of this literature quite skeptical with the rehabilitation procedures.

Efficiency arguments fail to explain why so many firms with such low probabilities of survival are reorganized. The existence of interest groups and rent-seeking behavior, often disguised as public interest efforts, provide one possible explanation. A firm may be conceived as a framework of interests and property rights. Property implies three different rights over the firm: the right to control it; ownership of the firm's assets; and the right to take possession of the firm's profits. According to a complex web of legal provisions and contracts, owners share these rights with creditors, employees, and the government.

Discussions over priorities in the use of these rights are a characteristic feature of bankruptcy procedure. Business experience reveals that the preference for reorganization or liquidation is often determined by the property right framework, as defined by law. The interests of secured creditors may be very different from those of unsecured creditors when faced with a choice between liquidation or reorganization. Employees and unions may think that reorganization is the most beneficial outcome for their interests. The incumbent managers may prefer reorganization if the procedure allows them to stay in charge of the reorganized firm (Gilson, 1990) but have reasons to be against reorganization if it seems likely that an external administrator will be appointed to lead the firm. Another argument for current managers to oppose liquidation could be that they may try to avoid being considered responsible for the failure of the company.

All these property rights and interests collide in bankruptcy procedures and each group follows its own strategies. Their relative success will depend on the value of their credit, the specific regulations of bankruptcy law, and the public support they can secure for their demands. Suppose that employees believe, as they usually do, that reorganization is the most convenient outcome for them. They will follow a strategy that puts pressure on decision makers, local politicians, and the media, in order to keep the firm in business. Some laws go even one step further and assign an active role to employees in the negotiations between debtors and the creditors (the French Bankruptcy Code being a good example). Public choice and rent-seeking models offer plausible explanations for the possible success of this strategy and account for the public subsidies that some companies receive in case of reorganization (Buchanan et al., 1980).

It is usual to present the liquidation-reorganization dilemma as a private vs. public interest problem. It is argued that the already complex framework of property rights and interests should be enlarged to include some kind of public interest in the survival of the bankrupt company. Unemployment or deindustrialization in a depressed area are the arguments more often used to justify the public interest in avoiding the liquidation of insolvent private firms. From an efficiency perspective it may be hard to justify these arguments. Bankruptcy law is not the best instrument to deal with problems such as unemployment or deindustrialization. There is no reason to consider the interests of unemployed employees or local interest groups more "public" or "social" than the welfare of the creditors, the taxpayers, or the whole society, which will eventually pay for the misallocation of factors of productions. The costs of liquidation and rehabilitation are often misperceived. It is easy to overestimate the short-run social costs of the liquidation of a firm, especially in cases of high rates of unemployment. It is, however, more difficult to assert the long-run costs of an inefficient allocation of resources. These long-run costs are usually downgraded by the public opinion, and public interest arguments often prevail over the efficiency aspects of the decision. It is true that a rehabilitation procedure may allow some efficient firms with short-term illiquidity problems to stay in the market; but it should be emphasized that more often it creates incentives to save inefficient firms that should be liquidated.

Firms Without Entrepreneurs?

As we have seen in the previous section, reorganization of a bankrupt firm often implies a change of management. It is true that the appointment of a new management does not always take place; for instance, under the chapter "History and Economic Theorizing" of the American Bankruptcy Law, management is usually allowed to continue operating the corporation. But other reorganization procedures insist on the removal of the incumbent management and the appointment of new managers under the supervision of the creditor's representatives. But are these managers real entrepreneurs?

Many economists think that the basic characteristic of firms in a competitive market is the existence of entrepreneurs that take risks and organize production, being both profit maximizers and discoverers of opportunities for gain. Some well-known models can be mentioned. In Schumpeter's theory of economic development entrepreneurs play a fundamental role when introducing to the market new goods or new methods of production or design new ways of organizing a company. Inventions per se are not relevant for economic progress. Only when they are put into practice do they become important. The role of entrepreneurs is to put together these "new combinations." Their effects are revolutionary changes that promote economic development. No one is an entrepreneur forever and there is not such a thing as a social class of entrepreneurs. Personal characteristics are required to be an entrepreneur. So, in his own words, one can inherit the entrepreneur's money, but not the claws of the lion. This first version of the theory was presented in Schumpeter's early book on the theory of economic development (Schumpeter, [1912] 1934). But some years later, in *Capitalism, Socialism and Democracy*, Schumpeter changed his theory at least in two relevant aspects: first, he put much greater emphasis on innovation than on entrepreneurship; and second, he said that the entrepreneur does not have to be a person. In this new approach to the study of economic development he accepted that a big corporation, a state company, or even a country itself might be the entrepreneur of the future. This idea explains his gloomy predictions about the future of capitalism: if the businessman entrepreneur is no longer necessary for economic progress, capitalism, as we know it, could cease to exist (Schumpeter, [1942] 1975).

A second approach to the role of the entrepreneur was presented by Frank Knight in his analysis of the role that risk and uncertainty play in business economics. Knight made a clear distinction between risk—that may be treated as an insurable cost—and uncertainty which cannot be. Workers are more risk averse than entrepreneurs. So the "essence of enterprise" is the specialization of the function of "responsible direction" of economic life. The role of businessmen in a market economy is to organize production in an uncertain world, in which they are forced to speculate on the price of their final products. So, according to Knight, uncertainty about the future allows entrepreneurs to earn profits even in cases of competitive equilibrium (Knight, [1921] 1971, esp. ch. 9 on "Enterprise and profit").

The third model I should mention is Prof. Kirzner's theory of entrepreneurship. Kirzner (1973) draws a sharp distinction between the means of production ordinarily conceived and entrepreneurship, in the sense that entrepreneurship implies the existence of a project and taking initiatives. If the project exists and the entrepreneur thinks that it is worth undertaking it, he will try to obtain the necessary factors of production. In principle, engineers have the knowledge to do it. But, according to this model, only the entrepreneur takes initiatives. Knowledge and factors of production may be bought in the market. But entrepreneurship cannot be purchased or hired and cannot be taught. Entrepreneurs detect market imperfections, caused by information asymmetries, and exploit them being their role to discover opportunities that other people in the market cannot see.

These three models are quite different from each other. But they share an important characteristic: all of them assert that it is difficult to explain the role of a firm in the marketplace without someone playing the role of entrepreneur. From this perspective, bankruptcy should be conceived as an entrepreneur's failure. And the point to be emphasized is that rehabilitation does not imply that a new entrepreneur takes over the firm—as it would happen if the company or part of it were sold to another efficient company with a sound business plan—and only means that creditors or workers appoint new managers. A manager usually is not an entrepreneur. So, according to the models that emphasize the role of the entrepreneur, it will be very difficult for a bankrupt firm to be saved by a group of managers, a trustee, or the representatives of workers or creditors. This is probably the best explanation of why so many failures occur in the rehabilitation procedures of companies in bankruptcy.

References

Baird, D. (1986). The Uneasy Case for Corporate Reorganization. *The Journal of Legal Studies, 15*, 127–147.

Bradley, M. (1992). The Untenable Case for Chapter 11. *Yale Law Journal, 101*, 1043–1095.

Buchanan, J. M., Tollison, R. D., & Tullock, G. (1980). *Toward a Theory of Rent Seeking Society*. Texas and A Press.

Frank, J., & Torous, W. (1989). An Empirical Investigation on U.S. Firms in Reorganization. *Journal of Finance, 44*, 747–769.

Gilson, S. (1990). Bankruptcy, Boards and Block Holders. *Journal of Financial Economics, 27*, 355–378.

Jackson. (1986). *The Logic and Limits of Bankruptcy Law*. Harvard University Press.

Kirzner, I. (1973). *Competition and Entrepreneurship*. University of Chicago Press.

Knight, F. ([1921] 1971). *Risk, Uncertainty and Profit*. University of Chicago Press.

Schumpeter, J. A. ([1912] 1934). *The Theory of Economic Development: An Inquiry into Capital, Profits and Interest and the Business Cycle*. Harvard University Press.

Schumpeter, J. A. ([1942] 1975). *Capitalism, Socialism and Democracy*. Harper.

The Place of *Money, Bank Credit, and Economic Cycles*, in the Austrian Tradition of Economic Treatises

Óscar R. Carreiro

I will try to assess the place of *Money, Bank Credit, and Economic Cycles* and, in general, Huerta de Soto's work within the context of the tradition of economic science and, more specifically, of the Austrian School of economics. First of all, we will have to consider a certain historical decline in the traditional practice of economics as a science (a decline that helps to explain the disappearance of the treatise as an important feature of economic research) to see that many elements that were an integral part of that tradition have been preserved in what we call "Austrian economics." Once we have identified those elements then we can see how well Huerta de Soto's work fares within that context.

In a lecture titled "The Essential Value of a Classical Education," Jeffrey Brenzel defines a classic book as a work that (1) addresses a permanent and universal concern about the human condition; (2) effected a significant

Ó. R. Carreiro (✉)
Universidad Rey Juan Carlos, Madrid, Spain
e-mail: oscar.carreiro@urjc.es

D. Howden, P. Bagus (eds.), *The Emergence of a Tradition: Essays in Honor of Jesús Huerta de Soto, Volume I*,
https://doi.org/10.1007/978-3-031-17414-8_8

shift in the way of thinking about something; (3) influenced other great works; (4) experts from later generations have respected it; and (5) is challenging to read yet rewarding.

Brenzel's definition falls within the broader cultural framework of the Great Books, the idea of great literary works that shaped the culture, values, and thought of the Western tradition. For example, according to educational philosopher Robert Hutchins (1952, xi): "Until lately the West has regarded it as self-evident that the road to education lay through great books. No man was educated unless he was acquainted with the masterpieces of his tradition."

Although the proponents of the idea of Great Books, generally speaking, did not pay much attention to the subject of economics, we could say that this field of human knowledge also advanced through the publication, reading, discussion, and recognition of great books, which, in this case, took the form of economic treatises such as Cantillon's *Essay on the Nature of Trade in General*, Adam Smith's *The Wealth of Nations* or J. B. Say's *A Treatise On Political Economy*. Thus, in the words of Murray Rothbard: "Before World War I, the standard method, both of presenting and advancing economic thought, was to write a disquisition setting forth one's vision of the corpus of economic science" ([2004] 2009, p. li).

What happened after World War I was a process of intellectual disintegration with two different but related aspects. On the one hand, a methodological shift toward positivism and, on the other, a split of economic science in different sub-fields compounded by the rise of hyper-specialization.

With regard to the first aspect, the methodological shift toward positivism meant the abandonment of the method of deduction using verbal logic and the triumph of the employment of unrealistic and complex mathematical models:

> For much of the post-World War II period, flexing one's mathematical and statistical muscles and stripping down one's argument to a formal and parsimonious set of equations was indeed the main path to establishing scientific purity in economics. (Fourcade et al., 2015, p. 92)

The side effect of this methodological shift was the fragmentation of economics in multiple sub-fields loosely connected if connected at all, starting with the division between microeconomics and macroeconomics. According to Joseph Salerno (2019), "failing to master the great praxeological system of economic theory that had taken shape in the interwar years, these postwar economists could now undertake research in the splintered, ultra-specialized areas of growth theory, labor economics, industrial organization, oligopoly theory and so on ad infinitum." This extreme specialization was a detriment to economic science because economics, by definition, deals with the interconnectedness of all the phenomena of action.

Harry Redner believes that the intellectual triumph of hyper-specialization was historically related to the birth and expansion of the nation-state and the concomitant control of science and knowledge through a statist process of institutionalization. With this process "the university was gradually acquiring a monopoly of knowledge, just as the state was acquiring a monopoly of power" (Redner, 1987, p. 47). According to Redner, the new bureaucratic system with its new forms of academic authority was fully realized only after the Second World War, in large part due to the intrusion of the state into education and research prompted by the War.

The institutionalization of science and knowledge came from the need of justifying the increasing state intervention. The state needed a class of intellectuals and specialists for providing rationalizations for various interventions into the market economy. On the side of the specialists, as Richard Harvey Brown (1993) explains, since institutionalization involves significant social investment, those who control the necessary resources can influence practitioners by proffering or withholding funds. According to Brown, such institutions serve several key functions: as settings for specialized discourse, as social mechanisms for training, licensing, and exclusion, and as defenders of professional prestige, property, and privilege. Thus, practitioners usually are inclined to promote institutionalization, and willing to adapt their discursive practices sufficiently to accord with the interests, and to maintain the support, of their sponsors.

Peter Burke, studying the decline of the polymath in the nineteenth and twentieth centuries, also links this process to the statist institutionalization of science and its research system:

> [N]ew academic specialties proliferated, often claiming the title of disciplines and taking institutional form in separate departments. The increasing emphasis on research, in other words on original contributions to knowledge, encouraged if it did not force individuals who hoped for an academic career to focus on limited fields. (Burke, 2020, p. 132)

As Rothbard notes, one of the unfortunate casualties of the institutional setting established after World War I was the old-fashioned treatise in economics which disappeared at the same time as the concept of economic science as an integrated field of knowledge. One does not need to be an Austrian economist to realize and regret the detrimental effects of the process of hyper-specialization in economics. For example, the post-Keynesian Imad Moosa, a staunch critic of the modern institutional setting which he subsumes in the aphorism "Publish or Perish" (POP) states:

> Under the POP culture, publications mean journal articles, and there is no place for books, whether they are textbooks or research monographs. Just as well that great economists such as Adam Smith, Karl Marx, David Ricardo and Alfred Marshall did not live under POP, otherwise we would not have seen *The Wealth of Nations*, *Das Kapital*, *Principles of Political Economy and Taxation*, and *Principles of Economics*. (Moosa, 2018, p. 175)

We can find critics of hyper-specialization in the natural sciences (see Cereijido, 2012) but it is significantly important with regard to the results of economic science. After all, as Hayek said, "nobody can be a great economist who is only an economist—and I am even tempted to add that the economist who is only an economist is likely to become a nuisance if not a positive danger" (Hayek, 1956, p. 463). Once again, one does not need to be an Austrian economist to agree with Hayek, as shown by the example of Edgar Morín:

> Economics, the most mathematically advanced social science is the most socially, humanly backward science because it has abstracted itself from the social, historical, political, psychological, and ecological conditions inseparable from economic activity. This is why the experts are increasingly unable to interpret the causes and consequences of monetary and stock market perturbations, or foresee and forecast economic trends, even on the short term. Thus, error in economics becomes a primary consequence of the science of economics. (1999, pp. 16–17)

Ludwig von Mises once thought that the label "Austrian economics" was no longer relevant because all its essential ideas were accepted as an integral part of the synthesis of economic theory that he called "modern subjectivist economics" (Salerno, 2009, p. xxiv). But the reality was that the triumph of the positivist ideal in the interwar period led to a continuous decline of the theoretical research employing verbal logic and the deduction method and the concept of economics as an integrated science. That fact can be seen as a reason to consider modern Austrian economics as the intellectual heir of what once was "the mainstream of an international economic tradition that originated in the Marginalist Revolution" (Salerno, 2009, p. xlix).

Even though we can trace the origins of the Austrian School back to the publishing of Carl Menger's *Principle of Economics* in 1871, Austrian economics constitutes a body of knowledge that has been discovered, refined, extended, and systematized collectively through the efforts of several generations of scholars:

> What we know today as the Austrian school of economics was not made in a day. This school has gone through years of evolution in which the wisdom of one generation was passed on to the next. Though the school has progressed and incorporated knowledge from outside sources, the core principles remain the same. (Hall, 2021)

Let us look at some of these core principles and see how well Huerta de Soto's *Money, Bank Credit, and Economic Cycles* fares within this tradition.

A Common Philosophical Background

Most of the theoretical elements considered as key features of Austrian economics, such as the application of intentionality to economic value (and therefore the subjectivity of economic value), the concept of methodological individualism, or the employment of the method of deduction, show how Austrian roots (and initially, economics in general) are grounded in Aristotelian philosophy (Gordon, 2020a).

We can see that Huerta de Soto acknowledges the Aristotelian philosophical roots of the Austrian School from the fact that he establishes a historical link between it and the Spanish scholastics of the School of Salamanca, moral philosophers trained in the theory of natural law in the Aristotelian-Thomistic tradition and considered by economic historians like Schumpeter (1954) as the founders of economics as a science. As stated by Huerta de Soto (2009, p. 209): "The Spanish scholastics were capable of developing the essential elements of what would later be the theoretical basis of the Austrian School of Economics."

A Systematic Development and Exposition of Economic Principles Which, in Many Instances, Took Place in the Form of Economic Treatises

We have many examples like Carl Menger's *Principles of Economics* (1871), Eugen von Böhm-Bawerk's *Capital and Interest* (1884), Frank Fetter's *Economic Principles* (1915), Ludwig von Mises' *Human Action* (1949), Murray Rothbard's *Man, Economy, and State* (1962), or George Reisman's *Capitalism* (1995).

To show some key features of some of these treatises, we can begin with Hayek's appraisal of Menger's work. Hayek thinks that in Menger's *Principles of Economics* the fundamental concepts of economics "become the powerful instrument of an analysis in which every step seems to result with inevitable necessity from the preceding one" (Hayek, 1934, p. 399). In a very similar fashion, Schumpeter states that in Menger's work "the focus lies on theory, which is entirely based on the phenomenon of value. [...] As such the endeavor is to be appreciated, since, if one is to base it on only one principle, it means a step towards the unification of the edifice of our science" (cited in Kirzner, 2018, p. 53).

In the case of *Human Action*, Peter Boettke thinks that one of the great achievements of this book is to present a unified body of theory through the systematic use of some fundamental economic principles:

> Mises united microeconomics and macroeconomics well before they were the terms of art in the economics profession, and he presented his readers with a coherent and unified body of theory grounded in the logic of choice, the role of relative prices, and the practice of rational economic calculation. Purposive human actors are at the center of the analysis from the first to the last page of this treatise, and along the way the reader is provided step by step with the intellectual tools necessary for understanding the operation of the unhampered market economy. (Boettke, 2020, p. 564)

And Hoppe, in the case of *Man, Economy, and State*, says that Rothbard "develops the entire body of economic theory, in a step by step fashion, beginning with incontestable axioms and proceeding to the most intricate problems of business cycle theory and fundamental breakthroughs in monopoly theory" (Hoppe, 1995, p. 33).

With regard to *Money, Bank Credit, and Economic Cycles*, Huerta de Soto states one of the objectives of his treatise:

> It is necessary to recognize economics as a unified whole, where macroeconomic elements are firmly rooted in their microeconomic foundations. In addition, I will attempt to demonstrate that the economic analysis of some juridical institutions yields critical implications and conclusions that are essentially macroeconomic [...] By closing the profound artificial gap between micro and macroeconomics, we arrive at a unified theoretical treatment of legal issues in the economic analysis of law. (Huerta de Soto, [1998] 2020, p. l)

This general objective, the treatment of economics as a unified science, and its applications to the analysis of institutions and law show how Huerta de Soto's work constitutes the continuation of the Austrian tradition. Furthermore, according to Hülsmann, "it is the first Misesian treatise on money and banking to appear since the publication of Mises's original work" and set new standards for Austrian scholars with its extensive treatment of subjects like the business cycle (Hülsmann, 2000, p. 86). The intellectual contributions of Huerta de Soto's treatise cannot be reduced to any subdiscipline in economics but, in the best Austrian tradition, establishes a coherently integrated picture capable of explaining a wide variety of juridical, historical, and economic phenomena:

> One of the main theses of the book is indeed that whereas the economic analysis of juridical institutions has thus far had almost exclusively microeconomic implications, the approach to the economic analysis of juridical institutions developed by the Austrian School yields critical implications and conclusions that are essentially macro-economic in nature, elucidating macro-economic phenomena like inflation, recurring boom-bust cycles and stagflation, besides their devastating consequences. (Van den Hauwe, 2006, p. 136)

The Use of Natural Language and the Deductive Method

Austrian methodology begins with the self-evident reality of human action and its immediate implications. It then introduces other empirical postulates that reflect the concrete conditions of action from which emerge the historically specific market phenomena that the economist seeks to analyze. Mises called this method Praxeology, which asserts the action axiom as true, and from this (together with a few empirical axioms—such as the existence of a variety of resources and individuals) are deduced, by the rules of logical inference, all the propositions of economics, each one of which is verbal and meaningful (Gordon, 2020b).

Money, Bank Credit, and Economic Cycles takes advantage of the corpus of knowledge discovered with the employment of this method and applies it to the economic analysis of banking. The use of praxeology and natural language, instead of artificial and unnecessary complex mathematical models, establishes a contrast between his treatise and other works. Samuel Gregg thinks that this contrast arises because of the way subjects like money, credit, and banking are taught in universities where much instruction is conducted in the language of econometrics and mathematics, whereas Huerta de Soto makes his subject "to come alive in a manner normally absent from most other texts addressing similar questions" (Gregg, 2007, p. 185).

The Idea That Economics Should Explain Real Economic Phenomena with Relevance to Real People

This is connected to the previous point. According to Salerno (2009, p. xxxii) the praxeological method is "necessarily about real things. It is for this reason that it has no use for fictions and figments like the 'representative firm', 'the perfectly competitive market', or 'the social welfare function'; nor does it concern itself with the existence, uniqueness, and stability of general equilibrium. The highly selective use that the praxeological method makes of imaginary constructs has a single aim: the systematic elaboration of a unified body of theory, comprising meaningful propositions about the causes of economic phenomena in the world as it is, has been, or is likely to be."

It was Menger who established this method by trying to discover cause-and-effect relationships that would explain the prices, wages, and interest rates observed in reality. His goal was to formulate an integrated theory of prices that would be valid for all times and places. This is the reason why the Austrian School does not fall to the Nirvana fallacy, that is, blaming the real world because it falls short of some impossible ideal instead of trying to assess which alternative real institutional arrangement seems best able to cope with the economic problem (Demsetz, 1969).

With regard to this point, Hülsmann states that Huerta de Soto's solid elaboration of his arguments along realist lines makes his treatise a model illustration of the Austrian approach to the study of the relationship between law and economics. In this approach, legal distinctions are fundamental and economic analysis is a derived analysis. The latter takes up the distinctions established by the former and explores their economic significance (Hülsmann, 2000, p. 88).

The Importance Granted to Institutional, Legal, and Historical Analysis

Praxeology is the method employed to deduce economic theorems that can be applied in the explanation and understanding of real economic phenomena. The emphasis put on realism explains why, since the beginning, Austrians (and originally all economists) have always put a high value on the study of actual economic and social institutions:

> Economists have always dealt with the impact of the law on human behavior and on the working of the economy at large. Roughly speaking until the end of the nineteenth century, the main purpose of economics was to come to grips with that impact. This in turn implied a certain prevalence of comparative methods. After all, to assess the impact of judges, legislators, and governments on the economy requires a comparison of this impact with the status quo ante; or, as some economists pointed out, it requires a comparison of this impact with what would have happened if judges, legislators, and governments had made other choices. (Hülsmann, 2004, p. 4)

Money, Bank Credit, and Economic Cycles examines the legal character of certain banking activities like credit banking and deposit banking, and then goes on, step by step, to point out their economic implications (Hülsmann, 2000, p. 86). This approach exemplifies Huerta de Soto's belief in the necessity of a multidisciplinary approach to the study of economic phenomena and economic institutions:

> Everything in the book, de Soto stresses, is examined from the three perspectives that he deems "necessary to correctly comprehend any social phenomenon: historical-evolutionary, theoretical, and ethical" (xxiv). This combination of insights from positive and normative sciences allows Huerta de Soto to do full justice to his topic as an economic, historical, and moral reality. (Gregg, 2007, p. 186)

In the eyes of Ludwig van den Hauwe, the detailed, systematic, and integrated way of performing this multidisciplinary analysis is one of the main virtues of Huerta de Soto's treatise:

> In conclusion, it should be stressed that the book under review has put the multidisciplinary method and approach into practice with great effectiveness. It is no exaggeration to assert that the strongest argument in support of the author's case ultimately derives from the fact that the results of the historical-evolutionary, the theoretical (or economic) and the juridico-ethical analyses converge on a similar overall conclusion. (Van den Hauwe, 2006, p. 140)

A Critical Analysis of Other Economic Theories

Given the fact that the objective of economic science is to discover knowledge about the real world that can be used to assess elements of the socio-economic organization of societies of significant importance to the well-being of people, one of the features of Austrian works since the foundation of the Austrian School was the intellectual critique of other theories. Prime examples are Böhm-Bawerk's detailed critical study of the theories of interest in *Capital and Interest* including a "crushing confutation" of the Marxist exploitation theory (Smart, 1890, p. xvi), Mises's critique of socialism in *Economic Calculation in the Socialist Commonwealth* (1920) and *Socialism* (1922), or Hazlitt's critique of Keynes in *The Failure of the "New Economics"* (1959).

In his treatise, Huerta de Soto "offers a thorough criticism of rival approaches to the understanding of business cycles" (Van den Hauwe, 2006, p. 138) including a critical analysis and refutation of the alternative explanations for business cycle phenomena offered by the monetarist and Keynesian schools. We can find also a highly interesting critique of the most important modern justification of fractional reserve banking, which stresses that credit contracts and deposit contracts are essentially the same thing.

A Conscious Effort Toward the Creation and Maintenance of a School of Thought

As reported by Guido Hülsmann (2007, p. 139) "Menger saw himself as the founder and leader of a new school of social research, and he strove to raise disciples and to spread them over the land." In a letter to the Austrian Ministry of Culture, he pointed out that many young scholars received their university professor's diploma under his auspices and that these scholars had obtained the majority of the chairs of political economy at the Austrian universities (Hülsmann, 2007, p. 139; Schulak & Unterköfler, 2011, pp. 53–62). Menger was also successful in establishing a network of like-minded young thinkers within the confines of Austria-Hungary. The effort of school building continued with the next generation with Mises private seminar which "became the nucleus for monetary and business cycle research and gained an international reputation" (Schulak & Unterköfler, 2011, p. 70) and had regular participants like Friedrich Hayek, Fritz Machlup, Alfred Schutz, Gottfried Haberler, and Oskar Morgenstern (Haberler, 1974). Later, the participants to Mises seminar in New York included people like Israel Kirzner, Hans Sennholz, Ralph Raico, Leonard Liggio, George Reisman, and Murray Rothbard. As Cristobal Matarán has studied, Huerta de Soto gathered together people interested in economics, politics, or philosophy from an Austrian perspective emulating the model that Ludwig von Mises instituted in Vienna and New York. These seminars aimed to establish a debatable framework around the Austrian principles applied to the current situation in Spain. This development was followed by the establishment of "Unión Editorial," the first publishing house of Austrian School essays in Spanish. Huerta de Soto's efforts culminated in the establishment of a Master's degree in Austrian Economics at Rey Juan Carlos University in Madrid in 2007. This process of development in Spain of a school of thought in the Austrian tradition led to a situation where "there had not been such a large group of researchers and thinkers [in Europe] about the Austrian School tradition since pre-World War I Vienna" (Matarán, 2021, p. 70).

Conclusion

After this examination, I think it is safe to say that Huerta de Soto's *Money, Bank Credit, and Economic Cycles* not only is firmly placed within the Austrian economics tradition but also fulfills the five points of Brenzel's definition of a classic. This consideration is supported by the popular success of the treatise, with translations to twenty-one languages, seven editions in Spanish and four editions for the English translation. It constitutes, as Lealand Yeager has said, "an impressive work of scholarship, synthesizing and criticizing legal and economic writings in numerous languages. It is probably the most thorough treatment in print of Austrian theories of banking and the business cycle" (Yeager, 2001, p. 255). For all these reasons, I completely agree with the following assessment of the book:

> There can be no doubt the book is destined to become a classic, both by virtue of the subject matters that are treated and in virtue of the manner in which they are treated: thoroughly and authoritatively. (Van den Hauwe, 2006, p. 141)

References

Boettke, P. (2020). *Mises's Human Action* and Its Place in Science and Intellectual Culture. *The Independent Review, 24*(4), 557–565.

Brown, R. H. (1993). Modern Science: Institutionalization of Knowledge and Rationalization of Power. *The Sociological Quarterly, 34*(1), 153–168.

Burke, P. (2020). *The Polymath. A Cultural History from Leonardo da Vinci to Susan Sontag*. Yale University Press.

Cereijido, M. (2012). Science is Not Balkanized in Different Disciplines: Being a Super-Specialist is Not an Excuse for Not Being a Wide Scientist. *International Journal of Psychological Research, 5*(2), 6–7.

Demsetz, H. (1969). Information and Efficiency: Another Viewpoint. *The Journal of Law and Economics, 12*(1), 1–22.

Fourcade, M., Ollion, E., & Algan, Y. (2015). The Superiority of Economists. *Journal of Economic Perspectives, 29*(1), 89–114.

Gordon, D. (2020a). *The Philosophical Origins of Austrian Economics*. Mises Institute.

Gordon, D. (2020b). *Praxeology and Mathematical Logic*. [online]. https://mises.org/wire/praxeology-and-mathematical-logic

Gregg, S. (2007). *Money, Bank Credit, and Economic Cycles*. Jesús Huerta de Soto. Translated by Melinda A. Stroup. Auburn, Alabama: Ludwig von Mises Institute, 2006 (876 pages). *Journal of Markets & Morality, 10*(1), 185–190.

Haberler, G. (1974). Mises' Private Seminar. In I. L. South Holland (Ed.), *Ludwig von Mises, Planning for Freedom* (pp. 190–192). Libertarian Press.

Hall, M. (2021). *The Austrian School of Economics*. [online]. https://www.investopedia.com/articles/economics/09/austrian-school-of-economics.asp

Hauwe, L. v. d. (2006). Book Review. Jesús Huerta de Soto. *Money, Bank Credit, and Economic Cycles*. Translated by Melinda A. Stroup. Auburn: Ludwig von Mises Institute, 2006. *New Perspectives on Political Economy, 2*(2), 135–141.
Hayek, F. A. (1934). Carl Menger. *Economica New Series, 1*(4), 393–420.
Hayek, F. A. (1956). The Dilemma of Specialization. In L. D. White (Ed.), *The State of Social Sciences* (pp. 462–474). University of Chicago Press.
Hoppe, H. H. (1995). Hans-Hermann Hoppe. In H. Llewellyn & J. Rockwell (Eds.), *Murray N. Rothbard: In Memoriam* (pp. 33–37). Mises Institute.
Huerta de Soto, J. (2009). *The Theory of Dynamic Efficiency*. Routledge.
Huerta de Soto, J. (2020). *Money, Bank Credit, and Economic Cycles*. Mises Institute.
Hülsmann, J. G. (2000). Dinero, crédito bancario y ciclos económicos. By Jesús Huerta de Soto. Madrid: Unión Editorial. 1998. *The Quarterly Journal of Austrian Economics, 3*(2), 85–88.
Hülsmann, J. G. (2004). Editorial. *The Quarterly Journal of Austrian Economics, 7*(4), 3–6.
Hülsmann, J. G. (2007). *Mises. The Last Knight of Liberalism*. Mises Institute.
Hutchins, R. M. (1952). *The Great Conversation*. Encyclopedia Britannica.
Kirzner, I. F. (2018). Schumpeter's Review of Frank A. Fetter's *Principles of Economics. Quarterly Journal of Austrian Economics, 21*(1), 52–59.
Matarán López, C. (2023). The Austrian School of Madrid. *Review of Austrian Economics, 36*, 1–79.
Moosa, I. (2018). *Publish or Perish*. Edward Elgar.
Morín, E. (1999). *Seven complex lessons in education for the future*. UNESCO.
Redner, H. (1987). The Institutionalization of Science: A Critical Synthesis. *Social Epistemology, 1*(1), 37–59.
Rothbard, M. N. (2009). *Man, Economy, and State with Power and Market*. Mises Institute.
Salerno, J. T. (2009). Introduction to the Second Edition of *Man, Economy, and State with Power and Market*. In M. N. Rothbard, *Man, Economy, and State with Power and Market* (pp. xix–l). Mises Institute.
Salerno, J. T. (2019). *Economics: Vocation or Profession?* [online]. https://mises.org/library/economics-vocation-or-profession
Schulak, E. M., & Unterköfler, H. (2011). *The Austrian School of Economics*. Mises Institute.
Schumpeter, J. (1954). *History of Economic Analysis*. Oxford University Press.
Smart, W. (1890). Translator's Preface. In E. von Böhm-Bawerk (Ed.), *Capital and Interest: A Critical History of Economical Theory*. Macmillan.
Yeager, L. B. (2001). The Perils of Base Money. *The Review of Austrian Economics, 14*(4), 251–266.

Human Behavior and Austrian Economics

Leef H. Dierks

In virtually every aspect of human life, decision-making features emotional components. Put simply, decisions are never based on strictly rational behavior alone. And still, an overwhelming number of economic models are based on this very assumption. Even contemporary models still understand the influence market participants' (unconscious) emotions exert on behavior to be moderate, at best. While classical investment theories assume that investment decisions are always based on a strictly rational process—and that an investor can forecast future developments in an undistorted manner, behavioral finance assumes that investors frequently

---

It was in Ancona, Italy, in December 2015 that I bumped into one of this Festschrift's fellow authors. For reasons which even several years later still remain unknown to us, the conference we attended, strongly resembled the Annual General Meeting of the John Maynard Keynes Society.

Over dinner (done in style, at least) my fellow author and I discussed the efforts related to organizing an academic conference (needless to say, on

---

L. H. Dierks (✉)
Lübeck University of Applied Sciences, Lübeck, Germany
e-mail: leef.dierks@th-luebeck.de

D. Howden, P. Bagus (eds.), *The Emergence of a Tradition: Essays in Honor of Jesús Huerta de Soto, Volume I*,
https://doi.org/10.1007/978-3-031-17414-8_9

act irrationally. This makes their behavior subject to considerable biases with regard to perception and evaluation. However, if market participants understand this phenomenon, inevitable consequences could a priori be accounted for (Dierks & Tiggelbeck, 2019).

A Potential Overlap of Behavioral and Austrian Economics

Behavioral economics present challenges to the neoclassical theory of individual behavior, which is based on individuals seeking to maximize their expected utility. However, behavioral economics has illustrated that, indeed, it is common for individuals to systematically deviate from this axiom. To a certain extent, Austrian economics is based on axiomatic theories of utility maximization, too, but the underlying assumptions are considerably weaker. In consequence, Austrian economics benefits from a (more realistic) behavioral foundation, which makes it less vulnerable to challenges by experimental and empirical approaches. Put differently, Austrian economics appears to be better suited for policy analyses. And yet, Austrian economics has often been criticized for its alleged inability to incorporate more modern economic paradigms. Particularly principles such as the *homo oeconomicus*, who strictly abides the concept of rationality, have been questioned. Critics claim that such approaches fail to adequately reflect reality—but instead are of mostly theoretical relevance. The concept of the *homo oeconomicus* is unrealistic; it can only be held upright in an environment of certainty or risk but not uncertainty (or ignorance).

Austrian Economics). It was not until we had drinks later that night that the scales fell from our eyes: Why not try and bring the conference to Madrid, i.e., to the "new Vienna" as my dear colleague appropriately referred to it.

It fell upon me to reach out to him who is honoured by this Festschrift. Reply was swift, reply was positive—and no later than autumn 2017 the inaugural Madrid Conference on Austrian Economics was held on the Vicálvaro campus of Universidad Rey Juan Carlos. That was when I first met Jesús Huerta de Soto.

Of course, I had heard the anecdotes long before we finally met. He would inevitably reach to his pocket, people claimed, seize a golden coin—and toss it to the ground, delightedly bathing in his audience's reaction, the amazement, and the emotions.

Still, in order to develop economic models, it is indispensable to make simplifying assumptions regarding decision-making. In extremis, the *homo oeconomicus* neither is subject to emotions, nor is his consciousness subject to limited absorption capacities. As models can merely depict an excerpt from reality it is inevitable to reduce complexity. However, more realistically (but contradicting the concept of the *homo oeconomicus*), market participants spontaneously adjust their preferences to environmental conditions. This ought to be taken into consideration. Whereas traditional models thus assume that market participants operate independently of any personal reference points, behavioral economics could show that decision-makers repeatedly behaved in contrast to the neoclassical axiom of rationality (Dierks & Tiggelbeck, 2021).

Limitations to Human Decision-Making

Behavioral economics refers to actual human decision-making through extending the neoclassical concept outlined above by methodological diversity, inter alia emphasizing the limitations of human thinking (Taffler, 2018). More recent research indicates that intuition and mental abbreviations (heuristics) can indeed be efficient tools for reaching a judgment. In an environment of uncertainty, they are not necessarily the origin of systematic errors in reasoning or of cognitive distortions.

The Influence of Emotions

In contrast to reasoning, emotions are an instinctive or intuitive feeling, which usually arises outside an individual's consciousness. It therefore cannot be directly influenced (Taffler, 2014, p. 2). However, a cognitive basis is a prerequisite for an emotion. Decisions made on the basis of emotions are usually not based on rational evaluations (i.e., maximizing expected utility in accordance with available fundamentals), but on the feelings which humans perceive in certain situations (Kahneman, 2011, p. 175).

Combining Behavioral and Austrian Economics

Austrian economics relies on praxeology (rather than empirical studies). Based on the action axiom, objective and universal conclusions about human behavior can be drawn, for example, the notion that investors engage in acts of choice implies that they have preferences. This must be true for anyone who exhibits intentional behavior. Austrian economics further suggests that individualism is non-existent in an environment in which subjectivism generates a spontaneous order by interacting with other investors. Notwithstanding unpredictable future developments, there will always be particular behavioral patterns repeatedly occurring.

Behavioral economics, in contrast, is primarily concerned with investors' bounded rationality—and seeks to explain how decisions are made, the explanatory power of any economic principle could ceteris paribus be greatly enhanced by combining these paradigms.

Parallels? Or Contradictions?

Behavioral economics appears to contradict Austrian economics with regard to influencing individuals' behavior in an attempt to arrive at a socially optimal outcome and to maximize economic welfare. Yet, among the essential characteristics of Austrian economics is its view of market competition in terms of processes and rationality—as opposed to merely an optimal equilibrium. This comes as Austrian economics' focus is on understanding the coordination of (eventually incompatible) plans among agents with limited knowledge, that is, in individual learning, effectively. This, in turn, is assessed in terms of the capacity to allow market participants to discover new solutions to market problems and to realize and correct individual mistakes (Muramatsu & Barbieri, 2017).

Behavioral economics, which typically benefits from a sound microeconomic foundation, attempts to answer the question to what extent unconscious processes influence individual investment decisions, that is, what significance emotions have for investment decisions and the perception of risk. From an Austrian perspective, however, behavioral economics could benefit from relaxing its restrictive and axiomatic definition of rationality—in an attempt to treat humans as *active* rather than passive recipients of (environmental and cognitive) influences (Whitman, 2021). It remains unclear to what extent this argument indeed is valid as behavioral economics being an interdisciplinary subdiscipline of economics, neurosciences, sociology, and psychology is inter alia based on a renunciation of the traditional concept of rationality in the sense of the *homo oeconomicus*. From the perspective of behavioral economics, in contrast, Austrian economics could benefit from better understanding the fundamental question of how individuals arrive at choices and to analyze how such choices interact with the agents' respective environment (Whitman, 2021).

Conclusion

Behavioral economics and Austrian economics feature considerable conceptual differences, which makes their relationship complex and multifaceted (Rizzo & Whitman, 2009). But as both behavioral economics and Austrian economics scrutinize the axiom of human rationality, a combination of the paradigms' essential features will undoubtedly create considerable academic value-added. A combination of Austrian economics and behavioral economics would considerably enhance the understanding of humans' sometimes erratic decision-making under uncertainty. This comes as economic models are but an axiomatic simplification of reality, whereas (a supposedly objective) reality ultimately is but a phenomenon of an individual's subjective perception.[1]

References

Dierks, L. H., & Tiggelbeck, S. (2019). (Ir-)Rationality of Investor Herding. *Procesos de Mercado: Revista Europea de Economía Política, 16*(2), 253–270.

Dierks, L. H., & Tiggelbeck, S. (2021). Emotional Finance—Zum Einfluss von Emotionen auf Investmententscheidungen. *Der Betriebswirt, 62*(2).

Kahneman, D. (2011). *Thinking, Fast and Slow*. Penguin.

Muramatsu, R., & Barbieri, F. (2017). Behavioral Economics and Austrian Economics: Lessons for Policy and the Prospects of Nudges. *Journal of Behavioral Economics for Policy, 1*(1), 73–78.

Rizzo, M. J., & Whitman, D. G. (2009). The Knowledge Problem of New Paternalism. *BYU Law Review, 2009*(4).

Taffler, R. (2014), *Emotional Finance: Theory and Application*.

Taffler, R. (2018). Emotional Finance: Investment and the Unconscious. *The European Journal of Finance, 24*(7–8), 630–653.

Whitman, G. (2021). Austrian Behavioral Economics. *Journal of Institutional Economics*, 1–18.

[1] Oh, and before I forget: After all, the coin he did toss. What did you think?

The Austrian Theory of Consumption Period Planning: Some Neglected Contributions from the Interwar Period

Richard M. Ebeling

In his famous *Essay on the Nature and Significance of Economic Science* (1932), Lionel Robbins showed through his footnote references that it was the writings of the Austrian economists in the 1920s who were among the primary originators of his own refined definition of economics as "the science which studies human behavior as a relationship between the ends

---

The revival of the Austrian School of Economics over the last fifty years has been due to a small handful of dedicated and insightful individuals who have successfully built upon the earlier Austrian tradition that ran from Carl Menger to Ludwig von Mises and Friedrich A. Hayek. One of the most outstanding of these contributors has been Jesús Huerta de Soto, and it is in appreciation of him as scholar and educator that this essay has been written.

R. M. Ebeling (✉)
The Citadel: Military College of South Carolina, Charleston, SC, USA
e-mail: rebeling@citadel.edu

D. Howden, P. Bagus (eds.), *The Emergence of a Tradition: Essays in Honor of Jesús Huerta de Soto, Volume I*,
https://doi.org/10.1007/978-3-031-17414-8_10

and scarce means which have alternative uses" (p. 15).[1] The leading Austrian authorities drawn upon by Robbins on this theme were very clearly Ludwig von Mises (1881–1973) and Hans Mayer (1879–1956). A year before his *Essay* appeared, Robbins referred, in the foreword he wrote for the first edition of Friedrich A. Hayek's *Prices and Production* (1931), to the "marvelous renaissance" the Austrian School had experienced in recent years "under the leadership of Professor Mayer and Professor Mises" (p. ix).[2]

Already in his essay on "Economic Calculation in the Socialist Commonwealth," (1920) and in *Socialism: An Economic and Sociological Analysis* (1922), Mises had outlined the logic of human action under the conditions of scarcity, that made all conscious conduct instances of "rational" decision-making between ends desired and means insufficient to serve all purposes. All "actions" were instances of exchange, the trading between more and less preferred circumstances, independent of their "material" or "non-material" natures, and always occurring in the passage of time, and under conditions of imperfect knowledge and uncertainty

[1] The footnote references in the first edition of Robbins' *Essay* show more clearly the strongly "Austrian" influence on his thinking than in the second edition (Robbins, 1935), in which modifications in the text and deletions in and additions to the footnote references create the impression of different authorities having influenced his ideas.

[2] Robbins made a point of saying in the preface to his *Essay on the Nature and Significance of Economic Science* (p. viii–ix), his "especial indebtedness to the works of Ludwig von Mises." But this was made even clearer in the letter that Robbins enclosed with the copy of the book that he sent to Mises on 20 May 1932, just after it was published: "I send you herewith a copy of my modest attempt to popularize for English readers the methodological implications of modern economic science. I hope you will not mind my especial mention of your name in the preface. I have no wish to make you in any way responsible for my crudities of exposition, but if there is anything of value in what I have said it would be most unjust that your name should not be associated with it. It is not easy for me to put into suitable words the magnitude of my intellectual debt to your work." Mises replied on 18 June 1932, expressing his thanks and complete agreement with Robbins' contribution: "Only today, I have the time to thank you for the pleasure that I found in having received your book. I have read it with great interest. It is needless to say that I fully agree with your arguments. I only regret that you did not expand your book to include the treatment of a number of other important problems. I am, however, convinced that your latest work will prove to be very successful." And as F. A. Hayek later pointed out, "Robbins' own most influential work, *The Nature and Significance of Economic Science*, made what had been the methodological approach to microeconomic theory established by the Austrian School the generally recognized standard [within the wider economics profession]" (Hayek, 1992, p. 53). On the Austrian School tradition, in general, and Ludwig von Mises's contributions to economic theory and policy, in particular, see, Ebeling (2003, 2010a, 2010b, 2014, 2016).

(1922, pp. 96–97). In a series of essays written during the 1920s and early 1930s, Mises elaborated on this theme, arguing its universality in explaining the logic of any and all human actions. Or as he expressed it in a 1931 essay on the, "Development of the Subjective Theory of Value":

> First, there is the realization that the economic principle is the fundamental principle of all rational action ... If, however, all conscious conduct is an act of rational economizing, then one must be able to exhibit the fundamental economic categories involved in every action, even in action that is called "non-economic" in popular usage. And, in fact, it is not difficult to point out in every conceivable human—that is, conscious—action the fundamental categories of catallactics, namely, value, good, exchange, price, and costs ....
>
> Action takes place only where decisions are to be made, where the necessity exists of choosing between possible goals, because all goals either cannot be achieved at all or not at the same time. Men act because they are affected by the flux of time. They are therefore not indifferent to the passage of time. They act because they are not fully satisfied and satiate and because by acting they are able to enhance the degree of their satisfaction. (1933, p. 148 & 150)

Hans Mayer was Friedrich von Wieser's (1851–1926) favorite student. He was appointed as Professor of Economic Theory and Public Finance as Wieser's replacement at the time of his retirement in 1923. Mayer was considered one of the leading figures of the Austrian School between two World Wars, in the 1920s and 1930s. His most notable contribution during this period was generally recognized to be a one-hundred-page monograph, "The Cognitive Value of Functional Theories of Price" (1932, pp. 55–168), in which he offered a fairly detailed critique of the mathematical equilibrium theories of Antoine Augustin Cournot, William Stanley Jevons, Leon Walras, Vilfredo Pareto, and Gustav Cassel. He contrasted what he called their "functional theories of price," which focused primarily on the determination and specification of the conditions for a given state of economic equilibrium to exist, with the more dynamic "causal-genetic" approach of the Austrian School, which was concerned with analyzing the origin and formation of prices through the interactions of individuals in the market process, out of which equilibriums may arise.

Because of this and other contributions by Hans Mayer during this period, Wilhelm Weber, in his biographical essay on Mayer for the *Handwörterbuch der Sozialwissenschaften* (1961), said:

> Hans Mayer, together with Ludwig von Mises and Joseph A. Schumpeter, formed the three stars of the "younger Austrian School," with certainly each of them reaching heights of distinction equal to the classic three stars of the older Austrian School [Carl Menger, Eugen von Böhm-Bawerk, and Friedrich von Wieser], out of which they grew. Mayer was, himself, the most consistent keeper and administrator of the inheritance of his teachers; and here, again, especially Wieser's system, which he continued and reshaped in his own work, and whose essential aspects he protected from all methodological criticism. (p. 264)[3]

However, the work by Hans Mayer that had the most impact on influencing Robbins' famous 1932 definition of economic science, evidently, was Mayer's 1921–1922 article, "Untersuchung zu dem Grundgesetz der wirtschaftlichen Wertrechnung" [Analysis of the Fundamental Law of Economic Calculation"][4] Mayer laid out what he considered to be the summary premises of what later became known as the formal "logic of choice":

> From now on, the elementary postulates [of economics] will be expressed in the following generalized form:
>
> 1. A *plurality* of given ends.
> 2. A quantitative *insufficiency* of given means.
> 3. An arrangement of all the given ends in *a system of ends in an order of importance.* (All the individual ends ranked in terms of significance.)
> 4. A *connection of all the realizable ends* dependent upon the same means.

Already contained in 1 and 3 is the norm: As many of all the ends should be attained as is possible. The very concept of ends to be attained implies such a norm. And the very essence of a rank ordering of ends implies the requirement that no attainable end of lesser importance is to be achieved before an end of higher importance:

> The presence of these postulates clearly necessitates economizing behavior. Behavior that incorporates the distribution of available means for the

[3] For more detailed overviews of Hans Mayer's life and contributions, see, Mahr (1956) and Klausinger (2015a).

[4] Hans Mayer, "Untersuchung zu dem Grundgesetz der wirtschaftlichen Wertrechnung," *Zeitschrift fur Volkswirtschaft und Sozialpolitik* (1921–1922). The following references to this article are taken from its reprint in the *Zeitschrift für Natonalökonomie*, Vol. XV, No. 3 (Mayer, 1956). All italics in the quotes from Mayer's article are in the original. All English translations of passages from this article are by me.

> realization of particular ends involves a disposal of the "goods" in an unequivocally determined manner. It is unequivocally determined because given the specific rank ordering of the ends (in terms of their importance: first, second, etc., within the entire array of ends) and given the means, the latter would be insufficient for any arbitrary application of any portion of the total means available. It is obvious that the scarcity of means limits the ends that ultimately can be achieved. Hence, economizing is perpetual problem-solving, a perpetual making up of one's mind: How shall I divide the total sum of means regularly available to me among the particular ends that, in general, would be most feasible to attain with the given means? This situation of realizing the problem of an insufficiency of the means in relation to the plurality of ends rest upon a clear knowledge of our ordering of the ends (Mayer 1921–22, p. 290)[5]

In the 1920s, a defining characteristic of Austrian theory became this emphasis on the "economizing" act as the unifying concept for the understanding of human decision-making. For instance, a year after Mayer's formulation, Richard Strigl (1893–1942), another leading member of the Austrian School during the interwar years in Vienna, offered a similar formulation of "the economic problem," in his work, *Die ökonomischen Kategorien und die Organisation der Wirtschaft* [*Economic Categories and the Organization of the Economy*] (1923):

> Suppose that an individual has control over a set of resources which can be devoted to the fulfillment of various ends; and suppose those ends have been arranged in scale of descending importance. The question then arises: How does this determine the ends to which the resources will be in fact devoted? This is the question to which theoretical economics must find the answer ... The formula "distribution of resources among given possible uses" expresses the unifying principle of economic theory. (p. 123)

[5] Mayer also emphasized that all economic action begins with the "wants" of individuals, but such wants were to be understood in the widest meaning, being anything to which the individual assigns importance as a basis of satisfaction, regardless of being it being "real" or "imagined," see, (Mayer, 1924, p. 450): "In the theory of economics the doctrine of wants has the task of depicting the final psychical determinants of economic action, of which the economic subjects are still conscious, and of deducing with their help the laws in the course of economic action ... The scientific notion of wants is wider than the customary language; it includes not only ... those desires which occur with great intensity, but every desire from the greatest to the least, and in particular also because in the reality of economic acts, equally, the effects of 'imagined wants', that is, things wanted not because you 'need' them, but because you 'want' them."

Carl Menger and Periods of Planning

Economic action is undertaken according to an individual human plan in which the actor has constructed a set of desired ends in a hierarchy of importance and for which he applies means at his disposal for their attainment. From the beginning of the Austrian School, this has been seen as central to the logic of human conduct. Carl Menger (1840–1921), the founder of the Austrian School of Economics, had emphasized that men needed to have a clear knowledge of both their "requirements" (ends) and the available goods (means) to service them. Without knowledge of the first, he argued, men would be acting "blind," since they would lack the goals to guide their actions in particular directions. And without knowledge of the second, their actions would be "planless," since they would not know what they had available to work with in bringing their goals to successful conclusion (1871, p. 80).

Menger also explained that the construction of a period of production is for the successful provision of future ends, for which it is necessary to plan ahead. The periods of production are guided by a conception of a "period of provision" for which individual plans to provide. Thus, the human actor designs both production plans and consumption plans. Menger's theory of consumption planning, as developed in his *Grundsätze der Volkswirtschaftslehre*, is constructed with one consumption period in mind. In his famous table (p. 127) of the logic of individual decision-making, Menger explains the allocation of an actor's means among alternative competing and complementary ends according to the principle of marginal significance in the context of a single period.

For example, (see Table 1) suppose that an individual has $100 to allocate among three alternative uses, with an ordering of the marginal

Table 1 Carl Menger's single period marginal income allocation

A	*B*	*C*
($10)	*($5)*	*($15)*
A_1		
A_2	B_1	
A_3	B_2	C_1
A_4	B_3	**C2**
A5	**B4**	C_3
A_6	B_5	C_4

significance of the goods as indicated below, given the prices at which units of the goods could be acquired:

The actor would allocate his $100 of means for the satisfaction of those ends indicated by the bold underlining. That is, five units of "A," four units of "B," and two units of "C."

Hans Mayer and Consumption Period Planning Guided by "The Law of the Periodic Recurrence of Wants"

In his 1921–1922 article, Hans Mayer tried to extend the logic of Menger's analysis in a setting of multi-period consumption planning. Mayer argued that the allocation of the individual's means among these alternative ends seemed "unequivocal," given the rank ordering of the ends and the means at his disposal. But the allocation that seemed most optimal changed its character if it was remembered that men make their allocational decisions subject to, what Mayer called, "the law of the periodic recurrence of wants":

> Hence, it is certain that because of the law of the periodic recurrence of wants the allocation of goods has to be related to a period of time. This is already verified from the general preconditions of the empirical economy, and not only for a highly developed economic culture with its tendency for as far as possible to make more and more distant future arrangements independent of "chance." However, the length of the time period over which the economic subjects allocate goods for the satisfaction of wants in the future seems, at the moment, to depend purely on the individual, i.e., on the foresightedness, imagination, and willpower of the individual economic subjects ...
>
> The representation of the system of ends by means of a scale of wants and curves of wants, which is commonly used in theory, does not take into account this characteristic feature of the system of ends of the empirical subjects: that they necessarily exist through a temporal succession of ends with a regular recurrence of the same ends. Scales of wants and curves of wants only capture a non-recurring, timeless representation of an uninterrupted stream of satisfaction for each type of want, from the highest to the lowest intensity of each want. As it were, they only provide a cross-section of an economic subject's system of ends ...

They are only an *elemental construction* – however indispensable – of the empirical system of ends, but not of the second part, the periodic recurrence of similar ends in time. *In the scale of wants (curves), each point of intensity is found only once in each type of want, but many times in the system of ends in the empirical economy.* (pp. 299–300)[6]

The logic of diminishing marginal utility is usually presented in textbooks by means of a diagram. Units of the available means are applied to serve the end in question, with each unit providing a lower degree of marginal utility than the previous unit, until that degree of marginal utility is reach at which the supply of the means is completely used up. Under the assumption that the individual was to allocate the entire supply of the means during the present period (period t_1), he would attain a level of marginal utility of MU_3.

Mayer's argument is that this ignores the fact that the same wants reappear with some periodic regularity. A time axis has to be added to the diagram to indicate the periodic recurrence of this particular want. It is assumed that during the income period over which the actor plans the use and allocation of the means at his disposal this particular want reappears three times, that is, three "consumption periods." An optimal allocation requires that he distribute the available means in such a way that no degree of marginal satisfaction is reached for this good in any one of the planned consumption periods lower than in the other two. Or in Mayer's words:

[The actor] satisfies at first wants of the highest intensity during the present consumption period (period of wants). But then, before he starts satisfying less intensive wants in the same (present) period of consumption – guided by the experience of the periodic recurrence of wants – he also secures for himself the satisfaction of the same wants of highest intensity for future periods of wants, over a certain range of time, approximately until the point in time at which he can expect a new inflow of goods (in the form of new output or new income).

[6] Or as Mayer expressed it more formally in a later reformulation of his theory, "Zur Frage der Rechenbarkeit des Subjectiven Wertes" ["On the Question of the Calculability of Subjective Values"] (Mayer, 1953, p. 73): "The introduction of the time factor into value theory and with it the assumption, consonant with empirical fact, that economic subjects in evaluating goods do so in relation to a space of time, leads to the following arrangement: if T denotes periods of the plan, $t_1, t_2, t_3 \dots t_n$, the needs for goods a, b, c … n, which emerge in the course of their periodic recurrence during the space of time, there results with every type of good a marginal stratum of utilization within which, in a homogeneous series, the marginal utility occurs t_n times."

> Only after securing the satisfaction of the top layer of wants within a certain range of time by the allocation of the fixed quantity of goods, does he begin to cover the layer of wants of next highest intensity; once more he evenly divides the goods among the present period of consumption and a number of future periods of consumption. Hence, he arrives at levels of wants of lower and lower intensity by dividing the total quantity of goods available equally among the wants of a longer period which enables several or many small periods of consumption (periods of wants). Finally, he attains a certain marginal layer of satisfaction for each type of want. (p. 297)

By following this rule, Mayer said, the individual "was proceeding strictly according to the norm of economic behavior. He also utilized no part of the supply of goods available to satisfy a less important want at the cost of a more important one. He secured the highest total satisfaction possible, though not only for one, the present period consumption, but for a period of longer duration."

Mayer's argument can be explained by using a modified version of Menger's table, Table 2. There are three consumption periods during which certain wants recur. If the income period over which means at the actor's disposal are being allocated covers all three of these consumption periods, the agent must allocate his income in such a manner that as many of his wants are satisfied in each consumption period without infringing upon one of those wants that is deemed more important in one of the consumption periods.

Table 2 Hans Mayer's multi-period consumption period planning

Income period = $100 = Three consumption periods								
Consumption period 1			*Consumption period 2*			*Consumption period 3*		
A.	*B.*	*C.*	*A.*	*B.*	*C.*	*A.*	*B.*	*C.*
($10)	*($5)*	*($15)*	*($10)*	*($5)*	*($15)*	*($10)*	*($5)*	*($15)*
A_1			A_1			A_1		
A_2			A_2			A_2		
A_3			A_3			A_3		
	B_1			B_1			B_1	
A_4	B_2	C_1	A_4	B_2	C_1	A_4	B_2	C_1
	B_3	C_2		B_3	C_2		B_3	C_2

The scale of value in this table has been modified from Menger's to emphasize that now the individual, in having to economize over several consumption periods, may possibly change his preference ordering. Hence, if category "A" represents food, he would wish to assure for himself three meals a day before satisfying any other want in the three periods over which he is allocating his income.

With an income period of once every three days, and each consumption period equal to a day, the actor would plan to allocate $30 per day to assure his "recurring" desire for food during the entire income period. The remaining $10 would be allocated among the three "B's" (a drink at a local bar, perhaps, which is also a recurring want). The decision as to the allocation among the "B's" would be indeterminate (unless more clearly specified). It could be "B_1" Period 1 and Period 2, or in Period 2 and Period 3, or in Period 1 and Period 3. This would depend upon his time preference (though this is an element to the allocational decision that Mayer does not discuss).

Paul N. Rosenstein-Rodan and Planning for "The Economic Period" Under Uncertainty

Paul N. Rosenstein-Rodan (1902–1985) is best known in the economics profession as a pioneer of the "Big Push Model" in the post-World War II period with his theory of economic development through large government planned and directed investment projects. However, in the period between the two World Wars, his focus and interest were more in the "Austrian" tradition of economic theory. He studied at the University of Vienna under Hans Mayer, and in the late 1920s, served as a managing editor, along with Oskar Morgenstern, of the Austrian journal, *Zeitschrift für Natonalökonomie*, under Hans Mayer's general editorship of the publication.

His 1927 article on, "Marginal Utility" ([1927] 1994) is considered a classic summary of the state of the theory up to that time, and in highlighting the "Austrian" contributions to the theory of marginal decision-making.[7] He also focused on the role and element of time in economic

[7] Rosenstein-Rodan remarked that, "Hans Mayer was the first to introduce the time factor with his 'law of the periodic recurrence of needs.' When making his economic plan, i.e., when choosing the most suitable allocations, the economic subject must indeed consider several or many need periods and evaluate the importance of his needs over a longer span of time" (p. 179).

decision-making and monetary processes. Part of this emphasis was in further developing themes formulated by Hans Mayer on consumption period planning. Rosenstein-Rodan moved to Great Britain in 1930, teaching at the London School of Economics, before going to work for the World Bank in 1947, and taking up a teaching position at MIT in 1953, which he held until 1968.

Rosenstein-Rodan attempted to develop Hans Mayer's theory of consumption period planning in an article on, "The Role of Time in Economic Theory," (1934), originally delivered as a lecture at the London Economics Club in 1932. He argued that "so far the time factor has not been sufficiently analyzed, and it is generally agreed that such analysis constitutes one of the main tasks of economics in the future." One of the problems concerning the role of time that has not been fully developed was "the determination of the length of time which economic activity has in view – the problem of the economic period." (p. 77).

Like Mayer, Rosenstein-Rodan emphasized that the optimal allocation of means among competing ends could not be determined until a time period over which the means were to be used was specified. "To each change in the period of time for which one is economizing, the economic period as it may be called, there corresponds a change in the optimal distribution of resources. The period of time for which one economizes must be defined in order that conduct may be unequivocally determined" (p. 78).

But the selection of the time-frame over which the economic period was to be defined, he said, was not arbitrary. It was determined by the individual's "system of wants." Rosenstein-Rodan argued that a principle for determining the period for which the individual planned for the satisfaction of his wants was "to be found in a certain quality of the imperfection of human foresight" (p. 80). Rosenstein-Rodan suggested:

> Let us consider an individual who establishes an economic plan on a certain definite date. He will estimate his concrete wants (wants for particular units of a good) in such a way as to envisage the most important ones as far in advance as possible. He will not be able to foresee his less important concrete wants so far in advance, but as they decrease in importance he will foresee them only for shorter and shorter periods. This is not because he underestimates future wants – in our opinion that is a false hypothesis – but because the risk factor, which where it can be isolated is represented by a slight modification of the intensity of the concrete wants, becomes so great the further one looks into the future that it becomes impossible in most

> cases to evaluate the intensity of such wants in isolation. The fact that the uncertainty factor enters in, makes it necessary to keep, as it were, a special account ("blocks of wants") in which the concrete wants of the future are lumped together. (pp. 80–81)

The uncertainty of the future, including the specific nature and circumstances in which one will concretely determine the types and characteristics of the goods the individual may desire to consume, therefore, set a limit for him concerning the details of the economic period for which he planned. The nearby Fig. 1, which Rosenstein-Rodan uses, helps to clarify his point.

The horizonal blocks represent concrete wants the satisfaction for which they are specifically planned. The vertical blocks represent "blocks of wants" of a more general and less specific type. The wants considered most important would be most concretely planned for from the perspective of the beginning of the economic period. While those wants of less importance whose character and detail would be less certain would be only planned for a general way.

In Consumption Period 1, the present period, within the wider economic planning period, the actor would have a fairly detailed idea of the particular shape of most of his wants, though even here there would be certain groups of wants about which only a general or blurry idea would be held in the mind of the actor. For example, the individual might have fairly detailed ideas about the food or clothing he wished to purchase during that consumption period (say, a "day"), but only a more general idea about the

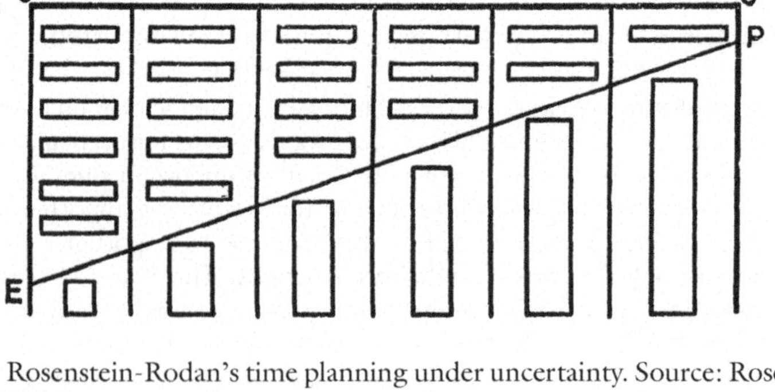

Fig. 1 Rosenstein-Rodan's time planning under uncertainty. Source: Rosenstein-Rodan (1934)

type of entertainment he would possibly pursue that evening (going to the movies, or going out dancing, or having a drink with friends).

As consumption periods extend further out into the future from the perspective of the point in time from which an economic plan is being constructed, more and more of the individual's wants become lumped together in general block categories. Finally, looking far into the future, the individual might only have the most general notion of any wants (say, Consumption Period 6 in the overall economic planning period), for example, that he will want various "somethings" under the general headings of "food," "clothing," "entertainment," "books," "time with friends," and so on. Only as those more distant consumption periods move closer to the present would those "blocks of wants" become disaggregated and particularized into concrete, or specific, wants.

In the diagram, Rosenstein-Rodan said, the diagonal line separating the horizontal blocks of concrete wants from the vertical general "blocks of wants" set the limit of the economic period for which specific multi-period consumption planning is made. Thus, the economic planning period extends over six consumption periods, beyond which the individual's planning takes on a completely non-specific character, that is, an intention to acquire income to assure the future satisfaction of wants, though the content takes on only the broadest of meanings.

Oskar Morgenstern and Multi-consumption Period Planning with Expectations

Oskar Morgenstern (1902–1977) is best known for his collaboration with mathematician, John von Neumann, in developing, *The Theory of Games and Economic Behavior* (1944). But Morgenstern's interests in the questions of planning coordination and expectations began under the mentorship of Hans Mayer at the University of Vienna. His first book was on *Wirtschaftsprognose* [*Economic Forecasting*] (1928), in which he challenged the ability for economic prediction solely through the use of quantitative and statistical methods.

This led him to analyzing how actors can successfully anticipate the actions of others for purposes of competition and cooperation. This also led him to question the assumption and use of the "perfect knowledge" postulate due to logical contradictions and absurdities when applied to actual market processes.

Morgenstern also attempted to extend Hans Mayer's theory of consumption period planning by introducing "expectations" into the analysis under a variety of alternative assumptions in his article, "The Time Moment in Economic Theory" (1935), which was originally delivered as a lecture at the Vienna Economic Association in 1933. Morgenstern also credited Hans Mayer with being, "the first author who clearly recognized the significance of the time element in value theory," and gave it a "precise formulation" (p. 151). While stating that he took Mayer's formulation as his own starting point, he believed that it represented, at best, only a first approximation for analyzing the nature and process of consumption period planning (p. 157).

Mayer's reference to the periodic recurrence of wants, Morgenstern pointed out, was constructed on the assumption of a uniform rhythmical repetition of all wants. As a result, the actor's task was merely to divide his income into equal portions to cover each consumption period within the wider income period. He suggested that under Mayer's construction there was only a "pseudo introduction of time into value theory."

The next logical step was to assume that wants, while repeating themselves, did not in a non-simultaneous and non-synchronized pattern. Thus, wants recurred during an income period, but with different frequency. For example, the desire for food would emerge each day, while other wants might reemerge only every other day, with still others appearing only once during, say, a three-day income period. The actor would have to allocate his income over the three consumption periods in unequal proportions to assure the maximum degree of satisfaction, or "utility," over the entire income period.

In Table 3, if the actor's income for the period was \$120, the "optimal" allocation, which would exhaust the available means and enable the achievement of the highest degree or ranked order of importance, would be \$35 in Period 1, \$45 in Period 2, and \$40 in Period 3. This allocation would assure optimal utility satisfaction over the entire income period.

However, the real meaning of income management over time, Morgenstern argued, only comes to the fore in the next extension of the theory. The new assumption is

> that the course of the recurrence of wants even if still dominated by a strong rhythm is so irregular, that the income periods are no longer mutually congruent. Should the individual totally use up his income in each income period, the income periods would show very dissimilar states of satisfaction

Table 3 Oskar Morgenstern's multi-period consumption period planning

Income period = \$120 = Three consumption periods									
Consumption period 1			*Consumption period 2*			*Consumption period 3*			
A.	*B.*	*C.*	*A.*	*B.*	*C.*	*A.*	*B.*	*C.*	*D.*
(\$10)	*(\$5)*	*(\$15)*	*(\$10)*	*(\$5)*	*(\$15)*	*(\$10)*	*(\$5)*	*(\$15)*	*(\$5)*
A_1			A_1			A_1			
A_2			A_2			A_2			
A_3			A_3			A_3			
	B_1				C_1		B_1		D_1

> or very different total welfare … Therefore, in each income period, already decisions have to be made which extend over this period … Herein lies the actual meaning of management over time … It seems that one must differentiate between the mere expectation of future events and the action in the present with regard to the future. (pp. 158–159)

The actor's wants may have a recurring rhythm, or a repeated pattern of reappearance, with their reemergence only in an income period after the present one. The individual must incorporate within his present income period planning some allocation of the means at his disposal into a future income period. Hence, the actor is required to undertake multi-period income planning to assure an optimal satisfaction of his wants.

In the previous example, the respective consumption periods for the respective wants (with the frequency with which each want reoccurred) were shorter than the income period. In this new case, the income periods are shorter than at least some of the consumption periods. The individual's consumption period planning horizon has to encompass several income periods, with the income allocation to any one income period including the entire *period of provision.*

In Table 4, with an assumed income of \$130 per period, an income allocation limited only to consumption periods within the income period (i.e., the wants that reoccur only with the given income period), would result, in Income Period 1 in complementarity of goods made up, at the margin, of "A_4," "B_2," and "C_1," in both consumption periods.

However, if the individual's economic period planning horizon extends beyond individual income periods to incorporate the recurrence of want, "D," which reappears only once in every two income periods (in

Consumption Period 2 in Income Period 2), a different allocation of income is required.

Suppose there is a transfer of $20 of income from Income Period I, with the foregoing of want-satisfactions, “A_4,” in Consumption Periods 1 and 2. From the perspective of a multi-income period of provision, that is, an economic plan covering both income periods, the want-satisfaction gain, “B_2” and “C_1” in Consumption Periods 1 and 2 in Income Period 2, results in a higher general degree of “utility” satisfaction, under the given assumptions.

Morgenstern also argued that the individuals do not always defer the satisfaction of wants in the present income period to satisfy want satisfactions in a future period, even when the importance of the want satisfaction in the future income period appears to have a higher ranked ordering than the want satisfactions in the more immediate income period. He said that this need not be taken as a demonstration of a positive time preference, that is, as the result of which the future want satisfaction is discounted against the present. Rather, it merely may be due to expectations on the part of the individual that anticipated income in the future will be sufficient to service those more highly ranked future wants. Tomorrow, in other words, will take care of itself, based on present expectations about the future (pp. 162–163).

Table 4 Oskar Morgenstern's economic period planning over multi-income periods

← *Economic period = $260 = Two income periods* →												
Income period 1—$130						*Income period 2—$130*						
Consumption period 1			*Consumption period 2*			*Consumption period 1*			*Consumption period 1*			
A	*B*	*C*	*A*	*B*	*C*	*A*	*B*	*C*	*A*	*B*	*C*	*D*
($10)	*($5)*	*($15)*	*($10)*	*($5)*	*($15)*	*($10)*	*($5)*	*($15)*	*($10)*	*($5)*	*($15)*	*($40)*
A_1			A_1			A_1			A_1			
A_2			A_2			A_2			A_2			
A_3			A_3			A_3			A_3			
	B_1			B_1			B_1			B_1		D_1
	B_2	C_1		B_2	C_1		B_2	C_1		B_2	C_1	
A_4	B_3	C_2	A_4	B_3	C_2	A_4	B_3	C_2	A_4	B_3	C_2	
A_5	B_4	C_3	A_5	B_4	C_3	A_5	B_4	C_3	A_5	B_4	C_3	

Morgenstern also challenged Rosenstein-Rodan's conception of consumption period planning. He stated that it was not necessarily true that the further off into the future one looks, the less certain the specific nature of what one's wants will be, so that various wants can only be closeted into general "blocks":

> It should be noted that the claim that there exists a uniform degree of diminution of the specification of all wants is at most a first approximation. Empirical observation of man teaches us rather that there are some wants which are determined in detail over very long time intervals, while others become already foggy after a few hours. At this point one should be warned not to make the mistake of assuming that needs which can be specified on a long-range basis are necessarily of a higher rank than other wants not itemized or not capable of specification.

> Rather, we will be able to show conclusively that these things, perhaps contrary to expectations, do not have to indicate any connection with each other ... The proof that many transactions of tomorrow are not at all organized to the last detail and made clear and that, on the other hand, I know exactly that in three months I will go to a health resort for a week in order to lead a well-defined life in an exactly specified sanitarium, etc., that is, that I will be able to determine this more accurately than where and what I will eat for dinner in a week, i.e., in a much shorter period, will lead one to discard the assumption that the crux of the matter had been hit by those writings which have hitherto been pre-occupied with the more global nature of needs seeing in it a solution to the problem of time in value theory. (p. 161)

For the remainder of his essay, Morgenstern merely touched upon the points that would require further development in a theory of consumption period planning. For example, not only did wants reoccur in an irregular rhythm, but an individual's income might be irregular, too, both in terms of amount and frequency of receipt. "Empirically, of course, both need and income, are subject to constant changes and the problem of it to attain a uniform state of welfare over time is evidently different in degree of difficulty according to the various layers and cases of consumers. In addition, economic managements take place usually in an unstable environment of changing prices. The components of expectations thus become more and more complicated," Morgenstern pointed out. "This is certainly a field that opens up a myriad of possibilities before the theorist" (p. 165).

There are also the complexities that arise from the fact that time periods when choices are made, when plans are executed, and when goods are consumed, may overlay in various different ways. There are also durable goods that can service wants several times before needing to be replaced through new acts of production. (pp. 165–166).

And, finally, there is the extension of the theory to the arena of market exchange. "A complete survey of the problems arising from the inclusion of time in value theory and the ways to their solution requires, however, further treatment of time management by the entrepreneur, because they show up a number of peculiarities," Morgenstern continued. "From the management of time by the consumer and the entrepreneur, then, results a genuine inclusion of the time element in theory of the exchange economy. Such an approach penetrates the problem much more than some introduction of time-parameters into some system of equations and the tagging of all economic processes with time indices" (p. 167).

The "End" to the Austrian School in Vienna

The types of questions and additional lines of inquiry raised by Oskar Morgenstern for an "Austrian" theory of consumption period planning were, seemingly, never developed further by any of the members of the Austrian School. And few historians of economic thought (particularly in English) have even taken notice of this interwar literature.[8] It may be reasonably asked, "Why"?

First, by the end of the 1930s, many of the active members of the Austrian School had left Vienna. For instance, in 1930 Rosenstein-Rodan moved to Great Britain, followed by Friedrich A. Hayek in autumn 1931, when he accepted a position at the London School of Economics. Gottfried Haberler left for a research position at the League of Nations in Geneva, Switzerland in 1933, and then took up a professorship at Harvard University in 1936. Fritz Machlup accepted a position at the University of Buffalo in New York State in 1934. Ludwig von Mises departed in the fall of 1934 for a visiting professor's position at the Graduate Institute of International Studies in Geneva, where he remained until leaving for the

[8] See Emil Kauder, *A History of Marginal Utility Theory* (Kauder, 1965, pp. 163–167), which is a notable exception. Kauder spends five pages very briefly outlining parts of Mayer's and Rosenstein-Rodan's discussions of "the time element and consumer strategy." He does not, however, refer to Morgenstern's article discussed in this essay.

United States in the summer of 1940. Oskar Morgenstern found himself exiled in the United States during a lecture tour, when Austria was being invaded and annexed by Nazi Germany; he found it politically impossible to return to Vienna. Several others associated with the Austrian School in Vienna found themselves in similar situations, and relocated to the United States during 1938 or 1939.

With this "Austrian" diaspora, the close proximity of like-minded thinkers interested in the same theoretical and applied questions was noticeably lost. They were dispersed to other parts of Europe and America, where economic questions and concerns into which they needed to be academically integrated were different than those they had shared with each other on a regular basis in Vienna. Remaining in Vienna, besides Hans Mayer, were only a handful of "Austrians" affiliated with him, including Leo-Schonfeld-Illy and Alexander Mahr, both prominent members in Mayer's circle. Richard Strigl died in Vienna in 1942.

Second, in the English-speaking world, theoretical interests surrounding consumer choice and marginal decision-making were increasingly focused on, especially, Pareto's "indifference curve" approach, as restated in J. R. Hicks and R. G. D. Allen's, "A Reconsideration of the Theory of Value" (1934), which soon became the dominant analytical framework in microeconomics. That Hans Mayer had offered trenchant criticisms of the assumptions and logic behind the Paretian indifference curve approach in his 1932 monograph on functional theories of price (pp. 109–125), did not go unnoticed. Hicks and Allen said, in passing, at the beginning of their "Reconsideration" that there had been "some very interesting inquiries into what may be called the dynamics of the subject, due to contemporary writers of the school of Vienna." (p. 52) But no other comments were made.[9]

The Pareto-Hicks indifference curves seemed to offer simplicity and conceptual elegance by capturing in one image the idea of the individual's field of ordered preferences superimposed on the trade-off constraints of relative prices in the form of the budget line. Through their interaction, there was offered a mathematical determination of both the "objective" and "subjective" marginal rates of substitution between alternatives, along with the (real) income effects resulting from shifts in relative prices at which alternatives were offered and taken.

[9] And even this comment was not repeated in Hicks' *Value and Capital* (Hicks & Allen, 1939), a few years later.

No such diagrams or mathematical formulations were found in the writings of the interwar Austrians. No similar easy to-read-off the diagram "solutions" to economic questions that were asked were offered to the reader. Besides, practically all the writings on this "Austrian" theory of consumption period planning were only available in German in the interwar period, most especially Hans Mayer's writings, a language in which most British and American economists were not always comfortably conversant.

But even if some of them were able to read German, any theoretical alternative to the growing appeal of the indifference curve approach for consumer choice theory was not brought forward by the "Austrians." Oskar Morgenstern's 1935 article seemed to end the discussion, even though the questions and problems he said remained open to debate with the introduction of the "time element" into consumer choice theory, failed to bring about any noticeable contributions. As the originating expositor of the theory, it would have been expected that Hans Mayer would have extended and developed his own "first approximation" to the idea. Yet, Mayer failed to add anything more to what he already had said in the 1920s.

Hans Mayer's "Betrayal" of the Austrian School

This gets us to a third reason for the theory remaining unfinished: Hans Mayer, himself. Many of the interwar generation of Austrian economists in Vienna later said that after suggesting so much early "promise," Mayer turned out to be, in their words, unreliable, "neurotic," and an "intriguer." He resented and envied what he considered to be the greater intellectual successes and the wider popularity with students of his "rivals" for influence on the faculty at the University of Vienna, and for the "leadership" of the Austrian School, especially in the person of Ludwig von Mises (Craver, 1986).[10]

Even worse, Hans Mayer chose to stay in Vienna and collaborate with the National Socialist regime following the annexation of Austria into the

[10] In a footnote in his essay on "Economics and Knowledge" as published in *Economica* (Hayek, 1937, p. 47), F. A. Hayek said, "It is true that Professor Mayer has held out before us the prospect of another, 'causal-genetic' approach, but it can hardly be denied that this is still largely a promise." It is noteworthy that when Hayek reprinted this essay in his collection, *Individualism and Economic Order* (Hayek, 1948, p. 35), this footnote had been removed.

Greater German Reich in early 1938. Indeed, as president of the Austrian Economics Association, Mayer sent out a letter to all members almost immediately after the arrival of the German Army and the Gestapo that under the new circumstances "non-Aryan members" were being expelled from the association (Mises, 1940, p. 99).[11]

Then at a meeting of German economists held in Berlin, Mayer participated in a symposium on, "Serving the National Economy as a Task of Economic Theory" (1939). While defending the "autonomy" and universal logic of economics in the form developed by the Austrian economists (in comparison to the Walrasian and Paretian mathematical general equilibrium approach), Mayer also made it clear that in the "new political reality" created by German National Socialism, the task of economic theory and its application was to serve the tasks set for the German people by the regime:

> There is a necessity of reformulating anew German economic theory in the context of the new purposes that exist for German political economy to solve, as these have materialized under National Socialism [...] Just as the "individualistic" theory of economics has shown the necessity of establishing a descending ordering of ends, given the scarce availability of means to serve them, the same logic applies now where the starting point is the national economic system as a whole, from which the particular features of a new "national" political economy may be understood, under new relevant assumptions ... Economic research methods are nothing but tactics on the battlefield of problems to solve, and must adapt themselves by various means to ever-changing situations [...] It will be possible to use many a brick of earlier [economic] theories for the construction of a new theory of a "national socialist" economy.

Through political intrigue and opportunistic maneuvering in the Nazi "new order," Mayer succeeded in maintaining his position as a senior professor at the University of Vienna during the National Socialist period of Austrian history (1938–1945). He was also able to successfully play the same games in the postwar period of the Allied occupation of Austria and Vienna, to maintain his professional standing, until his death in 1956.

Mayer's active accommodation with the Nazi regime lost a good part of his remaining stature and reputation both inside and outside the

[11] For a history of the Austrian Economics Society, including this episode and Mayer's conduct following the annexation of Austria and during the war, see, Klausinger (2015b).

Austrian School. Furthermore, the postwar period saw little new in the essays and articles that he wrote in the last ten years of his life. For the most part, they were restatements of his earlier writings from the interwar period (e.g., 1953). One exception was his, "John Maynard Keynes's 'New Foundation' to Economic Theory," (1952), in which he offered a micro-Austrian critique of Keynes's "aggregate" approach in *The General Theory*.

Those who had known and interacted with him in the Vienna of the interwar period often expressed contempt for his conduct during the Nazi era. He and his earlier contributions often lost all respect in their eyes. An especially strong instance of this is found in Lionel Robbins' *Autobiography of an Economist* (1971). He explained that his trips to Austria in the post-World War I period had made him deeply attached to the Vienna of that time. But ... his "love-affair" with the culture of the city had been imbittered by the National Socialist period and, especially, the conduct of someone like Hans Mayer:

> This [...] cemented [...] a love-affair with Vienna, its setting and its culture, which only terminated on the morrow of the *Anschluss* [the German annexation of Austria in March 1938] when, to his eternal shame, Hans Mayer, the senior Professor of Economics in the University of Menger, Wieser and Böhm-Bawerk, whom I myself had more than once heard denouncing Hitler and all his works, instead of closing it down as he honorably could have done, expelled the Jewish members from the famous Nationalökonomische Gesellschaft [the Austrian Economics Association] of which he was the president. (p. 91)

Thus, closed one of the chapters in the history of the Austrian School. The school's continuation and revival in the period since the Second World War has fallen to other hands, mainly in America and in a number of important centers in Europe.

References

Craver, E. (1986). The Emigration of the Austrian Economists. *History of Political Economy*, (*18*, 1), 1–32.

Ebeling, R. M. (2003). *Austrian Economics and the Political Economy of Freedom*. Edward Elgar.

Ebeling, R. M. (2010a). *Political Economy, Public Policy, and Monetary Economics: Ludwig von Mises and the Austrian Tradition*. Routledge.

Ebeling, R. M. (2010b). An 'Austrian' Interpretation of the Meaning of Austrian Economics: History, Method, and Theory. *Advances in Austrian Economics Fall*, 43–68.

Ebeling, R. M. (2014). Hayek and Mises: From Vienna Days to Conceptions of the Market Process. In R. W. Garrison & N. Barry (Eds.), *Elgar Companion to Hayekian Economics* (pp. 138–164). Edward Elgar.

Ebeling, R. M. (2016). *Austrian Economics and Public Policy.* Future of Freedom Foundation.

Hayek, F. A. (1931). *Prices and Production.* Macmillan.

Hayek, F. A. ([1937] 1973). Economics and Knowledge. In J. M. Buchanan & G. F. Thirlby (Eds.), *L.S.E. Essays on Cost* (pp. 43–68). Weidenfeld and Nicolson.

Hayek, F. A. (1948). *Individualism and Economic Order.* University of Chicago Press.

Hayek, F. A. (1992). *The Collected Works of F. A. Hayek.* In P. G. Klein (Ed.), *The Fortunes of Liberalism, Essays on Austrian Economics and the Ideal of Freedom* (Vol. 4). University of Chicago Press.

Hicks, J. R., & Allen, R. G. D. (1934). A Reconsideration of the Theory of Value. Parts I and II. In *Economica* (pp. 52–76, 196–218).

Hicks, J. R., & Allen, R. G. D. (1939). *Value and Capital: An Inquiry into Some Fundamental Principles of Economic Theory.* Clarendon Press.

Kauder, E. (1965). *A History of Marginal Utility Theory.* Princeton University Press.

Klausinger, H. (2015a). Hans Mayer, Last Knight of the Austrian School, Vienna Branch. *History of Political Economy, 47*(2), 271–305.

Klausinger, H. (2015b). The Nationalökonomische Gesellschaft (Austrian Economic Association) in the Interwar Period and Beyond. *University of Vienna, Department of Economics Working Paper No. 195.*

Mahr, A. (1956). Hans Mayer—Leben and Werk. *Zeitschrift für Natonalökonomie,* March, 3–16.

Mayer, H. ([1921–1922] 1956). Untersuchung zu dem Grundgesetz der wirtschaftlichen Wertrechnung. Reprinted in *Zeitschrift für Natonalökonomie, 15*(3), 265–303.

Mayer, H. (1924). Bedürfnis, *Handswörterbuch des Staatswissenschaften* (Vol. 2, pp. 450–456). Fischer.

Mayer, H. ([1932] 1994). The Cognitive Value of Functional Theories of Price. In I. M. Kirzner (Ed.), *Classics in Austrian Economics: A Sampling in the History of a Tradition* (pp. 55–168). William Pickering.

Mayer, H. (1939). Die Wendung zur Volkswirtschaft als Aufgabe volkswirtschaftlicher Theorie. *Weltwirtscaftliches Archiv,* March, 414–427.

Mayer, H. (1952). John Maynard Keynes's 'Neubegründung' der Wirtschaftstheorie. In E. Lugler & J. Messner (Eds.), *Entwickung und soziale Ordung: Festschrift für Ferdinand Degenfeld-Schonburg* (pp. 39–55). Julius Springer Verlag.

Mayer, H. (1953). Zur Frage der Rechenbarkeit des Subjectiven Wertes. In V. F. Wagner & F. Marbach (Eds.), *Wirtschaftstheorie und Wirtschaftspolitik: Festschrift für Alfred Amonn* (pp. 58–78). Franke Verlag.

Menger, C. ([1871] 1950). *Principles of Economics.* Free Press.

Mises, L. v. ([1920] 1935). Economic Calculation in the Socialist Commonwealth. In F. A. Hayek (Ed.), *Collectivist Economic Planning: Critical Studies on the Possibilities of Socialism* (pp. 87–130). George Routledge & Son.

Mises, L. v. ([1922] 1981). *Socialism: An Economic and Sociological Analysis.* Liberty Fund.

Mises, L. v. ([1933] 1981). *Epistemological Problems of Economics.* New York University Press.

Mises, L. v. ([1940] 1978). *Notes and Recollections.* Libertarian Press.

Morgenstern, O. (1928). *Wirtschaftsprognoses, eine Untersuchung ihrer Voraussetzungen und Morglichkeiten.* Julius Springer Verlag.

Morgenstern, O. ([1935] 1976). The Time Moment in Value Theory. In A. Schotter (Ed.), *Selected Economic Writings of Oskar Morgenstern* (pp. 151–166). New York University Press.

Morgenstern, O. & Neumann, J. v. ([1944] 1953). *The Theory of Games and Economic Behavior.* Princeton University Press.

Robbins, L. (1932). *An Essay on the Nature and Significance of Economic Science.* Macmillan.

Robbins, L. (1935). *An Essay on the Nature and Significance of Economic Science* (2nd ed.). Macmillan.

Robbins, L. (1971). *Autobiography of an Economist.* St. Martin's Press.

Rosenstein-Rodan, P. N. ([1927] 1994). Marginal Utility Theory. In I. M. Kirzner (Ed.), *Classics in Austrian Economics: A Sampling in the History of a Tradition* (pp. 171–212). William Pickering.

Rosenstein-Rodan, P. N. (1934, February). The Role of Time in Economic Theory. In *Economica* (pp. 77–97).

Strigl, R. (1923). *Die okonomischen Kategorien und die Organisation der Wirtschaft.* Gustav Fischer.

Weber, W. (1961). Hans Mayer. In *Handwörterbuch der Sozialwissenschaften* (Vol. VII, pp. 264–265). Fischer

History and Economic Theorizing

Carmelo Ferlito

Introduction

The only gift from my graduation which I still keep at hand is the Italian edition of Huerta de Soto's *The Austrian School. Market Order and Entrepreneurial Creativity* ([2000] 2008), which was given to me by a dear friend of mine.

It was my first encounter with the Spanish economist, undoubtedly the person who has done more than anybody else to spread the knowledge of the Austrian School in continental Europe. The book had a profound impact on me: its striking clarity made it a very important consultation tool and the fundamental volume to solidify the most important features of the school into the mind of a young student or scholar. The present condition of my copy of the book testifies to how much I used it.

While Huerta de Soto ([2000] 2008) played an important role in introducing me to a better understanding of the Austrian School, a taste of the great personality of the Spanish professor came to me years later, in 2010,

C. Ferlito (✉)
Center for Market Education, Kuala Lumpur, Malaysia
e-mail: carmelo@ideas.org.my

D. Howden, P. Bagus (eds.), *The Emergence of a Tradition: Essays in Honor of Jesús Huerta de Soto, Volume I*,
https://doi.org/10.1007/978-3-031-17414-8_11

when I published my first book in economic theory (Ferlito, 2010). As an unknown scholar, and fresh from a profound delusion about the Italian academic environment, I was seeking legitimacy; I then decided to contact Prof Huerta de Soto, asking him to write the preface for my book. "I have nothing to lose; in the worst-case scenario he will not reply to my email", was my thought. Unexpectedly, he decided to write a very kind preface, and he also did so for my Ferlito (2013).

Prior to any theoretical consideration, the humility shown by an already established international scholar in accepting to support a totally unknown young scholar, who had just lost his dream for an academic career, was something totally astonishing. It proved the stature of the man before that of the scholar.

Economics and History

In 2004 I entered a PhD program in Economic History, while never abandoning the passion for my first love: the history of economic thought. Even after moving away from economic history, my works in pure economics and the current ones in political economy mainly tackle problems with tools coming from the knowledge of past theories (the Austrian School in particular, it goes without saying), rather than with the tools of mainstream economics. So Huerta de Soto's way of doing economics could not be but congenial to my own way of thinking. His reference to the Salamanca School as a precursor to the Austrian School (Huerta de Soto, [2000] 2008, pp. 64–79) reasoned with the tools I had at my disposal.

It is clear that in Huerta de Soto's theoretical production there is no contradiction between economic theory, economic history, and the history of economic thought. Rather, his erudition—typical of the high tradition of continental Europe—allows him to navigate through different disciplines in a way that contemporary economists have lost, while it was very familiar to the masters who built the history of our discipline.

However, that link between historical facts and pure theory, which in Huerta de Soto appears to be so natural, is at the origin of the first controversy in which the Austrian School was involved against the German Historical School, the *Methodenstreit*; that "history of wasted energies" (Schumpeter, [1954] 2006, p. 782) is so well known to scholars that it need not be summarized here.

While it was never Carl Menger's intention to deny a role for history when dealing with economic theory (rather, Menger's "exact theory" called for a strong connection with what is real), the misunderstanding that emerged with the *methodenstreit* contributed to creating the myth according to which, for Austrian economists, the two disciplines need to be continually conceived as a sort of dichotomy rather than as a simple distinction (see Lavoie & Storr, 2011, whereby the authors use the word "distinction" to indicate a non-conflictual relationship, while using "dichotomy" as a sharp and conflictual separation).

Unfortunately, a certain lack of clarity in some of Ludwig von Mises's methodological statements helped perpetuate that myth. As pointed out by Lavoie and Storr (2011, p. 215), in *Human Action* Mises seemed to argue that history and theory are in strict dichotomy; in fact, while history deals with concrete and particular facts, praxeology "is a theoretical and systematic, not a historical, science. Its scope is human action as such, irrespective of all environmental, accidental, and individual circumstances of the concrete acts. Its cognition is purely formal and general without reference to the material content and the particular features of the actual case. It aims at knowledge valid for all instances in which the conditions exactly correspond to those implied in its assumptions and inferences. Its statements and propositions are not derived from experience. They are, like those of logic and mathematics, a priori" (Mises, [1949] 1998, p. 32).

With such statements, it seems Mises believed that history can never influence theory. But, Lavoie and Storr (2011, p. 215) wondered, did "Mises really need to draw an indelible line between conception and understanding in this way?" According to the authors, Mises was somehow intellectually forced to draw what seemed to be a dichotomy between *thymology* (understood by Mises, [1957] 2007, p. 266, as the "knowledge of the social environment in which a man lives and acts or, with historians, of a foreign milieu about which he has learned by studying special sources," to which realm history belongs) and *praxeology*, because economics was under attack on many fronts: positivists, historicists, and others were rejecting the teaching of economics.

A *Vision* as a Link

As explained by Lavoie and Storr (2011, pp. 221–222), in different passages of *Human Action*, Mises better clarified his position. According to Mises ([1949] 1998, p. 65), "the end of science is to know reality.... Therefore praxeology restricts its inquiries to the study of acting under those conditions and presuppositions which are given in reality.... Experience merely directs our curiosity toward certain problems and diverts it from other problems. It tells us what we should explore, but it does not tell us how we could proceed in our search for knowledge." He added that the system of economics is devoted to the *comprehension* of reality; it is not severed from any reference to reality (Mises, [1949] 1998, p. 66).

In these passages we can find a parallel with Schumpeter's emphasis on the role of what he called *vision* for economic theorizing. I always believed that it would be fruitful to further explore how Schumpeter's theory could be a source of enrichment for the Austrian School (and I tried to do so in Ferlito (2014, 2020b)). According to the Austrian economist, when we start our research work, "we should first have to visualize a distinct set of coherent phenomena as a worthwhile object of our analytic efforts. In other words, analytic effort is of necessity preceded by a preanalytical cognitive act that supplies the raw material for the analytic effort" (Schumpeter, [1954] 2006, pp. 38–39). Schumpeter called that preanalytical cognitive act *Vision*.

In other words, the economist is not an observer alien to reality. He or she lives in specific conditions of place and time, and his or her vision is shaped thanks to the interaction with and the observation of the reality typical of such conditions. The analytical effort is then the attempt to convert the vision into concepts, into a scheme; however, such analytical work contributes to making the vision evolve such that—to borrow Schumpeter's words—"[f]actual work and 'theoretical' work, in an endless relation of give and take, naturally testing one another and setting new tasks for each other, will eventually produce scientific models, the provisional joint products of their interaction with the surviving elements of the original vision, to which increasingly more rigorous standards of consistency and adequacy will be applied" (Schumpeter, [1954] 2006, p. 40).

While Mises was opposing a scientific environment in which theorizing was under attack by historicism and positivism, today we probably face the challenge of a theory that is decoupling itself from reality. It seems to me that a great part of contemporary scholarly work in economics is affected by the attempt—more or less conscious—to escape the need for Schumpeterian vision. The idea that economics should be "pure" has perhaps contributed to moving the researcher away from his or her own reality. And this seems to be more a contradiction today, when economics cannot be accused of not being empirical; quite the contrary: data collection and interpolation has almost entirely replaced the activity once known as theorizing.

What I see is that the content of the analytical work has been detached from its predecessor—vision—and consequently from theory. The time has come for the economist to sit back, look out the window, and let his or her astonished observation of the world shape that vision, which is so very needed if the blackboard work is to have any meaning at all.

This would bring us back to Mises's attempt, and that of the Austrian School in general: an economic science that aims to understand reality, as emphasized in particular by Ludwig Lachmann and his reprise of the Weberian research program, grounded on the concept of *Verstehen* (Lachmann, 1971), in which thymology and praxeology are distinct but complementary for a proper study of human action.

Economics as a Science of Meaning[1]

It is well known that Mises placed ***human action*** at the core of his economics and for him "[h]uman action is purposeful behavior. Or we may say: Action is will put into operation and transformed into an agency, is aiming at ends and goals, is the ego's meaningful response to stimuli and to the conditions of its environment, is a person's conscious adjustment to the state of the universe that determines his life" (Mises, [1949] 1998, p. 11).

Four expressions need to be emphasized here: purposeful behavior, will, agency, and meaningful. This last one is the one that the present paper will emphasize. As explained by Storr (2017, p. 65), we can stress that to be "an [...] economist is to be concerned with meaning. If we hope to understand human action, then we must pay attention to the meanings that individuals attach to their actions, and to the actions of others, and to the various choices that they are considering, and to the possible outcomes of those choices. Ours is at root a science of meaning."

[1] See Storr (2017), Ferlito (2020a).

A study of human action emphasizes that we must deal with the meaning that acting people attach to their actions. Mises ([1949] 1998, p. 92) clearly stated that economics "is not about things and tangible material objects ... [on the contrary] it is about men [sic], their meanings and actions. Goods, commodities, and wealth and all the other notions of conduct are not elements of nature; they are elements of human meaning and conduct. He who wants to deal with them must not look at the external world; he must search for them in the meaning of acting men."

By introducing the category of meaning we enter the world of interpretations, or *Verstehen* (understanding), central to the analysis of human action and on which the German economist Ludwig Lachmann and his followers built their most import contributions. Indeed, interpretation processes must be seen as the necessary subjective link between different objective facts and events. Human actions are objective facts; they are answers to other objective facts constituting the elements of reality. However, how such answers are defined is totally subjective, the outcome of interpretation processes, which we can define as hermeneutical actions (Ferlito, 2018).

Without the interpretative moment, reality could not take shape because no action would be decided. Storr (2017) reminded us that the importance of meaning, understanding, and interpretation is found both in Mises and Hayek. What does it mean that economists deal with meaning? Their main task is attempting to understand purposeful human actions, and thus "the emergence of social phenomena, [...] the opinions and beliefs that guide individual decision making" (Storr, 2017).

This implies that, although the category of understanding is linked with historical phenomena, economics cannot be deterministic; it cannot follow "the idea that everything that happens must happen as it does and could not have happened any other way" (Fullbrook, 2016, p. 1). If our science were deterministic, it would not be a science of human action, but just a science of human reaction.

Our human experience tells us that different persons react differently when facing the same situation, and even the same person can react differently when the same situation presents itself in different conditions of time and space. Time and space matter. Reality is not shaped by reactions whose content is a priori determined by the situation faced. Rather, the future is molded by how people interpret their reality; the action following such interpretive processes will entail intended and unintended consequences. As stressed by Storr (2017), life is characterized by open-endedness; we all face choices, determined by the specific content of information/knowledge available (in a unique way for each individual) in a precise condition of space and time.

It is therefore clear that, while market players are continuously involved with interpretive processes in an attempt to understand reality, economists themselves must deal with a different type of hermeneutical activity: the understanding of the meaning of human actions in the market and of the unintended consequences which go beyond players' intentions. Therefore, understanding is not limited to how players act. Their actions surely involve hermeneutical processes, but we should add, as explained by Prychitko (2018, pp. 162–163), that it also involves economists' interpretations and the visions subsequently emerging from them.

Hints for a New Synthesis

It seems to me that the introduction of the *Verstehen* category works well in order to build an economic science in which historical facts and pure theory are part of a unified approach to deal with "human meanings" (Lavoie & Storr, 2011, p. 232), while the Schumpeterian vision is the element that allows the social scientist to build his or her inner bridge between these two aspects of social sciences.

We cannot here dig into the topic, but even the last great member of the German Historical School, Arthur Spiethoff (1952, 1953, 1970), developed his "reconciliation" attempt with the introduction of an Economic Gestalt Theory, grounded on *real-types*, or the isolation of specific space-time phenomena that have significance for a unique economic style.

The process of synthesis seems to come to completion with Don Lavoie (2011), when he explained that interpretation and the search for meaning cannot be separated by the very facts to which meaning is attached. Lavoie (2011, p. 122) clarified that "[h]istory molds the direction of theoretical investigation, while theory is used as the interpretative framework with which the specific historical narratives can be told." History comes to be the "supplier" of facts, events, actions, and interactions on which the economist needs to place his or her interpretive lens.

The conception of "What can happen?" that we bring with us to an historical episode shapes the way we will work over the evidence as we ask the question "What did happen?" At the same time, the questions as to "What did happen?" influence the agendas of economists about which, of the infinite number of specific "What can happen?" questions he might be able to conjure up, are worthy of his serious attention.

Mises's discussion of history, like that of the Gadamer strand of the hermeneutics tradition, stresses that history always is and should be guided by enabling presuppositions derived from theory, including but not confined to the a priori theory that comes from reflection on the life-world (Lavoie, 2011, p. 122).

Conclusion

The infamous *methodenstreit* created a misunderstanding about the relationship between economics and history for the members of the Austrian School of Economics; certain radical methodological statements by Ludwig von Mises contributed to creating the myth of a dichotomy, rather than a distinction, between what he called thymology and praxeology. However, Mises himself never claimed that economic theorizing should be disconnected from (historical) reality.

On the contrary, by stressing the importance of looking to reality for the facts on which economic theory should be built, Mises paralleled Schumpeter closely in arguing that a vision, shaped by the observation of reality, is necessary, together with introspection, for praxeology.

Following Lachmann's research program, Don Lavoie and Virgil Storr explained that the category of *understanding* is the one that allows us to reconcile the two branches of social sciences into a unified effort for studying human meanings. In works such as Huerta de Soto ([1992] 2010; [1998] 2012), it is self-evident that such a reconciliation brings about important fruits for the progress of economic theory.

References

Ferlito, C. (2010). *Dentro la crisi. Combattere la crisi, difendere il mercato*. Preface by J. Huerta de Soto. Solfanelli.

Ferlito, C. (2013). *Economica fenice. Dalla crisi alla rinascenza*. Preface by J. Huerta de Soto. Solfanelli. English edition: *Phoenix economics. From crisis to renascence*. New York, NY: Nova, 2013.

Ferlito, C. (2014). The Natural Cycle: Why Economic Fluctuations are Inevitable. A Schumpeterian Extension of the Austrian Business Cycle Theory. *Journal of Reviews on Global Economics, 3*, 200–219.

Ferlito, C. (2018). For a New Capital Theory: A Hermeneutical Approach. *StoriaLibera, IV*(7), 11–61.

Ferlito, C. (2020a). *Economics: Human Action and Its Meaning*. CME EduPaper Nr 1. Center for Market Education.

Ferlito, C. (2020b). *The Entrepreneur: "One, No One and One Hundred Thousand"*. CME EduPaper Nr 2. Center for Market Education.

Fullbrook, E. (2016). *Narrative Fixation in Economics*. World Economics Association.

Huerta de Soto, J. ([1992] 2010). *Socialism, Economic Calculation and Entrepreneurship*. Edward Elgar. Italian edition (used here): *Socialismo, calcolo economico e imprenditorialità*. Edited by C. Ferlito. Chieti, IT: Solfanelli, 2012.

Huerta de Soto, J. ([1998] 2012). *Money, Bank Credit*, and *Economic Cycles*. Ludwig von Mises Institute. Italian edition (used here): *Moneta, credito bancario e cicli economici*. Soveria Mannelli, IT: Rubbettino, 2012.

Huerta de Soto, J. ([2000] 2008). *The Austrian School. Market Order and Entrepreneurial Creativity*. Edward Elgar. Italian edition (used here): *La Scuola Austriaca. Mercato e creatività imprenditoriale*. Edited by Paolo Zanotto and with a preface by Raimondo Cubeddu. Soveria Mannelli, IT: Rubbettino, 2003.

Lachmann, L. M. (1971). *The Legacy of Max Weber*. Glendessary Press.

Lavoie, D. (2011). The Interpretive Dimension of Economics: Science, Hermeneutics, and Praxeology. *The Review of Austrian Economics, 24*, 91–128.

Lavoie, D., & Storr, V. H. (2011). Distinction or Dichotomy: Rethinking the Line Between Thymology and Praxeology. *The Review of Austrian Economics, 24*, 213–233.

Mises, L. v. ([1949] 1998). *Human Action*. Ludwig von Mises Institute.

Mises, L. v. ([1957] 2007). *Theory and History: An Interpretation of Social and Economic Evolution*. Ludwig von Mises Institute.

Prychitko, D. L. (2018). Levels of Interpretation in a Hermeneutical Economic Theory: Comment on Ferlito. *StoriaLibera, IV*(7), 157–165.

Schumpeter, J. A. ([1954] 2006). *History of Economic Analysis*. Routledge.

Spiethoff, A. (1952). The "Historical" Character of Economic Theories. *The Journal of Economic History, 12*(2), 131–139.

Spiethoff, A. (1953). Pure Theory and Economic Gestalt Theory: Ideal Types and Real Types. In F. C. Lane & J. C. Riemersma (Eds.), *Enterprise and Secular Change* (pp. 444–463). George Allen and Unwin.

Spiethoff, A. (1970). Economic Styles. *The Journal of Economic History, 30*(3), 640–652.

Storr, V. H. (2017). Ludwig Lachmann's Peculiar Status Within Austrian economics. *The Review of Austrian Economics, 32*(1), 3–75.

Beyond Public Choice

Eduardo Fernández Luiña

Today it is impossible to dissociate anarcho-capitalist philosophy from the Austrian School of Economics. Murray Newton Rothbard and, subsequently, scholars such as Jesús Huerta de Soto, Hans-Hermann Hoppe and Miguel Anxo Bastos Boubeta have made contributions of considerable value in this respect. It is here where Jesús Huerta de Soto has stood out so prominently, both within the Spanish academic world and at the international level. Understanding anarcho-capitalism as the theoretical consequence of the Austrian School's approach also opens up a line of communication with the Public Choice School. At the beginning of the twenty-first century, the illustrious journal *Review of Austrian Economics* devoted a complete issue to reflect on the connections that existed between Public Choice and the Austrian School of Economics, effectively developing a new concept known as "Austrian Public Choice." This chapter seeks to pay homage to Jesús Huerta de Soto, as well as to his work and his approach when it comes to discovering the unique characteristics of Human Action. His work goes beyond the realm of Public Choice,

E. Fernández Luiña (✉)
Universidad Francisco Marroquín, Guatemala City, Guatemala
e-mail: efernandez@ufm.edu

D. Howden, P. Bagus (eds.), *The Emergence of a Tradition: Essays in Honor of Jesús Huerta de Soto, Volume I*,
https://doi.org/10.1007/978-3-031-17414-8_12

effectively integrating the contributions made by this School into the Austrian approach.

The chapter is structured in the following manner. In the first section, we present a brief review of the development of Public Choice, as well as introducing the concept of Austrian Public Choice. Subsequently, we establish Jesús Huerta de Soto's links with this School. All of this will attest to the statements we have made above. Today, Jesús Huerta de Soto is one of the key representatives of the Austrian School and his work has been able to integrate the contributions made by Public Choice, producing some fascinating results that enable us to understand the nature of interventionism and the predatory nature of the State.

The Public Choice School and Austrian School: A Reflection on the Existing Relationship Between the Two Schools

Public Choice is an analytical school that emerged in the early 1960s in the United States. We can trace back the roots of this particular approach to the work that Duncan Black produced at the time regarding committees and their collective decision-making (Black, 1958). We might also mention the famous Impossibility Theorem developed by Kenneth Arrow (1950). While recognizing the value of these early contributions, it is obvious that the School gained momentum and shape through the endeavors of scholars such as James Buchanan and Gordon Tullock (1999), Anthony Downs (1957), and William Niskanen (2007).

If we were to summarize the purposes of Public Choice in just a few words, we could confidently state that this is an approach that seeks to analyze the political process (of power) by using conceptual instruments and analytical tools taken from the field of economics.

Naturally, over a period of more than fifty years (the Public Choice Society was founded in the early 1960s), the School has been able to generate a varied range of contributions. Notions such as *free-riding* and *rent-seeking* have become classic themes for research. We might also mention the idea of *regulatory capture*, which has undoubtedly enhanced our understanding of the decision-making process inside the state and the incapability of public policies to resolve problems that affect our daily lives.

It is important to point out that Public Choice sought to address three aspects:

1) First, it analyzed legal issues. In societies characterized by the application of positive law, many people believe that by changing a law we can solve a problem. Unfortunately, this is completely false.
2) At the same time, Public Choice also reacted against approaches that originated from the Science of Public Administration. Studies produced within this field have a mechanistic view of the bureaucratic machinery. They are based on a belief that administration is made up of a human team of individuals who answer to a decision-maker, obeying every command. The evidence shows that, in a large number of situations, this view is also incorrect. The administrative machinery is made up of individuals who possess private and clearly defined interests. And these individuals sometimes tend to disobey.
3) Finally, the Public Choice School reacted against the assertions of the welfare economics school of thought. The most important representatives of this School consisted of scholars such as William Baumol (1952), Francis Bator (1958) and the widely recognized Arthur Cecile Pigou (1932). These scholars directed their efforts at presenting the failings of the market in order to justify the intervention of the state in different realms, thus enhancing the capacity of coercive power to design and implement public policies. The Public Choice scholars sought to demonstrate the opposite, namely that the state and the initiatives of bureaucrats present greater failings than the market. When it comes to administrating and allocating resources, they believed that it was better to trust in market forces and the free and voluntary actions of private individuals than in the state, the bureaucracy and relationships of a coercive nature.

For all of these reasons, the Public Choice School can help to improve our understanding of human action. Nevertheless, the methodologies that the authors belonging to this movement have employed over time have been subject to innumerable criticisms. If we were to summarize the foundations on which Public Choice has been built, these would be as follows:

1) Methodological individualism.
2) Rational choice.
3) Politics and public policies as a process of exchange.

In the early twenty-first century the *Review of Austrian Economics* devoted a special issue to analyzing and understanding the connections that exist (or could exist) between both schools.

In 2002, Peter Boettke published a text entitled *Austrian Economics and Public Choice* in conjunction with Edward López, the President of the Public Choice Society. In this paper, these American scholars presented the differences that exist between the two approaches. For example, in the case of methodological individualism, they indicated that "Austrian and public choice economics often differ regarding the role of information in the polity" (Boettke & López, 2002, p. 112). The Austrian School believes that information is imperfect, and knowledge is dispersed. In contrast, Public Choice believes that "political agents (voter, bureaucrat, politician) act in their own interest with perfect information" (Boettke & López, 2002, p. 112).

Having said that, both authors demonstrated the existence of "common ground" with a view to designing a method that might facilitate our knowledge and understanding regarding human action. The contribution made by Sandford Ikeda in this respect is of great significance. He believes that the points of departure of one school and the other are entirely different. If we are talking about political action, for the Austrian School the key aspect is the difference between the results achieved and the results that are desired. Authors who ascribe to the Public Choice approach think in an entirely different way, believing that what is truly important is the difference between the intentions that are declared and the real intentions that lie behind the action (Ikeda, 2003, p. 65).

When we analyze the failure of public policies that emanate from the state, the conclusions we can draw are also different, as we might expect. In the case of the Austrian School, the problem has to do with results that are achieved based on the scarce knowledge that exists regarding the economy; in the case of Public Choice, this school regards the failure of the state as the result of a series of unexpected (and expected) consequences deriving from human action (Ikeda, 2003, p. 67). The conclusion that Ikeda draws is of considerable interest: while the Austrian School has an evident distrust of the state's capacity to calculate properly, it reveals a sense of benevolence regarding the decision-maker. That is to say, the school does not perceive any untoward intentions among those who head the state. The problem is strictly one of knowledge, not perverse incentives and desire for power, status, or income (Downs, 1957).

In contrast, the adherents to Public Choice are aware of the problems that the political process entails, of the way in which asymmetrical information benefits perverse individuals who manipulate decision-making in order to obtain benefits of a private nature. Based on these conclusions, Sanford Ikeda (2003) believes that the approaches of the two schools should be combined:

- The Public Choice proponents should take into account the decentralized nature of knowledge and the subjective nature of individuals' evaluations and preferences. These are tenets that the Austrian School of Economics has advocated since it was founded.
- At the same time, the Austrian School should abandon its benevolent conception (of human nature) and its somewhat naïve vision of the state and the individuals who run it.

While agreeing with Ikeda in all aspects relating to this fusion, I believe there is sufficient evidence to state that the post-Rothbard Austrian School has already assimilated and adopted all of the contributions made by Public Choice. The works published by anarcho-capitalist authors are very clear in this respect. Murray Newton Rothbard (1977) does not believe that public policy problems solely derive from issues relating to access to information and knowledge. Perverse incentives certainly exist, as do individuals who act in their own benefit at the expense of others (taxpayers and voters). In fact, the American economist is fully aware of the evils that blight politics and the sense of perversity that surrounds the decision-making process, both of which affect regulators, decision-makers, bureaucrats, pressure groups, and voters.

The same could be said for the work of Hans-Hermann Hoppe. In this respect, it is the school's "classics" authors, figures such as Carl Menger, Eugen von Böhm-Bawerk, Ludwig von Mises, and Friedrich Hayek (although he might also be considered a transitional thinker), who might be considered the most "innocent" when it comes to interpreting the political power process and decision-making at a state level. Having said that, their "innocence" may simply have been the result of the upbringing and gentlemanly approach characteristic of the period in which these scholars published their works.

The post-Rothbard Austrian School, the one that Jesús Huerta de Soto has contributed to with his monumental work, consciously applies a realistic analysis of the predatory and coercive nature of the individuals who run the State. For this reason, scholars such as Huerta de Soto have currently gone beyond Public Choice, offering us a better understanding of the monster that the modern state has become for ordinary people who are trying to live their lives.

Jesús Huerta de Soto: Beyond Public Choice

When he received the Juan de Mariana Award for Freedom 2016, Jesús Huerta de Soto declared that he had devoted his life to three things: (i) studying the theory of freedom; (ii) conveying and teaching its principles at university; (iii) and disseminating and promoting freedom in all fields, without any reservations or concessions whatsoever. At the same ceremony, he expressed his profound gratitude to Friedrich Hayek for his help in enabling him to join the Mont Pelerin Society, as well as recognizing the influence that Murray Newton Rothbard had exercised over him. Luis Reig Albiol was another figure who influenced him greatly, since it was in his house that Huerta de Soto first heard the term "anarcho-capitalism" in 1974.

It was after this date that Huerta de Soto directed all of his research to a meticulous study of market forces, presenting a ferocious criticism of the state. His articles are innumerable, and they have been translated into more than eight languages. His books, as many of his readers know, analyze everything ranging from entrepreneurship, saving and life insurance provisions to economic history, money, credit, and economic cycles. His research articles go even further, delving into questions such as the euro, nationalist theory from the Austrian liberal perspective, the morality and justice of capitalism and the market and, more recently, the economic effects of the pandemic caused by the virus that the Chinese Communist Party has exported throughout the world.

Alongside his publications and always linked to the realm of research, Jesús Huerta de Soto has published and run the journal *Procesos de Mercado*, one of the key points of reference for anyone committed to research along the lines of the Austrian School. In addition to his work as a researcher, he has taught widely and disseminated his teachings extensively in the form of an endless series of videos, conferences, and short opinion articles.

If there is one aspect that we should highlight about his career, it is his commitment to the methodology of the Austrian School of Economics: methodological individualism and subjectivism. However, in addition, in the works of Jesús Huerta de Soto we can clearly perceive the difference between the declared intentions and the desired intentions of those responsible for decision-making, with this line of thought being highly tuned and compatible with what Peter Boettke, Edward López, and Sanford Ikeda define as "Austrian Public Choice."

The intellectual and academic work of Jesús Huerta de Soto reflects a distrust of decision-makers, bureaucrats, and politicians. But it also distrusts pressure groups that seek to obtain income from their political links and relationships with politicians. His work is fully conscious of the risks that can be observed in the competitive processes that revolve around policy (*free-riding* and *rent-seeking*). In fact, all the above explains his shift to anarcho-capitalism in the 1970s. The state is the problem. And this is nothing more than an organized minority of individuals who monopolize the power of coercion. The state is a monopoly of violence. Coercion eliminates spontaneous order, drastically curtailing the development of free and voluntary forms of cooperation that favor the material and spiritual growth of individuals. In Jesús Huerta de Soto's opinion, the state is unnecessary, and should it exist, in view of the (dual and problematic) nature of individuals, it never ceases to grow and, ultimately, it destroys freedom.

These beliefs are reflected in the thinker's most important works, such as *Money, Bank Credit, and Economic Cycles* (2006), as well as in his research articles and academic dissemination papers. For example, in his text "Liberalismo versus anarcocapitalismo" (2007), Huerta de Soto states that "a) the state is unnecessary; b) statism (even minimal) is theoretically impossible; c) in view of human nature, once the state exists, it is impossible to curtail its power" (2007, p. 15).

Points "b" and "c" are especially interesting for our analysis. In relation to point "b," we can state that, in effect, and fully in line with the Public Choice view, the Austrian School recognizes the distorting effect of any public policy and any coercive state measure. It is logical that the state should fail. And this is because of

> a) the enormous volume of information that it would need, information that can only be found in dispersed and disseminated form amongst the millions of individuals who take part in the social process each day. b) due to the predominantly tacit and non-articulable nature (and, therefore, non-transmissible in unequivocal form) of the information that the intervention body would need in order to provide its mandates with the necessary coordinating content. c) because the information that is used at a social level

> is not "given", but constantly changes as a result of human creativity, it being obviously impossible to convey information today that will only be created tomorrow, which is the very information the state intervention body requires in order to achieve its goals tomorrow. (2007, p. 20)

As we can see, the Austrian School goes much further by going beyond the problems that Public Choice encounters with regard to information. The following point is also of considerable interest, relating to the impossibility of curtailing the power of the state in view of the nature of human beings. This is where the work of Huerta de Soto entirely eclipses that of the early Austrian theorists, who are excessively benevolent with regard to human nature, while surpassing the analytical capacity of the Public Choice theorists:

> [T]he combination of the state, as the institution that has a monopoly over violence, with human nature is "explosive". Like a magnet with irresistible force, the state promotes and attracts passions, vices and the most perverse facets of human nature, which, on the one hand, seeks to evade its mandates and, on the other, takes advantage of the monopolistic power of the state as far as it can. Furthermore, and especially within democratic environments, the combined effect of the actions of privileged interest groups, government short-sightedness and "vote-buying", not to mention the megalomaniac nature of politicians and the irresponsibility and blindness of bureaucrats, creates a dangerously unstable and explosive cocktail, one that is constantly accompanied by social, economic and political crises, which, paradoxically, are always used by politicians and social "leaders" to justify subsequent doses of intervention that, instead of solving problems, simply aggravate them still further. (Huerta de Soto, 2007, p. 22)

As we can observe in this passage, the fusion of Public Choice and the Austrian School is quite evident, while also demonstrating that the analytical power of the Austrian School thinker is more effective by adding the school's subjectivism and its better understanding regarding information (disperse and imperfect) and the management and production of knowledge (totally decentralized). This helps us to acquire an appropriate and satisfactory understanding of the interventionist process, as well as the nature of the state as a political entity.

The work of Jesús Huerta de Soto goes beyond Public Choice, taking on the latter's contributions while incorporating those of the Austrian approach. As a result, his analyses pack a theoretical punch that is quite self-evident, helping us to understand the world we live in today.

Conclusion

This chapter pays homage to the magnificent and monumental work that Jesús Huerta de Soto has carried out over an academic career spanning more than forty years. Don Jesús, as we the disciples of Bastos Boubeta like to call him, has gone beyond Public Choice. He had been capable of integrating the significant contributions made by this theoretical school founded in the 1960s into the research project of the Austrian School.

His work, in line with that of one of his teachers, Murray Newton Rothbard, represents a milestone when it comes to understanding the predatory and coercive nature of the state as a political entity. In 2013, shortly after the passing of James M. Buchanan, Jesús Huerta de Soto wrote a marvelous and moving *Memoriam* in his honor. The fact is that, in spite of their methodological differences, the Spanish academic felt extremely grateful to the American scholar and held him in great esteem. The connections were and continue to be quite evident.

References

Arrow, K. (1950). A Difficulty in the Concept of Social Welfare. *Journal of Political Economy, 58*(4), 328–346.

Bator, F. (1958). The Anatomy of Market Failure. *The Quarterly Journal of Economics, 72*(3), 351–379.

Baumol, W. (1952). *Welfare Economics and the Theory of the State*. Green & Co.

Black, D. (1958). *Theory of Committees and Elections*. Cambridge University Press.

Boettke, P. J., & López, E. (2002). Austrian Economics and Public Choice. *Review of Austrian Economics, 15*, 111–119.

Buchanan, J., & Tullock, G. (1999). *The Calculus of Consent: Logical Foundations of Constitutional Democracy*. Liberty Fund.

Downs, A. (1957). *An Economic Theory of Democracy*. Harper and Row.

Huerta de Soto, J. (2006). *Money, Bank Credit, and Economic Cycles*. Ludwig von Mises Institute.

Huerta de Soto, J. (2007). Liberalismo versus anarcocapitalismo. *Procesos de Mercado: Revista Europea de Economía Política*, *4*(2), 13–32.

Huerta de Soto, J. (2013, January 3). *James M. Buchanan, "in memoriam"*. Libre Mercado.

Ikeda, S. (2003). How Compatible are Public Choice and Austrian Political Economy? *Review of Austrian Economics, 16*, 63–75.

Niskanen, W. (2007). *Bureaucracy and Representative Government*. Routledge.

Pigou, A. (1932). *The Economics of Welfare*. Macmillan.

Rothbard, M. N. (1977). *Power and Market: Government and the Economy*. Columbia University Press.

The Austrian Defense of the Euro in Light of Luigi Einaudi's Quest for Sound Money

Bernardo Ferrero

One of Huerta de Soto's most well-known essays is his 2012 "An Austrian Defense of the Euro," which has ignited a fruitful debate among Austrian economists (Hoffmann, 2013; Carrino, 2014; van den Hauwe, 2018;

Professor Huerta de Soto has been a great source of inspiration throughout these years. In order to give the reader an idea of the uniqueness of this man, I would like to recall a funny anecdote. In March of 2019 I travelled to Auburn for the Austrian Scholars Conference. It was a special occasion for the Mises Institute was celebrating the 70th birthday of Hans-Hermann Hoppe. I approached Prof. Hoppe and introduced myself as a student of Prof. Huerta de Soto. Hoppe immediately showed his admiration and friendship toward Huerta yet confessed that he was disappointed that he was never able to get him to Bodrum, Turkey, for the annual conference of the PFS. Upon returning to Madrid, I told Professor Huerta de Soto what Hoppe had said. With a smile on his face, he answered without hesitation: "I already told him that I never travel to third world countries!"

B. Ferrero (✉)
Ciencias Sociales y Juridicas, Universidad Rey Juan Carlos, Madrid, Spain

D. Howden, P. Bagus (eds.), *The Emergence of a Tradition: Essays in Honor of Jesús Huerta de Soto, Volume I*,
https://doi.org/10.1007/978-3-031-17414-8_13

Mingardi, 2019, pp. 162–184). Its central argument is that short of achieving a classical gold standard with a 100% free-banking system, one must aim toward "creating a monetary framework that disciplines as far as possible economic, political, and social agents." Viewed from this perspective, the introduction of the euro between 1999 and 2002 represented a step in the positive direction, in so far as an end was put to flexible exchange rates and monetary nationalism, which amounted to the possibility by the member states of "manipulating their local currency by placing it at the service of the political needs of the moment" (Huerta de Soto, 2012).

Far from being heterodox, this line of argument was presented more than seventy years ago by one of the intellectual fathers of the European Union: Luigi Einaudi. The aim of the following essay is to revive Einaudi's typically "Austrian" defense of the common currency and attempt to show that the abolition of monetary nationalism was one of the fundamental building blocks behind the process of European unification. This will prove to be an occasion, moreover, to touch on Einaudi's proximity to the Austrian economists, outline his admiration for the gold standard and evaluate his plan given the historical record of the ECB.

Einaudi, the Austrians, and the Quest for Sound Money

Luigi Einaudi (1874–1961) is mostly remembered as a statesman. He was elected governor of the Bank of Italy in 1945, member of the constituent assembly in 1946, Minister of Budget and Deputy prime minister in 1947, and finally President of the newborn republic in 1948—a charge that he occupied until 1955. In his brief yet intense career as a statesman, Einaudi was an instrumental figure in setting the foundations of Italy's post WWII economic miracle in so far as he stabilized the Italian *Lira* and pursued the necessary reforms to foster trust in market institutions. From 1948 to 1963—an epoch of relative monetary stability, light-touch regulation and low taxation—the Italian economy grew at an average of 6.5% annually (Mingardi, 2017, p. 36).

Less known, yet in no way less productive, was Einaudi's career as a scholar and journalist. Not only did he write scientific articles for prestigious journals like *La Critica sociale*, *La Riforma sociale*, and *La Rivista di storia economica*, but was also, between 1908 and 1946, a correspondent for *The Economist* and a regular contributor to *La Stampa* and il *Corriere della Sera*, where, just between 1903 and 1925, he wrote over 1700 articles (Pavanelli, 2012). Einaudi, in the words of Alberto Mingardi (2015), can thus be said to have been "the Italian Wilhelm Röpke and the Italian Konrad Adenauer in one man."

Einaudi continued the great tradition of Italian liberalism, which can be traced back to Antonio Genovesi (1713–1769), Ferdinando Galiani (1728–1787), Alessandro Manzoni (1785–1873) all the way to the father of the *scienze delle finanze*, Francesco Ferrara (1810–1900), and the *liberisti* of the late nineteenth century, the most important of which were Maffeo Pantaleoni (1857–1924), Vilfredo Pareto (1848–1923), and Antonio de Viti de Marco (1858–1943) (Buchanan, 2001; Sabetti, 1989; Mingardi, 2017; Masala & Cubeddu, 2011). Einaudi was the last representative of the second wave of *Liberisti* and in the aftermath of World War II was seen as "the best-known economic liberal in Europe" (Raico, 1996, p. 16).

While generally regarded as a neoclassical economist, influenced by the writings of Alfred Marshall, Vilfredo Pareto, Enrico Barone, Irving Fisher, and the above-mentioned authors, Einaudi was also highly receptive of the writings of the Austrian School economists. Einaudi played a very important role in translating, analyzing, and promoting key works of Carl Menger, William Smart, Philip Wicksteed, Ludwig von Mises, Wilhelm Röpke, Lionel Robbins, Friedrich Hayek, and Fritz Machlup for *La Riforma Sociale,* journal that he directed between 1908 and 1935 (Einaudi, 1933; Faucci, 1986).

What Einaudi found in the school of Carl Menger, Eugen von Böhm Bawerk, and Friedrich von Wieser was "a fertile breeding ground for conceptual tools and an extraordinary source of moral commitment" (Infantino, 2016). According to him, once his major works had come out, nobody had any excuse for not reading Menger, especially his 1883 *Untersuchungen über die Methode der Socialwissenschaften und der Politischen Oekonomie Insbesondere,* which he described as "a book of capital importance and not only for the social sciences [...]" (Einaudi, 1931). In the preface to the Italian edition of Lionel Robbins's "The Great Depression," which he described as "a lucid battling book," Einaudi referred to the "clarifying power of certain abstract concepts that it is the singular merit of the Viennese school of economics, old and new, to have elaborated and faceted endlessly." Referring to Ludwig von Mises and Friedrich Hayek, he concluded that they "give hope of becoming one of the world's major spiritual forces" (Einaudi, 1935, p. 14; 1937, p. 278).

When Einaudi was uttering these works he had already developed a personal relationship with many Austrians, starting from Ludwig von Mises, whom he first met in 1926 at Harvard University, during a debate hosted by Frank Taussig (Hülsmann, 2007, pp. 566–569). In the words of Margit von Mises, Einaudi was "a colleague and good friend of Lu's" (Mises, 1976, p. 146). When Mises fled from the Nazis and settled in New York, Einaudi's son Mario paid him a visit bringing him news from his father. On his part, in the summer of 1953, Einaudi hosted Mises at the *Quirinal Palace*, the official residence of the President of the Italian Republic and at his summer house in Dogliani in 1961 (Infantino, 2016). Einaudi developed a good relationship also with Wilhelm Röpke and Friedrich Hayek. Along with the Crocean philosopher Carlo Antoni and the economist Costantino Bresciani-Turroni, he was the only Italian scholar to become a member of the Mont Pelerin Society on its founding in 1947.

As for the Austrians, sound money or, as Hans Sennholz (2006) liked to put it, a "dependable medium of exchange" was a constant preoccupation of Einaudi, who could not see a return to sanity without a return to a monetary standard based on a commodity like gold: "Without a sound currency consisting of a fixed weight of gold of known fineness, and without a fiduciary currency convertible to the bearer on demand in that known fixed gold disc, it is vain to hope for a revival of trust and security; it is vain to believe that the competitions, wrath and envy of all classes [...] armed against each other, will cease" (Einaudi, 2001 [1944], p. 45). Einaudi, in fact, was aware that in so far as money is non-neutral with respect to the dynamics of the real economy, an inflationary currency would inevitably provoke all sorts of social tensions, economic disturbances, and redistributive processes (Einaudi, 1945; Einaudi, 1955).

In Einaudi's view, gold, unlike national fiat paper currencies, qua international commodity money enabled the fullest exploitation of the convenience of money over barter, with the corollary advantages of economic calculation, free trade, and international cooperation. This was only possible, however, due to gold's chief advantage: its unmanageability by the powers of the day, who could not engage in monetary debasement without abandoning the gold parity fixed by law. "Once upon a time," he wrote as if he was a grandmother telling his grandchild how the world was prior to WWI, "there was a magician [...] and this magician's name was gold [...] What was the magician of gold doing? He had taken the determination of the amount of money in circulation away from the arbitrariness of governments. After centuries of unsuccessful attempts to achieve the same result, the century between 1814 and 1914 [...] realized the ideal [...] Goods and men moved easily, without passports or visas, from one country to another. Technology was advancing very rapidly; and the results of technical advancement benefited everyone and especially the working classes. Never since [...] has national income and [...] wages [...] increased so much and so rapidly" (Einaudi, 1947, p. 1). The ever-increasing levels of trade as well as of savings, investment, and capital accumulation arose because, as a result of gold, "honesty, which had always been considered as one of the Ten Commandments, miraculously became the rule of action that not even men in government could fail to abide by" (Einaudi, 1947; quoted in Forte & Marchionatti, 2012, p. 26). Adhering to the classical gold standard was an assurance of both monetary and fiscal discipline, two factors that enhanced tremendously the propensity to save and thus the prospects for long term development.

Things changed radically, however, after 1914 when, tempted by what Friedrich Hayek (1977) would have called "the fatal conceit," "men imagined they could peep inside this mechanism, almost as if it were a toy; they wanted to see how this mechanism, this so carefully contrived and exquisitely delicate clock mechanism, really worked [...] and they broke it." In its place emerged an elastic, politically managed money as a result of which, Einaudi concluded, "we don't even know any more [...] whether there still exists a monetary unit" (Einaudi, 1947; quoted in Forte & Marchionatti, 2012, p. 26). Instead of fostering honesty, Einaudi was aware that this new managed currency, which substituted human will for the laws of nature, gave birth to a system based on lies, deception, and mischief, as a result of which uncertainty became the rule of the day: "Today [...] states and private individuals know that they no longer assume the same obligation when they contract bonds; and this is also known by savers [...] Certainty, mitigated by daily violation, has been replaced by the certainty of uncertainty. What was previously deplored as an error, as a necessity imposed by fate and circumstances, of war and peace, is now recognized as a sure fact" (Einaudi, 1956, p. 317).

European Federalism and the Centrality of the Common European Currency

Einaudi's reflection on the importance of sound money had a strong impact in shaping his political views, especially regarding international order. Although generally forgotten, Einaudi was an active proponent of

European unification, an interest that he manifested since 1897, when Greece declared war on the Ottoman empire for the possession of Crete and the united fleets of England, France, Russia, Italy, Germany, and Austria promptly intervened to stop the occupation. This event had given Einaudi the opportunity, following in the footsteps of the renowned English journalist William T. Stead who in the aftermath of the combined naval intervention by the six great powers had written an imaginary biography of the United States of Europe, to foresee for the first time the historical realization of a united Europe (Einaudi, 1897; Infantino, 2019). In this very same year the future Italian president came out with an article in *La Stampa* in which he concluded that "the birth of the European federation will not be less glorious just because it was born out of fear and mutual distrust and not out of brotherly love and humanitarian ideals" (Einaudi, 1973 [1897], p. 737).

In 1917 and 1918, Einaudi returned on this subject with two important articles that challenged the Wilsonian project of the *League of Nations* and what he called the dogma of sovereignty (Einaudi, 1918). The latter dogma, wrote the italian economist, "must be destroyed and banished forever" for, in his view, "the truth is the interdependence of free peoples, not their absolute independence [...] The isolated and sovereign state [...] is a fiction of the imagination [...]" (Einaudi, 1986 [1918], pp. 40–41). Through these writings Einaudi influenced Altiero Spinelli and Ernesto Rossi, two of the authors of the renowned 1941 Ventotene Manifesto *For a Free and United Europe*, something that has earned him the recognition as "the father of the fathers of Europe" (Santagostino, 2017). Nevertheless, while for Einaudi the European project had to preserve freedom and enhance liberalism, "for Spinelli and Rossi it had to pave the way for that socialist revolution that proved unfeasible within the framework of a national state" (Cofrancesco, 2017).

In unison with other classical liberals of his time like Mises and Hayek, Einaudi envisioned European federalism as a program capable at once of decentralizing European states and binding them into a supranational framework that would inhibit war and guarantee the free flows of goods, capital, and men between the states (Mingardi & Rohac, 2021). One of the central elements of this program was the creation of a common European currency, who's issuance would become a task assigned to the federation through an independent central bank. "Federalism," Einaudi made clear in one of his articles, "means many other things than those I have mentioned; but it certainly means the abolition of the right of each individual state to issue paper money" (Einaudi, 1986 [1945], p. 219). Imitating the functioning of the nineteenth century classical gold standard, the common European currency, according to Einaudi, would provide low transaction costs and stability in exchange rates, thus fostering harmonious financial and economic relations across state borders. With a single currency, in fact, a firm that was integrated in an extensive division of labor, say by having its base in Italy and its factories or suppliers spread between France and Spain, would not have to worry anymore about shifts in the exchange rates between the lira, the franc, and the peseta, and could thereby focus its entrepreneurial creativity on its customers and supply lines.

Einaudi was aware, however, that while real and significant, these advantages were relatively minor compared to another advantage of far greater value that would come from the introduction of a common currency: the abolition of monetary nationalism. In his own words: "The advantage of the system would not only be one of counting and convenience in inter-state payments and transactions. However great the advantage, it would be small in comparison with another, far greater in value, which is the abolition of the sovereignty of individual states in monetary matters." Einaudi agreed with Lionel Robbins that monetary nationalism must be considered the most pernicious form of nationalism since it underlies all subsequent forms of nationalism. Through its disruptive effects on the economy and society, in fact, monetary nationalism ultimately contributed to the rise in the 1920s of Mussolini in Italy and of Hitler in Germany in the 1930s: "Whoever remembers the bad use that many states have made and continue to make of the right to mint money cannot doubt the urgency of taking away that right [...] The devaluation of the Italian lira and the German mark, which ruined the middle classes and made the working classes unhappy, was one of the causes of the gangs of unemployed intellectuals and troublemakers who gave power to the dictators" (Einaudi, 1986 [1944], pp. 131–132).

In Einaudi's view, the abolition of monetary nationalism would be beneficial from an economic point of view because, lacking direct access to the printing press as a source of revenue, governments would find themselves obliged to tell the truth to their creditors and citizens and thus be forced to better economize on the resources at their disposal. As he explained: "When a state cannot, under any pretext whatsoever, have recourse to the easy means of raising revenue by the press of notes, it will be compelled to make good finance. Taxes and loans remain the only means of revenue at its disposal; and the state can have recourse to loans only within the limits in which it knows how to procure the confidence of savers, that is when it makes good finance" (Einaudi, 1986 [1943], p. 113). For this reason, Einaudi concluded, "If the European federation takes away from the individual federated states the possibility of coping with public deficits by making the ticket press groan and will force them to provide for them only with taxes and voluntary loans, it will have, for this only, accomplished something great" (Einaudi, 1986 [1944], pp. 131–132). One can see, therefore, how the argument given by the Italian economist parallels the one given by Huerta de Soto (2012) up to the point where one can even dare to say that the euro had an almost Austrian origin.

Albeit imperfectly, the Maastricht Treaty (1992), which was responsible for the creation of the EU, was loyal to Einaudi's plan: it established a European Central Bank with the primary objective of maintaining price stability, recognized its independence from elected officials and expressly forbid it to come to any defaulter's rescue by directing monetizing national debts. On top of this, in the no-bail out clause (Article 125 of the Treaty on the Functioning of the European Union), the signatories at Maastricht clarified that no member state would be liable to debts incurred by other euro states, while the Stability Pact stated that all states were bound to keep their deficits below 3% of GDP. "In its intentions at least," suggested Antonio Martino (2008, p. 267), "the Maastricht world is one of strict and impartial rules, a living monument to the market-liberal wisdom."

Since 2010, however, when the ECB openly rescued Greece by directly purchasing its sovereign bonds, Einaudi's great ideal, has been betrayed (Martino, 2010). This betrayal was brought to completion in 2015, when Mario Draghi implemented *quantitative easing*, bringing interest rates down to zero or more and purchasing sovereign and corporate bonds at a pace of 80 billion euros per month. Just like Einaudi had predicted more than 70 years ago, these moves led to excessive public indebtedness, financial fragility, and institutional rigidity, eliminating all political incentives to restore good finance and implement the required structural reforms of economic liberalization (Huerta de Soto, 2019). These expansionary policies, moreover, were significantly increased after the outbreak of the COVID-19 pandemic, and have brought the ECB down a blind alley, as the scenario of "Japanization" threatens to mutate into one of "Venezuelization," with significant price inflation on the horizon (Huerta de Soto, 2021; Huerta de Soto & Ferrero, 2022).

Was Einaudi's Plan Too Good to Be True? Huerta de Soto's Forgotten Alternative

We must then ask ourselves: was Einaudi's plan too good to be true? One thing we can accuse Einaudi is to have underestimated the possibility of currency manipulation at the supranational level. This was perhaps understandable for an economist who, within a half century, had seen the demise of the liberal "world of yesterday" at the hands of the worst possible abuses of national sovereignty—WWI, Fascism, Weimar Hyperinflation, The Great Austrian Inflation, The Great Depression, National Socialism, World War II, the Hungarian Hyperinflation of 1945–46 (Zweig, 2013 [1941]). The centralization of credit in a European central bank, nevertheless, breeds instability, for it ultimately means handing over the management of the monetary unit to a selected group of politically nominated, temporary caretakers (i.e., central bankers) with no skin in the game and who are completely unaccountable, thus severely compromising the quality of money as a means of exchange and store of wealth (Bagus, 2009, p. 35).

"If a workman spends all his wages on the day he receives them," reasoned Vilfredo Pareto (1896/7), "the next day hunger and privation will serve to impress upon his memory the usefulness of saving. But it will be extremely difficult for him to recognize in the evils from which he suffers the consequence [...] of the alteration of the currency" (Pareto, 1943, p. 61). In the private sphere, as Pareto well understood, the effect follows the cause more rapidly and visibly than in public life: a fact that is amplified when the monetary system is under the control of distant bureaucrats armed with the power of externalizing the costs of currency manipulation onto unknown people scattered throughout multiple, different countries (North, 2012).

What Einaudi failed to consider was the fact that the imposition of a new fiat money produced by a monopolistic central bank across Europe would represent an institutional change toward greater monetary central planning, thus inhibiting even more, given the ever-changing conditions of time and place, the determination and implementation of the optimal monetary policy (Ebeling, 2007; Huerta de Soto, 2020, pp. 647–661). As Hayek (2007, p. 224) pointed out, "the problems raised by a conscious direction of economic affairs on a national scale inevitably assume even greater dimensions when the same is attempted internationally."

Given the above and considering the nature of the state as a parasitic institution, in the long run the possibility for inflation and massive redistribution of income and wealth in favor of the political elites and their "feudal barons" at the expense of the general public is enhanced under a similar institutional setting (Hoppe, 2003). The existence of fewer central banks, in fact, makes it easier to pursue a policy of synchronized credit expansion and avoid the pains of devaluation (Herbener, 1999). As a result of there being one single currency imposed through legal tender laws, moreover, economic agents find themselves restricted in their ability to escape from inflationary policies by shifting their income and wealth to alternative media of exchange, a move which under currency competition they could otherwise conduct given the incentives and signals provided by the respective inflation rates and the related price differentials manifested in the foreign exchange market (Bagus, 2010).

For this reason, Friedrich Hayek, who had initially imagined a solution to Europe's monetary fiasco along Einaudi's lines (see, e.g., Hayek, 1948 [1939]), ultimately came to the realization that the best way to minimize the political abuse of the printing press, as Einaudi wanted, was to "deprive governments (or their monetary authorities) of all power to protect their money against competition" for "if they can no longer conceal that their money is becoming bad, they will have to restrict the issue" (Hayek, 1976, p. 18).

It is generally forgotten that a proposal along Hayek's line was presented by Huerta de Soto back in 1994, as he made the case for a freer Europe. Having sensed the problems that a higher degree of monetary central planning could bring to Europe, he argued explicitly that "the foundation of the European Central Bank needs to be reconsidered, and the priority of this objective must be replaced with the free choice of currencies from inside and outside of Europe in an environment in which, at most, we could allow a system of fixed parities between those currencies that have been freely chosen given their link with that national currency that in each historical circumstance offers greater assurance of independence and stability" (Huerta de Soto, 1994, p. 215).

References

Bagus, P. (2009). The Quality of Money. *The Quarterly Journal of Austrians Economics, 4*(2), 22–45.

Bagus, P. (2010). *The Tragedy of the Euro*. Ludwig von Mises Institute.

Buchanan, J. (2001 [1960]). La Scienza Delle Finanze: The Italian Tradition in Fiscal Theory. In G. Brennan, H. Kliemt, & R. D. Tollison (Eds.), *Externalities and Public Expenditure Theory (The Collected Works of James M. Buchanan* (Vol. 15, pp. 59–105). Liberty Fund.

Carrino, I. (2014). La Escuela Austriaca frente al Euro. *Procesos de Mercado: Revista Europea de Economía Politica, XI*(1), 273–284.

Cofrancesco, D. (2017). *Rossi, Spinelli, Einaudi e l'Equivoco Europeo.* il Giornale. https://www.ilgiornale.it/news/spettacoli/rossi-spinelli-einaudi-e-lequivoco europeo-1467273.html.

Ebeling, R. (2007). *The Euro versus Currency Competition.* The Freeman: Ideas on Liberty. https://fee.org/articles/the-euro-versus-currency-competition/?itm_source=parsely-api.

Einaudi, L. (1897). Un Sacerdote della Stampa e gli Stati Uniti d'Europa. *La Stampa..* http://www.luigieinaudi.it/percorsi-di-lettura/lib/percorso-7/un-sacerdote-della-stampa.html

Einaudi, L. (1918). Il dogma della sovranità e l'idea della Società. *Corriere della Sera.* http://www.luigieinaudi.it/percorsi-di-lettura/lib/percorso-7/il-dogma-della-sovranita.html.

Einaudi, L. (1931). Per una nuova collana di economisti. *La Riforma Sociale*, 394–399. http://www.luigieinaudi.it/doc/per-una-nuova-collana-di-economisti/?id=1938

Einaudi, L. (1933). Il mio piano non è quello di Keynes. *La Riforma Sociale, XLIV*(2), 129–142. http://www.luigieinaudi.it/doc/il-mio-piano-non-e-quello-di-keynes/

Einaudi, L. (1935). Prefazione a L. Robbins. *Di chi è la colpa della grande crisi?* Giulio Einaudi, 9–14. http://www.luigieinaudi.it/pubblicazione/prefazione-l-robbins-di-chi-la-colpa-della-grande-crisi/?id=4163.

Einaudi, L. (1937). Delle origini economiche della Grande Guerra, della Crisi e delle diverse specie di Piani. *Rivista di storia economica, 2*(3), 277–289.

Einaudi, L. (1945). L'alzamento della moneta. *Risorgimento liberale.* http://www.luigieinaudi.it/doc/lalzamento-della-moneta/

Einaudi, L. (1947). Bretton Woods. *Risorgimento Liberale.* http://www.luigieinaudi.it/doc/bretton-woods/?id=2351

Einaudi, L. (1955). Che cosa ha detto Cantillon. In R. Cantillon (Ed.), *Saggio sulla natura del commercio in generale* (pp. XI–XXV). Einaudi. http://www.luigieinaudi.it/pubblicazione/che-cosa-ha-detto-cantillon/?id=4087.

Einaudi, L. (1956). *Lo scrittoio del Presidente (1948-1955).* Einaudi.

Einaudi, L. (1986). *La Guerra e l'Unità Europea.* il Mulino.

Einaudi, L. (1973). *Il buongoverno. Saggi di economia e politica 1897-1954.* Laterza.

Einaudi, L. (2001). *Riflessioni di un liberale sulla democrazia 1943-1947.* Leo. S. Olschki.

Faucci, R. (1986). *Einaudi.* UTET.

Forte, F., & Marchionatti, R. (2012). Luigi Einaudi's Economics of Liberalism. *European Journal of the History of Economic Thought, 19*(4), 587–624.
Hauwe, L. v. (2018). Monetary Constitutionalism: Some Recent Developments. *Procesos de Mercado: Revista Europea de Economia Politica, XV* (2), 67–105.
Hayek, F. A. (1948 [1939]). The Economic Conditions of Interstate Federalism. *New Commonwealth Quarterly, 5*, 131–149. Now in *Individualism and Economic Order*, University of Chicago Press: Chicago, pp. 255–272.
Hayek, F. A. (1976). *Choice in Currency*. The Institute of Economic Affairs.
Hayek, F. A. (1977). *The Fatal Conceit: The Errors of Socialism*. Routledge.
Hayek, F. A. (2007 [1944]). *The Road to Serfdom*. The University of Chicago Press/Routledge.
Herbener, J. (1999). *Euro Inflation*. Ludwig von Mises Institute. https://mises.org/library/euro-inflation.
Hoffmann, A. (2013). The Euro as a Proxy for the Gold Standard? Government Debt Financing and Political Commitment in Historical Perspective. *Journal des Economistes et des Etudes Humaines, 19*(1), 41–61.
Hoppe, H. H. (2003). Government, Money and International Politics. *Etica & Politica / Ethics & Politics, 2*, 1–10.
Huerta de Soto, J. (1994). Por una Europa Libre. In *Estudios de Economia Politica* (pp. 214–217). Unión Editorial.
Huerta de Soto, J. (2012). *An Austrian Defense of the Euro*. Ludwig von Mises Institute. https://mises.org/library/austrian-defense-euro
Huerta de Soto, J. (2019). *The Japanization of the European Union*. Ludwig von Mises Institute. https://mises.org/wire/japanization-european-union
Huerta de Soto, J. (2020 [1998]). *Money, Bank Credit and Economic Cycles*. Ludwig von Mises Institute.
Huerta de Soto, J. (2021). *The Economic Effects of Pandemics. An Austrian Analysis*. Ludwig von Mises Institute. https://mises.org/wire/economic-effects-pandemics-austrian-analysis.
Huerta de Soto, J., & Ferrero, B. (2022). *Pandemia e dirigismo*. IBL Libri.
Hülsmann, J. G. (2007). *Mises: The Last Knight of Liberalism*. Ludwig von Mises Institute.
Infantino, L. (2016). *Einaudi l'austriaco*. Il Foglio. https://www.ilfoglio.it/gli-inserti-del-foglio/2016/06/13/news/einaudi laustriaco-97209/
Infantino, L. (2019). *Luigi Einaudi e il progetto europeista*. Luiss Open. https://open.luiss.it/2019/02/14/luigi-einaudi-e-il-progetto-europeista/.
Martino, A. (2008). Milton Friedman and the Euro. *Cato Journal, 28*(2), 263–273.
Martino, A. (2010). Einaudi Tradito. *Europa e l'Euro*. http://antoniomartino.org/einaudi-tradito/.
Masala, A., & Cubeddu, R. (2011). Liberalismo, Liberismo e Antistatalismo. *Cosmopolis: Rivista semestrale di cultura*, 17–27.

Mingardi, A. (2015). *A Quick Note on Luigi Einaudi.* The Library of Economics and Liberty. https://www.econlib.org/archives/2015/06/a_quick_note_on.html.
Mingardi, A. (2017). Classical Liberalism in Italian Economic Thought, from the Time of Unification. *ECON JOURNAL WATCH, 1*, 22–54.
Mingardi, A. (2019). *La verità, vi prego, sul neoliberismo.* Marsilio.
Mingardi, A., & Rohac, D. (2021). Hayek's Europe: The Austrian School and European Federalism. In F. Giavazzi, F. L. D'Ovidio, & A. Mingardi (Eds.), *The Liberal Heart of Europe* (pp. 67–80). Springer.
Mises, M. (1976). *My Years with Ludwig von Mises.* Arlington House Publishers.
North, G. (2012). Let the Euro Die… Soon. https://www.garynorth.com/public/9702.cfm.
Pavanelli, G. (2012). *The Economists and the Press in Italy: The Case of Luigi Einaudi.* ICER Working Papers 10-2012, ICER – International Centre for Economic Research.
Pareto, V. (1896/97 [1943]). *Corso di Economia Politica.* Einaudi.
Raico, R. (1996). Mises on Fascism, Democracy, and Other Questions. *Journal of Libertarian Studies, 12*(1), 1–28.
Sabetti, F. (1989). Un precursore siciliano di "Public Choice"? Francesco Ferrara e lo sviluppo delle scienze sociali in Nord-America. *Il Politico, 54*(3), 409–423.
Santagostino, A. (2017). *Luigi Einaudi, the Father of the Fathers of Europe.* Cambridge Scholars Publishing.
Sennholz, H. (2006). Milton Friedman: 1912-2006. *Mises Daily Articles*, Ludwig von Mises Institute. https://mises.org/library/milton-friedman-1912-2006.
Zweig, S. (2013 [1941]). *The World of Yesterday.* University of Nebraska Press.

Economic-Societal Order and Business Order: Efficient Configuration of the Business "Environment"

Santiago García Echevarría

One of the notable references of the academic events of all university students is manifested in the acts that reflect the persistent and incident activity both in the teaching and research contribution. A tribute work allows us to express, without ambiguity, that basic reference of the university professor, with the great reference that is friendship, the result of access to shared actions, both in knowledge and in teaching dimensions. In Professor Jesús Huerta de Soto, that has been precisely his great teaching work at the level of the development of the doctoral students' training, together with the great contribution that he has made in directing of doctoral theses. This is not only because of what participation in knowledge implies, as in the case of Professor Huerta de Soto and the Austrian School, but, above all, because of the work of teaching development in many doctoral students, as well as the dimension and contribution to the economic training of many university students as a basis for their intense research work and contribution to economic thought around the Austrian School. We join this tribute with appreciation for his efforts and excellent cooperation.

S. García Echevarría (✉)
Universidad de Alcalá, Alcalá de Henares, Spain
e-mail: santiago.garcia@uah.es

D. Howden, P. Bagus (eds.), *The Emergence of a Tradition: Essays in Honor of Jesús Huerta de Soto, Volume I*,
https://doi.org/10.1007/978-3-031-17414-8_14

All economic action basically implies the capacity *to coordinate* different types of knowledge in order to configure the *processes* in which the action of the person takes place, which requires a key value that is *trust*. It is the person who develops their action as a priority to *coordinate* with others, with their knowledge, but, in particular, as people who generate the certainty needed to *cooperate*. And it is people who, thanks to trust, develop the institutions that allow people to be openly integrated into the configuration of society. This is precisely the societal dimension of the economy, precisely based on people and the ability to generate trust.

And all this in the sense of Walter Eucken, who says that "the person not only needs protection and security, they need more, the development of his capacities according to his strength should not be hindered" (Eucken, 2017, p. 41).

The foundations of all economic action of the person and of institutions imply, in their configuration, a "vision" of action, that function of discovery of all human action that forces to formulate goals, objectives, which are framed in a "system of values" that ultimately determines the space of action that allows the development of the person, as well as in the entire independent development process, promoting capacities that allow cooperation between people, configuring the institutions.

That is the reason behind the need for a *"global vision,"* which frames individual action, individual capacities, and situations to develop. Sharing "the global vision," the integrating of people, is the necessary condition for the development of people and for the configuration of their institutions. This implies the broad interdisciplinarity of any economic action that necessarily matters and the broad economic-societal meaning that makes possible the coordination between people and their institutions in order to efficiently achieve, both economically and societally, the development of people.

The Interdependence of the Economic and the Societal Orders

There are very different ways through which people can coordinate themselves, their knowledge and, in particular, their "systems of values." The diversity of these forms of coordination decisively marks the way of understanding, on the one hand, the person in their own economic action and, on the other hand, the forms of coordination that are established to impart the development that is produced, according to the circumstances, according to the power and individual interests. Already *Walter Eucken* pointed this out with the concept of economic order, that is, the way of ordering these indicated coordination relations such that "the economic order is—as we know—the set of forms in which the concrete direction of the dominant economic processes takes place" (Eucken, 2017, p. 184).

But the economic order is framed and is, at the same time, determining a large part of the "order of society," since the forms of the economic order are close to the "order of society" (Eucken, 2017, p. 181), as "there are effects of mutual interdependence also between the economic Order and the Order of society" (Eucken, 2017, p. 183). It is, therefore, always an economic-societal dimension, which implies the development possibilities of the person and the configuration of their institutions.

According to the economic order that is developed in a country, "the global," and the dominant characteristics corresponding to this configuration of knowledge, the possibilities of development are opened or closed, both for people and for the development of their capacities and competencies, for their well-being. The economic order is imposed or developed around the possibility of the economic action of the person, in particular, when, from the partial consideration of the economic-social sphere, singular decisions are undertaken without considering the impact on the economic-societal group. Government action in partial sectors of the economy generate wide distortions in other areas with a growing deterioration of the whole.

The conception of the economic order as a concept of *the economic*, of the coordinating global action, is defined by Eucken (2017, pp. 19–33) thusly: "the economic order of a specific country is the set of corresponding forms carried out in which companies and domestic economies are linked and in which, therefore, the specific economic process takes place" (Eucken, 2017, p. 23). It is about the coordination of supply and demand, in macroeconomic terms, of the two key areas of the management of economic action through the institutions that generate the way of ordering and organizing the economic processes, and the behaviors of the people who act in them, so that "within the framework of the specific contribution of the management, each one of the economic institutions must be understood" (Eucken, 2017, p. 24), which is also why "it is shown that legal institutions—such as property, contractual freedom or responsibility, they change according to the form of the Order of their functions" (Eucken, 2017, p. 24).

Therefore, the conceptual development of the economic order is involved in the order of society and in the *systems of values* on which they rest, which implies a vision of the global, of the set with global objectives that must be carried out not only in the singular actions, in their singularity in the action, but from the economic-societal set respecting the order of interdependence between the different partial areas. That is, it is related to the great problems such as *"coordination costs"* between individual decisions and the global development of society, that is, the individual interest versus the interest of the whole, the common good.

Consequently, all economic action always implies a *social* impact, because "the problem of management policy does not result only from the economy, but also from changes in political and social situations" (Eucken, 2017, p. 30), since "there is no economic policy measure that does not have, simultaneously, directly or indirectly, effects and has a social meaning" (Eucken, 2017, p. 369) because "there is nothing that is not socially relevant" (Eucken, 2017, p. 369).

The Social Dimension, in the Economic Order and in the Economic Processes

The social dimension can be pointed out, the societal one is an indissoluble part of all economic activity, so social policy is part of economic policy and must be integrated with it in the economic-social order when configuring the action of the people and, all this, within the framework of the *"system of values,"* since "the Order, as a whole, should be in such a way that it enables people to live in accordance with ethical principles" (Eucken, 2017, p. 242). To which it must also be considered that in the evolution of the last decades, social decisions have dominated without their adequate integration into the economic-social order, causing serious coordination problems through their corresponding impact on behaviors, both institutional and individual. The separation of the social from the economic, or vice versa, seriously deteriorates *coordination*, creating grave mistrust for the economic-societal functioning, and it must be considered that "it is not possible to demand of people what only an economic Order can achieve: establishing an economic relationship between individual interest and general interest" (Eucken, 2017, p. 427).

The construction of coordination processes constitutes for Walter Eucken: the "...Order of a free society considers it consequently as a problem of legal Order..." that guarantees the functioning of a market economy "ensuring competition as a means of controlling economic power" (Streit & Wohlgemuth, 2000, p. 464). And it is precisely in the configuration of economic power that the achievement of a satisfactory and efficient order of competition is centered in order to have efficient open markets in a way that makes it possible to combine individual interests with the interests of the whole (García Echevarría, 2017, pp. LI). What defines Eucken precisely is the sense that "no one can have more or less economic power than is necessary to carry out an order of competition" (García Echevarría, 2017, pp. LI). Open competition, in the context of efficient markets, is the key to the socio-economic order within the framework of the *Ethical principles* necessary for the development of the person, of their capacities, and as can be seen in Röpke: "economic productivity, contrary to technical productivity, can only be measured in the production of those things that correspond to the scales of value and needs of society as a whole" (García Echevarría, 2017, pp. LI).

Conceptualization of Coordination Processes

From the perspective of the configuration of the economic-societal order, integrating economic and social policies with a government's actions, with its legal-institutional emphasis, rests, as a whole, on a series of *"principles"* that affect all economic-social and societal-political actions. This is decisive for the set of globally coordinating actions and also for singular, individual actions or "principles" under which all actions taken must be evaluated in the configuration and development of broader economic processes. These include both constituent and regulatory principles.

A) *Constituent Principles*, based on the economic-social and societal-political actions that affect the whole, and individual interests which articulate the order of competence, including:

- A *price system* capable of operating efficiently in terms of perfect competition (García Echevarría, 2017, pp. LI), which requires

  - Monetary policy stabilization
  - Open markets
  - Private property
  - Contractual freedom
  - Individual responsibility
  - Constancy in economic policy

- Considering perfect competition, a key to *Eucken*'s thinking, the main function of the State, focuses on the fact that "...competition deserves protection through law with its controlling effect on private power..." (Streit & Wohlgemuth, 2000, p. 466).

B) *Regulatory Principles* that affect, with a more instrumental nature, in the shaping action of the operational activity that affects the economic and social processes, whose fundamental mission is "to maintain the order of competence with the capacity to function" (García Echevarría, 2017, pp. LVI).

This is the key to the economic-social order that constitutes the *"economic constitution,"* as it is based on the *"Constituent Principles"* guaranteeing the long term generation of trust, in a framework of certainty, since the *"Regulatory Principles,"* that regulate specific situations, can cause problems, as well as adapt to certain transformation and adaptation processes that could influence the development of the person (Eucken, 2017, p. 291).

The Societal Economic Order and Business Dynamics

As has already been pointed out previously, the economic order involves both the processes of human action in the context of business activity, on the one hand, as well as human action in the context of domestic economies. In the business field, all economic-societal order, as well as the legal institutions that configure it, establish the framework in which all business processes are configured, from the definition of their global action possibilities to the individual action of each company and its multiple processes

(García Echevarría, 2021). This affects both the coordination processes between companies and the complex internal coordination processes of each one of them, of their organizational and directive forms oriented to the configuration of the markets, that is, to the generators of competitive capacity in order to contribute to their own business development, and their institutional-corporate interest (García Echevarría, 2020, p. 141) and their interest in contributing to society as a whole and to the development of the person.

The "Constituent Principles," both in their economic-social and institutional-legal dimensions, configure, in accordance with the *systems of values,* the coordination processes between the different public and private institutions that must create the context in which they can and have to configure both the action of the companies and the people who form them. This requires establishing the values and criteria in which the person, in their different actions in the company, generates the necessary confidence to provide "certainty" of a "constitutional" nature, for the creation and development of companies.

One of its fundamental characteristics for the development of business dynamics is to decisively address the *"long-term"* in business performance, the constancy of the context in which the company, each company, in its complexity, contrives in the face of "true" institutional expectations as a whole, which guarantees a stable, long-term environment. Key to the existence of a *business dynamic* that makes possible the development of both an established business culture is competition and the emergence of the business function of the key corporate culture in all market operations.

The totally dominant *vision* at present of a broad short-termism in the action of the company leads to upset the very figure of the company as a societal institution, beyond a strict economic approach, rather financial, thereby reducing dynamics business (García Echevarría, 2017, p. 117) to "business," in a vulgar sense. And, in particular, it goes beyond the mere interpretation that is frequently made of the business "environment" that is limited to the most immediate of the short-term adaptation processes, with which there is no place for the corporate institutional dimension that constitutes the "long term" of that long-standing coordination provided by the socio-economic order of a process involving, in the long term, the orientation of capacities and responsibilities.

The business "environment" goes beyond mere marquetry and is located in the long term in its corporate dimension, which contributes to a more efficient coordination, as an inter-institutional institution that facilitates the transformation and adaptation processes of people and their organizations.

One issue must be clear for the maintenance and operation of a market economy that must be considered especially dangerous for the planning of companies, inherent in their management, to shift to supra-corporate instances (Eucken, 2017, p. 376). For it is key, on the one hand, because the company sets objectives and generates the processes of social action through the planning process (García Echevarría, 2021, p. 285) for which it necessarily requires a "constitutional" framework, in the Euckenian sense, stable in the long term in search of the development of competition under the constancy of economic policy that allows business planning.

But, on the other hand, the planning action of the company could be shifted to the economic order, where entities outside the company of the legal, social, and economic order impose objectives and means to decide business activity. That is, a centralized economy, a directed economy, since there are different ways of understanding planning action, cancelling "business dynamics" and establishing an economic management that implies high "coordination costs" and eliminates development capacity, in the assumption of responsibilities and contribution to the development of people (Eucken, 2017, p. 19) and their capacities for action.

Reductionism, standardization, has supposed equalization of people and processes, which implies impoverishment in human action, in vision and in diversity, both in objectives and in the ways of configuring the processes, reducing the entire process, both in the economic-societal efficiency of business dynamics but also as a denial of diversity, as the vital fact of the development of the person and of the institutions.

The dominant short-termism and the consequent loss of institutional-corporate trust imply increasing "coordination costs," including the loss of responsibility capacities, the contribution of diversity to the development of companies, and the lack of creative processes in the capacity of human action in the company. It is necessary for the development of business dynamics, their contribution to the responsible development of the person and their organizations of an economic-societal order that makes the permanent action of the company sustainable and resilient beyond what it already implies to generate products and services to provide an efficient response to the needs of people and companies so as to take on the necessary transformation and permanent change processes. This is the societal dimension of the company.

It means governing a country around an economic-societal order based on the "Constituent Principles" that, in accordance with the *values* involved in society, always imply freedom for the development of the diversity of people and that of their institutions to help generate an "order of competence" that involves an efficient response to the needs of people, both in their economic, social, and societal dimension. An economic-social order defined by a set of "principles" is necessary, based on the value system that facilitates, on the one hand, a clear vision of the fundamental characteristics that should be the basis of legal and socio-economic institutions. But, on the other hand, it should also facilitate the interpretation of the coordination between all the institutions that make up the constitutional "environment," which affects all business dynamics, the action of the businessman, and the people involved in the company with their responsibilities and contributions in the ethical framework of human action.

And given the uncertainty in which all economic-social and ethical action always takes place, it must also be disposed, likewise, of the "regulatory principles" indicated (Eucken, 2017, p. 345) that must resolve the circumstances caused in the short term, always on the basis of the orientation to the "Constituent Principles" as its permanent reference. In this way, a situation of constancy of the "business environment" is established that does not mean immobility, but, precisely, the opposite, transformation and change, innovation and risk, individual and institutional responsibility that makes possible the business dynamics linked together to an order of competence that allows an efficient economic and social response to people's development.

Proposals for a Society Economically and Societally Efficient: Business Dynamics

As has been seen, the company, the business economy, constitutes together with the domestic economy the keys to the economic-social ordering of a country with all that this implies both in the economic context and in its effects on the social dimension. Both parties are constituents of the economic-social reality in which the wide and complex business diversity and the complexity of its institutions are involved, as well as the role of the state in the determination and maintenance of the economic-social order within which companies must arise, develop, and contribute, in their multiplicity and diversity of business forms, as well as their permanent dynamics of technical, economic, and social transformation. This occurs within the framework of the human complexity of their organizations and the forms of configuration both in the individual dimension and in their societal behavior.

That is why the "Constituent Principles" (Eucken, 2017, p. 305) mentioned not only guide legal, technical, economic, and social diversity, but also frame the reference to the action of the businessman and the company who can then contribute with their efforts to generate adequate competition that implies responsibility and efficiency to contribute to the development of technical, economic, and social efficiency of people.

Facing the economic-social order in search of the long term in determining the constancy of the economic policy and avoiding immobility, that is, an economic-social order is key to business dynamics, which is found in the wide diversity of business action, in the great differentiation of all its dimensions from business reality, which, on the one hand, as the singular, specific institution of concrete situations and, on the other hand, the joint field of action of the companies in their technical, economic, social, and corporate context in reference to their contribution to society, to the development of people. That is, what we could point to as *"business order"* that goes beyond representation in existing issues, in different institutions and associations that seek to unite and defend specific interests.

The "order of companies" goes beyond the singular legal dimensions. It is a set of "Constituent Principles" of the company. A "business order" that, in its societal dimension, facilitates the processes of "company coordination" with the society and the coordination between the different companies, facilitating the coordination processes, without prejudice to individual freedoms and responsibilities. This would facilitate greater cooperation, in many areas, always oriented to the "constituent principles" of the business environment. This includes the intensification of competition in order to facilitate and contribute to solving the systems of each company and the circumstance of the business as a whole, the common good valued in its contribution to the development of society and the person.

Although in the course of the last decades, attempts have been made to promote different ways of understanding the company–society relationship, it is necessary to establish, in the *Euckenian* style, a "business order," which goes beyond the political-social, technical, economic and legal aspects, among others, and define those principles that constitute the action of companies in the society. This is in order to reduce the *coordination costs* of the company with and in society, as well as the costs of coordination within and in each of the business organizations.

It is about the relationship between the person, in their actions in the company and their appreciation of the societal value of their contribution not only to the company as an organization, but as a company involved in the development of society. To appreciate the value that can drive the person to be included in business organizations, but, at the same time, to society, the assumption of what their contribution, effort and action means, implying their own personal development as the contribution of the company in what constitutes its social contribution.

It is about promoting the corporate role of the company, on the one hand, and the role, weight, and impulse that affects the valuation by each person in the contribution in which they are involved both in their own development and effort and in the incentive which means the value of their contribution.

It is the person who innovates, who transforms, who assumes responsibility, who contributes with others in processes that, without a doubt, are complex, that go beyond the business dimension itself, and that are key in the assessment and incidence of all socio-economic action in the company or institution in which it operates.

A "company order" that implies "Constituent Principles" that must be constitutive of the action of directing, organizing, configuring the economic-business processes, of a vision that goes beyond the traditional business borders, to influence the economic-social reality of the society in which people develop. The research program (García Echevarría, 2022) that is being carried out is dealing with these aspects, seeking that response centered on the person in the organizations and in the set of coordination processes in which they can contribute to give an efficient response, both economic and social and societally for the development of people and their inclusion, as well as the competence to ensure the common good shared with the individual good.

References

Eucken, W. (2017). *Principios de Política Económica*. Aranzadi.

García Echevarría, S. (2017). Cómo debe configurarse el Orden Económico-Societario. In W. Eucken (Ed.), *Principios de Política Económica* (pp. LI). Aranzadi.

García Echevarría, S. (2020). *Economía y Sociedad*. Díaz de Santos.

García Echevarría, S. (2021). *Teoría Económica de la Empresa*. Díaz de Santos.

García Echevarría, S. (2022). *Fundamentos de Política Económica de la Empresa*. (Manuscript in preparation).

Streit, M. E., & Wohlgemuth, M. (2000). Walter Eucken und Friedrich A. von Hayek: Initiator der Ordnungsökonomik. In B. Külp & V. Vanberg (Eds.), *Freiheit und Wettbewerliche Ordnung- Gedenkband zur Erinnerung an Walter Eucken* (pp. 461–498). Haufe Verlag.

Defining Money

David Howden

Walking down calle Villajimena on a beautiful early October evening in 2007, my arms were laden with books, too many to carry in any other situation. I just had my first meeting with Jesús Huerta de Soto. On his encouragement, I had moved to Madrid to study under him, an event that would drastically alter the course of my life. At this meeting Jesús gave to me in an almost haphazard way the books I carried, stressing that "you'll need to read this, and that, and this one for good measure." Those books formed the backbone of my own intellectual journey, as they did for countless other similar disciples of Don Jesús. They were also, as I discovered quickly, the foundation of his own intellectual tradition. Rothbard, Böhm-Bawerk, Hayek, Kirzner, and of course, Mises, all took central stage. (So too did his own books.) But he steered me towards other eclectic works that I would only appreciate much later as offering a rich complement to the normal list: Lachmann and Polanyi, to give two more well-known examples, but other names and "must read" books cropped up at every meeting. The result was a central pillar, a canon curated by Huerta de Soto, augmented and enriched in unusual and nonobvious but ultimately fulfilling ways. Jesús provided a complete education in economics, plus an emphasis on why one cannot view economics in isolation of law or the moral sciences. Don Jesús, for the continental ideas you inspired within this *anglosajon*, gracias.

D. Howden (✉)
Department of Business, Saint Louis University – Madrid Campus, Madrid, Spain
e-mail: david.howden@slu.edu

D. Howden, P. Bagus (eds.), *The Emergence of a Tradition: Essays in Honor of Jesús Huerta de Soto, Volume I*,
https://doi.org/10.1007/978-3-031-17414-8_15

Reception of Jesús Huerta de Soto's *Money, Bank Credit, and Economy Cycles* was nearly universally positive. Criticisms pertained mostly to the analysis of bank credit and its role in propagating economic cycles. Only one reviewer commented on the treatment of money in the book. Writing on the perils of base money, Leland Yeager (2001, p. 255) laments that Huerta de Soto takes "the concept of money for granted, as a primitive concept too obvious to require definition, especially before the emergence of banks." The omission of a satisfying definition of money has not gone completely unnoticed in broader circles. As I have discussed the book with others who use it as a text in money and banking courses there is a general feeling that the topics of "credit" and "economic cycles" are explored at great depth, at the expense of attention to the more fundamental concept of "money."

This chapter concerns the thorny issue of what money *is*. Money is most commonly defined today as "anything that is generally accepted as payment for goods or services or in the repayment of debts" (Mishkin, 2019, p. 57). There is not much for the Austrian economist to quibble with on this point. In various places of his tome, Huerta de Soto defines money as the generally accepted medium of exchange (2006, p. 739, p. 745n, p. 770n, and *passim*). Elsewhere he refers to money as the "only perfectly liquid asset" (*ibid.*, 186). Other authors also share the definition of money as the "generally accepted medium of exchange." The definition is, however, not without its drawbacks. As Rothbard (1962, pp. 192–93) notes:

> whereas the concept of a "medium of exchange" is a precise one, and indirect exchange can be distinctly separated from direct exchange, the concept of "money" is a less precise one. The point at which a medium of exchange comes into "common" or "general" use is not strictly definable, and whether or not a medium is a money can be decided only by historical inquiry and the judgment of the historian. However, for purposes of simplification, and since we have seen that there is a great impetus on the market for a medium of exchange to become money, we shall henceforth refer to all media of exchange as moneys.

Oftentimes, one gets the impression that authors put the cart before the horse when it comes to money. Defining money as the commonly accepted medium of exchange might be helpful, but it also begs a question. The economist takes a leap of faith by overlooking the important question of why a specific good is given this role. Glossing over the question of why a good serves as money leaves a hole in his theoretical corpus.[1] (And a serious

[1] Menger (1909, p. 5) also expresses similar objections to defining money as the generally accepted medium of exchange as a starting point in monetary analysis.

hole at that—there is broad agreement that money is the good with the most wide-reaching effects in the economy.)

Some approaches to money do try to rectify this problem by putting the horse firmly before the cart. Famously, Jevons's (1875, p. 3) focus on eliminating the problem of the double coincidence of wants started with the complicated economic problem of direct exchanges. Money emerges to solve this problem. Menger's (1871, ch. 8; 1892) emphasis on the evolution of money put empirical meat on the bones of Jevons's theory. By showing that commodity money evolved from specific goods valued for certain qualities and attributes, Menger takes the reader through a historical journey from the moneyless to the moneyed world. Mises's (1953, part II, ch. 1) regression theorem incorporates money into a general theory of pricing and allows the economist to understand where the value of modern fiat monies, which seem to lack any direct use value in the sense that gold or shells had, stems from.

This three-step process stemming from the Jevonsian ➔ Mengerian ➔ Misesian approaches to money correspond to the process of identifying the initial problem ➔ finding a solution to this problem by a good which we call money ➔ integrating and understanding the value of money within the scope of the broader economy. The process also forms the theoretical bedrock for the claim that money is the commonly accepted medium of exchange.

While not obviously incorrect, this process trivializes some important questions about the emergence of money. Some of these problems have been alluded to already, for example, does the double coincidence of wants problem require money in its solution? Credit transactions, at least in the modern economy with a well-functioning financial sector, seem to do the job just as well. (My credit card allows me to time the final payment of nearly all my consumption expenditures with the pay day of the fruits of my labor—could not my university pay for my consumption expenditures directly instead of offering me a salary in terms of money?)

Most troubling, one gets the feeling that money is just one good on the end of the liquidity spectrum, as in Keynesian liquidity preference theory, and now the most common view. Here money is demanded according to its liquidity relative to other financial assets, with the prevailing interest rate representing the opportunity cost of holding a money balance. While this view has been criticized handedly as getting the causality wrong in interest-rate determination (see Rothbard, 1962, pp. 786–87), the idea that money differs from other goods only according to its liquidity has survived with relative impunity.

In this liquidity-based view on money, we can reduce search costs and eliminate the double coincidence of wants problem by using money. But we can also do that by using any sufficiently liquid asset. Whether money is different from these other assets is just a question of liquidity. There is no objective way to differentiate money from other assets. In other words, the uniqueness of money is a question of degree and not of kind.

Although Huerta de Soto does not address this point directly, definitions of money as the generally accepted medium of exchange implicitly accept this liquidity view on money.[2] The Pandora's box that results from viewing money as the most liquid good has created the most difficulties for Huerta de Soto's core argument concerning the necessity of full bank reserves against the deposit base. Why must the full reserve be in terms of money if money is not fundamentally different from other assets? In other words, why cannot the bank substitute another good for money to complete its objectives (and even to satisfy its legal requirements), in the same way the consumer and producer substitute between various goods to do the same?[3]

One difficulty in the traditional view on money lies in identifying its particular role. On the one hand, money is held to facilitate transactions. On the other hand, it is held to hedge against felt uncertainty. In the first case, money has value from its ability to be exchanged for other goods and

[2] Two examples on this point, chosen only because of their clarity of exposition and representative view of the prevailing doctrine, claim that money is both the generally accepted medium of exchange and the most liquid asset. Huerta de Soto (2006, p. 186 fn. 9, p. 696 fn. 141, and p. 770 fn. 72) repeatedly stresses that money is the only perfectly liquid asset in the economy. Rothbard (1962, p. 375) does not refer to money as a perfectly liquid asset, instead focusing on its related feature as being the "present good *par excellence*." To the extent that a present good has a readily available market, the "best" present good becomes the most liquid asset. Both Huerta de Soto and Rothbard illustrate theories of money that amount to two sides of the same coin.

[3] In personal correspondence, one well-known member of the "free banking" school asked why I wanted to force the corner solution. In price theory, a corner solution is a common result of a consumption bundle containing a good with no substitutes. His question alluded to my own claim that the bank must hold full reserves in the form of money against its deposit base, and that this money cannot be substituted by other assets (even highly liquid bonds). The corner-solution rebuttal to full-reserve banking proposals has merit. The argument is the logical conclusion of a monetary theory which does not correctly identify the origin of money. The rebuttal also rests on the belief that money's specific role is not completely different in matters of kind but only in magnitude from that of other goods. This chapter rectifies these shortcomings.

services in the present. In the latter case, money has value because it protects the holder against the threat of a future expenditure arising and disrupting the individual's plans. The monetary tradition stemming from the double coincidence of wants problem views the demand for money as stemming from a demand to facilitate trades by minimizing transaction costs. Mises's (1949, pp. 245–51) use of the "evenly rotating economy" introduces a new tradition that views the demand to hold money as a demand to alleviate felt uncertainty. Under this chain of reasoning, money is not held for transactions in general. It is held to facilitate only those transactions that are unexpected, and thus could disrupt the individual's plans.

One way to deal with the tension these two traditions have with respect to the demand to hold money is to return to first principles. First, I will define what makes money unique compared with other financial assets. Building from Mises's use of the evenly rotating economy, I then define what types of uncertainties are relevant to the individual's plan coordination. From this understanding we can look at the specific functions of money to see which functions solve which coordination problems. Finally, we can look at what makes money unique as a financial asset. In this way, we will come full circle. Instead of defining money as the commonly accepted medium of exchange, we will see that this definition is the outcome of a good performing specific roles that solve concrete economic problems which would otherwise disrupt the coordination of the economic agent's plans.

Money in a World of Finance

All financial assets—stocks, bonds, money, and their derivatives—are means to transmit purchasing power intertemporally. Given this purchasing power transmission, the relevant questions that arise in their valuation are "what value do you get in the future" and "when in the future do you get it?" What type of value you get refers to an asset's ability to endow you with a fixed, or predetermined amount (i.e., par value), or a value determined by market conditions at the time of sale (i.e., market value).[4] When you get the value is either in the present (i.e., on demand by the owner of

[4] In almost all cases, the future value is defined in nominal terms. Although inflation-adjusted bonds exist, the market is small. In this chapter, I deal exclusively with financial assets with nominal claims in the future.

		Value of Asset	
		Par	Market
Availability	Present	Money	Equity
	Future	Bond	Future/Forward

Fig. 1 A categorization of financial assets. Source: Howden (2015a, p. 46)

the asset) or after some set amount of time (i.e., in the future). This amount of time can be predefined as a date in the future when the value must be realized, or a date after which the owner can realize the value (Bagus & Howden, 2012, p. 296).

Taken together these two attributes of the type of value and when it can be realized create a schema to categorize financial assets. The four financial assets commonly traded are the result, as outlined in Fig. 1.

Equity holders can access the value of their asset on demand (i.e., in the present). The specific value realized is contingent on the market conditions prevailing at that moment. Bond holders, in contrast, gain the ability to predefine how much value the sale of their asset will bring to them. But this benefit of guaranteeing the value ahead of time comes at a cost: they must wait a predefined (or at least minimum) period.[5] Futures and forwards give their owner a value dependent on future market conditions, and they also oblige their holder to wait for some time before realizing this value.

Money is unique in this categorization of financial assets because it is the only financial asset that endows its holder with a predefined value that is available on demand. One dollar of money will always settle an obligation of one dollar. (In contrast the number of shares needed to settle a debt of one dollar depends on the stock market's valuation at that moment.) Starting from this realization as to the nature of money, we find significant differences with other approaches that center on the use of money as the commonly accepted medium of exchange. One primary difference is that money is here not just an asset on the liquidity spectrum or

[5] A bond holder may, of course, sell their bond before maturity. But in that case, the value is governed by supply-demand conditions prevailing at the time. In effect, the bond is valued as if it were an equity. Futures similarly can be sold at any time, though not necessarily at their predefined value.

value scale. Instead it is an asset with definite qualities that differentiate it categorically from other assets.

Approaches that focus on money's use as an exchange medium commonly treat it as either (1) the most liquid of assets or (2) the most stable financial asset in terms of its nominal purchasing power. In this "medium of exchange" tradition, the only difference between money and bonds is that money is more liquid (i.e., its value can be realized without waiting), and that money normally exposes the holder to less credit risk.[6] Alternatively, the only difference between money and equities in this tradition is that money's value is more stable (i.e., that its bid-ask spread is minimal relative to other saleable goods). But in both cases, money is just seen as an asset on a scale from more to less liquid, and more to less stable in value terms. To give a concrete example, some authors in the "money as a medium of exchange" approach point to the fact that there is little difference between money and a bond with only a few minutes until its maturity. They alternatively point to the fact that money market mutual funds, or a blue-chip stock of stable value, is closer to money than a highly volatile technology share.

If some Austrian economists have found themselves down this path leading to monetary mayhem, they have been led by some well-respected peers. Machlup (1970, p. 225) writes not of money but of "moneyness." Hayek (1976, p. 56) echoes this view, lamenting that money is referred to as a noun (a thing that exists) and not as "an adjective describing a property which different things could possess to varying *degrees*." These economists, and those following them, have only taken the "money as a medium of exchange" logic to its full conclusion. Unfortunately, this conclusion—that money is not a distinct thing but rather a property that some goods have more of than others—leads the economist astray and beckons mistakes.[7]

[6] Whether money has less credit risk than bonds depends critically on the stability of the banking system. During the European debt crisis starting in 2009, the unstable banking system in Cyprus was resolved with a bail in. Under this scheme, depositors with more than €100,000 deposited in a Cypriot bank were forced to take a haircut. Even under less severe banking collapses, deposit insurance schemes pay out on deposits only up to a maximum amount to combat moral hazard. In contrast, US Treasury bonds have never defaulted, and fewer than 5% of high-risk bonds have defaulted over the past twenty years.

[7] Hayek (1976, p. 56) tries to solve the ambiguity problem of defining what money is by shifting the discussion to currency. This is particularly dangerous territory. Hayek prefers discussion of currency to money since the former is clearly defined. To the extent that currency is clearly defined through legal tender laws, such an argument seems to bring the economist back to the chartalism theory of the German Historical School.

By recognizing that money is the asset that is exchanged at par value on demand, we start the analysis by realizing that money is categorically different than other financial assets. It is not just one extreme of a liquidity or value spectrum, but actually defines the spectrums.

Money is not just a more liquid asset than bonds. If it were just this factor—the time before its value can be realized—there would be no significant difference between money and bonds. (In this respect note that money and bonds are column mates in Fig. 1.) It is only by referring to the continual availability of money that we can state that a bond has a greater or lesser degree of liquidity. We must also recognize that money is not just an asset that trades at a stable value relative to equities. If this were the only factor concerning us—the stability of the value that can be realized by the asset's sale—there would no significant difference between money and equities. (Here we see that money and equities are row mates in Fig. 1.) Instead, we now realize that the stability of money's nominal value is what allows us to refer to different equity classes as being more or less volatile in terms of their value dimension. It is only when we discuss money in terms of its two attributes simultaneously—the on demand and par value nature of its value—that we can pinpoint exactly how and in what ways money differs from other assets.

The difference between money and other assets is one of kind, and not only of degree. This helps shed light on the demand for money. It is only in a superficial sense that money is demanded because it is a highly liquid asset. This liquidity feature cannot be the sole reason money is demanded because it is a quality shared with other financial assets (e.g., equities). Money also cannot be demanded only because its purchasing power is predefined in nominal terms. Bonds also share this feature (abstracting from default risk). Money is demanded for its uniqueness. Money is the only asset that combines both value attributes—on demand availability at par value—in one package.

The second advantage of viewing money as not just the "commonly accepted medium of exchange" but the asset that sells at par value on demand is that it points to an analysis of its specific functions. This approach is the opposite to other approaches, which start by identifying money's functions and then uses those functions to define money.

In times past, a common mnemonic aided the student in remembering the functions of money. "Money is a matter of functions four: a medium, a unit, a standard, a store." This list of functions is not accidental. It is the result of looking at two fundamental roles of money both a- and inter-temporally.

If there is widespread agreement that money emerged and exists today to facilitate transactions, there is considerable disagreement as to how it performs this role. On the one hand are the economists who view money as fundamentally a medium to exchange to facilitate trade. This line of economists stems from Jevons. On the other hand, and less commonly, are those economists who view money's fundamental role as being the good that other goods are priced in. (A common denominator of sorts.) Walras was the first economist to broach the idea of a good serving as a numéraire to express the prices other goods within a general equilibrium setting. More recently, the idea that money serves only as a pricing unit has been revived under non-equilibrium conditions by Kocherlakota (1998), Kiyotaki and Moore (2002), and Yeager (2010). In this tradition, money serves only as a pricing unit to keep a track record of our past transactions. Taken together, the roles of pricing unit and exchange medium are in fact the defining characteristics that the previous mnemonic alludes to.

The four functions of money commonly listed in economics textbooks are the outcome of viewing money's two roles—pricing unit and exchange medium—in both the present and over time. The four resultant monetary roles are illustrated in Fig. 2.

First consider money's role as a pricing unit. When the economist thinks of money as being used to define prices, he typically has in mind the "unit" in the mnemonic: the unit of account. All goods are priced in terms of some other good. The comparison of relative prices, and the assessment of opportunity costs, is eased by giving all prices a common denominator to express them in.[8] This pricing unit can either define prices in the present (the unit of account) or in the future (the standard of deferred payments).

The previously mentioned mnemonic is not frequently encountered by modern students of economics. The standard of deferred payments is the use of a good to define prices payable in the future. With the advent of legal tender laws, this role was largely subsumed by the same good that serves as the unit of account. As debtors now have the option to repay future obligations in terms of the legal tender, the distinction between a good denominated in terms of another good in the present and a different

[8] The computational advantage using one good to determine all prices is obvious. An economy with n goods will have $n(n-1)/2$ prices under conditions of direct exchange but only $n-1$ prices if one good is used to express all prices.

		Monetary Role	
		Pricing Unit	Exchange Unit
Availability	Present	Unit of Account	Medium of Exchange
	Future	Standard of Deferred Payments	Store of Value

Fig. 2 Money's four roles revisited. Source: Howden (2015a, p. 49)

good in the future became unnecessary. Legal tender laws give the debtor an unfair advantage. He can select the less valued good to repay the debt and impose the cost on the lender. As a consequence, all future-dated contracts are denominated in terms of the current pricing unit (the unit of account) to put the debtor and creditor on even terms.

Likewise, the functions of the medium of exchange and store of value are two sides of the intertemporal coin. When the economist discusses the medium of exchange, he does so to refer to the exchange of one good for another in the present. When he discusses the store of value, the discussion centers on holding a good until some future date when it will be exchanged to settle an obligation.

While in the modern world the economist is accustomed to a unique good satisfying both monetary roles of the pricing and exchange units, there are many historical cases of the roles being fulfilled by separate goods.

Goods that have served as a pricing unit, both as a unit of account and a standard of deferred payments, have been numerous and varied over history. Gold and the other precious metals have served this role, but so too have less conventional goods. Of these unlikely goods are the commonly cited examples of cigarettes in POW camps (Radford, 1945), large circular Rai stones on the south Pacific islands of Palau and Yap (Bryan, 2004), and even slave women (kumal) in Early Medieval Ireland (Nolan, 1926).

Goods that have served as exchange units, both as the medium of exchange and the store of value, have been mostly confined to the precious metals. The qualities of commodity money, typically listed when the student of economics first learns the story of money's historical emergence, center on attributes such as divisibility, durability, rarity, ease of identification and transportation, and widespread demand. The precious metals have fulfilled these roles best among the goods serving the exchange role of money until now. These qualities do not, however, seem to describe the goods that have served as a monetary pricing unit. Cigarettes, large stones, and women, just to name a few, are indivisible, not easily transported, and of questionable durability. They are also not necessarily widely demanded or available.

The fact that the goods that have been used as pricing units that do not embody the common qualities of money is not problematic. For a pricing unit, the only qualities that matter are that the value of the good is widely recognized and that this value can be expressed in terms of some other good functioning as the exchange medium. In this way, opportunity costs and relative prices can still be established. It is a historical question whether it is easier to use one good for both monetary roles. Relatively recent examples of a different good being used to define prices than the one being exchanged to settle an obligation are also available (e.g., the use of US dollars to price goods in high inflation countries while the local currency is still exchanged at the prevailing exchange rate). There is no record that slave girls were ever exchanged in Early Medieval Ireland. There is widespread evidence that a standard list of "exchange rates" existed that allowed for prices denominated in kumals to be paid for by some other goods.[9]

While it is common to define money today as the "commonly accepted medium of exchange" we see that, theoretically and historically, this is only one half of the roles money performed. Consider what happens when the same good serves as a medium of exchange and unit of account, for example, gold during the gold standard. The outcome is that the exchange rate between gold as the unit of account and gold as the medium of exchange is 1:1. It is this outcome—the twinning of the monetary roles in one good—that creates the conditions under which the par value nature of money emerges.

When two goods serve separately as each of the monetary functions, an exchange rate must exist between them. Slave women may have been used as the pricing unit in Early Medieval Ireland, but they were never used to settle the obligations. Under the bimetallic standard in the United States, priced were defined in terms of gold, but silver could be exchanged in payment at the prevailing gold-to-silver exchange rate. The present discussion is not about whether the separation of the unit of account from the medium of exchange is beneficial or destabilizing. The answer to this

[9]Two legal texts, *Senchus Mor* and the *Book of Aicill* both contain tables outlining the prevailing "exchange rates" for a kumal. They also make clear that ultimate payment was to be made in either land or silver.

question is historical. It depends on the particulars of the time and place. (On this point, the interested reader can revisit the literature on New Monetary Economics, helpfully summarized in Cowen and Kroszner (1994)). With respect to the bimetallic period, evidence shows that the fixed gold-to-silver exchange rate proved destabilizing for the US economy relative to the gold standard period.

The discussion of what roles money performs is useful because it now allows us to shed light on the revised definition of money provided herein. We have previously seen that money is not necessarily the commonly accepted medium of exchange (although serving as a "medium of exchange" is one of the monetary roles). Money is unique because it is that asset that trades on demand and at par value. The twinning of these two attributes can only arise when one good serves as both the exchange unit and pricing unit. In this case, the exchange rate between the pricing unit and exchange unit becomes 1:1.

By way of example, consider what happens when you withdraw $100 from your checking account. If your checking account is defined in terms of US dollars, then you know that the transaction will be performed at an exchange rate of 1:1. The withdrawal changes the composition of your money balance but not the overall level. There is no risk that you will get less than $100 in currency because the units that define the checking account are the same as those being issued as medium of exchange. In a similar example, consider what happens when you buy a shirt priced at $20. In this case, you exchange $20 from your money balance to satisfy the obligation of $20 to buy the shirt. The 1:1 exchange rate between the exchange medium and unit of account leaves you with no risk that you will lose nominal purchasing power between the point where you accumulate (or earn) your medium of exchange and that point at which you exchange (or spend) it.

In a similar way, pricing goods in terms of the same good used in settlement allows for no wait time before you can realize the value in your money balance. If a good is priced in terms of the same good you hold as the exchange medium, there will always be a ready market available to sell (or exchange) it into. It is with this point in mind that Rothbard (1962, p. 375) referred to money as the "present good *par excellence*." This is not necessarily the case when two different goods perform the two monetary roles. In this case, an exchange between at least two goods must occur before the transaction is complete. The time between when the transaction is started and finalized exposes both sides of the exchange to risk.

This risk is analogous to the exchange-rate risk that occurs when someone uses their local currency to settle an obligation denominated in foreign currency.

It is not to be inferred from the discussion to this point that there is anything obviously wrong with defining money as the "commonly accepted medium of exchange." Instead, the preceding discussion serves to illustrate that doing so obscures important monetary roles that must be fulfilled before money earns this position. We also now have a framework to analyze historical cases where separate goods have been used simultaneously in different monetary roles.

Starting from the proposition that money is the unique financial asset that trades at par value on demand, we can then move to a discussion of what conditions are necessary for this to occur. The necessary and sufficient conditions for a good to trade at par value on demand are that it serves as both the exchange good and pricing unit simultaneously. Only when these two roles are fulfilled by the same good will that good be endowed with the properties necessary to be called money. By focusing on only one of money's roles (use in exchange or use in pricing) the good will not complete the conditions that make money unique relative to other goods.

The analysis thus far has answered one question—what is money?—by pointing to the ways that money is unique in a schema of financial assets. It has also shed light on the necessary and sufficient conditions for money to take on this definition. The question of why money would be valued and demanded for this uniqueness have been left unanswered. In the next section, we turn our attention to these questions.

Uncertainty, the Root of All Money

Mises (1949, pp. 244–51) uses the "evenly rotating economy" is a thought experiment that allows the economist to understand the conditions under which money would not be necessary. From this it is possible to infer the conditions under which money is necessary.

Consider a world in which each day repeats in terms of its income and expenditure streams. With full certainty of the cashflows, Mises shows that the demand for money falls to zero.[10] The reason is that if the individual

[10] Actually, Mises shows that the demand to hold money as a medium of exchange falls to zero. Money still exists as a numéraire to establish the prices of goods (Howden, 2009).

knew in what ways his expenditures would differ from his income he would either (1) buy a bond that matures in the relevant period to fund a future expense, or (2) settle the transaction in the present on the futures market at a discount (Howden, 2015b, p. 15).

When Mises writes of uncertainty as the guiding force behind the demand to hold money, he is actually speaking of a specific type of uncertainty. He extends[11] Knight's (1921) treatment of uncertainty by way of case and class probabilities. Building from these probabilities, we can categorize the origins of uncertainty and how they pertain to the demand for financial assets in general, and money in particular.

Financial assets are valued according to what income stream they endow their holder with, and when that income stream will be realized. This "what you get and when you get it" approach is most obvious in valuation models that discount future cash flows to determine an asset's present value. Rarely is a discussion broached as to why a given financial asset is demanded in lieu of another, for example, why invest in an equity and not a bond? Answers to this question have until now been answered only unsatisfactorily. An example of the confusion around this problem is found in the equity premium puzzle (Mehra & Prescott, 1985). Alternatively, the problem is skirted with any differences in demands between different financial assets distilled to nonmarket differences, for example, the differing tax treatments found in the Modigliani–Miller theorem.

Consider the typology of risks and uncertainty provided in Fig. 3. Here I differentiate the outcomes depending on whether the individual has knowledge of the timing or of the magnitude of a future expenditure. These attributes are chosen because in valuing financial assets, including money, the holder cares only of the form and the timing of the future payment.

Mises's (1949, ch. VI) introduction of case probabilities is best understood as elaborating on and making specific the conditions that Knight alluded to in his discussion of uncertainty. I offer a further refinement here, by specifying that case probabilities (or Knightian uncertainty) require a simultaneous lack of two specific types of knowledge. First, the individual must not know when (or if) a future event will happen. Second, he must not know the extent of the event. Since we are here dealing with financial assets, the future event in question will always be one of cashflow. A complete lack of knowledge with respect to both the timing and

[11] Unwittingly, as the case may be (see Herbener et al., 1998, p. xvi).

		Timing of Expenditure	
		Known	Unknown
Magnitude of Expenditure	Known	Certainty	Structural Risk
	Unknown	Class Probability, Systemic Risk	Case Probability, Knightian Uncertainty

Fig. 3 Risk and uncertainty types. Source: Howden (2015b, p. 15)

magnitude of an expenditure will leave one with a true case of Knightian uncertainty. The recent turmoil related to COVID-19 falls into this category. No one knew that the event would occur in the magnitude that it did, and there was no way to estimate the timing (or duration) of the event.

The less constrained case that Mises analyzes, class probability, requires that the individual lacks knowledge of only the magnitude of an event. The individual does know, however, when the event will occur. I refer to these types of risks as systemic. The term refers to the fact that the individual knows not how the specific parts of the state of the world will turn out, but he can take comfort in knowing that some future event will occur. Here we can point to the standard textbook risks such as casino games or recurring expenses, such as car insurance, which must be purchased by law but the amount of which is subject to change.

Mises does not analyze the north-east quadrant of Fig. 3. I refer to this specific risk as structural. Here the structure of the event is known (in this case, in terms of its magnitude) though the individual cannot say when or if the event will happen. As an example of this risk, we know that the roll of the die will yield a certain value one-sixth of the time, but not when or if that value will prevail.

This look at types of risks and uncertainty matters with respect to how the individual deals with the future events. In cases where the timing and magnitude of a future expenditure are known (the north-west quadrant of Fig. 3), the individual has two options to match the expense against his income. The first is to settle it early at a discount (i.e., prepay). The second is to buy a bond of appropriate duration that matures at the moment the expense arises. Note that both of these alternatives amount to the same operation in economic terms (the only difference is who the counterparty ultimately financing the expense is).

Structural and systemic risks can be hedged for, if only approximately, by buying a stock or bond. In the case of structural risk, an equity holding can be sold at any moment to provide the income necessary for the expense whose timing was unknown in advance.[12] Alternatively, if the timing of the expense was known in advance, then a bond could be purchased with a maturity consistent with the funding need. In both cases, the individual hedges his future risks in an efficient manner to reduce his opportunity costs.

Case probabilities, or Knightian uncertainty, create more difficult scenarios to hedge. Here the individual knows neither the magnitude nor timing of a future event.[13] Traditional financial products are not helpful in hedging since their owner will remain exposed to either timing risk or funding risk should the eventuality arise. Still, there is one option available to the individual. Money is the financial asset that is available on demand and at par value. Holding money endows him with the funds to meet a future nominal expense, regardless of when or whether it occurs. It is in this case that we see what Mises proved through his evenly rotating economy thought experiment. The "rotation" that must be "even" in his theoretical economy is across both the timing and magnitude of future cash flows. If either one of those streams is unknown while the other is known, the individual can hedge the risk by holding an alternative financial product (either a stock or a bond) instead of money. It is only in the constrained case of a complete lack of knowledge concerning the timing and magnitude of a future expense that the individual must resort to money to alleviate his felt uncertainty. The use of any other financial asset will forever leave him with some degree of residual risk which will not be able to be hedged away. This residual risk endangers the perceived coordination of his plans and, when taken to the extreme, imperils his ability to accomplish his goals.

[12] A bond could also be sold before maturity to the same effect. Recall that the value received from the sale of a bond sold before maturity will be the market value prevailing. This fact makes the early redemption of a bond an economically identical event to the sale of an equity.

[13] One strand of literature deals with Knightian uncertainty as an epistemological problem. Knowledge of certain future events is completely absent. While these cases are interesting from a theoretical perspective, they have no bearing on acting man. Man acts on what he perceives. Forces outside of the realm of his consciousness cannot shape the demand to hold an asset. In contrast, some degree of knowledge of the existence of a future state of the world is necessary to influence the demand for money. Such knowledge does not need to refer, however, to the exact temporal or value dimensions of the future state of the world.

Conclusion

We can now combine the insights of this chapter to understand why money exists and where its demand originates from. Since a lack of knowledge is unavoidable, individuals will always be exposed to certain risks and uncertainties. Sometimes the lack of knowledge will only concern the timing of a future event. Other times it will concern the magnitude of a future event. But sometimes a lack of both of these types of knowledge will be at hand, creating case probabilities or Knightian uncertainty.

These uncertainties are detrimental to the individual's plan coordination. The economist commonly realizes the reasons behind the demand to buy property insurance (alleviate a structural risk) or life insurance (alleviate a systemic risk) but has until now overlooked the way the individual combats Knightian uncertainty.[14] Uncertainty differs from structural and systemic risks because the individual lacks complete knowledge of both the timing and magnitude of the future expenditure. The only way to hedge against such unknowledge is to hold an asset that pays out (can be exchanged) at any time and at a predefined value. Money is the unique financial asset that enables such an exchange.

If money is unique among financial assets owing to its ability to be exchanged on demand and at par value, it is important to realize what attributes endow it with such features. It is only when a good is used to define prices and is also exchanged to settle those expenses that it can circulate on demand and at par value. This allows us to understand the items that must be included in the money supply much better. Instead of adjudicating what money "is" based on various liquidity concerns, as is common with the "M" measures, one can instead point to those goods circulating on demand and at par value and are denominated in the same terms as are prices.

As a simple first application, note that this quickly resolves the question of whether various cryptocurrencies should be considered as money. To the extent that they facilitate payment of various goods they are definitely media of exchange. But since they are not used to define prices, they cannot be considered money in the broad sense.[15]

[14] The reader may object to my characterization of death as a systemic risk. The purpose of pooling insurable lives by a life insurance company is to pinpoint, in probabilistic terms for a class of individuals, when a death will occur.

[15] I say "broad" sense here because in some narrow markets a price could be established in terms of, for example, bitcoin, and bitcoin could be exchanged to pay for this good. In practice, prices are established in terms of some other money, for example, US dollars, and then a cryptocurrency is exchanged for dollars at the prevailing market exchange rate. The transaction is no different than an individual selling his equity investment at the prevailing price to buy US dollars to complete a transaction. Given this fact, it is most correct to think of a cryptocurrency as a non-dividend paying stock.

As a second application of the theory contained in this chapter, consider the implications for bank reserves. Under one popular train of thought, money is just the most liquid asset on a liquidity spectrum. It is not differentiated from a house due to its nature, but instead is only considered to be a more liquid and readily saleable asset. Proponents of such reasoning see no reason why bank deposits must be on demand, par value assets. As a consequence, banks must make a best-efforts basis to create these qualities in order to attract customers, but they are under no legal obligation to do so. On the other hand, if one realizes that money is categorically different from other assets, he also realizes that the obligations governing its transactions are distinct. The purpose of money is to hedge uncertainties. This ability can only occur by way of a par value demandable asset. As such, money and money substitutes must retain these qualities, with implications for the obligation the bank faces when it converts a specific form of money (currency) into another (a demand deposit).

Finally, consider a third application. Efforts or restrictions that impact the "moneyness" of an asset do not just impair its monetary use quantitatively. They qualitatively change the nature of the asset into something else. The withdrawal clause, common in the nineteenth century British free-banking episode, was used to impose a waiting period between when a customer requested his deposit and when the bank was obliged to remit it to him. The withdrawal clause did not just cause money to lose its moneyness (i.e., lower its liquidity)—it converted depositors into creditors, bond holders to be specific. In a similar way, various movements in the wake of the Great Recession to give depositors a haircut on their deposits not only made the deposit a less liquid asset. They had the effect of converting the depositor into an equity investor in the bank. In both cases, the individual's plans would be disrupted as the outcome that motivated his original demand to hold money—to hedge an uncertainty—was frustrated by converting the means to alleviate this outcome (money) into an asset unsuited and unable to fulfill the task (an equity or a bond).

The economists of the Austrian School paved the way for monetary economics by showing that money emerged to solve specific problems, and that it can be valued in a general theory of pricing. These economists have also done much work in analyzing the effects of near monies, such as various credit instruments. This chapter has built on that tradition and augmented our understanding of the definition of money and the factors that affect its demand.

Money is not first and foremost the generally accepted medium of exchange, even though that statement is not entirely wrong. Money is a special financial asset that emerges to alleviate the definite economic problems of 1) plan disruption caused by uncertainty and 2) to facilitate the completion of previously conceived plans. The only way for a financial asset to perform these roles is to sell at par value and on demand. In order for a good to sell at par value and on demand this financial asset must be the good that is exchanged to settle transactions that are priced in terms of itself. Money is the specific good that embodies both of these monetary roles—as both the pricing unit and exchange medium. It is for this reason that money happens to be the generally accepted medium of exchange.

References

Bagus, P., & Howden, D. (2012). The Continuing Continuum Problem and Future Goods. *The Journal of Business Ethics, 106*(3), 295–300.

Bryan, M. F. (2004, February 1). Island Money. *Federal Reserve Bank of Cleveland Commentary.*

Cowen, T., & Kroszner, R. (1994). *Explorations in New Monetary Economics.* Blackwell.

Hayek, F. A. (1990 [1976]). *Denationalisation of Money – the Argument Refined* (3rd ed.). The Institute of Economic Affairs.

Herbener, J. M., Hoppe, H.-H., & Salerno, J. T. (1998). Introduction to the Scholar's Edition. In L. von Mises (Ed.), *Human Action.* Ludwig von Mises Institute.

Howden, D. (2009). Fama's Efficient Market Hypothesis and Mises' Evenly Rotating Economy: Comparative Constructs. *The Quarterly Journal of Austrian Economics, 12*(2), 17–26.

Howden, D. (2015a). Money. In P. Bylund & D. Howden (Eds.), *The Next Generation of Austrian Economics: Essays in Honor of Joseph T. Salerno* (pp. 43–58). Ludwig von Mises Institute.

Howden, D. (2015b). Money in a World of Finance. *Journal of Prices & Markets, 4*(1). Papers *&* Proceedings of the 3rd Annual International Conference of Prices & Markets, Toronto, ON, November 6–7, 2014: 13–20.

Huerta de Soto, J. (2006). *Money, Bank Credit, and Economic Cycles* (M. Stroup, Trans.). Mises Institute.

Jevons, W. S. (1875). *Money and the Mechanism of Exchange.* C. Kegan Paul.

Knight, F. (1921). *Risk, Uncertainty, and Profit.* Houghton Mifflin.

Kiyotaki, N., & Moore, J. (2002). Evil is the root of all money. *The American Economic Review, 92*(2). Papers and Proceedings of the One Hundred Fourteenth Annual Meeting of the American Economic Association (May 2002): 62–66.

Kocherlakota, N. R. (1998). Money is Memory. *Journal of Economic Theory, 81*(2), 232–251.

Machlup, F. (1970). Euro-Dollar Creation: A Mystery Story. *Banca Nazionale del Lavoro Quarterly Review, 94*, 219–260.

Mehra, R., & Prescott, E. C. (1985). The Equity Premium: A Puzzle. *Journal of Monetary Economics, 15*(2), 145–161.

Menger, C. (1871 [2007]). *Principles of Economics* (J. Dingwall & B. F. Hoselitz, Trans.). Mises Institute.

Menger, C. (1892). On the Origin of Money. *Economic Journal, 2*(1), 239–255.

Menger, C. (1977 [1909]). *Money, chapters V–XIV* (A. H. Zlabinger, Trans.). As prepared for the "Carl Menger Symposium" at Claremont Men's College, May 26–28.

Mises, L. v. (1953 [2009]). *The Theory of Money and Credit* (J. E. Batson, Trans.). Mises Institute.

Mises, L. v. (1998 [1949]). *Human Action: A Treatise on Economics* (Scholars Edition). Mises Institute.

Mishkin, F. C. (2019). *The Economics of Money, Banking, and Financial Markets* (12th ed.). Pearson.

Nolan, P. (1926). *A Monetary History of Ireland*. King.

Radford, R. A. (1945). The Economic Organisation of a P.O.W. Camp. *Economica, 12*(48), 189–201.

Rothbard, M. N. (2009 [1962]). *Man, Economy, and State with Power and Market* (Scholar's Edition). Ludwig von Mises Institute.

Yeager, L. B. (2001). The Perils of Base Money. *Review of Austrian Economics, 14*(4), 251–266.

Yeager, L. B. (2010). Bank Reserves: A Dispute over Words and Classification. *Review of Austrian Economics, 23*(2), 183–191.

Investment Under the Theoretical Framework of the Austrian School of Economics

Juan Huerta de Soto Huarte

Most people know my father as Prof. Huerta de Soto. An intellectual mentor, a thoughtful and inspirational economist, an energetic teacher and a comprehensive PhD thesis director. However, I am lucky enough to know him from three very different angles: as a father, as a professor and most recently as a professional. It is the professional aspect I have mentioned above the one which has shaped my character the most. Everybody will agree that my father's passion is the academic world, but what most people don't know is that first and foremost he is a businessman, an entrepreneur, who has been successfully managing the over ninety-year-old family business for several decades now. In a nutshell, he has taught me through his example some very valuable lessons. First and foremost, that perseverance is the secret sauce for success in life. Secondly, that passion is great, but duty comes first. Finally, that intellectual curiosity and a critical spirit are the key to pursue the quest for the search of truth. Above all, he is a great father and a formidable person, with whom I have a very close relationship, as well as the best mentor of life one could have.

J. Huerta de Soto Huarte (✉)
Cobas Asset Management, Madrid, Spain
e-mail: jhuertadesoto@cobasam.com

D. Howden, P. Bagus (eds.), *The Emergence of a Tradition: Essays in Honor of Jesús Huerta de Soto, Volume I*,
https://doi.org/10.1007/978-3-031-17414-8_16

My personal perception is that not much has been written regarding the role of the investor as an entrepreneur and subjectivity. In this regard, the best contributions I have found are the ones from Mayer (2018) and García Iborra (2020), whose interesting books shed some light on these still obscure matters and have been very useful to write this short chapter. However, before we jump into the theoretical framework, I think it is useful to make a brief summary of what I consider sensible investing and its main characteristics.

Sensible Investing

Almost everybody is more familiar with the term value investing, which has been extensively written about and is commonly associated with very famous investors as Benjamin Graham, Warren Buffett, Charles Manger, John Templeton, Peter Lynch, and Francisco García Paramés, just to name a few. In a nutshell, it consists of investing in assets taking advantage of subjectively considered mispricing in the marketplace to obtain a higher expected future value. If successful, the investor should attain a reward in the shape of returns which are subjectively pondered as appropriate under his plan of action to achieve his specific future goals. It can be applied to all type of securities, like public and private equities, bonds, derivatives, and distressed debt. Still, for the sake of simplicity, because most well-known value investors apply it to public equities and because it is my personal area of expertise, all subsequent explanations will be based on investment in shares of publicly listed companies.

Nevertheless, I personally think that the term value investing is a pleonasm, as the word value seems somewhat redundant. Any acting individual takes a course of action to try to achieve his own personal goals, that he subjectively considers as the most appropriate to improve his current situation. To do so he comes up with a combination of scarce means that he considers to be the most appropriate to reach his previously established goal. Therefore, by definition, every investor is an entrepreneur, as correctly stated by Huerta de Soto (2010, p. 18): "In a broad or general sense, entrepreneurship actually coincides with human action. In this respect, it could be said that any person who acts to modify the present and achieve his objectives in the future exercises entrepreneurship." Through their role as long-term capital allocators, of either personal or third-party savings, investors try to detect those capital goods that, under a specific combination within a firm, will produce the goods and services that better satisfy the needs and desires of future consumers, which will be translated into pure entrepreneurial profits. As such, investors are always trying to generate a higher subjective value from accumulated savings that have been deterred from current consumption, via a successful capital allocation process that increases the initially invested savings in real terms and enlarges the future consumption capacity, facilitating the achievement of their future goals, whatever these may be. If successful, the investor will increase his wealth, expanding the spectrum of potential future goals that he can satisfy. But if he fails, wealth will have been destroyed. This is the ultimate reason why investment management is always linked to value generation and, therefore, the term value investing seems like a pleonasm.

But why should there be any adjective, be it value or sensible, attached to the term investing? Doesn't this imply that not everybody that invests is acting sensibly or rationally? Mises clearly explained that all human action is rational by definition, and I wouldn't dare contradict this statement. So even though all economic agents act rationally when they take their investment decisions, it also seems to be a fact that inevitable differences exist on the capabilities of individuals to identify, process, and draw conclusions from available information dispersed in the market and, consequently, apply their own subjective knowledge to reach their long-term goals. This has been better explained by Thomas Mayer when describing economic agents as subjectively rational (emphasis added):

> Instead, economic agents are seen to collect only that information they regard as relevant and can access. They evaluate this information with their own cognitive capabilities and act on the basis of their specific knowledge about the relationship among the facts they have collected and the economic goals they want to achieve. Thus, agents are **subjectively rational**. Incomplete knowledge of facts and insufficient understanding of economic circumstance is supplemented by intuition. [...] **Since individuals differ in their capabilities of recognition and evaluation of facts relevant for the attainment of their objectives as well as in their knowledge of the relationship between facts and goals, their capabilities of reaching goals are different**. (Mayer, 2018, p. 165)

From this it can be drawn that, in the same way that not all entrepreneurs succeed in obtaining their much-desired business profits, not all investors are able to achieve their targeted investment returns and many of them even suffer losses. The main reason is that not all economic agents have the same entrepreneurial capabilities but, also very importantly, most don't have the appropriate theoretical framework, nor do they apply the adequate principles to put the odds on their side. Hence, there is a distinction between investing in general terms and sensible investing, based on the principles explained below, which can be easily seen from a theoretical angle, as most economic agents are unaware of what is discussed here and still follow the guidelines of Modern Finance Theory (MFT). Even more remarkable perhaps is the difference in real investment returns that have been obtained historically between those who exercise sensible investing and those who don't. In this regard, the list of investors mentioned in Warren Buffett's famous speech to Columbia Business School students titled "The Superinvestors of Graham-and-Doddsville" (Buffett, 1984) has been frequently used as a good piece of evidence on how those investors who apply sensible investing, even if they don't actively know they are doing so, have generated above average returns and beaten their respective benchmarks during long periods of time. However, this is something which has not only occurred during the 1950–1980 timeframe as depicted on the mentioned speech, as there is a nurtured list of sensible investors that have also beaten their benchmarks comfortably during the last 30 years. Just to name a few: Mohnish Pabrai, Guy Spier, Bill Ackman, Tom Gayner, Francisco García Paramés, Joel Greenblatt, François Rochon, Li Lu, Francis Chou, Jean-Marie Eveillard, Didier le Menestrel, and Christian Gueugnier. But what is the correct conceptual framework and principles of what I define as sensible investing? I will enumerate them and try to explain it with more detail hereafter.

Principles

- The focus of study in finance is the acting subject, the same as in economics. Therefore, the methodology under which it should be studied is not the one of natural sciences but the one of social sciences. This emphasizes the importance of subjectivism vs. objectivism.
- The value of business processes and firms is always subjective and never objective. There are valuation methods governed by the premises of objectivity established by MFT, which are usually too time consuming and give a false perception of precision, as, for example, the discounted cash flow model (DCF), which is based on erroneous premises like the capital asset pricing model (CAPM) for the calcula-

tion of the weighted average cost of capital (WACC), as well as beta (volatility equaling risk).

- The acting subject in finance is the investor, who exercises his entrepreneurship to analyze disperse and incomplete information, with the aim of achieving an investment return, subjectively determined, using those scarce means he considers most appropriate. In this specific case, the means are the totality of investable public equity stocks, and the goal is to achieve an investment return which is usually higher than the average obtained by the market.
- To obtain better returns than the market, the sensible investor must be ready to apply a contrarian mindset and not follow the herd. This requires better judgment and use of his entrepreneurial skills.
- The market is always in dynamic disequilibrium and never in the imaginary state of neoclassical equilibrium. This generates opportunities for those investors that successfully exercise their entrepreneurship. Therefore, it is possible to obtain higher returns than the market.
- Time is the scarcest and most important means within sensible investing. The investment horizon must be sufficiently long (at least 10 years) so that companies can culminate their business plans and generate long-term value. Thus, the sensible investor needs to be patient.
- Investors are business owners, and it is irrelevant if they own a meaningful percentage of the firm or just a minority stake. As owners, investors "will concentrate on developing the business model in such a way that economic success is guaranteed for the long term" (Mayer, 2018, p. 99). As highlighted in the previous point, it is key to investing for the long term.
- The sensible investor must recognize the difference between risk and uncertainty and incorporate it in his investment management process through an adequate level of diversification and focusing on the margin of safety within the individual investments that make up his portfolio.
- The best economic framework to understand the reality of financial markets is the one established by the Austrian School of Economics. Understanding Austrian Business Cycle Theory is key.
- All of the above have to be incorporated in the investor's investment process, which is dynamic, continuously evolving through time and improving as the circumstances change and he learns from his mistakes and successes.

Entrepreneurship and Dynamic Efficiency

I have already given some hints on how the investor exercises his entrepreneurship within the investment management process. He discovers profit opportunities in the marketplace and acts "accordingly to take advantage of these opportunities" (Huerta de Soto, 2010, pp. 25–26). These profit opportunities arise from deficiencies subjectively detected by the investor and reflected in the market prices of common stocks. As Mayer (2018, p. 165) reminds us: "[p]rices are the medium for the transfer of knowledge, and they are formed through the exchange of subjective knowledge." The relationship between price and value is the main pillar of investing. In essence, investors have to subjectively appraise publicly listed companies, which are the means to achieve a desired end, in this case a specific return deemed appropriate by the investor and generally above the one that could be obtained by the market index. After estimating the value, or more precisely the utility, of each investment, the sensible investor has to compare it with the price reflected in the market and conclude if the difference between both is sufficient to proceed with the investment. This is what is commonly known in finance as the margin of safety, that we will discuss in more detail below.

But to compare price and value, the latter has to be estimated from a subjective standpoint, and this adds another layer of complexity to the exercise of entrepreneurship by the sensible investor. He has to evaluate the entrepreneurship capabilities of the businessmen that own and manage the firms in which he invests, and if these will bear its fruits, translating into pure entrepreneurial profits in the future. To do so he has to analyze all aspects of the business, including the competitive landscape, value chain, economic moats, management quality, capital allocation and financial statements, among others. Finally, the same as if it was as a complicated jigsaw puzzle, he must put everything together and use his subjective knowledge to try to foresee if the companies' goods and services will be demanded in the future in a given quantity, resulting into higher cash flows which do not seem to be reflected in the current market price. To be successful the investor has to correctly apply his entrepreneurship and, in parallel, determine with certain accuracy if the entrepreneurs behind the companies in which he has invested will also exercise their entrepreneurship successfully. Thus, the sensible investor has to adopt a multidisciplinary role, concurrently acting as an investor and as a businessman with as many areas of expertise as sectors in which the companies he has invested are present. He must be an entrepreneur in the industrial, retail, telecommunications, technology, mining, and many other economic areas. This is commonly defined in the investment world as the circle of competence, and it is the investor's duty to keep growing and strengthening it over time. It is not an easy task, and this is probably the main reason why most people cannot be sensible investors, added to the necessary temperament to act against the crowd and overcome other behavioral biases.

When entrepreneurship results in pure economic profits, it produces three main effects: "First, entrepreneurship has created new information which did not exist before. Second, this information has been transmitted throughout the market. Third, the above entrepreneurial act has taught the economic agents involved to tune their behavior to that of the others" (Huerta de Soto, 2010, p. 35). When an investor invests in a company, he is transmitting the information to the market that, from his point of view, there is a clear mismatch between his appraisement of such company and the current market price, which can result in pure economic profits if taken advantage of. This may not be completely new information, but in general terms this information did not exist in the minds of most economic agents. Finally, if he is proven right, it teaches the other economic agents to adapt their behavior and this eventually reflects in the company's share price, which tends to converge toward the investor's appraisement. Altogether, the coordination role of sensible investors in financial markets seems clear and of utmost importance.

This whole process of creation and transmission of information, as well as coordination and adjustment of the rest of economic agents, "necessarily modifies among all of the actors involved the general perception of ends and means. This shift in turn gives rise to the appearance of a limitless number of new maladjustments which represent new opportunities for entrepreneurial profit, and this dynamic process spreads, never comes to a halt, and results in the constant advancement of civilization" (Huerta de Soto, 2010, p. 48). This is what Mayer has correctly defined as dynamic disequilibria and constitutes a core characteristic of investment.

There is a very popular question nowadays regarding the death of value investing. My personal appreciation is that, if you agree with the concept of entrepreneurship and the role of investors as entrepreneurs in the marketplace, value or sensible investing cannot be dead by definition, as new investment opportunities will constantly be created in a process that never ends.

Uncertainty, Diversification, and Marginal Utility

Due to the nature of human action and entrepreneurship, the economy and financial markets are in constant change and, consequently, the future is never determined but, on the contrary, it is yet to be built by the actions taken by the entrepreneur and his interaction with other actors. Hence, investors have to work in an environment of permanent uncertainty. The problem is that uncertainty cannot be quantified or measured. How could it possibly be, if the myriad of future alternatives and events that could impact our investment have not been created yet, or even thought by the economic agents involved. As an example, let us consider the Covid-19 pandemic which has impacted our lives and financial markets in such a drastic manner during the last two years. Nobody was able to predict this event and less so quantify it and incorporate it as a measurable risk within their portfolios. Nassim Taleb (2007) calls these type of events black swans, but in reality, this is nothing else than uncertainty.

Modern finance has created a pernicious situation by which the concept of risk, associated with class probability as defined by Mises (1949, pp. 107–113), has absorbed the notion of uncertainty in investment management. The origin of this has to do with the inadequate use of natural science methodology in finance. In order to try and give a false sense of control, mathematical probabilities to measure risk are widely used in financial markets, creating the wrong perception to investors that the "risky" future events are well known and can be quantified to try to avoid them. A very clear example of human hubris or the fatal conceit described by Hayek. But we must never forget about the difference of subjective risk and uncertainty, as it has been very well described by Mayer (emphases added):

> Former US Defense Secretary Donald Rumsfeld has given a lucid description of the difference between risk and uncertainty. He called the former the "**known unknowns**" and the latter the "**unknowns**". In the first case, we know the event but we don't know whether it will happen. In addition, we have a fairly precise view of the probability of the event actually happening, which we derive from the experience or from the probability distribution of similar events in the past. This has been called risk. In the second case we do not know the event and hence cannot even have a vague idea of the probability of its occurrence. All we know is that something unexpected can happen. **It is the latter type of uncertainty that investors really need to take into account.** (Mayer, 2018, pp. 169–170)

Unknowns or uncertainty is what really can destroy an investment thesis. There are three main ways in which an investor can deal with uncertainty. First, through better exercise of his entrepreneurship. As long as the sensible investor follows the principles we have described, is able to interpret better the incomplete and disperse information reflected through market prices and combines everything with his own subjective private knowledge, he may have an edge versus the average investor in the marketplace. But let us face it, there is only a handful of Bill Gates and Steve Jobs in every generation and there is probably just one Warren Buffett every one hundred years. The chances are that we as investors will not have a higher-than-average entrepreneurial skillset and, therefore, the next tools I will explain seem to have a higher relevance.

The second element to deal with permanent uncertainty is diversification. No matter how well the investor thinks he may know a specific company and how many hours of work he has spent analyzing all the variables he considers relevant, it is impossible for him to eliminate the uncertain events that may negatively affect the company in a future which is still to be created by human actors. Hence, if he wants to achieve his investment return, he must consider adding more investments that will increase the marginal utility of his portfolio as a means to achieve his targeted end. There is no magic number to attain the optimal level of diversification in a portfolio. This idea comes from the erroneous application of objectivism to the study of finance, which we have already commented. Following the law of declining marginal utility, the sensible investor will only increase the number of companies that he owns, if the last marginal investment he can add increases the utility of his portfolio to achieve his goal of a specific return. In other words, he will refrain from including an additional (marginal) investment unless he considers that it can reduce the aggregate uncertainty of his portfolio. This is a subjective appreciation for each individual, so some will be comfortable with ten companies and others with one hundred. Yet we must consider that the number of companies within a portfolio is negatively correlated with how well anyone can get to know those companies. Time is a scarce resource and too much diversification can act in detriment of our entrepreneurship, as there is just so much brain power and entrepreneurial capabilities that we can dedicate as human beings to analyze each of the companies.

It is important to highlight that diversification is not just a matter of numbers, but what really matters is the perceived diversification brought by each company due to their different business models, sectors, and variables that affect them. For example, it adds little value if someone has a portfolio of 1000 stocks, but all of them will suffer similarly if the price of commodities increases. Diversification would be better with a lower number of companies that have uncorrelated business drivers. The same applies to the weights of individual stocks within the portfolio. It matters little if we have a decent number of uncorrelated companies but two or three of them represent 50% of our portfolio, as if an unexpected event heavily impacts one of them, we risk being unable to attain our investment goal.

The third and final element is the margin of safety, defined as the difference between the appraisement of a company and its market price. A higher margin gives more headroom for being wrong in our subjective valuation of the company, either because we have failed in the exercise of our entrepreneurial skills or due to unexpected future events, that is, uncertainty. Thus, sensible investors should always seek to invest in companies with a high margin of safety and persistently try to improve the aggregate margin of safety of the portfolio.

The law of marginal utility also encloses the theoretical justification behind the dilemma of when to buy and sell a specific company. In practice, everyone has a different way to proceed, which is generally determined by the accumulated knowledge embedded in their own personal investment process, as well as their own intuition. However, a sensible investor should only buy a new company, or a larger amount of an existing one within the portfolio, if it increases the marginal utility of the portfolio. For example, if the investor's goal is to beat the market index, without setting a specific numerical return (e.g., 10% per annum for the next 10 years), he should allocate his capital to those companies that A) he subjectively considers that will reduce the overall level of uncertainty and B) increase the aggregate expected return of the portfolio. In practice, the sensible investor will sell companies to substitute them for others that he considers that reduce the uncertainty and also increase the expected return of the portfolio. The companies added do not necessarily need to be new, but they can be existing stocks in the portfolio that the investor decides to increase in weight.

The Current Investment Environment

I think it is appropriate to end this essay with some thoughts on the complex situation that investors are experiencing in financial markets due to the unprecedented manipulation of money and credit orchestrated by central banks in collusion with governments. This is not the place to discuss with great detail the numerous socialist policies that have been implemented and, unfortunately, are still being implemented at a worldwide scale.

Still, from a professional standpoint I feel quite confident to say that the biggest difficulty that investors are facing today are artificially low—even negative—interest rates. If we follow the theoretical arguments laid out before, the universe of market inefficiencies that hide potential entrepreneurial profits and move investors to act is being strongly impacted nowadays. Investors are being stopped from an efficient execution of their entrepreneurship to discover these opportunities, take advantage of them and, in doing so, coordinate the whole financial markets.

As I explained before, the difference between market prices and appraisement is the main pillar of sensible investing, as well as one of the main elements to deal with uncertainty. Currently, companies′ and assets′ appraisement is becoming increasingly difficult because the manipulation of interest rates and the denominated "risk free rate" (usually associated with the 10-year sovereign debt of a developed economy) has affected the discount rates used by investors to estimate the current fair value of future cash flows. In general terms, the discount rate used by most market participants has been lowered, with very few exceptions like in extremely unpopular sectors like oil and gas, where a risk premium is compensating a lower discount rate. The direct consequence of a lower discount rate is that those cash flows that the investor estimates will be generated in the most distant future are usually valued considerably higher than if a normalized, non-manipulated, discount rate was used. This is especially true with the terminal value of those cash flows, which is the value to perpetuity calculated in a discounted cash flow model (the most generally accepted valuation method in finance), for example, in the fifth or tenth year counted from the current moment. In conclusion, the biggest percentage of the estimated value of a firm now comes from the most distant cash flows, making current cash flow generation less relevant. Consequently, this makes those companies which do not generate much cash flow (or even zero) today but will supposedly generate very high cash flows ten years from now, comparatively more attractive than those which generate a robust cash flow currently, but most probably will not grow that cash flow at a very high rate in the most distant future. Thus, the denominated "growth companies" are being attributed much higher market prices, favoring them versus "value companies."

The effect just described is being augmented by the complete oblivion of the permanent uncertainty that all investors face. Artificially low interest rates and unprecedented money creation by central banks have made most investors eliminate from the equation the uncertainty inherent to any investment, pushing them to invest in those growth companies that precisely face bigger uncertainties as their cash flows will be generated in the most distant future. More distant cash flow estimation demands an increasingly difficult exercise of entrepreneurship, as we are trying to foresee events, needs, and demands from consumers, very far away in time. On top of this, "growth companies" tend to be valued at very high multiples of future expected earnings, which translates into higher present market prices, leaving a very thin margin of safety, or even sometimes its disappearance.

Altogether, the current context has forced many sensible investors to throw in the towel and capitulate, forgetting about the principles I explained before and jumping into a very dangerous terrain that can end in huge losses for most of them. However, it is precidsely in these extreme situations that sensible investors have to stick to their principles and the theoretical framework made available by the Austrian School of Economics with a greater determination. Big rewards or losses are at stake.

References

Buffett, W. (1984). *The Superinvestors of Graham-and-Doddsville*. Columbia Business School.

García Iborra, R. (2020). *Principios de Economía Financiera, un Enfoque Austriaco*. Unión Editorial.

Huerta de Soto, J. (2010). *Socialism, Economic Calculation and Entrepreneurship*. Edward Elgar.

Mayer, T. (2018). *Austrian Economics, Money and Finance*. Routledge.

Mises, L. v. (1949). *Human Action*. Yale University.

Taleb, N. (2007). *Black Swan: The Impact of the Highly Improbable*. Penguin.

Financial Markets and the Production of Law

Jörg Guido Hülsmann

Huerta de Soto's brilliant book *Money, Bank Credit, and Economic Cycles* stands at the intersection of law and economics. In our present contribution, we shall try to follow in his footsteps by analyzing the impact of government interventions on the production of legal claims. We will focus

It is a great pleasure and honor to contribute the present paper to the Festschrift for Jesús Huerta de Soto. He is a true gentleman, one of the most eminent economists of our time, and a staunch defender of the Austrian School. Although I have met him only a few times, what I have seen and heard is more than enough to instill in me a deep admiration, not only for his scholarly output, but also for his many achievements in all walks of life: as a Catholic, as a father, as the head of an important family business, as the inspirator and leader of a thriving and vigorous scholarly movement, and as a public intellectual. Last but not least, like all great men, he had the good sense, and the fortune, to find a magnificent spouse to match and support him. Clearly, the Almighty has blessed him abundantly. May He continue to bless him, his family, and his intellectual descendants. Ad multos annos, dear Jesús!

J. G. Hülsmann (✉)
University of Angers, Angers, France
e-mail: guido.hulsmann@univ-angers.fr

D. Howden, P. Bagus (eds.), *The Emergence of a Tradition: Essays in Honor of Jesús Huerta de Soto, Volume I*,
https://doi.org/10.1007/978-3-031-17414-8_17

on an area where economics and law most visibly overlap, namely on financial markets. The latter can be defined as exchanges of legally enforceable promises of future cash payments. The beneficiaries of such promises own legal claims on future payments of money. The different financial claims—also known as financial titles and products—are different specifications of the conditions under which the promised future payments can be obtained.

Financial markets are the birthplace of a great number of legal claims and corresponding obligations (and financial firms also employ a great number of lawyers). Thus they are a promising though neglected field to study the economics of the production of "claims" in the sense of Bruno Leoni (1991, p. 192). We shall argue that the economics of financial markets is in several respects a special case of the economics of law. The impact of government interventions in finance is a special case of the impact of government interventions in the "production of law" (Leoni, 1991, p. 205).

This chapter is organized as follows. We will start off by revisiting the work of Bruno Leoni, who we have just cited, in a bit more detail. Leoni has not only drawn some of his own inspiration from economics, but the himself greatly influenced the development of economics during the past fifty years. Then we shall turn to financial markets, stressing that financial titles are a special subset of legal claims and analyzing how government-imposed financial titles modify the scope and the workings of financial markets. Finally, we will point out the analogies of these findings within the field of law making.

Felicitous Cross-Fertilization

Bruno Leoni made a famous "economic" case for competitive law making and against legislation. For the assessment of conflicting legal claims, it was not necessary to endow lawyers, judges, and other professionals in the field with any monopoly powers. He went on to demonstrate that the monopolized legislative process was likely to produce results contrary to the very purpose of the law, especially in creating greater uncertainty about the future law than would prevail without legislation.

His argument was recognizably inspired by the writings of Ludwig von Mises (1981, 1998) and Friedrich August von Hayek (1935). Mises stressed that all social phenomena ultimately result from individual human choices. Leoni (1991, p. 192) thought this also held true for the raw material of jurisprudence, namely for legal claims. Mises argued that government interventions tended to be counter-productive. As we have stated above, Leoni held that the same thing was true in the field of law making. Mises stressed that government-imposed, immaterial "fiat" money undermined the operation of the market economy and was a severe threat to political liberty. Similarly, Leoni (1991, p. 206) contrasted "two ways of 'producing law'," namely the natural way and the way of government fiat, and he highlighted the adverse legal and political implications of the latter.

Bruno Leoni thereby shed new light on the importance of the common law. He gave a new theoretical legitimacy to this traditional law-making process, relying as it were on custom, contract, and jurisprudence, rather than on the power of the state.

But Leoni also provided an important illustration of the fertility of the "praxeological" approach developed by Mises. Economic science, as the latter understood it, was not confined to the analysis of exchange, prices, and the production of economic goods. It was the science of human action. Law making too is a branch of human action. The principles that determine the production of all other goods also determine the activities of those human beings who define the law and adjudicate legal claims. Mises had not seen this connection, but Leoni did. He radicalized the application of Mises' ideas, and this radicalization had great influence on the further development of economic science and social philosophy. For example, it prompted F.A. Hayek to abandon his legislation-focused approach to the creation of a *Constitution of Liberty* (1960) and to explore the evolution of legal and political institutions through competitive processes, most notably in his *Law, Legislation and Liberty* (2012). Leoni had a similar impact on Murray Rothbard (1973, 1998) who set out to analyze the economic mechanisms of a competitive juridical order, thus laying the foundations for the contemporary scholarship on these questions (e.g., Benson, 1990; Hoppe, 2012; Lottieri, 2002; Osterfeld, 1989; Stringham, 2011; Van Dun, 2004, 2009).

In what follows our purpose is to analyze the impact of government interventions on the production of financial claims and to argue that this analysis can be generalized along the lines that Bruno Leoni highlighted more than fifty years ago.

The Production of Financial Claims

Financial titles are claims on future payments of money to be made by natural or juridical persons (e.g., corporations). The different financial claims or "products" are different contractual specifications of the conditions under which a promisee can obtain a future payment from a promisor. For example, by purchasing shares of a company on the stock market, one acquires a claim on receiving any dividends that the shareholder assembly decides to pay out of the annual profit. By purchasing a government bond, one typically buys a claim on interest payments and the eventual restitution (at maturity) of the principal, both of which are specified in advance.

Financial claims and the corresponding obligations can be produced under the respect of private-property rights. In this case, we shall speak of the ***natural production of financial claims and obligations***, which are part and parcel of natural finance. However, financial claims can also be modified and created through the violation of private-property rights. In that case we shall speak of ***fiat financial claims*** (FFCs) and fiat financial obligations (FFOs), respectively of fiat finance.

To study of the impact of government intervention on financial markets, we shall therefore compare natural financial claims (NFCs) and natural financial obligations (NFOs) to FFCs and FFOs. Due to space limitations, our analysis does not purport to be systematic or exhaustive. Rather, we shall focus on five central questions and discuss them only as much as necessary in order to clarify the differences between the natural and the fiat production of financial claims. These five questions concern 1) the origin of financial claims, 2) their conditions, 3) their role within overall finance, 4) their limitations, and 5) how they are in tune with the general nature of markets and of financial markets in particular.

The Natural Production of Financial Claims

(1) The origin of financial claims. Natural financial claims are created under the consent of the liable party. Usually they have their origin in contracts. When Smith lends money to Brown, Smith sells (a part of) his monetary savings to Brown, and he buys a financial claim on the latter. Brown buys Smith's savings in exchange for his promise to make a future payment to the latter.

Not all financial claims are initially bought with money. Sometimes people exchange one promise of a future payment against another such promise, for example, in financial-derivative contracts. Similarly, not all financial claims are written; not all are negotiable and thus can be exchanged on financial markets; not all are fungible and also endowed with those additional guaranties that turn them into "securities" and qualify them for organized exchanges.

Financial claims may also have other origins. They may be created one-sidedly. For example, a company selling a product of type X may announce that it will pay its customers a certain amount of money if the latter find X at a lower price elsewhere. Some financial claims have their origin in customs, for example, in religious customs (such as the tithe) and in the customs of extended families in sub-Saharan Africa and other places.

In what follows we shall focus on contractual origin, which seems to be most important in practice. One crucial characteristic of this contractual origin is that it puts private individuals in charge. Private individuals, in their capacity as savers, control the overall volume of financial markets. They also choose the immediate users of their savings, though not necessarily the final users. In short, natural finance works bottom-up.

(2) Necessary conditions for financial exchanges to take place. The creation of a financial claim is per se costless. Promises are cheap. Anybody may promise anything, the difficulty is to find people who believe the promise and are willing to buy it. In other words, the real question is when and why financial titles have any subjective value, and especially when and why they can command a monetary market price. We cannot answer these questions here in any detail, but the overriding answer is that a person X who wishes to buy and own the promise given by another person Y must *trust* that other person. While this fundamental role of trust in financial exchanges is well known, it is appropriate to add two further clarifications.

The first one is that trust depends in turn on a great number of causes, most notably on objective factors such as the track record of the promisor and his current ability to honor his financial obligations. Subjective factors also come into play, in particular, the *judgment* of the promisee about the character of the promisor and about the latter's future ability to honor his financial obligations. However, these subjective factors ultimately depend, in large part, on the aforementioned objective factors.

The second point that needs some clarification is that, within the setting of a market economy, the word "trust" has a rather special meaning.

Saying that A trusts B does not only imply that A believes the promises made by B, but that A also backs up this good faith with his own money. In the terminology proposed by Murray Rothbard (1956), we might say that natural trust is ***demonstrated*** through action, rather than being merely declaratory. Person A might say that he has profound trust in the word of person B, but unless A takes action we can never know whether this is true (rather than a lie) and we can never compare the extent of his trust.

In other words, the trust that we put into someone is not some sort of mere declaration, certifying his or her trustworthiness. It is first of all a personal choice we make. We choose to trust someone, and we demonstrate our choice through the use of our property. In short, trust bears a subjective value component and all financial claims therefore have subjective value.

In the normal state of affairs, there is *no consensus* on the trustworthiness of the different households and firms. Each saver-investor applies his own judgment and his own criteria. There are overlapping networks of judgments and of trust.

(3) The structure of finance. Financial exchanges—exchanges of promises of future payments—are neither the only nor the most important way to finance human activities. The most important source of finance for households, firms, and governments is past revenue. In advanced economies, the aggregate *gross* revenue of all sectors is typically twice as high as GDP. By contrast, financial exchanges in most cases only serve to refinance already existing credits. *Net* issues of financial products through financial markets are very volatile, and quantitatively they are much less significant. In the United States, before the financial crisis of 2007–08, net issues of securities represented about one third of GDP, thus six times less than aggregate gross revenue resulting from selling goods and services.

Financial exchanges are the most visible mechanism of interpersonal finance. They allow savings of one person to finance the activities of another person, and they facilitate the sharing of uncertainty. But they are not the only way to achieve this. The other main mechanism of interpersonal finance, surprisingly, is cash hoarding. An increased demand for cash balances on the side of one group of people brings about a tendency for the price level to drop. This means that the purchasing power of the money units that are not being hoarded, but continue to be exchanged, is increased. Hence, savings in the form of cash hoarding serve to finance in an indirect way the activities of other people. There are in this respect no differences between this form of saving and saving in the form of financial investments (see Hülsmann, 2013, ch. 2).

To sum up, in a free-market economy, financial exchanges are just one way to finance human activities. They are a very important mechanism of interpersonal finance, but not the only one and not the most important one. They are part and parcel of a whole "structure of finance" and this structure is constantly being changed through the competitive market process. This brings us to the next point.

(4) The limits of financial markets. Financial exchanges are constrained by the same legal rules as all other exchanges. Nobody is obliged to buy and keep financial claims. There are always at least four basic alternatives. The money that could be spent on a financial claim can just as well be 1) spent on consumers' goods, 2) spent on real estate, 3) spent on factors of production, or 4) held in cash. Financial exchanges take place *if and only if* in the eyes of both partners they appear to be more useful than those four alternatives.

This implies that both the aggregate volume of financial markets and the volume of each type of financial exchange are determined by a great number of causes, many of which lay outside of the financial markets. For example, if the quality of money improves, then saving in the form of cash hoarding will tend to increase, and this is likely to diminish the amount of savings exchanged against financial claims. Similarly, if business regulations increase and deter people from creating and running a business, then the amount of savings spent on factors of production is likely to diminish, and this could very well go in hand with increased financial investments. The financial structure that results from the unhampered market process might be called a natural financial order.

To sum up, in a free-market economy, the boundaries of financial markets are established through the competitive market process. Financial claims then exist only to the extent that they provide greater services to savers, and to the users of savings, than all other forms of using one's income. Financial markets therefore tend to encourage additional savings and to improve the use of available savings. They thereby contribute to increasing aggregate production and economic growth.

Let us now see how these characteristics change under the impact of violations of private-property rights.

Fiat Finance

We can define fiat financial claims (FFC) as such claims on future payments that do not originate from consent of the liable party. The person liable to a fiat financial obligation (FFO) is therefore not strictly speaking a "promisor" because he or she never consented in the first place. But what does it mean for a person A to be liable without his or her consent? It means that some other person or group B decides that A shall make that payment *and* enforce this decision with violence or under the threat of violence.

FFCs and the corresponding FFOs cannot exist without some aggressor that forces the non-consenting party to make the payment. In practice, the aggressor must be a government or some similar social authority (church, labor union, etc.). Today FFCs and FFOs are typically products of government intervention in the sense of Mises (1929, p. 6; 1998, pp. 714–715).

Governments very often are the immediate beneficiaries of such interventions, most notably in the case of loans to the state. In this case, we may speak of "binary" intervention in the sense of Rothbard (1970, chs. 4 and 5). But governments may also create FFCs and FFOs between third parties, for example, in the form of inheritance laws, divorce laws, or mandatory pension plans in firms. In these cases we may speak of "trilateral" intervention in the sense of Rothbard (1970, ch. 3). In finance, trilateral interventions usually involve financial intermediaries such as commercial banks and insurance companies. For example, in many countries, governments force households to buy health insurance policies or pension plans from insurance companies; and in most countries the citizens today are forced to have bank accounts if they wish to conduct certain types of transactions, for example, purchase real estate or vehicles.

Hence, the creation of FFCs and FFOs tends to inflate the scope of the activities of financial intermediaries. This in turn greatly facilitates subsequent binary interventions and fills the public purse without much political resistance. Rather than forcing millions of households to directly buy government bonds, antagonizing the voting public in the process, the government has just to force the banks and insurance companies to do so. These financial firms usually have no self-interest in opposing such policies. After all, they are themselves the beneficiaries of various trilateral interventions that force the public into contracts with intermediaries.

How do such interventions modify the characteristics of financial markets?

(1) The origin of financial claims. It is clear that we are here confronted with a new and distinct origin of financial claims, namely coercion. The implication is that the quantity of financial claims increases beyond the quantity that would be created in the unhampered market.

(2) Necessary conditions for financial exchanges to take place. A further implication is that the role of trust in finance is diminished and perverted. FFCs and the corresponding FFOs do not spring from an exchange between a saver and a borrower. They do not presuppose on the side of the victim a free choice to save and a free choice to exchange those savings against a financial claim. Those who buy and hold FFCs do not necessarily trust the counterparty. But they may trust that the counterparty will pay under the threat of coercion. In other words, trust in the counterparty is replaced by trust in the government to honor its pledge of violence. Trust is centralized and homogenized.

It follows that the role of trust-building "objective" factors such as track records, revenues, and wealth is weakened. On a free market, such factors are paramount. In fiat finance, they become dispensable *for the creation* of FFCs, though not for the eventual payment of these FFCs. This implies that the overall risks involved in financial exchanges tend to increase and that more savings be wasted.

(3) The structure of finance. As we have stated, under the impact of fiat finance, the supply of financial claims is artificially increased. Financial exchanges increase relative to cash hoarding, and thus the autonomy of savers is eroded. More savings are allocated to the state. Therefore, less savings are available to finance the activities of private households and firms.

We have pointed out already that the overall risks involved in financial exchanges tend to increase and that more savings are wasted because of the diminished role of objective factors in the creation of financial claims. There is a related reason why FFCs tend to be riskier than NFCs, namely reduced liquidity. Government coercion may create FFCs of a certain nominal market price, but this does not imply in the least that these products are exchangeable at those nominal amounts on the market. Quite to the contrary, just as the initial "buyers" of the FFCs did not themselves value them at that amount, but had to be forced to buy them, subsequent buyers are also likely to refuse to buy them at that price. Secondary markets for FFCs therefore tend to be either inexistent or small. In other words, FFCs have very low market liquidity and are relatively risky to own on this account.

(4) The limits of financial markets. Above we have stressed that NFCs tend to encourage additional savings. By contrast, FFCs at best have no impact on the overall volume of savings and as a rule they tend to discourage savings and the investment of savings. The foremost reason is that people will try to evade being subject to FFCs, for example, through emigration. But even without emigration, FFCs tend to reduce the overall volume of savings. As long as the FFCs are credible—that is, as long as their beneficiaries expect them to be paid in the future—these beneficiaries are likely to reduce their present savings. They will tend to consider the FFCs as a part of their overall portfolio of invested savings, and thus are likely to reduce the other elements of that portfolio in order to spend more money now on consumers' goods (this is particularly pernicious when the FFCs are being issued by a pay-as-you-go public pension system, see Garello, 2014). By contrast, if the FFCs are *not* credible, their beneficiaries will probably not take account of them in choosing their level of present spending and in composing their portfolio.

The foregoing investigation can be summed up in three points.

1. Fiat finance without the backing from fiat money is severely constrained by the objective ability of the liable parties to make the mandatory payments. Creating more fiat obligations without any improvement to the ability to pay ends up in not financing anything, but merely increases the likelihood of default (increased counterparty risk). Other limitations result from the fact that the market prices for FFCs are inflated, which prevents the development of secondary markets, and from evasions of the fiat obligations.

2. Fiat finance absorbs a part of the overall savings and (fully or partially) wastes those savings. To waste savings means to use them in projects that the savers consider to be less important than known or imagined alternatives. In the case of fiat finance, there are always more important alternatives, otherwise it would not be necessary to resort to coercion in the first place.

3. Credible FFCs tend to provoke a reduction of the overall volume of savings, while non-credible FFCs may lead to increased saving in alternative forms such as cash hoards.

Let us now see how these results are modified under the impact of fiat money.

Fiat Finance Within a Fiat-Money System

Fiat money is a generally used medium of exchange (money) the use of which is being imposed on the citizens, typically through monopoly privilege or through legal-tender laws. While governments have imposed many different types of money, the most important cases are the ones of irredeemable paper notes and of irredeemable accounting money. Today nearly all countries of the world have fiat monies that are produced by central banks in the form of banknotes and accounts. This state of affairs is no historical accident (see Hoppe, 1994). Governments have imposed banknotes and accounting money because these types of money can be produced *ad libitum* to the benefit of the treasury.

The production of additional money units brings about a tendency for all money prices to rise, causing a reduction of the purchasing power of all (old and new) money units. But this price inflation does not happen in the way of a single and simultaneous change of all prices. It occurs through a great number of subsequent exchanges (Cantillon effects). It follows that the first users of the new money units—those who can exchange them first—stand to benefit from the fact that their purchasing power is still relatively high. This goes in hand with corresponding losses for other money users, and especially for the last users of the new money units. The latter have to wait until their monetary revenue increases when they receive some of these new units, but until this happens they already have to pay higher money prices out of their old revenue.

In short, the production of money creates winners and losers. Fiat money can be produced *ad libitum* and therefore offers the possibility to extent this redistribution virtually without limits. Furthermore, central banks—the appointed producers of fiat money—have the power to pick the first users of new money. Thus they can make sure that the government is always in a pole position among the winners. The general economic, political, and moral dimensions of these facts have been analyzed in some detail (see, e.g., Rothbard, 2008; Hoppe, 1990; Hülsmann, 2008). In what follows we shall highlight their impact on finance and financial markets.

The starting point for our analysis is the fact that fiat money greatly boosts the development of financial markets, through at least four distinct channels (there is a detailed exposition in Hülsmann, 2013, ch. 8).

Central banks may create fiat money to purchase financial claims, thus increasing both the demand for those claims and their prices (the monetization channel). Central banks may create fiat money in order to lend it to other market participants. Such lending is usually "collateralized" or secured by the temporary transfer of already-existing financial claims to the central bank. Thus the demand for such claims increases because they may serve as collateral in central bank lending operations (the collateral channel). The permanent increase of the fiat money supply typically creates a positive price-inflation rate. In this case, savings in the form of cash hoarding are no longer a suitable way to preserve wealth, and thus savers and investors increasingly turn to financial markets (the price-inflation channel). Finally, central banks usually try to stabilize the purchasing power of money, which involves a stabilization of the commercial-banking system. Because the commercial banks know that they can count on support from the central bank, they have an incentive to increase their financial exchanges beyond what would otherwise be their precautionary limits (the moral-hazard channel).

Let us stress again that central banks may create fiat money without any technical or commercial limitation. Apart from political resistance, the only long-run limit of fiat-money creation is a runaway or hyperinflation (see Bernholz, 2003 for historical overviews). When money prices rise fast and high, the market participants have very strong incentives to reject their money and turn to using other media of exchange. But in the short run, central banks are virtually always able to create more money as they see fit without losing too many customers. This has four major implications for financial markets and the production of financial claims.

First off, as we have already stated, under a fiat money system, there is a very strong tendency for cash hoarding to diminish because the permanent increases of the price level (the aforementioned price-inflation channel). Rather than hoard their savings in cash, the citizens start to buy financial claims, in the hope that the associated dividends and interest payments compensate for the shrinking purchasing power of money. Yet this implies that the direct personal control over the final use of one's savings diminishes. In practice, this control is usually being turned over to government-licensed intermediaries such as banks and insurance companies.

Second, fiat money completely erodes the role of trust on financial markets. As we have seen, in a fiat-finance system *without* fiat money, overlapping networks of individual trust relations are being partially replaced by trust in a single agent's (the government's) ability to honor its promise of coercing payments from other market participants. But coercion does not create any goods, and the victims' objective ability to pay is therefore still a limitation of any fiat finance system. This limitation evaporates once fiat money comes into play. Then *even if* the citizens are unable to meet their fiat financial obligations, and *even if* the government is unable to do anything about this by wielding sheer force, the central bank still has the technical possibility to simply create the money necessary to buy and hold indefinitely all FFCs, respectively, to redeem all financial obligations. The central bank itself does not need to trust the commercial banks, or local government, or whoever else might have an account at the central bank. It does not need to believe that the obliged parties are objectively able and willing to make the future payment. It can provide them with any amount of fresh credit out of the printing press, at zero or negative interest rates, and for unlimited time. In short, under a fiat money system "trust" tends to be severed from the objective ability to make payments. *In extremis*, trust under a fiat system means trust in the central bank's willingness to buy this or that financial claim, respectively, to bail out the counterparties of these claims.

Third, the foregoing analysis does not imply that the objective abilities of the counterparties to financial claims are no longer relevant. They certainly are relevant from the point of view of the economy as a whole. Rather, the point is that they are comparatively less important *in the judgment of the individual market participants*. The latter are more likely to engage in particularly risky financial exchanges if they have reasons to believe that they might get away with it thanks to help from the central banks. In short, resources tend to be wasted, while each individual saver-investor behaves perfectly rationally under the given circumstances (i.e., a rationality trap).

Fourth, this tendency is reinforced by the fact that central banks can buy—and do buy—FFCs at nominal prices, thus creating veritable secondary markets for those FFCs. This implies a stronger demand for FFCs, along with higher prices and correspondingly lower interest rates. This may come at the expense of other types of investment, but it is also likely to reduce the overall volume of savings. The beneficiaries of a fiat public pension plan might have doubts that the payments will ever come forth, and thus they are likely to build up savings outside of the pension system. But under a fiat money system, it is virtually certain that the nominal payments will be made, and thus the incentives to save outside of the system tend to diminish. They would not diminish only if the purchasing power of the forthcoming payments was expected to fall.

To sum up, a fiat money system destroys the two major limitations of fiat finance that we highlighted in the preceding section. Most importantly, it undermines the role that objective factors play in the individual decision-making process. It thereby destroys the reality check of success and failure, while the economic system as a whole is still subject to objective limitations. Furthermore, the permanent price inflation that typically results from fiat money production destroys one major alternative to financial investments, namely cash hoarding and thus discourages savings.

In short, savings fall below the level they would otherwise have reached, and the savings that remain tend to be wasted to a greater extent. How long can this go on? We have already stated that one remaining limitation is hyperinflation (or at least uncomfortably high rates of price inflation). Another limitation is the complete destruction of savings. But these limitations may play out in the very long run and only if there are no countervailing tendencies such as technology-driven growth or a strong savings culture, as in Japan or Italy. Hence, although a fiat-money-backed fiat-finance system is very destructive, it can potentially last a long time, especially if it can parasitically live on the economic and financial virtues of the citizens.

Financial Markets and Statutory Law Making

The foregoing analysis can be generalized along the lines suggested by Bruno Leoni more than fifty years ago. Leoni (1991, pp. 205–206) distinguished between a natural law-making process and a fiat law-making process. The natural law-making process is based on individual claims that usually emerge out of contracts. The adjudication of conflicting claims works bottom-up and is driven in the first place by the concerned citizens themselves and only secondarily by professional specialists (lawyers, judges) who assist the citizens. By contrast, the fiat law-making process works top-down and involves the imposition of claims without the consent and against the will of the liable citizens. Its tool is statutory law, that is, legislation. In Leoni's (1991, p. 206) words:

> Lawyers and judges produce law by working on some materials that are considered to be given to them in order to condition their own production. To adopt a happy metaphor of a great contemporary scholar, Sir Carleton Kemp Allen, they 'make' law in the same sense that a man who chops a tree into logs has 'made' the logs. On the contrary, the ambition of the legislators

> is to make the law without being conditioned that way. They not only 'produce' law, but they also want to produce it by a kind of fiat, regardless of materials and even of contrary wills and opinions of other people. What they mean is not sheer production, but [...] *creation* of the law.

Leoni's analysis of the consequences of statutory law can be summarized by saying that statutory law tends to destroy the law. More precisely, under the impact of legislation, the law tends to become disconnected from the opinions and the will of the citizens, thus undermining their autonomy. The organic and "grown" structure of the law—involving contracts, customs, expert opinion, and previous judgements—gives way to one unique and homogenous source of claims, namely legislation. Most importantly, legislated law undermines the certainty of the law, and thus one of its basic functions. Leoni highlighted the fact that *in the short run*, legislation might very well clarify the law and thus increase its certainty. However, precisely because legislation allows to create laws *ad libitum* it entails greater uncertainty *in the long run*. Leoni states (1991, p. 80):

> The more intense and accelerated is the process of law-making, the more uncertain will it be that present legislation will last for any length of time. Moreover, there is nothing to prevent a law, certain in the above-mentioned sense, from being unpredictably changed by another law no less 'certain' than the previous one.

The parallels to our foregoing analysis of fiat-money-based financial systems are striking. In fact, we found exactly the same tendencies that Leoni highlighted in the more general case of legislation. Fiat money increases the financial capacity of the system in the short run, yet destroys the financial autonomy of the citizens and the organic bottom-up structure of financial exchanges; and it facilitates the waste of savings, thus undermining the financial capacity of the system in the long run.

Let us conclude with three additional remarks on the interrelations between the production of law and the production of financial claims.

1. Statutory law (legislation) is fundamental. Without statutory law, there can be no fiat financial claims and corresponding obligations. Without statutory law there can be no such thing as immaterial money that can be produced *ad libitum*. Historically, all paper monies and all accounting monies have been introduced by legislative fiat. There is some current debate about the theoretical *possibility* of a purely voluntary

emergence of immaterial money, spurred by the success of bitcoin (see Murphy, 2013). But the plain fact is that bitcoin owes its success to the fact that it cannot be produced without limit, because the production function contains an in-built ceiling. Thus our above statement remains valid: Without statutory law there can be no such thing as immaterial money that can be produced *ad libitum*.

2. As statutory law diminishes the certainty of the law, it also undermines the certainty of financial claims. Legislators may decide to unilaterally revoke or redefine the financial obligations of banks, insurance companies, nonfinancial firms, and of the state. Historical examples are legion.

3. Fiat money systems greatly boost the capacity of the legislative process. Without fiat money, the legislator is strongly limited in his capacity to create rights and obligations out of nothing, because the objective ability of the state and of the citizens to honor financial and other obligations is limited. But as we have seen, fiat money allows one to redeem all nominal financial obligations, though at the cost of a shrinking purchasing power per unit of money. Legislators, especially legislators caught up in the political process and the election cycle, have a strong incentive to create all sorts of rights (e.g., public welfare services) for their constituents and to make the corresponding payments through credit financed directly or indirectly by of the printing press. In the United States, periods of high rates of money creation (1970s, late 1990s, 2020s) have gone in hand with a particularly strong legislative activity, while periods of moderate monetary expansion (1980s, early 1990s) featured a lower production of statutory law.

Conclusion

In this chapter, we have argued that the economics of financial markets is in several respects a special case of the economics of law. In particular, we have shown that government interventions in money and finance, creating fiat claims and obligations, entail the same characteristic consequences as the production of statutory law and which were highlighted by Bruno Leoni more than fifty years ago. Just as statutory law tends to create short-term certainty at the expense of the ultimate destruction of the law, fiat-money-based finance tends to create short-term funding possibilities at the expense of an ultimate destruction of savings and productive investments. We have also briefly discussed the mutual interdependence of financial markets and statutory law making, underlining the fact that legislation benefits from the short-run lending facilities of a fiat-money system.

References

Benson, B. L. (1990). *The Enterprise of Law: Justice Without the State*. Pacific Research Institute for Public Policy.

Bernholz, P. (2003). *Monetary Regimes and Inflation*. Edward Elgar.

Garello, J. (2014). *Comment sauver vos retraites*. Nizza.

Hayek, F. A. (2012). *Law, Legislation, and Liberty*. Routledge.

Hayek, F. A. (1960). *Constitution of Liberty*. University of Chicago Press.

Hayek, F. A. (Ed.). (1935). *Collectivist Economic Planning*. Routledge.

Hoppe, H.-H. (2012). *The Great Fiction*. Laissez-Faire Books.

Hoppe, H.-H. (1994). How is Fiat Money Possible?—or, The Devolution of Money and Credit. *Review of Austrian Economics*, 7(2), 49–74.

Hoppe, H.-H. (1990). Banking, Nation States, and International Politics: A Sociological Reconstruction of the Present Economic Order. *Review of Austrian Economics*, 4, 55–87.

Hülsmann, J. G. (2013). *Krise der Inflationskultur*. Finanzbuch-Verlag.

Hülsmann, J. G. (2008). *The Ethics of Money Production*. Mises Institute.

Leoni, B. (1991 [1961]). *Freedom and the Law* (3rd ed.). Liberty Fund.

Lottieri, C. (2002). European Unification as the New Frontier of Collectivism: The Case for Competitive Federalism and Polycentric Law. *Journal of Libertarian Studies, 16*(1), 23–44.

Mises, L. v. (1998). *Human Action*. Mises Institute.

Mises, L. v. (1981). *Socialism*. Liberty Fund.

Mises, L. v. (2011 [1929]). *A Critique of Interventionism*. Mises Institute.

Murphy, R. P. (2013, June 3). *The Economics of Bitcoin*. Library of Economics and Liberty. http://www.econlib.org/library/Columns/y2013/Murphybitcoin.html.

Osterfeld, D. (1989). Anarchism and the Public Goods Issue: Law, Courts and the Police. *Journal of Libertarian Studies, 9*(1), 47–68.

Rothbard, M. N. (2008 [1983]). *The Mystery of Banking*. Mises Institute.

Rothbard, M. N. (1998 [1982]). *The Ethics of Liberty*. New York University Press.

Rothbard, M. N. (1973). *For a New Liberty*. Collier Macmillan.

Rothbard, M. N. (1970). *Power and Market*. Institute for Humane Studies.

Rothbard, M. N. (1956). Toward a Reconstruction of Welfare and Utility Economics. In M. Sennholz (Ed.), *On Freedom and Free Enterprise*. Van Nostrand.

Stringham, E. P. (Ed.). (2011). *Anarchy and the Law: The Political Economy of Choice*. Transaction Publishers.

Van Dun, F. (2009). The Logic of Law. *Libertarian Papers, 1*(36).

Van Dun, F. (2004). Natural Law and the Jurisprudence of Freedom. *Journal of Libertarian Studies, 18*(2), 31–54.

The Capital Asset Pricing Model: Dead and Kicking

Massimiliano Neri

The capital asset pricing model (CAPM) is the result of the works of Sharpe(1964), Litner (1965), and Mossin (1966). By working independently, they came up with the same model based on the earlier work of Harry Markovitz. In 1990 Professor Sharpe won the Nobel Prize for Economics for this contribution, and sixty years after his seminal paper no innovation has been able to displace it. It is still the centrepiece of MBA investment courses, and it is often the only asset pricing model taught in these courses.

Professor Huerta de Soto had on his radar a critique of the CAPM for decades. He has always been obsessed with researching alternatives to the CAPM that would be consistent with the Austrian School. During the period in which I attended his graduate seminar, from 2002 to 2005, every time a new doctoral student or a finance professional appeared in his class, the professor would systematically test the ground: "Are you familiar with the CAPM? There is a big opportunity in researching alternatives!" I

M. Neri (✉)
Universidad Francisco Marroquín, Guatemala City, Guatemala
e-mail: mn@ufm.edu

D. Howden, P. Bagus (eds.), *The Emergence of a Tradition: Essays in Honor of Jesús Huerta de Soto, Volume I*,
https://doi.org/10.1007/978-3-031-17414-8_18

was committed to another research subject, so I did not pick it up myself, but a few years later, David Howden focused his PhD thesis on this subject, laying down the map for an Austrian alternative to the CAPM.

In the financial world, the CAPM has two prominent use cases. First, it is used to estimate the cost of equity of firms. The traditional method for evaluating the present value of an asset (discounted cash flow model, or DCF) requires that one discounts the stream of future cash flows with a "discount rate" that represents an appropriate industry return expectation for such asset. In corporate finance, this discount rate corresponds to the cost of capital, which reflects the return expectations of shareholders. The cost of capital is traditionally estimated using the weighted average cost of capital (WACC), which is the sum of the cost of equity and the cost of debt. The cost of equity is traditionally estimated with the CAPM. Secondly, the CAPM is used to assess the performance of an investment portfolio. Portfolio managers use terminologies such as the "beta" and other "risk factors" to evaluate current portfolios, both in terms of past performance and expected return. Every portfolio manager embeds this number in their calculations, and today there is an ecosystem of modeling and data providers that offer results based on the CAPM and its successive multifactor evolutions.

What Is the CAPM?

The CAPM rests on three pillars. The first one is portfolio selection theory, introduced by Harry Markowitz with the famous original paper in 1952. According to this theory, investors make portfolio decisions based only on the mean and variance of the investment return. As a result, investors adopt a framework (mean-variance framework) where they choose "mean-variance efficient" portfolios.

The second pillar is the direct outcome of a collaboration between William Sharpe and Markowitz to overcome a limitation of portfolio selection. The calculation of an efficient portfolio consists essentially of a mathematical optimization exercise, where the expected inputs are the returns, variances, and correlations among all the individual assets of the portfolio. With the computational power available in the twenty-first century, this is a trivial exercise, but in the fifties and early sixties, this calculation was extremely onerous, being highly time-consuming as well as costly in terms of computing resources. Sharpe found that by estimating the sensitivity of each security against the market as a whole, the problem was completely bypassed. This idea led to the CAPM, with *beta* representing the volatility of a stock against the market portfolio. Fama and French (2004) provide a helpful diagram of how the CAPM works (Fig. 1).

The horizontal axis describes the portfolio risk (measured by the standard deviation of portfolio return), while the vertical axis shows the portfolio expected return. The curve *abc* represents the portfolio's possibilities curve. The *ab* portion is called the minimum variance frontier (or efficient frontier) since for every level of risk, it is more efficient to pick the portfolio with the highest expected return. The traditional trade-off between risk and return is apparent in the diagram (to obtain a high return one needs to accept high risk). This trade-off is obviously the outcome of defining risk as the volatility of excepted return, and it is rejected by those, like the value investors, who believe that risk and volatility are different concepts, and that it is possible to achieve high return with low volatility (meaning that it is possible to invest in a portfolio that sits outside the portfolio's possibilities curve).

If we introduce the assumption that an investor can borrow and lend infinite amounts at a risk-free rate, we add a line to the diagram. A risk-free

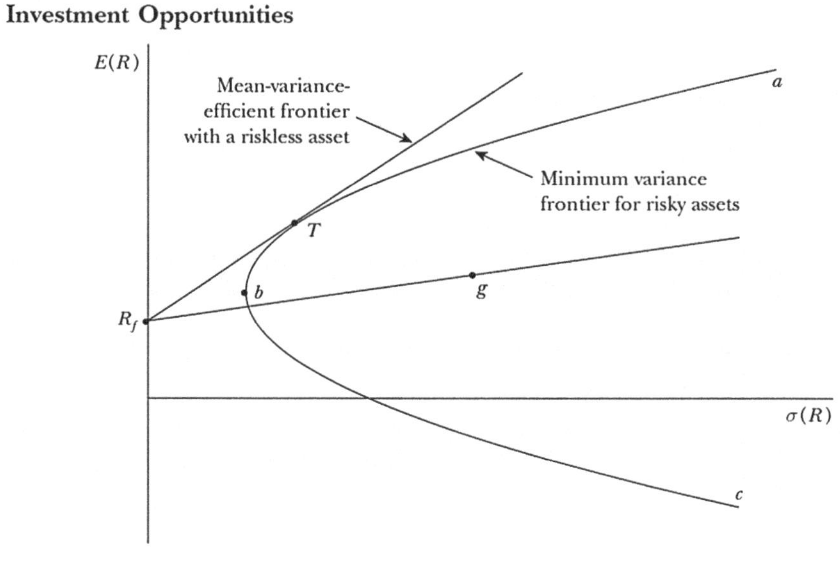

Fig. 1 The efficient frontier. Source: Fama and French (2004)

asset (which could be approximate to an AAA government bond or to a savings account) has zero volatility by default (point R_f). If an investor places a portion of his funds in a risk-free asset and the rest in a portfolio of risky assets (point *g*), these two points allow to draw the line describing all the possible combinations between these two alternatives. If the investor picks a portfolio on the efficient frontier (meaning, a mean-variance efficient portfolio), the line becomes tangential to the curve at point *T*.

As a third pillar, the CAPM introduces one of the strictest assumptions: all investors agree on the distribution of expected returns at t+1, therefore they all see the same opportunity set. Hence, all investors hold the same portfolio of risky assets (*T*), and this portfolio must be the market portfolio. As a result, the expected return on a portfolio consisting of riskless and risky assets is:

$$R_i = R_f + \beta_{iM}\left[R_M - R_f\right]$$

where R_i is the expected return on asset *i*, R_f is the return on a risk-free asset, R_M is the expected return of the market portfolio, and β_i is the market beta of asset *i*. Beta is often interpreted as the sensitivity of the asset's return to the market portfolio's return (technically speaking, beta is the covariance of the asset return with the market return divided by the variance of the market return). Beta is often called *systematic risk*, which is the risk that cannot be eliminated through diversification.

The assumption of risk-free borrowing and lending was so unrealistic that Fischer Black (1972) developed a version of the CAPM without it, by allowing unrestricted short sales of risky assets instead. In other words, Black was able to show that the market portfolio is efficient and it represents the minimum variance portfolio. As Fama and French (2004) point out, the assumption that short selling is unrestricted is as unrealistic as the assumption of unrestricted risk-free borrowing and lending. However, the relationship between expected return and beta is lost without this assumption, and the CAPM falls.

CAPM Assumptions

In summary, the CAPM introduces a weighty set of assumptions:

1) **All investors make decisions based on the mean-variance framework**

According to the mean-variance framework, investors make decisions solely in terms of expected values and standard deviations of portfolio returns. Using this framework, they construct efficient portfolios, built with optimization techniques that aim to maximize expected return while minimizing variance on the return. This framework implicitly embeds the assumption of normal distribution of expected returns because this is the only probability distribution that can be described with only two parameters (mean and variance).

2) **All investors have homogeneous expectations of asset returns**

All investors have the same expectations about expected asset returns, hence they have identical expected probability distributions concerning the future. Consequently, all investors have identical expectations of inputs required for portfolio decisions: expected return, variance on return, and the correlation matrix (between pairs of assets). This generates a unique and optimal risky portfolio (the market portfolio with expected return R_M).

3) **All investors look forward with the same time horizon**

Investors plan to hold a portfolio for one single period (one year) and assume that all other investors base their decision-making on the same time horizon.

4) **Unlimited risk-free borrowing or lending privileges**

Each investor can lend or borrow any amount of funds at an interest rate equal to the rate of risk-free securities. Black et al. (1972) substituted this assumption with unlimited short selling, where investors can short any asset, and hold any fraction of an asset. This implicitly means that assets are infinitely divisible.

5) **Investors do not affect prices with their trading activity, they are price takers**

An individual cannot affect the price of a stock by buying or selling it. This is analogous to the assumption of perfect competition. While no individual investor can influence individual stock prices, investors determine the total share prices.

6) **All assets are marketable**

All asset types and securities, and all assets, including human capital, can be bought and sold on the market, and all investors have equal access to them.

7) **No taxes nor transaction costs**

The first implies that the investor is indifferent to dividends versus capital gains. The second means there are no commission costs.

The Empirical Critique of the CAPM

After the CAPM was published, the academic literature was flooded with studies testing its predictions. Testing the CAPM is not a simple task. Beta is not observable from market data and must be estimated. Early tests of the CAPM were usually done in two steps: first, estimating the betas, and second, testing the model's predictions. The beta of a stock can be estimated in two ways: a) as the covariance between the stock's excess return (over risk-free rate) and the market portfolio's excess return, divided by the variance of the market portfolio's excess return; b) by running a time-series regression of the stock's excess returns on the market portfolio's excess returns separately for each stock (the slope estimate will correspond to the beta).

The first empirical tests were quite supportive. The University of Chicago economists Eugene Fama and James D. MacBeth published the most supportive study in 1973. Based on monthly stock returns from 1926 to 1968, they showed that the portfolio's average return was positively related to its beta (Fama & MacBeth, 1973).

Other studies found significant discrepancies. For example, Black et al. (1972) used the same data set from 1931 to 1965 and found that portfolios with low beta stocks had higher returns than the CAPM predicted (and vice versa for portfolios with high beta). The authors concluded that such evidence was "sufficiently strong to warrant rejection of the traditional form" of the CAPM. Black et al. (1972) proposed an alternative form that would be compatible with the empirical results. He found that by dropping Sharpe's assumption of unlimited borrowing at the risk-free rate, it was still possible to find an equilibrium with restricted borrowing compatible with the data.

Several early empirical tests supported the Black et al. (1972) version of the CAPM. According to Fama and French (2004), these early results "coupled with the model's simplicity and intuitive appeal, pushed the CAPM to the forefront of finance." MacKenzie (2006) describes the role of Wells Fargo, and in particular of John A. McQuown, in attracting and supporting financial economists engaged with financial innovation. "Wells Fargo Bank supported Black, Jensen, and Scholes's research financially and sponsored the conference at which it was first presented, held at the University of Rochester (where Jensen then taught) in August 1969. Probably at Black's suggestion, McQuown's group at Wells Fargo saw a way to exploit the result of the research. If the anomalous finding was the result of restrictions on borrowing, perhaps it could be exploited by an investment company, which could borrow more easily and more cheaply than an individual could? The idea was to invest in low-beta stocks, with what the study by Black, Jensen, and Scholes had suggested was their high return relative to risk, and to use 'leverage' (in other words, borrowing) to increase the portfolio's level of risk to somewhat more than the risk of simply holding the overall market, so also magnifying returns (McQuown interview)."

The push toward CAPM-oriented financial innovation happened even if the same studies consistently rejected the original formulation of the CAPM (by Sharpe (1964), Lintner (1965), and Black et al. (1972)), where the risk premium corresponds to the expected excess market return multiplied by beta. For example, they found that, although a positive relation between beta and average return exists, it is "flatter" than the CAPM prediction.

Empirical evidence against the CAPM piled up in the late 1970s and during the 1980s, even rejecting the Black version of the CAPM. Research showed that expected market return is "unrelated" (term used in Fama and French (2004)) to market beta and is rather sensitive to several other factors. For example, Basu (1977) showed evidence that earnings-price ratios can explain expected return; Banz (1981) documented the size effect (in terms of market capitalization); Bhandari (1988) found that high debt-equity ratios provide higher expected returns; finally, Stattman

(1980) and Rosenberg et al. (1985) showed that stocks with high book-to-market equity ratios have higher average returns than the CAPM prediction.

Even early supporters like Professor Fama changed their minds. In 1992 he published, with his University of Chicago colleague Kenneth R. French, what MacKenzie (2006, p. 91) defined as "the most influential empirical critique." They showed that the relationship between beta and average return predicted by the CAPM holds from 1941 to1965 (and even then, the relationship would drop by modifying the portfolio according to the firm's size). However, after 1965 the data undeniably falsify the model. At the time, the CAPM was already the most prominent model used in the investment industry, so Fama and French (1992) received significant media attention: *The Economist* headlined the news as "Beta beaten," and in an interview with the *New York Times,* Fama declared that "beta as the sole variable explaining returns on stocks is dead." Ultimately, it became known as "the 'beta is dead' paper."

In their 1992 paper, Fama and French accomplished two primary objectives: first, they showed that the data supports the CAPM predictions only in certain historical periods; second, they demonstrated that beta alone could not explain stock returns. Indeed, they found that beta alone cannot explain the stock's expected return. Rather, one must also consider other factors such as size, price-earnings, debt-equity, and book-to-market ratios. Their findings were challenged by studies such as Kothari et al. (1995). The latter was rebutted in Fama and French (2004).

Fama and French (1992) further show that "the contradictions of the CAPM associated with price ratios are not sample-specific." In Fama and French (2004, p. 36), they finally affirm: "If betas do not suffice to explain expected returns, the market portfolio is not efficient, and the CAPM is dead in its tracks."

The Theoretical Critique of CAPM

The empirical evidence against the CAPM supported numerous explanations about why the model is faulty. The first explanation relates to the number of factors required to build a good predictive model.

Fama and French (1992) had demonstrated two clear facts. First, the original formulation of the CAPM with one factor (beta) has been disproven. Second, adding additional explanatory factors makes it possible to improve the model predictions. Their 1992 paper proposed a three-factor model based on the *beta*, the *size* factor (outperformance of small versus big companies), and the *value* factor (outperformance of high book/market versus low book/market companies). The latter factor implicitly recognized the point that value investors had always defended: that the CAPM is based on the Efficient Market Hypothesis (EMH), where the market price is always equal to the fundamental (or intrinsic) value, while value investors affirm there is a gap between the two (called "margin of safety"), that can be exploited as an investment opportunity.

All the major accounts of value investing history, such as Buffett (1984), Lowenstein (1995), and MacKenzie (2006), provide an account of the famous 1984 conference at Columbia Business School celebrating the 50th anniversary of the book by Graham and Dodd (1934), which became known as the debate between Michael Jensen and Warren Buffet. Jensen represented the stereotypical position of efficient marketers, claiming that value investors' success was simply a matter of luck, like the happy winners of a coin-flipping contest. Buffet memorably responded: "I think you will find that a disproportionate number of successful coin-flippers in the investment world came from a very small village that could be called 'Graham and Doddville'."

Fama and French (1992) became the catalyst for more empirical studies exploring additional factors that could explain stocks' expected returns. Carhart (1997) extended their model with the additional *momentum* factor (which promotes an investment strategy involving buying winners and selling losers). Momentum was first introduced by Jegadeesh and Titman (1993) and by Cliff Asness in his PhD thesis, completed in 1994 under Eugene Fama (Asness, 1994). Fama never liked the results of Asness's research, and in Asness (2016) he recognized that momentum is one of the most challenging factors to reconcile with the EMH. In Fama and French (2004), Fama had previously admitted that the momentum effect was their three-factor model's most serious problem. They also insisted that while the original version of the CAPM was doomed, if one identifies the right factors it is possible to build a good predictive model based on regressive historical data. Later, Fama and French (2015) extended their original model by adding two further factors: *profitability* and *investment*.

A second explanation is based on Roll (1977). Richard Roll was another of Eugene Fama's PhD students. In the CAPM, everything rotates around the sensitivity of asset returns to the market portfolio, and Roll was puzzled by how to define it. Econometric tests were based on the S&P 500, the best available proxy for the market portfolio, but one could also have included other types of assets such as corporate bonds, real estate, movable capital, even unobservable elements like the "human capital." Therefore, while the market portfolio is supposed to be in an optimal equilibrium (on the minimum variance efficient frontier), we will never be able to observe and test it in practice. MacKenzie (2006) explains that Professor Sharpe himself admitted that Roll's critique was essentially correct. Fama and French (2004) responded pragmatically to this challenge. If one can identify a proxy sitting on the minimum variance frontier, it can be used in a multi-factor asset pricing model to predict expected returns. Besides, Stambaugh (1982), another PhD student at Chicago, had shown that the CAPM is not sensitive to the expansion of the market portfolio to other assets, essentially because the portfolio's volatility is dominated by stock volatility.

A third explanation is based on behavioral finance. In the market, we can observe stocks with high book value to market price (B/M), which are considered underpriced and called "value stocks." Eventually, a market correction will result in high growth (vice versa, with low B/M stocks). According to behaviorists, these violations of the CAPM are due to economic agents' bias, and as a result, assets in capital markets are mispriced (DeBondt & Thaler, 1987; Lakonishok et al., 1994; Haugen, 1995). Consequently, the EMH does not hold, and markets are irrational, meaning that they do not behave according to the neoclassical definition of Rational Choice Theory. Fama and French (2004) concede that when a test rejects the CAPM, one cannot recognize whether one is facing a violation of the rational pricing assumption (the behaviorist view) or a breach of the asset pricing model (Fama and French's view).

According to the fourth explanation, the CAPM assumptions are unrealistic and over-simplistic. When he first published the CAPM, Sharpe was aware that the model's assumptions were "highly restrictive and undoubtedly unrealistic" (cited in Mackenzie, 2006, p. 54). He defended this opinion by invoking Milton Friedman's 1953 essay "The Methodology of Positive Economics." Revisiting the debate on Friedman's epistemological viewpoint is not in the scope of this chapter. However, we cannot fail to mention that Professor Markovitz, the father of the foundations upon which the EMH and the CAPM are built, in Markovitz (2005) attacked two of the basic CAPM assumptions: i) investors can borrow risk-free with no limits; ii) investors can sell short without limit to take on long positions. By relaxing these assumptions, the market portfolio no longer needs to be an efficient portfolio. As Bernstein (2007) points out, if the market portfolio is not efficient, then "indexing makes no sense, and perhaps no strategy of broad diversification makes sense."

The fifth explanation is the Austrian one, and it can be seen as a more sophisticated version of the previous one. It should not come as a surprise that the Austrian stance is identical to the behaviorist critique of the CAPM's unrealistic assumptions (as expressed, for example, in Ang (2014), a key reference-point for factor investing). After all, both take issue with Chicago's Rational Choice Theory (to which the EMH and the CAPM belong). Let's start with the assumptions related to the market (the first two are identical to Markovitz (2005)):

a) Availability of unlimited resources in the market to be lent at a risk-free rate: this is a simplification that does not occur.
b) Unlimited short selling is possible in any market: this is not the case in real life. In many securities, such a market simply does not exist.
c) Negotiability of any asset: any asset can be bought or sold by anyone under the same conditions.
d) The CAPM ignores transaction costs (commissions), which undoubtedly have a powerful impact on the result of any portfolio.
e) The CAPM also ignores taxes (which have a much more significant impact than in the previous case).
f) Investors' activities do not influence market price movements: this is false since the formation of prices emanates precisely from who buys and sells at any given moment.

Furthermore, the following two assumptions on the behavior of the economic agent are in sharp contrast with Austrian subjective valuation applied to investment decisions (to be precise: Mises subjective valuation assumption and Huerta de Soto's entrepreneurial function):

g) All investors have the same forecasts about market behavior (probability distribution) and analyze it in the same way (mean-variance framework): in reality, everyone has their subjective expectations. If everyone believed that a given asset was worth the same price, no buying and selling would ever take place.
h) The CAPM assumes that all investors invest with the same time horizon, which is not true in real life either. Such time horizons undoubtedly affect buying and selling decisions, which the CAPM completely ignores.

In addition to the above, the Austrians (and other schools of thought) do not agree with the mainstream definition of risk as the variance of the event under observation. First, if one measures the risk of return as its standard deviation, then the risk of any event can be measured, and *risk* and *uncertainty* end up conflated instead of being kept separated according to the well-known Knightian dichotomy. Secondly, standard deviation treats upsides and downsides equally, and while the former is desirable, the latter corresponds precisely to the potential loss the investor seeks to avoid. A significant literature studies the "downside risk," which defines risk as the negative half of the distribution of return probabilities. According to Grabowski and Pratt (2014), this literature focuses on the risks of an investment loss, as opposed to the symmetrical likelihood of a loss or gain. Finally, from a methodological perspective, the whole CAPM models' ecosystem is based on the idea that expected future returns could be deduced from the movement of past prices.

Alternatives to the CAPM

The Factors' Zoo

The proliferation of studies to identify risk factors that explain stock returns has opened the path to the main evolution of the CAPM: "multi-factor models." The first one to popularize this term was Ross (1976), who developed Arbitrage Pricing Theory (APT). According to this theory, multiple factors best explain security returns. An asset represents a portfolio of risk factors; therefore, its price corresponds to the weighted sum of the risk factors' price, where the weights are proportional to the exposure to each factor.

In the CAPM and its multi-factor extensions (Fama and French's three or five factors model, Carhart (1997), etc.), the risk factors are predefined. In the APT, the number and nature of these factors are undefined and can vary over time and across markets. This allows the creation of models in which the expected return of a financial asset is a function of various macroeconomic factors (including inflation, gross domestic product (GDP), gross national product (GNP), yield curves, etc.) or market indices.

The risk factors cannot be directly observed, therefore they must be identified and estimated with statistical techniques (such as principal components' analysis), where the factors are not pre-specified in advance. This triggers vigorous debates and relegates the challenge of building multi-factor models to essentially a statistical exercise, distinct from the asset's fundamental or economic valuation. If one wants to explore the issues with factor's estimation errors, Damodaran (2013), chapter 8, is an excellent place to start.

Since Fama and MacBeth (1973), hundreds of papers have been published to explain expected returns. The trend among those that seek to go beyond the original formulation of the CAPM is to adopt a multi-factor model. The most prevalent factors today are value, growth, size, momentum, low volatility, yield, and quality. However, the number of factors that have been identified (in the decade following Fama and French (2004)) has grown exponentially, since scholars and practitioners have the incentive to gain a reputation for discovering a new factor that explains returns. Cochrane (2011) warned that this body of literature has created a "zoo of new factors," populated with all sorts of creatures: "at current production rates, in the near future we will have more sources of empirically 'identified' risk than stock returns to price with these factors—the so-called factors' zoo phenomenon" Bryzgalova et al. (2019, p. 3).

To provide a map for this ecosystem, Harvey et al. (2016) and Harvey and Liu (2019) have created a census of the zoo, where all the known factors (almost 400 factors published in top academic journals) are classified and traced in terms of the literature that generated them.

Forward-Looking Alternatives

All the ramifications of the CAPM illustrated so far have one thing in common. They are backward-looking because the model predicts expected return based on stock return's past behavior. There is a vast literature that warns about the dangers of this approach, emphasizing the fact that past prices are not a good indication of future risks. Therefore, an alternative body of literature has grown to study forward-looking models.

In asset valuation, a key element is the cost of equity, which can be estimated with a forward-looking technique in different ways. The first way is to solve the dividend discount model (DDM) for the cost of equity, assuming that the present value is the market price and forecasting somehow future dividends. This technique is not recommended to value a company since it would lead to circular reasoning: the starting assumption is that the current value is the market price, therefore we would obtain that as a result of the valuation. Instead, the resulting cost of equity (either of the individual company or of the sector it belongs to) can be used as a benchmark. For example, Damodaran (2013) has developed a well-known technique to estimate the market-implied cost of equity of a sector, against which we can compare a beta estimated with the CAPM. There are various similar approaches based on reverse engineering the discounted cashflow model (DCM), accounting based methods, and so on. The reference for this approach is Frank and Shen (2016). The weakest side of the market-implied alternatives is the difficulty of estimating future dividends or cash flows. Some scholars attempted to address that challenge by using equity analysts' estimates, but we know those analysts' projections are biased since they tend to overstate the long-term growth of earnings or dividends.

A second way is to use derivative prices to estimate beta (option-implied beta). This family of techniques still relies on the original CAPM idea that expected returns can be estimated based on one or more betas, but instead of estimating betas using regressions on past prices, they rely on option prices. There is a body of literature dedicated to this approach. For example, according to Hollstein and Prokopczuk (2016), a combination of option-implied beta and historical beta outperforms all other techniques. Baule et al. (2016) have found that the predictive performance of implied beta estimators is superior if the time horizon is short (one month), or if options market activity is high.

Conclusions: The CAPM Condrum

Despite its shortcomings and all the available alternatives, the CAPM remains the most widely used method for estimating the cost of equity and for making investment decisions.

Brotherson et al. (2013) surveyed nineteen corporates,[1] ten financial advisors and investment bankers,[2] and the six main textbooks. Among their conclusions, two takeaways stand out: i) the CAPM was the dominant model, and only one respondent did not use the CAPM; ii) the variety of cost of equity estimations from different providers is stunning,

[1] AmerisourceBergen, Caterpillar, Chevron, Coca Cola, Costco Wholesale, IBM, International Paper, Intuit, Johnson Controls, PepsiCo, Qualcomm, Sysco, Target, Texas Instruments, Union Pacific, United Technologies, UPS, W.W. Grainger, Walt Disney.

[2] Bank of America Merrill Lynch, Barclays Capital, Credit Suisse, Deutsche Bank AG, Evercore Partners, Goldman Sachs & Co., Greenhill & Co, LLC, JP Morgan, Lazard, Morgan Stanley, UBS.

which is an indicator of how complex and prone to errors are the techniques to estimate beta.

The CAPM is also the preferred model for classroom use in MBA and other advanced finance courses, as Fernandez (2020) confirmed. Finally, the CAPM is still the reference model in courtrooms. For example, Dane (2014, p. 62) shows that when facing the dilemma about which valuation model to use, the Delaware Chancery Court (regarded as a reference for disputes over valuation-related issues associated with merger, acquisition, and recapitalization) did not accept results from alternatives to the CAPM, since they "are not well accepted by mainstream corporate finance theory."

Brotherson et al. (2013) remind us that in business, we measure with a micrometer, mark with chalk and cut with an axe. In the end, a financial analyst and a portfolio manager need a number (cost of equity) to make a decision. Despite decades of development of sophisticated alternatives to the CAPM, the complexity of these alternatives and the lack of consensus in the academic community mean that an imperfect and even erroneous reference like the CAPM is better than nothing.

This is probably the reason why a commentator cited in Grabowski and Pratt (2014, p. 220) said: "In spite of the lack of empirical support, the CAPM is still the preferred model for classroom use in MBA and other managerial finance courses. In a way it reminds us of cartoon characters like Wile E. Coyote who have the ability to come back to original shape after being blown to pieces or hammered out of shape."

References

Ang, A. (2014). *Asset Management: A Systematic Approach to Factor Investing.* Oxford University Press.

Asness, C. S. (1994). *Variables That Explain Stock Returns.* Ph.D. Dissertation, University of Chicago.

Asness, C. (2016, February 5). *Fama on Momentum.* Cliff's Perspective, AQR Insights. Retrieved January 9, 2021, from https://www.aqr.com/Insights/Perspectives/Fama-on-Momentum

Banz, R. (1981). The Relationship Between Return and Market Value of Common Stock. *Journal of Financial Economics, 9*, 3–18.

Basu, S. (1977). Investment Performance of Common Stocks in Relation to Their Price-Earnings Ratios: A Test of the Efficient Market Hypothesis. *Journal of Finance, 12*(3), 129–156.

Baule, R., Korn, O., & Saßning, S. (2016, June). Which Beta Is Best? On the Information Content of Option-Implied Betas. *European Financial Management*. European Financial Management Association, *22*(3), 450–483.
Bernstein, P. L. (2007). *Capital Ideas Evolving (a review)*. Wiley.
Bhandari, L. C. (1988). Debt/Equity Ratio and Expected Common Stock Returns: Empirical Evidence. *Journal of Finance.*, *43*(2), 507–528.
Black, F. (1972). Capital Market Equilibrium with Restricted Borrowing. *Journal of Business*, *45*(3), 444–454.
Black, F., Jensen, M. C., & Scholes, M. S. (1972). The Capital Asset Pricing Model: Some Empirical Tests. In M. Jensen (Ed.), *Studies in the Theory of Capital Markets*. Praeger.
Bryzgalova, S., Huang, J., & Julliard, C. (2019, November 18). *Bayesian Solutions for the Factor Zoo: We Just Ran Two Quadrillion Models*. Available at SSRN: https://ssrn.com/abstract=3481736
Brotherson, T., Eades, K., Harris, R., & Higgins, R. (2013). "'Best Practices' in Estimating the Cost of Capital: An Update". *Journal of Applied Finance*, *23*(1), 15–33.
Buffett, W. E. (1984). The Superinvestors of Graham-and-Doddsville. *Hermes, the Columbia Business School Magazine*.
Carhart, M. M. (1997). On Persistence in Mutual Fund Performance. *The Journal of Finance*, *52*(1), 57–82.
Cochrane, J. H. (2011). Presidential Address: Discount Rates. *Journal of Finance*, *66*, 1047–1108.
Damodaran, A. (2013). Equity Risk Premiums (ERP): Determinants, Estimation and Implications–The 2013 Edition. In *Managing and Measuring Risk: Emerging Global Standards and Regulations After the Financial Crisis* (pp. 343–455).
Dane, C. G. (2014, SUMMER). Valuation-Related Issues as Decided by the Delaware Chancery Court. *Judicial Decision Insights*.
DeBondt, W. F. M., & Thaler, R. H. (1987, July). Further Evidence on Investor Overreaction and Stock Market Seasonality. *The Journal of Finance*.
Fama, E. F., & French, K. R. (1992). The Cross-Section of Expected Stock Returns. *Journal of Finance*, *47*(2), 427–465.
Fama, E. F., & French, K. R. (2004). The Capital Asset Pricing Model: Theory and Evidence. *Journal of Economic Perspectives*, *18*(3), 25–46.
Fama, E. F., & French, K. R. (2015). A Five-Factor Asset Pricing Model. *Journal of Financial Economics*, *116*, 1–22.
Fama, E. F., & MacBeth, J. (1973). Risk, Return and Equilibrium: Some Empirical Tests. *Journal of Political Economy*, *8*(1973), 607–636.
Fernandez, P. (2020). The Equity Premium in 150 Textbooks. *Journal of New Finance*, *1*(3), Article 3. https://doi.org/10.46671/2521-2486.1009
Frank, M., & Shen, T. (2016). "Investment and the Weigthed Average Cost of Capital". *Journal of Financial Economics*, *119*(2), 300–315.

Grabowski, R. J., & Pratt, S. P. (2014). *Cost of Capital: Applications and Examples*. Wiley.

Graham, B., & Dodd, D. (1934). *Security Analysis*. Whittlesey House.

Harvey, C. R., & Liu, Y. (2019, February 25). *A Census of the Factor Zoo*. Available at SSRN: https://ssrn.com/abstract=3341728

Harvey, C., Liu, Y., & Zhu, H. (2016). … and the Cross-Section of Expected Returns. *Review of Financial Studies, 29*(1), 5–68.

Haugen, R. (1995). *The New Finance: The Case against Efficient Markets*. Prentice Hall.

Hollstein, F., & Prokopczuk, M. (2016). Estimating Beta. *The Journal of Financial and Quantitative Analysis, 51*(4), 1437–1466.

Jegadeesh, N., & Titman, S. (1993). Returns to Buying Winners and Selling Losers: Implications for Stock Market Efficiency. *Journal of Finance, 48*, 65–91.

Kothari, S. P., Shanken, J., & Sloan, R. G. (1995). Another Look at the Cross-Section of Expected Stock Returns. *Journal of Finance, 50*(1), 185–224.

Lakonishok, J., Shleifer, A., & Vishny, R. W. (1994). Contrarian Investment, Extrapolation, and Risk. *Journal of Finance, 49*, 1541–1578.

Lintner, J. (1965). The Valuation of Risk Assets and the Selection of Risky Investments in Stock Portfolios and Capital Budgets. *Review of Economics and Statistics., 47*(1), 13–37.

Lowenstein, R. (1995). "Buffett: The Making of an American Capitalist". Random House.

MacKenzie, D. (2006). *An Engine, Not a Camera: How Financial Models Shape Markets*. The MIT Press.

Markowitz, H. M. (2005). Market Efficiency: A Theoretical Distinction and so What? *Financial Analysts Journal, 61*(5), 17–30.

Mossin, J. (1966, October). Equilibrium in a Capital Asset Market. *Econometrica, 34*(4), 768–783.

Roll, R. (1977). A Critique of the Asset Pricing Theory's Tests. Part I: On Past and Potential Testability of the Theory. *Journal of Financial Economics, 4*, 129–176.

Rosenberg, B., Reid, K., & Lanstein, R. (1985, Spring). Persuasive Evidence of Market Inefficiency. *Journal of Portfolio Management, 11*, 9–17.

Ross, S. A. (1976). The Arbitrage Theory of Capital Asset Pricing. *Journal of Finance, 13*(3), 341–360.

Sharpe, W. F. (1964). Capital Asset Prices: A Theory of Market Equilibrium under Conditions of Risk. *Journal of Finance, 19*(3), 425–442.

Stambaugh, R. F. (1982). On the Exclusion of Assets from Tests of the Two-Parameter Model: A Sensitivity Analysis. *Journal of Financial Economics., 10*(3), 237–268.

Stattman, D. (1980). Book Values and Stock Returns. *The Chicago MBA: A Journal of Selected Papers, 4*, 25–45.

A Brief Note on Bank Circulation Credit and Time Preference

Thorsten Polleit

The Austrian Business Cycle Theory (ABCT) points out the impact of an increase in bank circulation credit (credit that is not backed by real savings) on economic activity; that is, how it affects the intertemporal choices of market agents in terms of parceling out income on consumption, savings, and investment, and what effect it has on prices, production, and employment (Mises, 1998 [1949], pp. 535–583; Hayek, 1933 [1929]; Rothbard, 2006 [1973], pp. 213–240; Garrison, 2001, pp. 57–83; Huerta de Soto, 2006, pp. 347–384). ABCT holds that an increase in bank circulation credit lowers the market-clearing interest rate *below* society's *true* time preference rate. This causes a decline in savings, a rise in consumption and, in addition, encourages new investment. Taken together, this leads to an economic "boom" which, however, must come to an end (turn into "bust").

Important questions in this context are: *How does the injection of additional credit and fiat money, created through bank credit expansion, affect*

T. Polleit (✉)
University of Bayreuth, Bayreuth, Germany
e-mail: thorsten.polleit@uni-bayreuth.de

D. Howden, P. Bagus (eds.), *The Emergence of a Tradition: Essays in Honor of Jesús Huerta de Soto, Volume I*,
https://doi.org/10.1007/978-3-031-17414-8_19

the rate of societal time preference? and *How does the societal time preference rate relate to the market interest rate in the course of a boom-and-bust-cycle?* This article argues that the expansion of bank circulation credit—which is a key feature of a fiat money system—*artificially raises* societal time preference, something that all too often goes by the board or is ignored in illustrations of the ABCT. This detail deserves attention as it helps to understand not only the economic but also the wider social-political consequences of bank circulation credit expansion—namely the distortive "revaluation of all values" it entails and which affect all fields of human action.

Time Preference and the Originary Interest Rate

The irrefutably true proposition that "humans act" means that acting man substitutes a more satisfactory state of affairs by a less satisfactory state of affairs (Mises, 1998 [1949], part One, and pp. 480–487). It implies that human action takes *time* (Rothbard, 2009 [1962], pp. 13–17). Time is a *requisite* for achieving *ends*, and there is no human action possible that wouldn't take time. If and when human action does not require time, an actor's ends would be achieved instantaneously. This, however, would mean that human action is no longer possible—which is, (praxeo-)logically speaking, impossible. As a means, time is *scarce*. This is why man prefers his ends to be achieved in the shortest possible time—which is expressive of the universal fact of *time preference.*[1]

The *originary interest rate* is the manifestation of time preference and as such a category of inherent in any human valuation (Mises, 1998 [1949], p. 523): "Originary interest is the ratio of the value assigned to want-satisfaction in the immediate future and the value assigned to want-satisfaction in remoter periods of the future." The originary interest rate (or the pure time preference rate) is the price discount future want satisfactions suffer—from the viewpoint of the individual human actor—vis-à-vis present satisfactions.[2] Time preference and the originary interest rate are always and everywhere positive; one cannot, for (praxeo-)logical

[1] The term time preference was introduced by Frank A. Fetter in his 1915 Economic Principles (Fetter, 1915, p. 236). Rothbard (1977, p. 4) credits Fetter to be the first economist to explain the interest rate phenomenon solely by time preference.

[2] For a detailed discussion of the pure time preference theory and its critique, see Herbener (2011).

reason, think that the originary interest rate could ever fall to zero, let alone become negative (Mises, 1998, p. 524; Polleit, 2020, p. 167; Polleit, 2015).

This can also be exemplified by taking recourse to the *Modus* (or: *Tollendo*) *Tollens* (Cohen & Nagel, 2002, pp. 101–105): An accepted conditional statement says "if *p* then *q*." If, however, we observe "not-*q*," then we infer the negation of the antecedent, that is "not-*p*." Assume *p* represents the statement "Humans act" and *q* the statement "The originary interest rate is always and everywhere positive." If we say "*non-q*" (meaning "The originary interest rate is *not* positive"), then *non-p* must hold (meaning "Humans cannot act"). This, however, is (praxeo-)logically false.

If people prefer to consume a great deal and save little of their income, their time preference and thus their originary interest rates are *high*; and if they prefer to save a great deal of their income and consume little, their time preference and thus their originary interest rates are *low* (Hoppe, 2006a, pp. 1–3; Rothbard, 2006, pp. 233–235). In other words, a high ratio of consumption to savings (out of income) is expressive of high time preference and a high originary interest rate; and a small ratio of consumption to savings signals a low time preference and thus low originary interest rate. In what follows, the impact of an increase in so-called *bank circulation credit* on the societal time preference rate will be analyzed.

Bank Circulation Credit Expansion and Time Preference

Bank *circulation credit* denotes bank credit that is not backed by real savings (Mises, 1998 [1949], p. 430; 1953, pp. 268–69 and pp. 271–72). If and when bank circulation credit is expanded, the outstanding quantity of money (*fiduciary media*) is increased. Bank *commodity credit*, in contrast, denotes a form of credit that is 100 percent backed by real savings (money proper); its expansion doesn't increase the outstanding quantity of money in the economy but merely changes its composition.

The societal time preference and—as its manifestation—the societal originary interest rate are the results of the aggregation of all individual supply schedules for savings and all individual demand schedules for investment, respectively, in the *time market*, where present goods are exchanged against future goods (Rothbard, 2009 [1962], pp. 375–389).

To illustrate this, let us assume that people have a *given income*. They can use their income for consumption *C* and/or savings *S*, and savings will be used for investment *I*. *S* is positively and *I* negatively related to the interest rate *i* in Fig. 1.

The market-clearing interest rate i^* is determined by the interplay of *S* and *I*. In equilibrium, savings amount to S^* and investment to I^* (right-hand side of the graph), while the corresponding level of consumption is C^* (with the axis in the left-hand side of the graph running from right to left). The market-clearing interest rate i^* is expressive of the societal time preference rate. It ensures that there are sufficient savings available to realize investments. In other words: i^* puts the economy firmly on the road toward higher material prosperity.

As a first step, let us now assume a *decline* in peoples' time preference (people become less present-oriented and more future-oriented). In Fig. 1, *S* moves to the right, to *S*': For any given level of the interest rate, savings are now higher, so that savings and investment increase to S_1 and I_1, respectively, while the consumption schedule *C* moves to the right, to *C*'; the amount of consumption declines to C_1. The new market-clearing interest rate—which is in line with the *true* societal time preference rate—is i_1.

As a second step we assume that there is an increase in bank circulation credit, as illustrated in Fig. 2. The increase in bank credit moves *S* to the right, to *S*' (which is $S+\Delta M$). As *I* is unchanged, the market-clearing

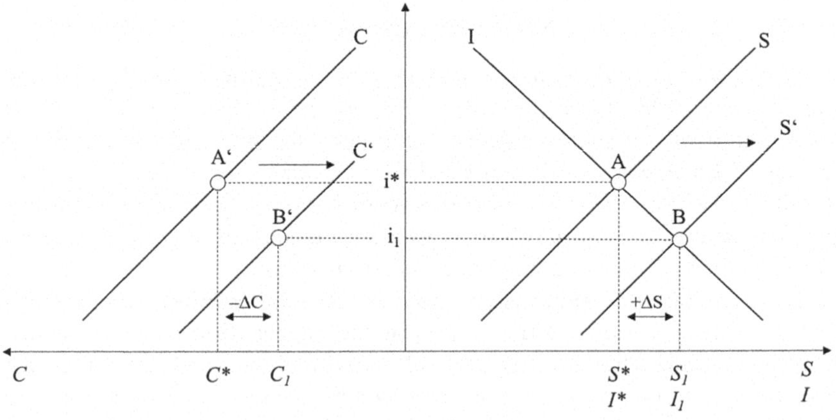

Fig. 1 Decline in time preference

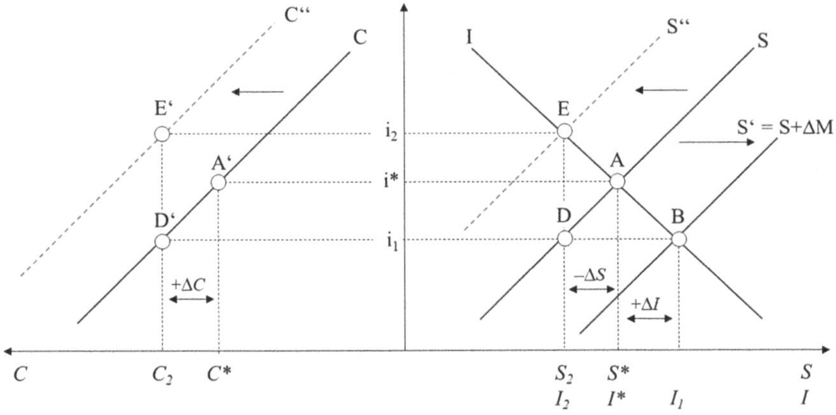

Fig. 2 Increase in bank circulation credit and the societal time preference rate

interest rate falls to i_1. Accordingly, savings decline from S^* to S_2, while consumption rises from C^* to C_2. In addition, investment increases from I^* to I_1. This sets into motion the notorious boom-and-bust-cycle. *What has happened to peoples' time preference rate?* The answer is: *It has effectively gone up* (Rothbard, 2006 [1973], pp. 233–234).

The graphical explanation is as follows (Garrison, 2001, pp. 67–69): The drop in the market-clearing interest rate from i^* to i_1 lowers savings from S^* to S_2. For a given level of income, this implies a rise in consumption, which increases from C^* to C_2. However, C_2/S_2 implies a higher societal time preference and originary interest rate than C^*/S^*, for $C_2/S_2 > C^*/S^*$. Yet, C_2/S_2 is accompanied by i_1, which is lower than i^* at C^*/S^*. How can that be? To provide an intelligible answer to this question, an additional analytical step is required.

The decline in savings from S^* to S_2, caused by an increase in bank circulation credit, implies that the savings schedule S moves to the left, to S", and this is accompanied by the consumption schedule C shifting to the left, to C". The resulting (artificially increased) societal time preference rate is therefore i_2 ($>i^* >i_1$). In other words, the issuance of circulation credit makes people behave *as if* their time preference has actually increased (raising consumption and lowering savings), but in truth it has not!

In most illustrations of the ABCT it is shown that under bank circulation credit expansion, the market interest rate falls below the original societal time preference rate, namely to i_1 from i^*. However, this does not give the full picture. It overlooks that the issuance of bank circulation credit *artificially raises* the societal time preference rate to i_2. Bank circulation credit expansion does not only drive a wedge between the *given* societal time preference rate and the market interest rate, it actually also pushes up peoples' societal time preference rate.

Market agents' dispositions of parceling out their income in terms of savings, consumption, and investment correspond to the market-clearing interest rate, that is i_1 in Fig. 2. i_2 can be interpreted as the *acted-upon* social time preference rate: It is the *unobservable* social time preference rate that corresponds to the increase in *actual* consumption that comes at the expense of *actual* savings. It stands for the time preference rate that *actually* governs peoples' actions if and when the market interest rate has been artificially lowered as a result of the issuance of fiat money.

As a final note, the exposition above can actually reconcile the ABCT as interpreted by Ludwig von Mises and Friedrich August Hayek (Garrison, 2004). In his interpretation of the ABCT, Mises stressed "overconsumption and malinvestment" as a result of the artificial lowering of the interest rate (Mises, 1998 [1949], p. 560, 562). The term "forced savings," as used widely by Hayek in this context, can simply be understood as *investment in excess of savings* (Hayek, 1975 [1939], p. 197). From this point of view, "overconsumption and forced saving′ are cognates," as Garrison (2004) rightly points out.

Revaluation of All Values

The issuance of bank circulation credit leads to a far-reaching "revaluation of all values," to borrow a term from the German philosopher Friedrich W. Nietzsche (1844–1900).[3] It makes people value want satisfaction in the present even more highly than want satisfaction in the future. Such an *artificial* increase in societal time preference does not only affect the economic and financial sphere (as shown earlier) but all forms of human action.

Human action is inextricably linked to the phenomenon of time preference and its manifestation, the originary interest rate. It should be noted here that time preference and the originary interest rate are not confined to a monetary economy. They also exist in a non-monetary, or barter

[3] "Revalution of all values" (in German: "Umwertung aller Werte") is a catch-phrase and a central term in Nietzsche's philosophy and moral critique.

economy; and they determine the valuation of monetary as well as non-monetary goods (or want satisfactions, for that matter). That said, the truth is that changes in time preference do affect peoples' valuation of all walks of life (Howden & Kampe, 2016).[4]

As was shown earlier, an artificial lowering of the market interest rates—brought about through circulation credit expansion—translates into an increase in peoples' time preference, manifested as a rise of their originary interest rates. This, in turn, pushes further up the (subjective) value individual actors ascribe to present monetary and non-monetary goods relative to future monetary and non-monetary goods. From this we can deduce a number of general conclusions regarding how fiat money affects the value people see in various modes of action.

For instance, in a fiat money regime it will be less attractive for the individual to spend hours learning (compared with the situation in a commodity money system), as it means reducing present consumption at the expense of future consumption. As a result, the quality of general education can be expected to decline. Also, starting a family becomes more self-sacrificing and burdensome—as parents must forego highly valued present want satisfaction, and so the family as an institution is weakened in society.

What is more, for people whose time preference has increased divorce increasingly seems to be an appealing way out of current relationship problems—which otherwise could only be solved by time-consuming efforts. Furthermore, having good manners—saying good morning, helping a stranger across the street, getting out of somebody's way, and so on—is considered less rewarding in a "high time preference society," as it means restricting present want satisfaction with any potential rewards occurring at a future point in time (and is therefore less valued).

The artificially lowering of the market interest rate in a fiat money system has also a bearing on how people economize scarce natural resources. It does not only cause a boom which drives up the demand for scare natural resources, it also leads to wasteful usage of them—for the boom leads to malinvestment. In addition, the owners of scarce non-permanent resources (say, gravel pits or oil fields) wish to maximize the capital value of their property (Rothbard, 2009 [1962], pp. 488). A rise in property

[4] The authors provide, inter alia, an in-depth discussion of the factors affecting time preference (i.e., personal factors, biological factors, environmental (or external) factors, institutional factors, economic institutions, juridical institutions, and moral institutions (pp. 386–391)); they also discuss the effects of changes in time preference (pp. 391–393).

owners' time preference therefore means that they will increasingly exploit their resources in the present at the expense of resources available in the future. To put it differently: The artificial increase in peoples' time preference (as a direct result of the fiat money system) speeds up the depletion of scarce resources, posing an additional burden for the environment.

Finally, let us have a brief thought about *aggression* and *war*. Any state seeks to increase its power, to expand its territory—by military means or, as a common effort pursed by the states themselves, by reducing the number of states (Hoppe, 2006b, p. 107). Having the option to create new money through bank circulation credit expansion, it becomes relatively appealing for the state to become aggressive and go to war (Mises, 1919, esp. pp. 123–134).

This becomes obvious if one compares the economic consequences of credit financing in a bank circulation credit regime and a commodity credit regime. In a commodity credit regime, the state's demand for loans would (other things being equal) drive up the market interest rate. This, in turn, does not only increase the state's costs of borrowing, but it also hurts private investment and employment and lowers income. Consumers and producers do not enjoy this much!

Things are different in a bank circulation credit regime. As the state's demand for credit goes up, so does the supply of credit—and the market interest rate remains unchanged.[5] The additional demand from the state, accompanied by an increase in the quantity of money and an unchanged market interest rate, sets into motion a *boom*. Consumers as well as entrepreneurs enjoy this, and their opposition to making war will be greatly reduced!

A Case Against Fiat Money

The purpose of revisiting ABCT was to make explicit that bank credit expansion—which is at the heart of today's fiat money regime—directly affects the societal time preference rate. Bank circulation credit expansion not only lowers the market interest rate vis-à-vis peoples' original time preference rate, setting into motion a boom must end in a bust, but it also raises peoples' time preference.

[5] This, of course, assumes that neither inflation nor risk premia, which are typically components of the market interest rate, go up. In any case, in a fiat money system the central bank can, if deemed necessary, fix the market interest rate at a politically desired level.

In other words, if and when manipulating the market interest rate, central banks arrogate to themselves the power to influence peoples' valuations of present good versus future goods. It is in that sense that central banks' interest rate policies amount to basically a "revaluation of all values": Through bank credit expansion people are made to be more present-oriented and less future-oriented.

A fiat money induced boom leads to impoverishment in the sense that output does no longer correspond to satisfying consumer demand in the best possible way or that it causes a waste of scarce resources—compared with a state of affairs in which bank circulation credit expansion had not taken place (Mises, 1998 [1949], p. 562). Both outcomes are the inexorable result of an artificially increased societal time preference caused by monetary policy.

A (praxeo-)logical analysis thus reveals that a fiat money regime hampers rather than advances economic (and cultural) progress: For it lowers peoples' savings to the benefit of higher consumption, thereby hampering capital accumulation, productivity gains and higher real incomes in the future: The economy is actually prevented from living up to its full potential; people would be better off without bank circulation credit expansion.

As the analysis in this article has pointed out the problem is not just an artificially lowered market interest rate as a result of bank circulation credit expansion. The actual problem is that bank circulation credit expansion raises peoples' time preference and, at the same time, lowers market interest rates. What happens is trouble—and this insight can be interpreted as yet another argument, a case against fiat money.

References

Cohen, M., & Nagel, E. (2002 [1934]). *An Introduction to Logic and Scientific Method*. Simon Publications.

Fetter, F. (1915). *Economic Principles*. The Century Company.

Garrison, R. W. (2004). Overconsumption and Forced Saving in the Mises-Hayek Theory of the Business Cycle. *History of Political Economy, 36*(2).

Garrison, R. W. (2001). *Time and Money. The Macroeconomics of Capital Structure. Foundations of the Market Economy*. Routledge.

Hayek, F. A. (1933 [1929]). *Monetary Theory and the Trade Cycle*. Harcourt, Brace.

Hayek, F. A. (1975 [1939]). *Profits, Interest and Investment*. Augustus M. Kelley.

Herbener, J. (Ed.). (2011). *The Pure Time Preference Theory of Interest*. Ludwig von Mises Institute.

Hoppe, H.-H. (2006a). *Democracy. The God That Failed. The Economics and Politics of Monarchy, Democracy, and Natural Order*. Transaction Publisher.
Hoppe, H.-H. (2006b). *Banking, Nation States, and International Politics: A Sociological Reconstruction of the Present Order. The Economics and Ethics of Private Property. Studies in Political Economy and Philosophy* (2nd ed., pp. 77–116). Ludwig von Mises Institute.
Howden, D., & Kampe, J. (2016). Time Preference and the Process of Civilization. *International Journal of Social Economics, 43*(4), 382–399.
Huerta de Soto, J. (2006). *Money, Bank Credit, and Economic Cycles*. Ludwig von Mises Institute.
Mises, L. v. (1998 [1949]). *Human Action: A Treatise on Economics*. The Scholar's Edition. Ludwig von Mises Institute.
Mises, L. v. (1953). *Theory of Money and Credit*. Yale University Press.
Mises, L. v. (1919). *Nation, Staat, und Wirtschaft. Beiträge zur Politik und Geschichte der Zeit*. Manzsche Verlags- und Universitäts-Buchhandlung.
Polleit, T. (2020). *Der Antikapitalist. Ein Weltverbesserer, der keiner ist*. Finanzbuch Verlag.
Polleit, T. (2015, March 21). The "Natural Interest Rate" Is Always Positive and Cannot Be Negative. *Mises Daily Articles*. Ludwig von Mises Institute.
Rothbard, M. N. (2009 [1962]). *Man, Economy, and State*. The Scholar's Edition. Ludwig von Mises Institute.
Rothbard, M. N. (2006 [1973]). *For A New Liberty. The Libertarian Manifesto*. Ludwig von Mises Institute.
Rothbard, M. N. (1977). Introduction to Capital, Interest, and Rent. In F. A. Fetter (Ed.), *Essays in the Theory of Distribution*. Sheed Andrews and McMeel, Inc..

Dynamic Efficiency, Economic Development, and the Ethics of Property

Shawn Ritenour

Economic development is a process. It is not a static state, nor is it a momentary snapshot. It is not a timeless equilibrium. It is a process that plays out in real history, as real people interact with each other and their environment over time. By the very nature of economic development, therefore, a general theory explaining economic progress must be holistic.

I have appreciated Jesús Huerta de Soto from afar since 2007 when I read his *Money, Bank Credit, and Economic Cycles* and began using it in my Intermediate Macroeconomics course at Grove City College.

The more of his work I read, the more I became impressed with Professor Huerta de Soto as a model scholar. He is an excellent researcher and extremely well read. In his work he shows himself to be both an outstanding analyst as well as superior synthesizer. And he is never afraid to defend his intellectual convictions wherever they may lead.

S. Ritenour (✉)
Grove City College, Grove City, PA, USA
e-mail: ritenoursr@gcc.edu

D. Howden, P. Bagus (eds.), *The Emergence of a Tradition: Essays in Honor of Jesús Huerta de Soto, Volume I*,
https://doi.org/10.1007/978-3-031-17414-8_20

Developing such a theory requires effort both at analysis and synthesis. Understanding the process of economic progress requires identifying and explaining the various processes that contribute to economic prosperity. Such research necessitates investigating the various sources that contribute to prosperity in isolation. This is a work of analysis.

However, because economic development is an historical process, a good general theory of economic prosperity needs also to explain why and how all these processes must work together to generate economic progress. This is a necessary work of synthesis.

Such a theory both helps to understand and provide forward guidance for those who desire to enable societies to improve or maintain their standard of living. A satisfactory general theory of economic progress, therefore, is both able to identify the various causal factors that contribute to development and explain how they do so through time in the real world. A good, causal-realist theory of economic prosperity additionally allows for identifying and explaining the nature and consequences of institutions necessary for the effective flourishing of the identified processes.

As will be seen, such a general, causal-realist theory of economic prosperity provides a sharp contrast with modern neoclassical growth theory. An Austrian understanding of economic progress derived from pillars of the Austrian tradition such as Menger, Böhm-Bawerk, Mises, Hayek, and Rothbard results in a theory of what Huerta de Soto (2009) calls dynamic efficiency.

The theory of dynamic efficiency understands economic progress as a result from entrepreneurial creativity and coordination. In any

---

What made him most appealing was that in all of this he was a humane economist. His economic analysis is always firmly connected to the action of real human beings. He also, importantly, does not neglect ethics. While understanding that economic laws are value free, describing what is, he nevertheless recognizes that economic policies, institutions, and even the actions of humans within society all have ethical components.

Huerta de Soto is a Christian Scholar and gentleman. He takes all his callings—spiritual, familial, entrepreneurial, and intellectual—very seriously. His scholarly, academic, and commercial successes are tremendous, providing for a persistently expanding legacy of sound economic analysis. I was thrilled to personally meet Jesús not long ago at an economics conference and learned experientially that, while enjoying the fruit of civilization, he is not ensnared by self-importance. To me he remains generous and encouraging, and the picture of what a scholar and gentlemen should be.

entrepreneurial process, new maladjustments will always appear. A certain amount of waste is inevitable and inherent in any human endeavor and that includes the market economy. Society may not achieve static Pareto optimality, but all its members may nevertheless profit if entrepreneurial creativity constantly improves everyone's productive possibilities with a continuous, creative flow of new ends and means which, prior to their entrepreneurial discovery, had yet even to be envisioned (Espinosa, 2020). Additionally, the same entrepreneurial force which propels dynamic efficiency through the creation and discovery of new profit opportunities is precisely the one which achieves the highest degree of static efficiency humanly possible at each moment by coordinating pre-existing maladjustments.

Sources of Prosperity

Economic theory has identified four sources of economic progress: the market division of labor, capital accumulation, technological advance, and entrepreneurship. From very early in history people have recognized that cooperation in the division of labor contributes to prosperity (Plato, 1888, pp. 50–53; Cantillon, 2009; Chafuen, 2003, p. 74).

There are generally two ways of increasing one's satisfaction through the use of economic goods: violence or voluntarism. Violent acquisition of goods is socially destructive, breeding enmity, fear, and bitterness at best and injury and death at worst. Thankfully for those who prefer civilization to barbarism, a more socially productive path to prosperity is peaceful production and voluntary exchange.

Production combines factors of production and transforms them into a new economic good (Shapiro, 2007, pp. 59–61). As such, while creative, it is never absolutely new creation, *ex nihilo*, but rather transforms previously existing matter is such a way that it can satisfy a want.

The use of factors of production including labor are limited in their ability to provide continuous production due to their finiteness and the law of returns. There are technical limitations constraining how many units of a variable factor can be helpfully combined with a fixed number of complementary factors. Additionally, there are only so many able workers in existence at any one time and there is a finite number of hours each can work before they must rest. Further increases in productivity through the application of labor and other factors must be found through something else than merely increasing their magnitude.

One such source is the division of labor which opens the door to increased productivity by allowing people to specialize according to efficiency. The market division of labor as a social phenomenon is the historical manifestation of the Law of Association: each factor of production is most efficient in some line of production. This law is a development and universalization of the Law of Comparative Advantage by Mises (1998, pp. 158–63) and applies not only to labor, but also to land and capital goods. As each factor is employed according to efficiency, people will reap the most output from the resources used. This increased productivity results in higher real incomes and societal wealth.

Note, however, that people can only benefit from the division of labor if they are free to exchange the goods that they produce. Perhaps the best sentence Smith (1965, p. 17) gave us in *The Wealth of Nations* is "the division of labor is limited by the extent of market." To extend division of labor, we only need to bring others into the market. Specializing according to efficiency increases personal productivity and, hence, social productivity, providing for higher real incomes, increased purchasing power, and increased demand for a wider variety of goods. As the extent of the market increases, the division of labor can expand, which further increases productivity, wealth, and standards of living. This in turn provides for a further extension of the market, which enables even more specialization and division of labor.

A second source of economic prosperity, which is the other side of the market division of labor coin, is the formation of capital. Capital is the sum of monetary value of the whole complex of goods used by a firm in production A firm's capital is, therefore, intimately related to its stock of capital goods (Mises, 1998, p. 261, p. 500). Before capital goods can be used, however, they must be produced. To accumulate capital, people must be willing to delay present consumption so that they will have resources available to invest in production of capital goods. The lower are people's time preferences, the more they will save and invest, accumulating more capital goods, resulting in increased productivity, incomes, and wealth (Mises, 1998, pp. 292–97; Rothbard, 2004, pp. 626–27; Garrison, 2001, pp. 57–83; Huerta de Soto, 2006, pp. 317–44).

Within the production structure, producers must make many choices about capital goods. They can arrange production to be more or less capital-intensive. Each factor has a different degree of specificity. Factor durability also needs to be considered. All of these are decision variables chosen by the producer.

The nature of the capital structure points to an important difference between the Austrian understanding of the economic order and the approach of modern macro (Foss, 2012, pp. 154–66). The aggregation inherent in Keynesian, Monetarist, and Neoclassical models obscures all the insights from Austrian capital theory (Huerta de Soto, 2006, pp. 509–83). Economic capital is a structure of heterogeneous capital goods with different uses, specificity, and durability appraised at their market value. To be effective, every capital good must be used in the right place, at the right time, in the right combination with other complementary factors. What is usually called the macroeconomy is really a general *economic order*. Capital, therefore, is neither best represented by a generic stock nor a flow, but as a structure in which all parts are interrelated through production decisions made at every stage.

With more capital investment usually comes better technology, which is a third contributor to economic prosperity. Technological advance aids in economic growth, because it allows the same quantity of factors to yield more output. It has presently become almost axiomatic in the mainstream literature that almost all economic development and all continued economic growth is the result of improved technology (Abramovitz, 1956; Helpman, 2004, pp. 19–54; Solow, 2000).

In order for economic progress to continue over time, however, it is important not to squander opportunities provided by technology and the capital in which it embodies. Wise entrepreneurship, consequently, is the fourth major contributor to economic development. Waste of resources is possible, because production decisions in the present are based on a forecast of uncertain future market conditions. If the producer forecasts incorrectly, he will use his capital making something people do not want and will not be able to sell his output at the price needed to cover his costs.

Entrepreneurs need to use economic calculation if they are to direct factors of production toward their most valued uses. Monetary market prices allow entrepreneurs to make meaningful comparisons of subjective value between different consumer and producer goods because money prices are all expressed in the same monetary unit. These same objective prices are determined by the subjective preferences of buyers and sellers. If the expected price of a final product is greater than the sum of the prices of the factors of production, the entrepreneur will produce that good. When entrepreneurs reap a profit, they do it precisely by providing those goods that people value the most in the least costly manner.

Economic Progress as a Process of Dynamic Efficiency

Economic progress occurs over time, and, therefore, it is more than an analytical puzzle to be solved. It is not a timeless static equilibrium condition. Economic development is the result of dynamic efficiency for two reasons, both of which are due to production taking place in the flux of time. Production must bridge the gap between the known present and an uncertain future. As such, profitable production requires successful entrepreneurship. Additionally, as Sudha Shenoy (2010, pp. 157–59; pp. 184–85) helpfully reminds us, economic progress is a real historical process. It is the product of the four sources of prosperity working together in specific ways in history resulting in higher standards of living for the society in question.

In explaining the actual process of economic development, therefore, we cannot neatly sever the components responsible for economic expansion from one another and find a single key that explains economic progress. Synthesis is required. A highly developed division of labor, for example, would be impossible without the accumulation and use of capital goods, and the specialized production within the market division of labor makes investing in more expensive, capital-intensive production economical viable (Shenoy, 2010, pp. 240–44).

Likewise, the necessary coordination of the market division of labor requires wise entrepreneurship. At the same time, in his pursuit of profit the entrepreneur must invest capital, and his capital goods all embody a specific level of technology.

It is important to recognize, however, that, contra-neoclassical growth theory, technology is not autonomous. Discovering and implementing better technology require research and development which requires saving and capital investment in laboratories, equipment, and prototypes (Mises, 1977, pp. 126–27). Additionally, in order to be operational, technology must always be bound up in real capital goods. Technological advance occurs as capital goods that wear out are replaced by capital goods embodying a higher level of technology.

Additionally, research, development, innovation, and the implementation of new technology are all entrepreneurial decisions. An increase in technological knowledge does not necessarily imply it is economical to use it. The decision to implement new technology is determined by the difference between the expected gains through more efficient production and the price of the new machine. Production decisions with respect to technology must also be coordinated with other investment decisions.

At the same time, capital *per se* never guarantees economic progress either. Capital does not "beget profit" (Mises, 1998, p. 265). Capital investment is profitable if it is wisely employed from the point of view of consumers. All of the coordination of production within the division of labor, the accumulation and application of capital goods, and the selection and use of specific technology require entrepreneurial judgment. Economic progress, then, is the happy consequence of a highly developed division of labor, taking advantage of an increasing stock of better capital goods, wisely invested by entrepreneurs.

The Importance of Institutions

That economic development is a process of dynamic efficiency implies that there are important social institutions necessary for the sources of prosperity to function together generating economic progress. If we want society to enjoy the fruit of economic expansion, we need social institutions that foster the development of the division of labor, the accumulation of capital, technological improvement, and successful entrepreneurship. We need what David Osterfeld (1992, pp. 221–30) calls the "enabling environment." How do social institutions aid in the process of dynamic efficiency? How do they provide the environment that enables economic progress?

Both Douglass North and Jesús Huerta de Soto see a key function of institutions to be that of reducing uncertainty. North (1986, p. 231; 1991, p. 97) views them as humanly devised constraints that structure repetitive social interaction. Following North, Acemoglu and Robinson (2008, 2) see three important features of institutions: (1) they are "humanly devised," not determined by things outside of human control, such as geography; (2) they are "the rules of the game" setting "constraints" on human behavior; and (3) their major effect will be through incentives.

Huerta de Soto (2009, p. 24; 2010, p. 44) simply defines an institution as "any repetitive pattern, rule, or model of conduct, regardless of its sphere" or "any generalized pattern of conduct or behavior." Such institutions are humanly devised, but they emerge as the result of a process of social interaction, without design by any single person. They are said to communicate a large quantity of practical knowledge. Such is the case regarding language, morality, law, and money. Institutions reduce uncertainty resulting from the complexity of magnitude of transactions in a highly developed market division of labor, thereby increasing dynamic efficiency. This helps explain why societies adhering to stronger ethical principles that support certain institutions tend to be more dynamically efficient.

What are these certain institutions? The functioning of the process of dynamic efficiency requires the social institutions of private property and sound money. Remember that a prerequisite for participating in and benefitting from the market division of labor is voluntary exchange. People can only benefit from the market division of labor if they are free to exchange the excess supply of the goods that they produce. Because we cannot trade what we do not own, an environment of private property is needed to foster a flourishing exchange culture. We, therefore, can only enjoy a society of flourishing exchange in an environment of private property. Hence, to benefit from the division of labor and the economic development that flows from it, members of society must be secure in their property.

Likewise, for capitalists to have the incentive to accumulate capital, they must be secure in their property. Confiscatory taxation hinders capital accumulation because taxes reduce net incomes. With higher taxes, capitalists have a smaller disposable income available for savings and investment. Additionally, capitalists have less incentive to save and invest, because, as taxes are a cost of doing business, they guarantee a smaller return on their investment.

While incentives matter as North (1991, pp. 100–1) stresses, institutions more importantly effect the very ability of entrepreneurs to use economic calculation. For economic calculation to be a useful tool in guiding producers, two necessary conditions must be met: 1) the prices must be free market prices, and 2) they must be monetary prices. Because market prices are manifestations of people's subjective preferences, when entrepreneurs reap a profit, they do it precisely by providing those goods that people value the most in the least costly manner. Only prices resulting from voluntary exchange are manifestations of the subjective values of the buyers and sellers in society. Only such prices provide a practical link between economic profit and loss and social productivity. Prices arbitrarily fixed by the state can yield profit and loss calculations, but production determined according to calculations in this case would direct the use of scarce factors in ways contrary to the preferences of people in society. Private property once again proves indispensable.

The institution of sound money—money unmanipulated by the state—is also crucial. Sound money is a corollary of private property. The emergence of money itself required the right to property because it was also a process of voluntary exchange (Menger, 1994, pp. 257–62; 1985, pp. 152–55; Mises, 1953, pp. 29–33; Rothbard, 2004, pp. 189–93). Due to the lack of coincidence of wants that occurred relatively frequently in barter societies, people traded away goods that were less marketable for goods that were more easily tradeable. As more people demanded such goods for their exchange value, the demand for relatively more marketable goods increased, raising their exchange value even more, making them even more marketable. As people continued this process of trading away relatively less marketable goods for relatively more marketable goods, this process of voluntary exchange culminated in people using a single commodity as the general medium of exchange.

This same institution also provides entrepreneurs the freedom to act on their conclusions from economic calculation to the benefit of society. Indeed, the beauty of the market price system is that the entrepreneur reaps a profit for doing precisely what people in market want, and all the coordinated production satisfying people's preferences occurs peacefully.

If through statist intervention, however, the purchasing power of money continually fluctuates at a rapid rate, it becomes harder to calculate profit and loss magnitudes that will be relevant to actual production decisions. If the central bank expands credit not funded by voluntary savings, it falsifies interest rates and encourages malinvestment, resulting in the business cycle, capital consumption, and relatively impoverishment (Mises, 1998, pp. 547–62; Hayek, 1967; Rothbard, 2004, pp. 994–1004; Huerta de Soto, 2006, pp. 347–84; Strigl, 2000, pp. 120–33; Garrison, 2001; Salerno, 2012).

An implication of our understanding of the importance of private property and sound money for economic progress is that an economic policy that involves aggression against a person's property will hamper the market. It will distort prices, reduce the ability and incentive to save and invest in capital formation, and make it more difficult for entrepreneurs to meaningfully calculate profit and loss. To enable and promote economic progress, specific economic policies must reflect private property. Real private property is incompatible with interventionist policy.

Ethics and Economic Prosperity

The influence of economic institutions points to the further importance of ethics. Economic institutions do not appear fully formed *ex nihilo*. They are habits of human action. As such, they are ultimately determined by the preferences that motivate action. While the origination and definition of property were partly a by-product of people seeking out beneficial ways to reduce or mitigate potential conflicts arising from the appropriation, use, and exchange of economic goods, (Hoppe, 2010, pp. 17–30; North, 1984), human ideologies and worldviews also influence preferences. Here is a link between culture and dynamic efficiency. Culture is the manifestation of worldview, which is a systemization of all the theorems and theories guiding the conduct of people and groups (Mises, 1998, p. 178). As a theory, a worldview is an explanation that interprets all things. As a technology, a worldview is a precept for action concerning the best means for achieving ends.

Worldviews are formed based on religion and philosophy. One's theology and philosophy of life, therefore, have a large impact on our action. The late Roger Scruton (2000, p. 5) notes that "The core of common culture is religion." It affects ends we seek to fulfill, the means we deem suitable for achieving such ends, and the social institutions that constrain human action. People's attitudes toward education, work itself, progress, and change all have an impact on the willingness of people to engage in the productive behavior that is the fountainhead of economic prosperity (Sowell, 2016, pp. 135–54).

Worldview and ideology also affect the sort of economic and political institutions that are affirmed. Whether a society pursues statist institutions or free market institutions are largely a matter of ideology (Mises, 1990a, 1990b, 1991, 1998, p. 141, pp. 188–89; North, 1984). Some societies opt for interventionism due to historical inheritance of political centralization and tradition (Osterfeld, 1992, pp. 43–46). Additionally, a sense of injustice in market institutions have led some to curtail economic freedom with some degree of intervention (North, 1978, pp. 971–74).

A reverence for equality is a primary driving force for the contemporary lurching toward interventionism and socialism (Rothbard, 1971; Schlossberg, 1983, pp. 55–56). Egalitarianism requires that stamping out of many individual differences and cannot coexist with liberty and prosperity. In a free society, there will be inequality of incomes because people will be paid according to their marginal contribution to society as determined by society and not everyone is equally suited toward that end.

Along with economic and political reasons, ideology also is a significant reason some societies opt for free market institutions. In the history of Western Civilization, the embracing of market institutions partially resulted from increases in labor scarcity during the fourteenth century due to war, the black death, and famine as well as the independence of city-states (Rosenberg & Birdzell, 1986, pp. 37–70; Osterfeld, 1992, pp. 43–46).

Importantly, however, religious and philosophical beliefs and ethics played a primary part. Huerta de Soto (2009, pp. 18–22) has clearly explained the important relationship between the natural law ethics of property and dynamic efficiency. For the rest of this chapter, I desire to demonstrate how an explicitly Christian ethic of property and personal responsibility incorporates and complements the natural law regarding the right to property.

Historically, a majority of Christian theologians recognized that private property is a Christian social institution. The morality of private property was recognized as necessary for providing charity to the poor by patriarchs such as Turtullian, Ambrose, and John Chrysostomos, while Clement of Alexandria, Cyprian, and Augustine also endorsed private property and allowed for the possession of riches (Clement, 1995, p. 595; Koehler, 2017, Rothbard, 1995, pp. 33–36; Swift, 1979; Tertullian, 1986, p. 368).

Thomas Aquinas and the scholastic tradition also affirmed the superiority of private property over communal property, basing his convictions on both natural and divine law. *Quia vir reprobus*, Pope John XXII's 1329 papal bull, appealed to the Scriptures in explicitly and without qualification affirming the right to property, proclaiming that God's dominion over the earth is reflected by Man's dominion or property over his material possessions (Koehler, 2017, pp. 120–23). Property rights, therefore, were rooted in man's nature as created by divine law. The Thomistic tradition culminated with late scholastics Pedro de Aragon, Juan de Medina, Miguel Salon, and Domingo de Soto all defending the ethical legitimacy of private property (Chafuen, 2003, pp. 31–50).

Likewise, the mainstream Protestant tradition affirmed the right to property, drawing primarily from the Bible. John Calvin (1960, pp. 408–11), for example, argues that the commandment against stealing commands everyone to "strive faithfully to help every man to keep his own possessions." The Reformed Christian confessions such as the Heidelberg and Westminster Larger Catechisms also teach that Christian justice demands the protection of property from the aggression of others. Nineteenth century Princeton theologian Charles Hodge (1999, p. 421), in his discussion of the commandment against theft, concludes that "the right of property, [is] ordained by God, and cannot be violated without incurring His displeasure and the certain inflictions of His divine punishment."

The majority of Christians advocated the right to property, because, while there are many warnings against greed, trusting riches, and the love of money, and exhortations to share with those less fortunate, God has nevertheless revealed the justness of the right to property. Baptist minister and President of Brown University Francis Wayland summed up the Christian case for private property in his treatise on ethics, *The Elements of Moral Science* (1844, pp. 231–34). Wayland explains that the right to property is founded on God's will that He makes known to us through both general and special revelation. Not only do we inherently know in our natural conscience that the right to property is just, but the general consequences of either upholding or violating the right to property results in certain consequences. Without society embracing the right to property, the human race must perish or exist in wretchedness.

Additionally, Wayland notes that the Christian ethic of the right to property is communicated to us in the Scriptures. The Biblical view of property begins with the understanding that humans hold property as stewards of God, who ultimately owns all there is (Ps. 24:1; 50:10; 95:4–5). As owner of all that exists, God has the right to confer the use of property on whomsoever and under whatsoever restrictions he pleases.

In laying down constraints regarding the lawful obtaining of property, both the Old and New Testaments contain many precepts against acts of theft (Exod. 20:15; Deut. 5:11; Lev. 19:11, 13; Prov. 30:9; Jer. 7:9; Matt. 19:18; Mark 10:29; Luke 18:20; Rom. 13:9; Eph. 4:28). Fraud is considered an abomination and keeping back wages due laborers is sinful (Lev. 19:13; Prov. 11:1; 20:10). The encroachment of someone else's property by moving recognized property boundaries is likewise prohibited (Deut. 19:14; Prov. 22:28; 23:10-11). In the Old Testament, restitution for theft was a requirement (Exod. 22:1-4). The Bible even condemns thoughts from which stealing proceeds (Exod. 20:17, Deut. 5:21; Col. 3:5).

The Scriptures also instruct that the Christian ethic of property includes right to voluntary exchange. In Acts 5 we have the sad account of Ananias and Sapphira, a husband and wife who sold a piece of property and conspired to lie to the Church, telling it that they were giving all the proceeds to the Church for it to distribute to those in need. They were found out and sequentially struck dead by God.

Some have argued that in this incident, we find a mandate for Christian socialism. However, in the biblical account, after Ananias lied to the Church, Peter replies, referring to the land, "While it remained unsold, did it not remain your own? And after it was sold, was it not at your disposal? Why is it that you have contrived this deed in your heart? You have not lied to man but to God." (Acts 5:4). Note that Peter expressly says that their property was theirs to do with as they saw fit. Both Ananias and Sapphira were struck dead by God, not for keeping their property, but by lying to God about it. It should also be noted that when exhorting churches to contribute to the common charity fund, there were never calls for coercive extraction of property, but voluntary giving (2 Cor. 9:7).

This same right to property that constrains individuals, constrains the state. God does not say, "Thou shalt not steal, except by majority vote." Rather, God is very concerned that rulers execute their office with justice (Ps. 2:10–11; 2 Sam. 23:3–4). Ruling and judging with justice require upholding the right to property. The Christian ethic of property is, happily, one that provides for the environment enabling the sources of prosperity to work together promoting dynamic efficiency and the flourishing of human civilization.

Personal Ethics and Prosperity

Private property, however, does not guarantee economic progress. It only makes it possible. A free society cannot force people to save and invest their incomes. They are free to spend it all on consumption if they wish. Therefore, in a free market, society participates in just as much economic growth as individuals want. If they prefer more present consumption and less economic progress, they can achieve this. If, however, they prefer to put off present consumption so they can consume more in the future as a result of economic development, they can do this too.

In addition to the right to life and property, Christianity also fosters various personal virtues that are conducive to the functioning of the sources of prosperity identified above. Christian virtues of self-control (Prov. 25:28; 1 Cor. 9:25; Gal. 5:23; 2 Tim. 1:7) and patience (2 Cor. 6:6; Gal. 5:22; Col. 3:12) manifest themselves in lower relative time preferences. Additionally, Christianity is forward looking and emphasizes planning for the future, thriftiness, and being diligent in labor. Historian David Landes (1999, pp. 174–79) identifies the stress seventeenth century Protestants placed on time as a significant reason for the flourishing of economic development in Northern Europe.

Ethical vices also make it more difficult to maintain private property. If market participants are driven by greed, they become more likely to lobby for state granted privileges via market regulation, reducing the scope of private property. Government corruption and bribery to subvert justice (Exod. 23:8; Prov. 17:23; Is. 1:23) contribute toward the overthrowing of the rule of law and the free society (Osterfeld, 1992, pp. 210–11, pp. 214–17). If theft and fraud become rampant, uncertainty related to exchange increases and more resources will be directed toward protecting property and away from producing goods.

Christian ethics work toward reducing statist intervention, corruption, violence, fraud and theft, and instead promote peace, honesty, and trust between our neighbors, which provides a more inviting exchange environment. Interestingly, some recent economic research has found evidence that serious religious faith (proxied by a fear of hell) has been positively correlated with economic expansion and negatively correlated with corruption (Kliesen & Schmid, 2004).

Conclusion

Human flourishing is the consequence of dynamic efficiency. The only way to further human civilization and avoid descending into a barbaric struggle for survival is to take advantage of the social division of labor, capital accumulation, technological improvement, and wise entrepreneurship. Allowing these sources of economic progress to flourish requires the security provided by peace and private property sustained by and combined with cultural values such as a forsaking of theft and low social time preferences.

Personal reflection upon our own conscience and the created order and careful study of the Scriptures conclusively demonstrates that not only is the social institution of private property generally beneficial, but also it is morally imperative. This conclusion has great consequences for social thought. It is the basis for the free society that manifests voluntary exchange, social cooperation, and the human flourishing that follows.

References

Abramovitz, M. (1956). *Resource and Output Trends in the United States since 1870.* Occasional Paper No. 52, National Bureau of Economic Research, New York, NY.

Acemoglu, D., & Robinson, J. (2008). *The Role of Institutions in Growth and Development.* Working Paper No. 10, Commission on Growth and Development.

Chafuen, A. A. (2003). *Faith and Liberty: The Economic Thought of the Late Scholastics*. Lexington Books.

Calvin, J. (1960). In J. T. McNeil (Ed.), *Institutes of the Christian Religion*. The Westminster Press.

Cantillon, R. (2009). *Essay on the Nature of Commerce in General*. Transaction Publishers.

Clement of Alexandria. (1995). Who is the Rich Man that Shall Be Saved? (W. Wilson, Trans.). In A. Roberts, & J. Donaldson (Eds.), *The Ante-Nicene Fathers* (P. Holmes, Trans., Vol. II, pp. 591–604). Hendrickson Publishers.

Espinosa, V. I. (2020). Epistemological problems of development economics. *Procesos de Mercado: Revista Europea de Economía Política, XVII*(1), 55–93.

Foss, N. J. (2012). The Continuing Relevance of Austrian Capital Theory. *Quarterly Journal of Austrian Economics, 15*(2), 151–171.

Garrison, R. W. (2001). *Time and Money: The Macroeconomics of Capital Structure*. New York, Routledge.

Hayek, F. A. (1967 [1931]). *Prices and Production*. Augustus M. Kelley.

Helpman, E. (2004). *The Mystery of Growth*. The Belknap Press of Harvard University Press.

Huerta de Soto, J. (2006). *Money, Bank Credit, and Economic Cycles*. The Ludwig von Mises Institute.

Huerta de Soto, J. (2009). *Dynamic Efficiency*. Routledge.

Huerta de Soto, J. (2010). *Socialism, Economic Calculation and Entrepreneurship*. Edward Elgar.

Hodge, C. (1999). *Systematic Theology* (Vol. 3). Hendrickson Publishers.

Hoppe, H.-H. (2010). *A Theory of Socialism and Capitalism*. The Ludwig von Mises Institute.

Kliesen, K., & Schmid, F. A. (2004, July). Fear of Hell Might Fire Up the Economy. *The Regional Economist*, 10–11.

Koehler, B. (2017). The Economics of Property Rights in Early and Medieval Christianity. *Economic Affairs, 37*(1), 112–124.

Landes, D. (1999). *The Wealth and Poverty of Nations*. W. W. Norton.

Menger, C. (1985 [1883]). *Investigations into the Method of the Social Sciences with Special Reference to Economics*. New York, New York University Press.

Menger, C. (1994 [1871]). *Principles of Economics*. Libertarian Press.

Mises, L.v. (1953). *The Theory of Money and Credit*. Yale University Press.

Mises, L.v. (1990a). The Role of Doctrine in Human History. In R. M. Ebeling (Ed.), *Money, Method, and the Market Process* (pp. 289–302). Kluwer Academic Publishers.

Mises, L.v. (1990b). The Idea of Liberty is Western. In R. M. Ebeling (Ed.), *Money, Method, and the Market Process* (pp. 303–312). Kluwer Academic Publishers.

Mises, L.v. (1991). Liberty and Property. In *Two Essays by Ludwig von Mises* (pp. 15–43). The Ludwig von Mises Institute.

Mises, L. v. (1977 [1929]). *A Critique of Interventionism*. New Rochelle, NY: Arlington House Publishers.
Mises, L. v. (1998 [1949]). *Human Action*. Scholars Edition. The Ludwig von Mises Institute.
North, D. C. (1978, September). Structure and Performance: The Task of Economic History. *Journal of Economic Literature, XVI*, 963–978.
North, D. C. (1984). Transaction Costs, Institutions, and Economic History. *Journal of Institutional and Theoretical Economics, 140*, 7–17.
North, D. C. (1986). The New Institutional Economics. *Journal of Institutional and Theoretical Economics, 142*, 230–37.
North, D. C. (1991). Institutions. *Journal of Economic Perspectives, 5*(1), 97–112.
Osterfeld, D. (1992). *Prosperity Versus Planning: How Government Stifles Economic Growth*. Oxford University Press.
Plato. (1888). *The Republic* (B. Jowett, Trans.). The Clarendon Press.
Rosenberg, N., & Birdzell, L. E., Jr. (1986). *How the West Grew Rich: The Economic Transformation of the Industrial World*. Basic Books.
Rothbard, M. N. (1971). Freedom, Inequality, Primitivism, and the Division of Labor. *Modern Age, 15*(3), 226–243.
Rothbard, M. N. (1995). *Economic Thought Before Adam Smith*. Edward Elgar.
Rothbard, M. N. (2004). *Man, Economy, and State with Power and Market*. The Ludwig von Mises Institute.
Salerno, J. (2012). A Reformulation of Austrian Business Cycle Theory in Light of the Financial Crisis. *The Quarterly Journal of Austrian Economics, 15*(1), 3–44.
Schlossberg, H. (1983). *Idols for Destruction: Christian Faith and Its Confrontation with American Society*. Thomas Nelson Publishers.
Scruton, R. (2000). *An Intelligent Person's Guide to Modern Culture*. St. Augustine's Press.
Shapiro, M. M. (2007). *Foundations of the Market Price System*. The Ludwig von Mises Institute.
Shenoy, Sudha R. (2010). *Towards a Theoretical Framework for British and International Economic History: Early Modern England. A Case Study*. Auburn, AL: The Ludwig von Mises Institute.
Smith, A. (1965 [1776]). *An Inquiry into the Nature and Causes of the Wealth of Nations*. The Modern Library.
Strigl, R. (2000). *Capital and Production*. The Ludwig von Mises Institute.
Solow, R. (2000). *Growth Theory* (2nd ed.). Oxford University Press.
Sowell, T. (2016). *Wealth, Poverty, and Politics*. Basic Books.
Swift, L. J. (1979). Iustitia and Ius Privatum: Ambrose on Private Property. *The American Journal of Philology, 100*(1), 176–187.
Tertullian. (1986). In A. Roberts, & J. Donaldson (Eds.), *The Ante-Nicene Fathers* (Vol. III, P. Holmes, Trans.). Wm. B. Eerdmans Publishing Company.
Wayland, F. (1844). *The Elements of Moral Science*. Gould, Kendall, and Lincoln.

Puviani on Smith on Taxes

Carlos Rodríguez Braun

Taxation is not and has not been only
an act of violence but also of astuteness.
Amilcare Puviani

The Italian economist Amilcare Puviani (1854–1907) graduated in Law from the University of Bologna, where he subsequently taught Political Economy, Public Finance and Financial Law. He moved afterwards to the

In 1992 I was a member of the committee that examined Jesús Huerta de Soto's doctoral dissertation at the Universidad Complutense in Madrid. I remember his excellent text, the brilliance of his speech, and the energy with which Jesús instructed the members of the committee about how we should think! He deservedly achieved the *cum laude* distinction. All these years I have been a friend of Jesús, and I have participated in some of his numerous academic initiatives and backed his indefatigable struggle for the cause of liberty.

C. Rodríguez Braun (✉)
Complutense University of Madrid (Retired), Madrid, Spain
e-mail: carlos@rodriguezbraun.com

D. Howden, P. Bagus (eds.), *The Emergence of a Tradition: Essays in Honor of Jesús Huerta de Soto, Volume I*,
https://doi.org/10.1007/978-3-031-17414-8_21

University of Perugia, where he remained as professor of Public Finance until his death.

Puviani wrote to Jevons offering himself as translator of the latter's *Primer of Political Economy*, but Luigi Cossa had already been commissioned to undertake the job (Jevons, 1977, p. 37). Puviani had also no luck with the English translation of *Teoria della illusione finanziaria*, his own *opus magnum*, which had nevertheless German and Spanish versions (Puviani, 1903).

He was the first to show that the state creates fiscal illusions through both taxes and expenditures, and was much appreciated by James Buchanan, who summarized his work and announced an English translation of his book which, however, was never done (Buchanan, 1960, pp. 59–64; 1975, p. 393; Eusepi, 1989, p. 819; Goetz, 1977, p. 177; Wagner, 2006, p. 238).

In this chapter I shall first present Puviani's theory of fiscal illusion, and then consider his analysis of Adam Smith and taxation in *The Wealth of Nations*. A section on Puviani on socialism precedes the conclusion.

Puviani and the *Illusione Finanziaria*

The late nineteenth-century scholars who researched into the theory of public finance in Italy coincided in the importance they assigned to individual valuation. The aim of the *scienza delle finanze* was, in Puviani's words: "Look for the psychological tax movements and the objective conditions that determine them" (Puviani, 1896, p. 299; Kavaalp, 1989, p. 155).

These scholars were considered by Buchanan to be precursors of the public choice theory because they included the public finances in the realm of economic theory and underscored the productivity of the public services:

> The Italian fiscal theorists seem to have totally rejected Adam Smith's relegation of collective services to the category of the unproductive. They were motivated to ask, and did ask the basic questions: What is the state? To what extent is the state separated from the citizenry? What are the motivations of those who act as decision makers for the collectivity? To what degree can collective action be factored down into participatory roles for individuals subject to such action? (Buchanan, 2008, p. 259; Smith, 1981, p. 862)

The notion of public productiveness is linked to the fiscal illusion, the *illusione finanziaria*, that Puviani first presented in 1896, stating that taxation poses a hedonic difficulty that economists had not yet been able to sort out:

> The fundamental problem, which we must solve, is to find the reasons why large masses of people induce themselves to pay large sums of tax and to undertake enormous sacrifices in cases in which the benefits obtained or expected in return from the state don't seem profitable. (Puviani, 1896, p. 298)

According to Puviani, the state manages to conceal its characteristics in such a manner that the people tend to overestimate the benefit of public expenditure and underestimate the burden of taxes. This has to do with deception or self-deception, but not necessarily with ignorance or irrationality. Fiscal illusion is more like a mirage: when in the desert we are sure that we see water in the distance, and the water is not there, this phenomenon is not absurd, and can be logically accounted for. We are dealing with a subjective dimension that can exert an important influence in the political ideas and reactions of the people (Buchanan, 1999, pp. 126–130; Rodríguez Braun et al., 2021, pp. 90–100).

Mirages last more or less, and accordingly a hedonistic, rational, and free people may revolt against taxes, but they may also accept them, and do so "not under the fear of threats of the strongest; but because of an eclipse in their consciousness" (Puviani, 1896, p. 304).

Tax analysis, Puviani said, failed to come to grips with fiscal subjectivity, and so the rationale of taxation was not discussed. Contributions in the *ancien régime* were paid by subjects obedient to God and King, but analytically nothing really seemed to be different after the French Revolution. Taxes supposedly provided then for the needs of society, "but even here the motives for imposing taxes were not to be found in the mind of a real man; it is precisely in the period of the highest exaltation of the individual that the individual appears as an element which is not conscious of the great results of his own work." A Hegelian state turned out to be the new god demanding the resources of the faithful, and no questions were to be asked—"What need was there to seek the opinion of the individual taxpayers since the state was to look after the common good?" Marginalist economics suggests that "given the high degree of final utility which single units of wealth have for the disadvantaged, at all times, the lower classes ought to have contributed very little to the paying of taxes" (Puviani, 1901, pp. 16–17, p. 29). This was never so.

To explore fully the reasons for such a lot of the inferior ranks, Puviani gathered the elements of his previous research and published in 1903 *Teoria della illusione finanziaria*, that pointed out the essential change undergone by taxation since the old feudal illusions of lords and religion:

> In the feudal stage, fundamentally authoritarian, the public financier did not have to face the formidable problem that the next epoch had to solve, that consisted in hiding from the masses of taxpayers a great part of the real fiscal situation, making almost ephemeral controls, while at the same time proclaiming the sovereignty of the people and the democratization of the tax administration. (Puviani, 1903, p. 220)

In modern times, accordingly, the ruling classes do not exploit the people blatantly but stealthily, pretending to serve the people's interest and gaining their consent through several expedients that disguise the real fiscal pressure.

There is a wide range of strategies, such as: charge indirect taxes included in the prices of goods and services; debase the coin; increase the public debt; divide taxes into smaller ones, or payments in smaller installments; grant subsidies; trade with bureaucratic places; collect money via selling or lending public estates, charging the people with the corresponding opportunity costs, that should also include the relative inefficiency of the public sector vis-à-vis the private one (Puviani, 1903, chapters 2 and 3). James Buchanan remarked: "Although not imagined by Puviani, withholding of taxes at source would almost ideally fit his criteria" (Buchanan, 2008, p. 259; Wagner, 2006, p. 247). Plain lies should be included, such as unfulfilled promises of lowering taxes or levy temporal taxes that turn to be permanent. Budgets will become increasingly obscure and, as taxpayers do not discriminate between their private resources and the public ones, they will usually exaggerate the value of public services and gradually become accustomed to pay more and more taxes without resistance (Puviani, 1903, p. 173, p. 224).

Puviani on Smith on Taxes

Adam Smith was aware of the hiding possibilities of taxes. As he taught in his Glasgow lessons:

> The taxes on consumptions are not so much murmured against, because they are laid upon the merchant, who lays them on the price of goods, and thus they are insensibly paid by the people. (Smith, 1982, p. 533)

This was also recognized by the classical economists:

> If all taxes were direct, taxation would be much more perceived than at present, and there would be a security, which now there is not, for economy in the public expenditure. (Mill, 1909, p. 864)

> The burden of direct taxation is palpable and obvious. It admits of no disguise or concealment but makes everyone fully sensible of the exact amount of the demand made upon him by government. We are all, however, extremely averse from parting with property, except we obtain some more acceptable equivalent in its stead. ... [indirect taxes] this ingenious plan, while it conceals the amount of taxation, makes its payment in some measure voluntary. (McCulloch, 1863, p. 152)

Puviani acknowledges in the *Teoria* that Smith had grasped what he calls positive and negative illusions, that is, to see things that do not exist and not to see things that do exist. The first correspond to the ignorance of the causes of public expenditures and the second to the insensibility about the weight of the taxes that people really pay (Puviani, 1903, p. 13, pp. 20–21, p. 201, p. 214). Smith had mentioned, among other measures, debt and the division of taxes to finance a larger public expenditure, like in war; and the debasing of the coin to achieve a "pretended payment" of the public debt (Smith, 1981, p. 925, p. 929).

In the article he had dedicated five years before to Smith and taxation, Puviani synthesized his objections thus: "just as Smith did not delve into the precise *concept* of imposition, so he did not study its *causes*" (Puviani, 1898, p. 14; this same point was made much later by Stigler, 1982, p. 139).

Smith's theory of taxes can be interpreted as if taxes were payments for services: "The expence of government to the individuals of a great nation, is like the expence of management to the joint tenants of a great estate, who are all obliged to contribute in proportion to their respective interests in the estate" (Smith, 1981, p. 825). Puviani underscored Smith's last words but put them into context, following Bonar. Smith did not present a strictly juridical theory of the state, but "he conceives, although within certain rather narrow limits, a certain solidarity among all the citizens of a great state, so that order and general prosperity result from a complex of sacrifices not always proportionate to the special public benefits received"; accordingly, the rich should contribute to the relief of the less well-off, and Smith seems to be "very sober in his proposals for tax reforms," viewing them from the premises of public needs, which does not fit very well with a liberal standpoint: "It seems that the influence of mercantilist finance, trusting in the paternal state, and in particular the influence of James Steuart penetrated into Smithian financial theory" (Puviani, 1898, p. 10, p. 12, p. 13). This lack of tax-reform initiatives could stem from Smith's notion that the British tax system of his time was a relatively good one (Smith, 1981, p. 899).

Although he does not analyze the causes of taxation, "Smith's tax theory is primarily a study of their economic effects...this profound view of the connection of finance with economics constitutes the pre-eminent title of honor that Smith had over his predecessors." Puviani adds that Smith detected the opposition between privileged groups versus the common interest, and the former's control of the state, but the conflict is not "something necessary, continuous, organic, systematic...but something fragmentary, occasional, arbitrary" (Puviani, 1898, p. 16).

Smith was too optimistic, in Puviani's view, because he saw a natural agreement between the classes in an economic evolution where inequalities would be corrected, and everyone could better their own condition in a divine plan devised by a very wise mind and led by an invisible hand. The Italian economist, on the contrary, saw "the defeat of the workers and the enslavement of the government to the interests of the richest." For Smith, on the other hand, the state is not a vile instrument of certain classes but in general a force in favor of the common good, which finally ennobles taxation, and designates the taxpayer as a free person (Puviani, 1898, p. 18, p. 20; Smith, 1981, p. 857). It seems that Puviani exaggerates Smith's ideas, as when he states that Smith predicted a considerable reduction of public expenditure due to the peaceful impulses of economic prosperity (Puviani, 1898, p. 25; Paganelli & Schumacher, 2019; Rodríguez Braun, 2019).

Arguing that Smith could not be aware of what the future held in store, Puviani saw deeply negative forces in the capitalism of his own times, forces that tended to oppress workers, suppress liberty, limit science, squander resources, and push industry aggressively overseas to conquer new markets (Puviani, 1903, p. 230; Dallera, 1987, p. 99).

Puviani's Socialism

From what we have seen, it would seem that Puviani, independently of his more or less precise analysis of Smith and taxation, was a clear socialist.

He criticizes capitalism, speaks about the state as serf of the bourgeoisie against the poor, in a conspiracy to put Parliament at the mercy of the owners, who in fact organize budgets and taxes, and prevent wages from rising and the workers from being educated, or even born (Puviani, 1895, p. 885; 1903, p. 61, p. 95, p. 204, p. 240). He favored a progressive income tax as "a formidable weapon against capital" (Dallera, 1987, p. 140).

But he also praises liberals like Cobden and Bastiat, while upholding a liberal view of the state: "An essential first step toward an appreciation of and adherence to libertarianism requires that we shed all vestiges of the romantic vision of how politics works" (Jevons, 1977, p. 41; Buchanan, 2008, p. 258).

Puviani denounces socialism precisely for spreading this romanticism and "a great sentimental optimism" about the state (Puviani, 1896, p. 307). His theory of the state in the hands of capitalists and his view of the world in terms on ruling and ruled classes has Marxist echoes, but he is also an individualist that combines materialism with subjective utilitarianism (Buchanan, 1999, p. 128; Dallera, 1987, p. 198, pp. 116–7; Puviani, 1903, p. xxvii).

Conclusion

Although marked with distortions and excesses, Amilcare Puviani's analysis of Adam Smith on taxes is ultimately right in the sense that the Scottish thinker fell short of the possibilities of considering the state as a bilateral result from the interactions between power and subjects, combining objective reality and subjective appreciations. The overcoming of this deficiency can help to explain why so many taxpayers pay sums that are larger than the benefits supplied by the government, and through what mechanisms individuals take fiscal decisions and, in some way, "determine the size of the public sector, along with the distribution of costs and benefits" (Buchanan, 1999, p. 175).

References

Buchanan, J. M. (1960). *Fiscal Theory and Political Economy. Selected Essays.* The University of North Carolina Press.

Buchanan, J. M. (1975). Public Finance and Public Choice. *National Tax Journal, 28*(4), 383–394.

Buchanan, J. M. (1999). *Public Finance in Democratic Process: Fiscal Institutions and Individual Choice.* The Collected Works of James M. Buchanan, (Vol. 4). Liberty Fund.

Buchanan, J. M. (2008). Italian Fiscal Theorists. In R. Hamowy (Ed.), *The Encyclopedia of Libertarianism* (pp. 258–260). SAGE Publications.

Dallera, G. (1987). *Amilcare Puviani.* Benucci Editore.

Eusepi, G. (1989). Buchanan's Critique of the Neoclassical Model and the Rediscovery of the Italian Tradition in Public Finance. *Rivista Internazionale di Scienze Economiche e Commerciali, 36*(9), 801–822.

Goetz, C. J. (1977). Fiscal Illusion in State and Local Finance. In T. E. Borcherding (Ed.), *Budgets and Bureaucrats: The Sources of Government Growth* (pp. 176–187). Duke University Press.

Jevons, W. S. (1977). In R. D. Collison Black (Ed.), *Papers and Correspondence of William Stanley Jevons* (Vol. V, Correspondence 1879–1882). Macmillan.

Kayaalp, O. (1989). Early Italian Contributions to the Theory of Public Finance: Pantaleoni, De Viti de Marco, and Mazzola. In D. Walker (Ed.), *Perspectives on the History of Economic Thought* (Vol. 1, pp. 155–166). Edward Elgar.

McCulloch, J. R. (1863). *A Treatise on the Practical Influence of Taxation and the Funding System* (3rd ed.). Adam and Charles Black.

Mill, J. S. (1909). In W. J. Ashley (Ed.), *Principles of Political Economy.* Longmans.

Paganelli, M. P., & Schumacher, R. (2019). Do Not Take Peace for Granted: Adam Smith's Warning on the Relation Between Commerce and War, *43*(3), 785–798.

Puviani, A. (1895, December). Moventi e fenomeni economici in una casa di forza. *La Riforma Sociale, II*(IV, fasc. 12), 873–889.

Puviani, A. (1896). Il problema edonistico nella scienza delle finanze. *La Riforma Sociale, III*(VI, fasc. 5), 297–309.

Puviani, A. (1898). Sulle idee finanziarie di Adamo Smith. *La Riforma Sociale, V*(VIII), 5–28.

Puviani, A. (1901). Sulla ragione dell'imposta. *Giornale degli Economiste, 22*(12), 14–34. English translation in *Giornale degli Economisti e Annali di Economia*, December 2012.

Puviani, A. (1903). In F. Volpi (Ed.), *Teoria della illusione finanziaria.* Istituto Editoriale Internazionale, 1973; German translation: *Die Illusionen in der öffentlichen Finanzwirtschaft*, G. Schmölders ed., Berlin, Duncker & Humblot, 1960; Spanish translation: *Teoría de la ilusión financiera*, Álvaro Rodríguez Bereijo ed., Madrid, Instituto de Estudios Fiscales, 1972.

Rodríguez Braun, C. (2019). Adam Smith's Liberalism. *Review of Austrian Economics, 34*(4), 465–478.

Rodríguez Braun, C., Blanco, M., & Ávila, L. D. (2021). *Hacienda somos todos, cariño*. Deusto.

Smith, A. (1981). In R. H. Campbell & A. S. Skinner (Eds.), *An Inquiry into the Nature and Causes of the Wealth of Nations*. Liberty Fund.

Smith, A. (1982). In R. L. Meek, D. D. Raphael, & P. G. Stein (Eds.), *Lectures on Jurisprudence*. Liberty Fund.

Stigler, G. J. (1982). Smith's Travels on the Ship of State. In *The Economist as Preacher and Other Essays* (pp. 136–145). Chicago University Press.

Wagner, R. E. (2006). Choice, Catallaxy, and Just Taxation: Contrasting Architectonics or Fiscal Theorizing. *Social Philosophy and Policy, 23*(2), 235–254.

Milton Friedman's Views on Method and Money Reconsidered in Light of the Housing Bubble

Joseph T. Salerno

Milton Friedman passed away on November 16, 2006. Although he had not added much to his corpus of scientific research since the early 1980s, Friedman continued to contribute to the public debate over monetary policy with op-ed pieces, media interviews, and letters to the editor right up until his death (Nelson, 2007). In this chapter, I will argue that Friedman's failure to recognize the housing and financial asset bubbles leading up to the financial crisis of 2007–2008 was rooted in the inductivist method that Friedman and Anna Schwartz ([1963] 1971) used to

J. T. Salerno (✉)
Mises Institute, Auburn, AL, USA
e-mail: salerno@mises.org

D. Howden, P. Bagus (eds.), *The Emergence of a Tradition: Essays in Honor of Jesús Huerta de Soto, Volume I*,
https://doi.org/10.1007/978-3-031-17414-8_22

formulate the theory at the heart of the monetary doctrine of "monetarism."[1] Because Friedman's method relies heavily on statistical correlations between the money supply and other aggregate variables, monetarist theory is not only inductive but also macroeconomic. The serious shortcoming of such a theory is well known to Austrian economists and it was trenchantly summarized by Friedrich A. Hayek (1978, p. 215):

> My chief objection against [Friedman's] theory is that, as what is called a 'macro-theory', it pays attention only to the effects of changes in the quantity of money on the general price level and not to the effects on the structure of relative prices. In consequence, it tends to disregard . . . the most harmful effects of inflation: the misdirection of resources it causes and the unemployment which ultimately results from it.

Friedman's method of theory construction thus led to a simplistic and truncated theory of the monetary transmission mechanism which completely neglects its complex "microeconomic" network of channels and pathways, especially as they affect the structure of capital and production. Friedman's limited vision of the monetary adjustment process, in turn, led to his most notable, and now generally accepted, theoretical claim, namely that contraction of the money supply is the main cause of depression. The crucial link between Friedman's method and his purely monetary explanation of economic fluctuations was perceived by Professor Jesús Huerta de Soto (1998, p. 527) who bluntly declared:

> Attributing crises to a monetary contraction is like attributing measles to the fever and rash which accompany it. This explanation of cycles can only be upheld by the scientistic, ultra-empirical methodology of monetarist macroeconomics, an approach which lacks a temporal theory of capital.

We now turn to a consideration of the nature and development of the methodological foundation of Friedman's monetary theory.

[1] I shall henceforth refer to "Friedman" in general discussion of monetarist method, theory, and policy.

The Nature and Sources of Friedman's Method

Over the last three decades, there have been several valuable studies by former students and followers of Friedman as well as interviews with Friedman himself. The effect of these publications, if not their intent, has been to reveal and clarify the actual *method* Friedman used in his monetary research as opposed to the formal *methodology* he proposed in his classic article, "The Methodology of Positive Economics" (Friedman, 1953). These articles and interviews indicate that statisticians such as Henry Schultz, Harold Hotelling, and especially Wesley Clair Mitchell were much more influential on Friedman's thinking on method than the philosopher Karl Popper. The authors of these articles include George Tavlas (2014); James Lothian (2009, 2011); Robert Hetzel (2007); Edward Nelson (2007); Hugh Rockoff (2006); Kevin Hoover (2004); and Michael Bordo and Anna Schwartz (2003). Interviews with Friedman (1992, 2001) by Daniel Hammond and John Taylor, respectively, as well as the memoirs of Milton and Rose Friedman (1998) are also important to this project of clarification.

When engaging Friedman's positive method of deriving economic theory, it is important to recognize that Friedman was first and foremost a statistician. Lothian (2009, p. 1087) observed that Friedman's "command of price theory" and "his intuition for statistics and its practical research applications" were "exceptional" and "the two informed everything he did in economics, including monetary economics." Tavlas (2014, p. 9) remarked on Friedman's "capacity and proclivity to apply statistical analysis to economic data" and observed: "By the mid-1940s, Friedman had demonstrated the potential to become a statistician of considerable stature." While Friedman's primary influences in technical economics were Jacob Viner (price theory), Lloyd Mints (monetary theory), and Henry Simons (monetary theory), he was most heavily influenced in his approach to statistical work by Schultz, Mitchell, and the mathematical statistician Hotelling (Friedman, 1992, pp. 111–112; Friedman & Friedman, 1998, pp. 35–39, 43–44; Rockoff, 2006, pp. 26–31).

As a research assistant to Schultz at the University of Chicago, Friedman (1992, p. 98) wrote sections—although not the statistical parts—of Schultz's classic, *The Theory and Measurement of Demand* (Schultz,

1938).[2] While a visiting faculty member at the University of Wisconsin in 1941, Friedman and Alan Wallis "were tentatively committed to writing a statistics text" (Friedman & Friedman, 1998, p. 100).[3]

Friedman (1952, p. 237) considered Mitchell's empirical work "a contribution to economic theory . . . of the first magnitude" and "an invaluable body of tested knowledge about these phenomena [prices and business cycles] for the formulation of new theories and the testing of old theories." Friedman (1952, p. 237, n. 1) clearly saw Mitchell as a mentor, expressing his indebtedness to Mitchell "for his part, as teacher, colleague, and friend, in my intellectual development in general, and in my understanding of his own scientific creed in particular." Friedman (1992, p. 108) did stress the differences between himself and Mitchell, especially regarding economic theory. However, these differences as Friedman presented them were quite ambiguous. Contending that Mitchell "was not a natural theorist," Friedman strained to identify where the distinction between him and his mentor lay:

> [T]he difference between Mitchell and me is not at all in our abstract ideas of what theory ought to do or what its role is. In that sense Mitchell was as much of a theorist as I am. The difference is that my natural instincts are theoretical and his natural instincts are not. . . . I don't mean he didn't have respect for theory or that he wasn't concerned with theory. . . . He couldn't make theory. He could do theory but he couldn't make it.

Be that as it may, Friedman's contemporary followers see a continuity between Friedman and Schwartz's method of analysis in their classic *Monetary History* and Mitchell's method of "descriptive analysis," which Friedman (1952, p. 243) depicts as "bringing together an enormous mass of material, putting it into systematic form, and giving an orderly, lucid and meaningful account of it." This was the case study method that

[2] Interestingly, Friedman (1992, p. 98, p. 108) characterized Schultz as "a good mechanic" but not "really very smart." In fact, Friedman confided that as a brash young research assistant he "had close to contempt for [Schultz], because he just wasn't very smart," although his respect for Schultz and his work grew as he matured.

[3] Friedman had written a controversial memo arguing that a student at Wisconsin would not be able to "secure training . . . sufficient to qualify him to teach advanced statistics or to do independent work in the field of statistical methods." The ensuing imbroglio caused to withdraw his name from consideration for an associate professorship in the economics department (Friedman & Friedman, 1998, pp. 91–104).

Mitchell (1913) pioneered in his book *Business Cycles*,[4] a volume that contained what Friedman (1952, pp. 243–44) considered the "finest and fullest expression" of the Mitchellian method, which was to become the template for research carried out at the National Bureau of Economic Research. Indeed, Rockoff (2006, pp. 44–45) notes "[t]he similarity in methodology between *Business Cycles* and *Monetary History*" and concludes:

> Although Friedman and Schwartz were more systematic and self conscious than Mitchell about using historical case studies as raw materials for drawing conclusions about the effectiveness of monetary policy, the inductive methodology is clearly an extension of the practices of Mitchell and the other business cycle researchers at the National Bureau.[5]

In *Monetary History*, Friedman and Schwartz use Mitchell's "clinical methodology" and proceed as "monetary clinicians" (Rockoff, 2006, p. 5, pp. 42–43). Following Mitchell, Friedman and Schwartz eschew the modern econometric penchant for building large complex models,

[4] An abridged version of the book containing only the analytical section was published in 1941 under the title of *Business Cycles and Their Causes* (Mitchell, [1941] 1963).

[5] That Friedman shared Mitchell's affinity for the raw inductivist approach explains Friedman's heated reaction to the classic review essay by the econometrician Tjalling Koopmans (1947) of Burns and Mitchell's book *Measuring Business Cycles* (1946). Koopmans took Burns and Mitchell to task for their relentlessly a-theoretical inductivism. Koopmans (1947, pp. 163–64) wrote of the book:

> The toolkit of the theoretical economist is deliberately spurned. Not a single demand or supply schedule or other equation expressing the behavior of men or the technical laws of production is employed explicitly in the book, and the cases of implicit use are few and far between. . . . Instead [the authors] study the 'behavior' (in a more mechanical sense) of certain measurable joint effects of several of those actions and responses. This shift of attention from underlying human responses to their combined effects is a decisive step. It eliminates all benefits . . . that might be received from economic theory. . . .

Friedman was queried about his methodological sympathies in the dispute between Koopmans and Burns-Mitchell in an interview 45 years after the publication of Koopmans' essay. Friedman (1992, p. 109) acidly responded:

> Koopmans was just foolish. There is no doubt whatsoever that . . . my sympathies were entirely on the Burns-Mitchell side. I thought that Koopmans' was a very sophomoric attack and had no effective positive content. . . .

estimating the model on a small body of data, and then extrapolating outside the data set of the model.[6] As Friedman (2001, pp. 121–22) puts it:

> Some of the modern approaches involve data mining and exploring a single body of evidence all within itself. When you try to apply statistical tests of significance, you never know how many degrees of freedom you have because you're taking the best out of many tries [of a large number of alternative hypotheses]. I believe that you have a more secure basis if, instead of relying on extremely sophisticated analysis of a small fixed body of data, you rely on cruder analysis of a much broader and wider body of data, which will include different circumstances. The natural experiments that come up over a wide range provide a source of evidence that is stronger and more reliable than any single very limited body of data.[7]

Thus in *Monetary History*, Friedman and Schwartz shun hypothesis-testing using formal models and multiple regression analysis as a method for deriving causal propositions about economic phenomena. Instead, they apply correlation analysis to a wide range of data supplemented with historical narrative to accumulate quantitative and qualitative evidence which then leads "to the formulation of broad hypotheses and informal testing based on data other than those used to derive the hypotheses" (Tavlas, 2014, pp. 9–10).

Lothian (2009, p. 1091) incisively summarized the method used in *Monetary History* as

> a combination of historical narrative and careful analysis of the monetary and other economic data. They provide no tests of hypotheses in the formal statistical sense. Instead, they let history design the experiments, which they then use in quite ingenious ways to investigate the impact of money on

[6] In his interview with John Taylor, Friedman (2001, p. 111, p. 120) agrees that "most of his articles are empirical rather than theoretical" and that, at least in his early work, he "was trying to explain data, but not through models . . . but through more informal stories."

[7] Elsewhere Friedman (1990, p. 20) argues:

> In my view, regression analysis is a good tool for deriving hypotheses. But any hypothesis must be tested with data or nonquantitative evidence other than that used in deriving the regression or available when the regression was derived. Low standard errors of estimate, high t-values, and the like are often tributes to the ingenuity and tenacity of the statistician rather than reliable evidence of the ability of the regression to predict data not used in constructing it.

prices and business conditions and to separate these monetary effects from other influences.

From Mitchellian Method to Monetarist Theory

Thomas Sargent (1987) keenly observed that the project of the *Monetary History* was to inductively identify the causal factor in Burns and Mitchell's empirical account of the business cycle:

> In tying their method of presentation to that of Burns and Mitchell, Friedman and Schwartz assembled an impressive body of evidence that their money supply series is the hidden common factor underlying Burns and Mitchell's business cycle or that it is closely correlated with it. There is impressive evidence in favor of a one-dimensional (or at least a low-dimensional) factor *explanation* of business fluctuations, much of the evidence being organized by Burns and Mitchell. [Emphasis added]

So how exactly do Friedman and Schwartz surmount the problem confronting all inductivists, that of extracting cause-and-effect relationships from the data? The answer is revealed in the concluding chapter of *Monetary History* (Friedman & Schwartz, [1963] 1971, pp. 676–700) where they summarize their findings and seek to establish their significance for monetary policy. There, Friedman and Schwartz ([1963] 1971, p. 676) state three propositions that they describe as "common elements of monetary experience" that "can be expected to characterize our future as well as our past." These are, in their words:

1. Changes in the behavior of the money stock have been closely associated with changes in economic activity, money income, and prices.
2. The interrelation between monetary and economic change has been highly stable.
3. Monetary changes have often had an independent origin; they have not been simply a reflection of changes of economic activity.

The first two propositions are based purely on correlations that were observed over a wide variety of (U.S.) monetary experience. The third proposition is derived from historical narratives and "natural experiments" and is an attempt to infer causation from these correlations, that is, to establish the validity of the quantity *theory* of money.[8] Friedman and Schwartz conduct their research as monetary clinicians, approaching each historical episode as a clinical case study which provides evidence that bears on the propositions above but on its own proves nothing about causation. Causation is only inferred from an accumulation of natural experiments yielded by history in which the individual cases can be compared. According to Rockoff (2006, pp. 42–44):

> Each episode that Mitchell or Friedman and Schwartz investigate is a case study. The Great Contraction taken as a whole . . . is essentially a single case history. By itself it proves little. . . . The natural point at which to draw conclusions about causation from case studies is at the point when cases can be compared and contrasted. . . . The next step in a clinical study is to summarize the weight of the evidence suggested by the individual cases.

Friedman and Schwartz do this in the last chapter of their treatise. Let us examine the way in which they establish the close covariation of the money stock with money income, prices and, to a lesser extent, real economic activity. From the 93-year period they investigate (1867–1960), they develop 10 case studies. Four periods exhibit "economic stability": 1882–92; 1903–13; 1923–29; and 1948–1960. The remaining six periods feature severe economic contraction and unemployment: 1873–79; 1893–97; 1907–08; 1920–21; 1929–1933; and 1937–1938. Friedman and Schwartz ([1963] 1971, p. 677) find that, in the four periods marked by economic stability, there was "a high degree of stability in year-to-year change in the money stock," while the six severe contractions were "accompanied by an appreciable decline in the stock of money." For two of the severe contractions (1920–21 and 1937–38) the fall in the money supply was due to policy actions of the Fed and did not involve a banking crisis; the other four were accompanied by "major banking or monetary disturbances." Thus, a change in the money stock, regardless of its source

[8] In an influential article, James Tobin (1970) criticized Friedman's inductivist methodological approach on much the same grounds as Koopmans had earlier criticized Burns and Mitchell (see footnote 5 above). As Bordo and Schwartz (2003, p. 18 fn. 6) point out: "Tobin's critique essentially condemned Friedman's work because it lacked an explicit model that specified cause and effect relations before undertaking measurement and estimation." Friedman's approach thus contradicted Popper's method. For Popper (1965, p. 30) "opposed . . . all attempts to operate with the ideas of inductive logic," describing his own theory as "*the theory of the deductive method of testing*, or as the view that a hypothesis can only be empirically *tested*—and only *after* it has been advanced."

and the accompanying concrete circumstances, is associated with changes in nominal income, prices, and economic activity. From these ten data points, Friedman and Schwartz ([1963] 1971, p. 678) derive proposition 1 above and discover especially close correlations "on the one hand between secular and cyclical movements in the money stock, and, on the other, corresponding movements in money income and prices." Proposition 2 relates to the stability of the velocity of money and is also teased out using correlation analysis and historical narrative (Friedman & Schwartz, [1963] 1971, pp. 678–86).

Now, in order to establish the causal role of money in these covariations and validate the quantity theory, it is necessary to demonstrate proposition 3, according to which changes in the money stock originate independently of the other variables. Ben Bernanke (2002) recognized this as the crowning achievement of Friedman and Schwartz when he wrote:

> The special genius of the *Monetary History* is the authors' use of what some today would call 'natural experiments'—in this context, episodes in which money moves for reasons that are plausibly unrelated to the current state of the economy. By locating such episodes, then observing what subsequently occurred in the economy, Friedman and Schwartz laboriously built the case that the causality can be interpreted as running (mostly) from money to output and prices. . . .

Friedman and Schwartz identified four such episodes. One occurred under the gold standard (1897–1914). But since gold is a commodity whose production and international movements are partly determined by market forces, variations in the national quantity of gold money are never fully independent of economic activity. The authors therefore find most compelling the three episodes that occurred after the Federal Reserve was established. They label these as "crucial experiments" and compare them to experiments conducted in the physical sciences. They argue that, in the physical sciences "no experiment is completely controlled" and most "add little to tested and confirmed knowledge about the subject of the experiment." A crucial experiment is one that "throws a flood of light on its subject—a light that blinds us to many less important experiments that were necessary before the one crucial experiment could be made." The three counterparts of such crucial experiments that Friedman and Schwartz ([1963] 1971, p. 688) identify occurred: January–June 1920; October 1931; and July 1936–January 1937. According to Friedman and Schwartz

([1963] 1971, p. 688), "these are the three occasions—and the only three—when the Reserve System engaged in acts of commission that were sharply restrictive." In the first two cases, the Fed sharply increased rediscount rates when the banking system was either heavily indebted to the Fed or undergoing a wave of failures. In the third case, the Fed doubled reserve requirements while gold inflows were being sterilized via restrictive open market operations.

Friedman and Schwartz ([1963] 1971, p. 688–89) are emphatic in describing the significance of these episodes:

> On three occasions the [Federal Reserve] System deliberately took policy steps of major magnitude which cannot be regarded as necessary or inevitable economic consequences of contemporary changes in money income and prices. Like the crucial experiments of the physical scientist, the results are so consistent and sharp to leave little doubt about their interpretation. . . . There is no other occasion in Federal Reserve history when it has taken restrictive measures of comparable magnitude—we cannot even suggest possible parallels.

Friedman and Schwartz ([1963] 1971, p. 689) go on to argue that, on all three occasions, both the purely monetary changes and the economic changes "associated" with the Fed's monetary actions were "equally sharp and distinctive." To reinforce their attribution of the causal role to money on the basis of these "three quasi-controlled experiments," Friedman and Schwartz ([1963] 1971, pp. 689–90) seemingly abandon their Mitchellian "clinical methodology" and seek to indirectly calculate probabilities by way of a medical analogy:

> Suppose 3 men and four women were found to have a specified illness. Suppose 3 of the 4 women turned out to be the wives of the 3 men with the same illness. The presumption that the illness was contagious would certainly be very strong especially so if it were discovered that the husband of the fourth woman was the only remaining man to have a biologically related but not identical illness.[9]

[9] The fourth married couple refers to the 1929–31 period which exhibits features very similar to but not identical with the three episodes identified as "crucial experiments." In this period there was a severe economic contraction, but the Fed did not *deliberately* commit a restrictive monetary act and, therefore, strictly speaking, the monetary change did not originate independently of economic changes.

According to their calculations, the probability that the disease was not contagious—that is, that the matching of independent monetary decline and subsequent economic decline was random—range from 1 in 2870 to 1 in 30, depending on the number of discrete observations that are assumed.[10] Friedman and Schwartz ([1963] 1971, p. 690) conclude from this analogy:

> Similarly, the three episodes . . . establish a comparably strong presumption that the economic changes were the consequence of the deliberately undertaken monetary actions, and hence that our finding of a close covariation between the stock of money and income reflects the existence of an influence running from money to income.[11]

Friedman's Monetary Theory and Its Critics

Thus, Friedman's monetary theory as delineated and "tested" in the *Monetary History* is a highly aggregative and mechanical version of the quantity theory of money with very few variables and relationships. In particular, there are no correlations or crucial experiments establishing the significance of the financial markets in disseminating monetary impulses to the economy. This is a little surprising because in reconstructing his mentor's theory of business cycles early in his career, Friedman (1952, pp. 267–71) recognized that Mitchell regarded "the cost and availability of loans" as an important element in the cyclical process. As Rockoff (2006, pp. 22, 45) notes, however, Friedman and Schwartz "rejected Mitchell's bank-centric view of the transmission mechanism," instead emphasizing a "transmission mechanism running from money to economic activity that relied on a more direct channel connecting changes in money with changes in income." Thus Friedman (1969) formulated his helicopter model to lay bare the linkages between changes in money,

[10] The lower probability of non-contagion relates to 42 observations which reflect the 42 years of the Fed's existence covered in the *Monetary History*. The higher probability is based on ten observations reflecting the ten complete NBER "reference cycles" occurring during the period, with the reduced set of observations intended to eliminate serial correlation among successive years.

[11] Friedman and Schwartz ([1963] 1971, p. 694) regard the economic contraction of 1929–31, which they attribute mainly to acts of omission rather than commission by the Fed, "as a fourth crucial experiment, making the matching of independent monetary decline and subsequent economic decline 4 to 4." For 42 observations, the probability that the matching is random declines to 1 in 111,930 and for 10 observations, to 1 in 120.

spending, nominal income, and prices, maintaining that his conclusion holds even as the simplified model is modified to account for "more sophisticated institutional arrangements" (Rockoff, 2006, p. 23). In other words, the Friedman-Schwartz transmission mechanism operated "as if" financial markets were absent or, at least, neutral to the process consequent upon the infusion of new money into the economy.

In light of the foregoing, it comes as no surprise that Friedman, in sharp contrast to the Austrians, dismisses the significance of changes in interest rates, real and financial asset prices, and the temporal structure of production in his account of the inflation-adjustment process. This, in part explains why Friedman (2001, p. 123) disagrees with both his mentor Mitchell and the Austrians about the existence of business cycles:

> I do believe that short-run fluctuations in the economy are simply the accumulation of random shocks I don't believe that there is such a thing as a business cycle. . . . [I]n the sense of regularly recurring cycles, the kind of thing that Mitchell was trying to describe, I don't think they exist.[12]

Thus, the Friedmanite quantity theory is in effect a theory of monetary income whose sole aim is to explain the long-run movements in a single-valued price index by movements in a monetary aggregate, that is, the "money stock." Friedman's theory is mute on the subject of the short-run adjustment of the two variables on the right side of the equation of exchange, namely prices and real output, to changes in the money stock.[13] Friedman's approach consequently yields an extremely restricted concept

[12] Elsewhere, Friedman ([1998] 1999) reiterated his position, sardonically commenting: "[B]oth the Austrians and the Keynesians . . . added to our understanding of business cycles. Only I don't think there are business cycles." Rockoff (2006, p. 20), however, believes that Friedman and Schwartz simply assumed "a nonmonetary cycle that would continue in the absence of monetary disturbances." He conjectures that the reason for this was the strict division of labor at the NBER in which they were assigned to "clarify the role of money in the business cycle" and hence sought "to describe how monetary forces pushed or pulled a cycle determined by non-monetary forces." Friedman's "plucking model" of economic fluctuations seems to run counter to Rockoff's surmise (Friedman, 1993; Garrison, 1996).

[13] Although Friedman (1974, pp. 40–61) attempted to set out what Lothian (2009, p. 1093) calls "a generalized dynamic model of the short-run adjustment of inflation and nominal and real income growth to shocks," it has been almost completely ignored. Moreover Friedman (quoted in Lothian, 2009, p. 1093) himself acknowledged that it was a provisional attempt "to outline a general approach that could suggest what empirical issues required study." It was not to be considered "as the final word."

of inflation, which refers exclusively to the general movement of prices and completely ignores other, more momentous effects of changes in the money supply. It is these effects that the logical-deductive economist, not restricted to correlations between aggregate time series data, is able to detect by logical inference from broadly empirical facts. These include an interest rate artificially suppressed by the central bank below its "natural" level, a distorted structure of relative prices and wages, and the falsification of capitalist-entrepreneurs' profit and wealth calculations. The "natural" rate of interest, a coordinated structure of relative prices and wage rates, and undistorted profit and wealth calculations are, of course, unobservable phenomena that characterize a counterfactual market process unhindered by expansionary monetary policy. Yet economic analysis based on these concepts allows us to comprehend asset price bubbles, malinvestments, cyclical unemployment, overconsumption, and financial crises as a predictable qualitative pattern in the observed data.

Hayek's critical remarks on the positivist method are pertinent in this respect:

> We know, of course, with respect to the market and many social structures a great many facts which we cannot measure. . . . And because the effects of these facts in any particular instance cannot be confirmed by quantitative evidence, they are simply disregarded by [positivists]; they thereupon happily proceed on the fiction that the factors which they can measure are the only ones that are relevant. . . . On this standard there may thus well exist better 'scientific' evidence for a false theory, which will be accepted because it is more 'scientific', than for a valid explanation, which is rejected because there is no sufficient quantitative evidence for it. (Hayek, [1975] 1978, pp. 24–25)

It is not just those unsympathetic to Friedman's inductivist method, such as the Austrians, who are critical of his monetary theory for its narrow focus on a few macroeconomic variables. Even fellow monetarists like Karl Brunner[14] and Allan Meltzer object to Friedman's exceedingly sparse account of the monetary transmission mechanism, especially as it plays out over the short run. In their very insightful comment on the attempt by Friedman (1974) to recast his monetary framework in terms of short-run

[14] It was Brunner (1968) who, in 1968, coined the term "monetarist," although he capitalized it.

neo-Keynesian IS-LM analysis, Brunner and Meltzer (1974, pp. 64–65) note the "thinness" of Friedman's theoretical framework, arguing

> [T]he absence of an explicitly stated theory capable of generating the propositions that have been supported by empirical investigation [presumably in the *Monetary History*] has impeded the further development of monetary theory. . . . Friedman's statement of monetary theory does not seem to us an adequate underpinning for monetary theory or a particularly useful basis for empirical work.

In particular, the authors criticize the complete absence of relative prices, interest rates, and credit markets in Friedman's discussion of the transmission mechanism. Thus, Brunner and Meltzer (1974, p. 66) contend that the (then) contemporary search for microfoundations of macroeconomics implies that "macrotheories that seek to explain the underutilization of resources must take account of changes in relative prices, including but not limited to changes in interest rates." Furthermore, Brunner and Meltzer (1974, pp. 70–71) argue, Friedman's failure to distinguish between "money and bank credit" and include "the market for bank credit in his analysis of the markets for money and output" undermines his effort to transcend "the *IS-LM* framework and Keynesian paradigm" that he adopts for expositional purposes.[15]

Perhaps most important from the standpoint of Austrian business cycle theory is the recognition by Brunner and Meltzer (1974, p. 68, p. 73) that Friedman assumes that real interest rates are constant over the cycle and market rates adapt rapidly to changes in expectations in the short run. Not only does Friedman neglect to distinguish between real and market rates, but he does not acknowledge that interest rates are "a proxy for relative prices of assets and output." Friedman's framework is thus unable to explain the fact that "market interest rates generally rise during economic

[15] In a paper discussing monetarist objections to the IS-LM model, Bordo and Schwartz (2003) focus on the works of Friedman and co-authors Brunner and Meltzer. According to Bordo and Schwartz (2003, abstract page), Friedman never articulated his objections to the model, although he generally refrained from using it. In contrast, "Brunner and Meltzer's objections to IS-LM were explicit. They found it too spare, so they elaborated it. . . ." Curiously, Bordo and Schwartz (2003) never mention that Brunner and Meltzer's objections and elaborations were directed specifically at Friedman's use of the model to present the monetarist version of the quantity theory in a framework common to all macroeconomists. Nor do they cite the article by Brunner and Meltzer (1974) that contains the criticisms of Friedman discussed in the text above.

expansion and fall during economic contraction." I might add here that treating the real interest rate as constant and not as a variable market price subject to manipulation by monetary policy would also prevent Friedman from predicting, or even recognizing, the asset booms or bubbles that are an integral part of the cyclical pattern of economic activity. As Brunner and Meltzer (1974, p. 73) conclude:

> By keeping real rates constant, ignoring fiscal variables, and relative prices, Friedman's 'common model' neglects the variables that, we believe, explain many of the short-run changes in expenditures and market interest rates.

At the end of the day, Friedman (2001, p. 122) himself is not very bold in his claims for the predictive ability of his clinical methodology. Thus, he declares:

> I do not believe that we can possibly understand enough about the economy as a whole to be able to predict or interpret small changes. The best we can hope for is to be able to understand significant larger changes.

In this statement, Friedman sounds very much like Austrian and other logical-deductive economists, whose methodology he spurns as unscientific, and who uphold the ultimate rationale of economic science as "pattern prediction," especially with regard to the consequences of economic policy measures.[16] This similarity between their claims for the predictive power of economic theory invites a comparative test of pattern predictions between Friedman and the Austrians with respect to their interpretations of economic events in the five years leading up to the bursting of the housing and financial bubbles and its financial consequences. Constraints of

[16] As Ludwig von Mises (1978, p. 67) put it:

> Economics can predict the effects to be expected from resorting to definite measures of economic policies. It can answer the question of whether a definite policy is able to attain the ends aimed at and, if the answer is in the negative, what its real effects will be. But, of course, this prediction can only be "qualitative." It cannot be quantitative because there are no constant relations between the factors and effects concerned. The practical value of economics is to be seen in this neatly circumscribed power of predicting the outcome of definite measures.

On pattern prediction, also see Robbins ([1935] 1969, pp. 121–26); Hayek ([1964] 1967); and Rothbard (2006, pp. 311–14).

space prevent such an exercise in this essay. Our purpose here is rather to demonstrate that Friedman's inductivist theory was inadequate in predicting such a constellation of events.

Prelude: Milton Friedman on Monetary Policy 1981–2001

The extreme sparseness of Friedman's theoretical account of the monetary transmission mechanism and its neglect of important but difficult to measure variables such as relative prices, the real interest rate, asset markets, and so on, emphasized by both Brunner and Meltzer and the Austrians, were bound to lead Friedman astray in his pattern predictions of economic events. Indeed, his predictions began to go dramatically awry in the early 1980s. In every year from 1982 to 1985, Friedman predicted that Fed monetary policy would reignite a major (consumer price) inflation. These forecasts were repeatedly falsified, as inflation never reached 5 percent in any month from 1983 to 1986. In fact, inflation continually declined during this period except for a mini-spike in 1984. The reason for these inaccurate forecasts was that velocity had not remained stable during these years despite the laboriously calculated correlations of the *Monetary History*. Also, in 1983 Friedman forecast a recession in early 1984 based on a sharp decline in the money supply in late 1983. The recession never materialized and economic growth was particularly strong in the first quarter of 1984. Friedman (quoted in Nelson, 2007, p. 165) conceded, "I have no easy explanation of what went wrong."

As the New Year dawned in 1990, Friedman (quoted in Nelson, 2007, p. 168) expressed optimism about the new decade, opining: "There's no reason why we shouldn't have a decade of rapid growth and relatively low inflation." Seven months later the economy slipped into a recession that cost President George H. Bush re-election, devastated the S&L industry, and ended in a prolonged "jobless recovery."[17]

During the 1990s, possibly chastened by his forecasting errors in the previous decade, Friedman the forecaster was uncharacteristically subdued. In 1992, Friedman (1992) exhorted the Greenspan Fed to shift to a more expansionary monetary policy in order to push M2 growth into its announced policy range. Despite Friedman's handwringing about tight monetary policy, the economy took off in 1993 and continued its seemingly strong performance for the next 6 years. By 1998, Friedman began to recognize that the empirical findings of the *Monetary History*—at least regarding the stability of velocity—could no longer "be expected to characterize our future as well as our past" as he and Schwartz had so confidently maintained in the *Monetary History*. Thus, at the end of the decade Friedman ([1998] 1999) effusively praised Greenspan in an interview, stating that Greenspan "has been doing a splendid job so far." Obliquely admitting the error of his own prescription in 1992 that the Fed should increase the rate of growth of M2 to promote recovery, Friedman remarked:

> I think there is no doubt that, from 1992 to 1995, around there, there was a very sharp uptick in the velocity of M2 and that targeting the money supply in a rigid fashion would not have been a good thing to do. . . . I don't know what I would have done. . . . I only say in retrospect that Greenspan did the right thing in abandoning primary reliance on M2 during that period. Whether I would have had the sense to do that or not, I don't know.

In May of the following year, Friedman told Peter Brimelow (1999a) in an interview that he saw "no sign of a recession" and mentioned that the Fed had been too expansionary. Friedman did, however, recognize the Dot-com bubble stating: "Amazon.com worth more than Barnes and Noble? . . . . It's a bubble part of the Internet bubble" (Brimelow, 1999b).

[17] By way of contrast, I wrote an article in 1988 and based on Austrian business cycle theory, I concluded:

> [M]y summary outlook for the U.S. economy for the next year . . . includes accelerating price inflation, coinciding with rising interest rates and a declining dollar for the first two or three quarters of 1989. . . . [T]he Fed will be compelled to tighten monetary policy before the end of the year [1989]. This will usher in a recession in late 1989 or early 1990, which would strike the U.S. economy with particularly heavy impact on the thrift and banking industries. (Salerno, [1988] 2010, p. 466)

But Friedman did not make the connection between the asset bubble and monetary policy. In fact, in an interview with John Taylor in 2000 but published the following year, Friedman (2001, p. 105) credited Greenspan and the Fed for "the dramatic reduction in the variability of GDP" that began in 1992 despite the breakdown between money and real GDP that began in the same year. This left him "baffled" and wondering if the Fed had "installed a new and improved thermostatic controller" (Friedman, 2001, p. 103). In an article published well after the collapse of the bubble and the subsequent recession (which he failed to foresee), Friedman (2002) explicitly attributed the bubble not to monetary policy, but to "technological change" that "produced extraordinary economic growth . . . triggering a bull market in stocks that terminated in a market collapse."[18]

Milton Friedman on Monetary Policy 2002–2006

For most of his career Friedman staunchly advocated that monetary policy be based on a "simple rule" and not be entrusted to the discretion of the monetary authorities. The rule, which was to be legislatively mandated, would entail that the Fed steadily increase the money supply at a rate sufficient to offset the secular decline in prices caused by the long-run growth of real output and decline in velocity. As we shall see, Friedman changed his mind near the end of his life, instead trusting to the discretion of the Fed, particularly in the person of Alan Greenspan.

In a series of articles and interviews between 2002 and 2006, Friedman effusively praised the Fed, and especially Greenspan, for finally learning how to maintain price stability. He further argued that the Fed's monetary policy was significant in promoting three decades of unprecedented prosperity and growth in the U.S. economy beginning in the late 1980s. In these writings, Friedman was totally oblivious to the formation of one of the greatest asset bubbles in U.S. history and its consequences for the economy. His inductivist monetary theory led to a wildly inaccurate interpretation of the development of economic events in the twenty years leading up to the bursting of the housing bubble and the near collapse of the financial system.

[18] Nelson (2007, p. 171) claims, "Friedman attributed some of the stock market's strength [in the late 1990s] to higher M2 growth." Nowhere in the two sources that Nelson cites does Friedman explicitly state such a position.

A. Friedman 2002

In a *Wall Street Journal* article in 2002, Friedman (2002) argued that the Fed under Greenspan was acting properly to avoid a repeat of the Great Depression after the recession of 2001 by rapidly expanding the money supply to prevent deflation. He contended "the current rate of monetary growth *of more than 10%* is sustainable and perhaps even desirable as a defense against economic contraction and in reaction to the events of Sept. 11." (Emphasis added.) He did concede, however, that "continuation of anything like that rate of monetary growth will ensure that inflation rears its ugly head once again."

B. Friedman 2003

In another *Wall Street Journal* article published the following year, Friedman (2003) completely ignored the expanding housing bubble and the rapid run-up in stock prices that were becoming apparent even to many media commentators. Housing prices by early 2003 were increasing at a 12.5 percent rate year-over-year (YOY) and had undergone a cumulative increase of 55 percent from the beginning of 2000 to early 2003. The S&P 500 index had risen from 800 to 1000 or by 25 percent in the four months (from early March to early July 2003) preceding the publication of Friedman's article. In addition, the money supply (M2) had grown by over $1 trillion or about 8.8 percent annually (uncompounded) from the beginning of 2001. But because Friedman was exclusively focused on the CPI, which was increasing at the time by 2.3 percent YOY, he chose to address the question of why the macroeconomic performance of the US economy had become so good after 1985.

Friedman's answer ran as follows. The Fed and other central banks had found the correct "thermostat," which was embodied in the quantity equation. The primary responsibility of the Fed is to ensure "as close an approximation as possible to price stability." But it wasn't until "sometime around 1985" that "the Fed appears to have acquired the thermostat that it had been seeking the whole of its life." According to Friedman, the problem the Fed faced was encapsulated in the "truism called the quantity equation of money," that is, $MV = Py$. In order to maintain the stability of the price level (P) the Fed is required to vary the quantity of money (M) to offset movements in both velocity of circulation (V) and real output (y). As long as velocity fluctuates "mildly and rather randomly" around a gentle long-run trend, which was one of the main empirical findings of the *Monetary History*, then the quantity of money per unit of real output is the dominant factor in determining the price level.

Friedman (2003) was greatly pleased with the Fed for finally having seen the light:

> Prior to the 1980s, the Fed got into trouble because it generated wide fluctuations in monetary growth per unit of output. Far from promoting price stability, it was itself a major source of instability. . . . Yet since the mid '80s, it has managed to control the money supply in such a way as to offset changes not only in output but also in velocity. The improvement in performance is all the more remarkable because velocity behaved atypically, rising sharply from 1990 to 1997 and then declining sharply—a veritable bubble in velocity.

This passage is a striking illustration of the Mitchellian methodology of the *Monetary History*. Friedman is here focused on a "bubble" in the meaningless but measurable macroeconomic variable of velocity while ignoring the bubble in real prices actually paid on asset markets. Indeed, Friedman admonished his readers not to worry that the continuing high rate of monetary growth would cause inflation, because "velocity was precisely back to trend" and there was "no overhang to be concerned about."

Friedman (2003) then posed "the obvious question" of why the new thermostat was implemented at precisely the time that it was. His answer was basically that central banks had abandoned the original Keynesian vision and finally learned the monetarist lessons of the *Monetary History*: "that inflation is always and everywhere a monetary phenomenon; that monetary policy has important effects on real magnitudes in the short run but no important effects in the long run . . . .[that] the crucial function of a central bank is to produce price stability." Friedman acknowledged that there were several other factors that also played a role in improving monetary policy but, he believed, "they were nowhere near as important as the shift in the theoretical paradigm. The MV=Py key to a good thermostat was there all along."

Friedman thus did not spy any clouds on the economic horizon in 2003 and believed that, with the Fed calibrating monetary policy according to the quantity theory thermostat, the future was rosy indeed.

C. Friedman 2004

In 2004, Friedman (2004) published a retrospective marking the 40th anniversary of the *Monetary History*. Friedman was positively glowing in assessing the performance of the Fed and other central banks. He still saw no ominous clouds gathering on the horizon, only an onward and upward movement toward greater macroeconomic stability as central bankers continued to learn and implement the policies of price stabilization taught by his book and its numerous devotees. Friedman (2004, pp. 349–50) triumphantly reported:

> Since the mid-1980s, central banks around the world have reacted to the mounting evidence of monetary research by accepting the view that their basic responsibility is to produce price stability. . . . The variability of prices is less by an order of magnitude since the mid-1980s than it was before, not only in the United States, but also in New Zealand (the first country to adopt an explicit inflation target), Great Britain, Euroland, Japan, and elsewhere.

Indeed, the adoption of monetarism by central bankers had not only stabilized the economy, but had altered monetary theory and the nature of money itself, radically transforming it from an exogenous to an endogenous variable. According to Friedman (2004, p. 350):

> Their success in controlling inflation has altered the empirical relation between short-term movements in money and in nominal income. Achieving price stability requires offsetting changes in velocity by opposite changes in the quantity of money, which reduces sharply the correlation between short-term movements in money and short-term movements in nominal income. To put it differently, short-term changes in the quantity of money can no longer be regarded as largely exogenous. They have become largely endogenous.

For Friedman, then, central bank actions were no longer the cause of macroeconomic fluctuations; rather, they "converted the quantity of money from an unruly master to an obedient servant." Since central bank bureaucrats had finally discovered the magic monetarist formula that enabled them to deftly fine tune the money supply to neutralize velocity shocks, they no longer needed to be constrained by a monetarist growth rule. Notice that here Friedman has given the game away to the Keynesians who claimed all along that the quantity theory was useless precisely because V was volatile. In fact, the dominant New Keynesian macroeconomic textbooks teach that the primary cause of "aggregate demand shocks" to which the Fed must react are caused by short-run fluctuations in velocity.

D. Friedman 2005

In December 2005, Friedman sat for a remarkable televised interview with Charlie Rose which covered a broad range of topics, including the performance of the Fed under Alan Greenspan. He gave no indication even at that late date that he had a clue that monetary policy had stimulated a dangerous housing bubble or that a bubble even existed.

In the interview, Friedman (2005b) lavishly praised Alan Greenspan and gave his approval to the Fed's recent monetary policy. The interview is worth quoting at length because it demonstrates how flawed monetary theory gives rise to profoundly inaccurate interpretations of the economy's performance. Note Friedman's almost monomaniacal focus on price stability and how this drives his entire appraisal of the state of the U.S. economy:

Milton Friedman: The United States is at the peak of its performance in its history. There has never been a time in the United States when we have had the state of prosperity, its level and its spread, that we have had in the last ten or fifteen years. There has never been a fifteen-year period in which there has been so little fluctuation in prices, in inflation. Inflation has stayed around 2 or 3 percent or less for the last 15 years. It's unprecedented. I certainly do [give credit to Alan Greenspan for that]. I think monetary policy is primarily responsible for it.

Charlie Rose: You think that Alan Greenspan . . . was the greatest Federal Reserve Chairman ever . . . ?

Milton Friedman: There has been no Chairman since [the founding of the Fed] who has anything like as good an outcome. Because he took the containing of inflation as the chief task of the Fed. . . . [L]et me put it this way, in the first 75 years of its existence, the Fed on the average was a major negative feature in the economy. We never would have had the Great Depression if there hadn't been a Fed. Since then, since 1982 or 1983 the Fed has been a beneficiary [sic, benefactor] for the economy. . . . I very seldom had anything good to say about the Fed before the 1980s. But since Alan Greenspan took over I've very little but good to say.

I think his successor [Ben Bernanke] is a very able man and he like Greenspan takes keeping stable prices as the major function of the Fed. And I have a good deal of confidence that he will continue in Alan Greenspan's path.

You can make a good argument that the Fed overdid easing money a little, that they kept the [Fed] Fund[s] rate at one percent a little too long. And you know that it's a natural tendency that you overdo things. You almost never go right along [on a stable path] like this. You go up, you go too far. It's very hard to calibrate. That was Greenspan's genius. . . .

In a letter to the *Wall Street Journal* in April of the same year, Friedman (2005a) had defended Greenspan against the charge that he was "reigniting inflation." To the contrary, argued Friedman, the growth rate of the money supply had been "trending downward" since 2000 and by 2005 was consistently "in the range of 4% to 6%, just about the rate required for a rapidly growing non-inflationary economy." Friedman failed to mention that the growth rate of the money supply (M2) fluctuated in a range roughly between 7 percent and 10 percent from the beginning of 2001 through 2004. More important, he did not find it noteworthy that the Fed Funds rate was pegged below 2 percent for almost three years or that the real interest rate, as measured by the difference between the federal funds rate and headline CPI, was negative from roughly 2003 to 2005. Lacking a realistic and robust theory of the monetary transmission mechanism that encompasses financial markets, Friedman was not concerned with short-run movements of the interest rate, except as a secondary gauge of monetary policy.

E. Friedman 2006 (Posthumously)

On November 17, 2006, one day after his death, an article by Milton Friedman (2006) was posthumously published in the *Wall Street Journal*.[19] Its title was "Why Money Matters." In this article, Friedman compared three episodes in monetary policy which he called, using inductivist jargon, a "major natural experiment." These episodes were the booms of the 1920s and 1990s in the U.S. and of the 1980s in Japan. All three booms occurred during periods of rapid economic growth sparked by technological change and were accompanied by a stock market boom that terminated in a crash. Monetary policy, accord-

[19] This article was based on a journal article Friedman (2005c) had published the year before.

ing to Friedman, was also very similar during all three booms. But monetary policy diverged greatly across all three episodes after the boom ended. The money supply contracted sharply after the 1920s boom collapsed in the U.S.; after the Japanese boom of the 1980s ended, the money supply stagnated and then began to grow very slowly; following the collapse of the 1990s dot-com bubble in the U.S., the money supply continued to grow rapidly.

The conclusion that Friedman drew from this "natural experiment" was that the highly expansionary monetary policy that the Fed pursued after the 1990s boom caused the U.S. recession of 2000–2001 to be very mild and allowed the U.S. economy to avoid a 1930s-style Great Depression or a 1990s Japanese-style Great Recession. Now this article vividly illustrates the reason for Friedman's remarkable failure to recognize the housing and financial bubbles that were clearly evident and peaking by 2006. For Friedman did not give the slightest indication that he viewed the rapid growth in the money supply as a major factor driving the boom phases of these three episodes. Rather, he concluded,

> Monetary policy played a role in these booms, but only a supporting role. Technological change appears to be a major player.

This judgment is a direct implication of Friedman's inductivist monetary theory: since there was very little change in some selected price level index in the US in the 1920s and 1990s and in Japan in the 1980s, well, then, monetary policy could not have been the main cause of the boom.[20]

Conclusion

Milton Friedman was perhaps the leading practitioner and proponent of empirical economics of his era. But, ignoring the Popperian methodology he propounded in his famous essay, Friedman instead developed theory

[20] Lothian (2011, p. 180, p. 186) offers as a "fourth episode" to bolster Friedman's "controlled experiment" the "recession that began in the fourth quarter of 2007 and the boom period that preceded it." Like Friedman six years earlier, Lothian completely ignores the sustained negative real interest rates and asset bubbles that marked the preceding boom. He does conclude, nonetheless, based on his own correlations between money supply, national income and stock prices over the four episodes, that "monetary shocks" rather than "credit shocks" continue to operate as the "senior partner" in "influencing" cyclical declines.

using the inductivist case study method pioneered by his revered "teacher, colleague and friend" Wesley Mitchell. Thus, in their *magnum opus*, *Monetary History*, Friedman and Schwartz eschew the econometric method of formulating and testing hypotheses using a selected body of data. Rather they use history as their laboratory, identifying historical episodes in which the handful of measurable variables they are interested in change with minimal influence from other changes occurring during the episode. These case studies are then treated as "natural" or "quasi-controlled" experiments comparable to laboratory experiments in the natural sciences, which, Friedman insists, are never "completely controlled" either. While correlations based on an accumulation of these case studies provide extremely useful material for theory construction, they do not establish a definite direction of influence among the variables, that is, "cause and effect" to non-inductivists. What is needed to rule out mutual interaction among variables is a "crucial experiment," by which Friedman and Schwartz mean an episode in which a clearly exogenous change occurs in one of the variables. With causality thus established, a "valid" theory emerges explaining the correlations among the variables. As pointed out above, for Friedman and Schwartz, the validity of the quantity theory of money, at least for the U.S., hinges on three crucial experiments, in January–June 1920, October 1931, July 1936–January 1937. In these three instances, the Fed autonomously restricted the money supply.

The artifice of the "crucial experiment" permitted Friedman to explicitly assign causality to the role of money in Mitchell's "descriptive analysis" of the business cycle. However, the result was the development of a simplistic and misleading monetary transmission mechanism that linked money directly to nominal income. This departed from Mitchell's bank-centric view and suppressed the role of financial markets and the interest rate in the mechanism. Austrians such as Hayek criticized Friedman's approach for narrowly focusing on measurable macro variables while totally ignoring the effect of money creation in reshaping the structure of relative prices and, thereby, distorting the pattern of allocation of labor and other resources. Fellow monetarists Brunner and Meltzer faulted Friedman's model for assuming the real interest rate is acyclical and ignoring relative prices and fiscal variables.

Friedman's reconstructed quantity theory led him to the conclusion that stabilization of "economy activity," as reflected in the macro variables of the price level and aggregate output, requires a stable money supply. Friedman advocated, therefore, that monetary authorities under a fiat standard should be subject to a rule mandating a policy of low and steady growth rate of the money supply that roughly offsets the secular growth rates of velocity and real output. Stability of an arbitrarily selected price index thus became, for Friedman, the single indicator of a stable economy. The relative price level stability of the 1980s and early 1990s in the face of unprecedented volatility of velocity, however, prompted Friedman to abandon his rule-based approach to monetary policy at the dawn of the new century. He then began to retrospectively hail the Greenspan Fed's discovery of the monetary "thermostat." This thermostat was the quantity theory, which guided the Fed to deftly manipulate the money supply to neutralize velocity fluctuations, stabilize prices, and maintain the real economy on an even keel through the 1990s. According to Friedman, this discovery effected a revolution in monetary theory and policy, transmuting money from an exogenous to an endogenous variable. But this innovation only intensified Friedman's implacable focus on stability of the price level as the desideratum of monetary policy and promoted his newfound trust in a discretionary Fed to achieve it. Thus was Friedman blinded to an asset bubble of epic proportions which was certainly apparent by 2004–2005 in the coexistence of rapid monetary expansion, negative real interest rates, and overheated housing and financial markets. We thus may agree with the judgment of Brunner and Meltzer (1974, p. 65)—although not for precisely the same reasons—that Friedman's reformulation of the quantity theory "does not seem to [be] an adequate underpinning for monetary theory or a particularly useful basis for empirical work." Ironically, Friedman's monumental failure in predicting the pattern of economic facts caused by Greenspan's monetary policy is attributable to his adoption of the inductivist method for deriving economic theory.

References

Bernanke, B. S. (2002). *Remarks at the Conference to Honor Milton Friedman.* University of Chicago. Board of Governors of the Federal Reserve System, November 8.

Bordo, M. D., & Schwartz, A. J. (2003). *IS-LM and Monetarism.* NBER Working Paper 9713.

Brimelow, P. (1999a). Beware the Funny Money. *Forbes*, May 3, p. 138.

Brimelow, P. (1999b). Bubblenomics. *Forbes*, May 3, p. 138.

Brunner, K. (1968). The Role of Money and Monetary Policy. *Federal Reserve Bank of St. Louis Review., 50*, 8–24.

Brunner, K., & Meltzer, A. H. (1974). Friedman's Monetary Theory. In R. J. Gordon (Ed.), *Milton Friedman's Monetary Framework: A Debate with His Critics* (pp. 63–76). University of Chicago Press.

Burns, A. F., & Mitchell, W. C. (1946). *Measuring Business Cycles.* National Bureau of Economic Research.

Friedman, M. (1952). The Economic Theorist. In A. F. Burns (Ed.), *Wesley Clair Mitchell: The Economic Scientist* (pp. 237–282). National Bureau of Economic Research.

Friedman, M. (1953). The Methodology of Positive Economics. In M. Friedman (Ed.), *Essays in Positive Economics* (pp. 3–43). Chicago University Press.

Friedman, M. (1969). The Optimum Quantity of Money. In M. Friedman (Ed.), *The Optimum Quantity of Money and Other Essays* (pp. 1–50). Aldine.

Friedman, M. (1974). A Theoretical Framework for Monetary Analysis. In R. J. Gordon (Ed.), *Milton Friedman's Monetary Framework: A Debate with His Critics* (pp. 1–62). University of Chicago Press.

Friedman, M. (1990). A Cautionary Tale about Multiple Regressions. Addendum to "Alternative Approaches to Analyzing Monetary Data" by Milton Friedman and Anna J. Schwartz. The Hoover Institution. Working Papers in Economics E-90-10 (March), 27 pp.

Friedman, M. (1992). An Interview with Milton Friedman on Methodology. By J. Daniel Hammond. *Research in the History of Though and Methodology* (Vol. 10, pp. 91–118).

Friedman, M. (1993). The 'Plucking Model' of Business Fluctuations Revisited. *Economic Inquiry., 31*(2), 171–177.

Friedman, M. ([1998] 1999). Mr. Market. *Hoover Digest*, No. 1 (January). Retrieved December 1, 2021 http://www.hoover.org/research/mr-market. Reprinted from Gene Epstein, "Mr. Market: A Nobelist Views Today's Fed, Currencies, Social Security, Regulation." Barron's (August 24, 1998). p. 30.

Friedman, M. (2001). An Interview with Milton Friedman. By John B. Taylor on May 2, 2000. *Macroeconomic Dynamics* (Vol. 5, pp. 101–131).

Friedman, M. (2002). The 1990s' Boom Went Bust. What's Next? *WSJ.com*, January 22. Retrieved October 10, 2021, from http://interactive.wsj.com/archive/retrieve.cgi?id=SB1011663602461321440.djm.

Friedman, M. (2003). The Fed's Thermostat. *The Wall Street Journal*, August 19. Retrieved October 9, 2021, from http://online.wsj.com/articles/SB106125694925954100.

Friedman, M. (2004). Reflections on a Monetary History. *Cato Journal, 23*(3), 349–351.

Friedman, M. (2005a). No Cause to Berate the Fed for 'Reigniting Inflation.' Letter to the Editor. *The Wall Street Journal.* Retrieved November 3, 2022, from http://online.wsj.com/articles/SB111284021842000451.

Friedman, M. (2005b). Interview with Charlie Rose. *Charlie Rose*. Television, December 29. Retrieved October 1, 2021 from Becker Friedman Institute for Research in Economics http://bfi.uchicago.edu/video/milton-friedman-charlie-rose.

Friedman, M. (2005c). A Natural Experiment in Monetary Policy Covering Three Episodes of Growth and Decline in the Economy and the Stock Market. *Journal of Economic Perspectives.*, *19*(4), 145–150.

Friedman, M. (2006). Why Money Matters. *The Wall Street Journal*, November 17. Retrieved October 9, 2021, from http://online.wsj.com/articles/SB116372965543825880.

Friedman, M., & Friedman, R. D. (1998). *Two Lucky People: Memoirs*. University of Chicago Press.

Friedman, M., & Schwartz, A. J. ([1962] 1971). *A Monetary History of the United States, 1867-1960*. Princeton University Press.

Garrison, R. W. (1996, October). Friedman's 'Plucking Model.' *Economic Inquiry*, *34*(4).

Hayek, F. A. ([1964] 1967). The Theory of Complex Phenomena. In idem, *Studies in Philosophy, Politics and Economics* (pp. 22–42). Simon and Schuster.

Hayek, F. A. ([1975] 1978). The Pretense of Knowledge. In F. A. Hayek (Ed.), *New Studies in Philosophy, Politics, Economics and the History of Ideas* (pp. 23–34). University of Chicago Press.

Hayek, F. A. (1978). *New Studies in Philosophy, Politics, Economics and the History of Ideas*. University of Chicago Press.

Hetzel, R. I. (2007). The Contributions of Milton Friedman to Economics. Federal Reserve Bank of Richmond. *Economic Quarterly*, *93*(1), 1–30.

Hoover, K. (2004). *Milton Friedman's Stance: The Methodology of Causal Realism*. University of California Department of Economics Working Paper Series, Paper # 06-6.

Huerta de Soto, J. (1998). *Money, Bank Credit, and Economic Cycles* (M. A. Stroup, Trans.).

Koopmans, T. C. (1947). Measurement Without Theory. *The Review of Economics and Statistics.*, *29*(3), 161–172.

Lothian, J. R. (2009). Milton Friedman's Monetary Economics and the Quantity-Theory Tradition. *Journal of International Money and Finance.*, *28*(7), 1086–1096.

Lothian, J. R. (2011). Why Money Matters: A Fourth Natural Experiment. *Open Economies Review*, *22*, 179–187.

Mises, L. v. (1978). *Notes and Recollections* (H. F. Sennholz, Trans.). Libertarian Press.

Mitchell, W. C. (1913). *Business Cycles*. University of California Press.

Mitchell, W. C. ([1941] 1963). *Business Cycles and Their Causes*. University of California Press.

Nelson, E. (2007). Milton Friedman and U.S. Monetary History: 1961-2006. Federal Reserve Bank of St. Louis. *Review, 89*(3), 153–182.

Popper, K. R. (1965). *The Logic of Scientific Discovery* (2nd ed.). Harper & Row.

Robbins, L. ([1935] 1969). *An Essay on the Nature and Significance of Economic Science* (2nd ed.). Macmillan.

Rockoff, H. (2006). On the Origins of *A Monetary History*. National Bureau of Economic Research Working Paper 12666.

Rothbard, M. N. (2006). *Power and Market: Government and the Economy* (4th ed.). Mises Institute.

Salerno, J. T. ([1988] 2010). A Monetary Explanation of the October Stock Market Crash: An Essay in Applied Austrian Economics. In J. T. Salerno (Ed.), *Money: Sound and Unsound* (pp. 449–466). Mises Institute.

Sargent, T. J. (1987). *Some of Milton Friedman's Scientific Contributions of Macroeconomics*. Hoover Institution. Remarks delivered at the Symposium to Celebrate Milton Friedman's 75th Birthday.

Schultz, H. (1938). *The Theory and Measurement of Demand*. University of Chicago Press.

Tavlas, G. S. (2014). *In Old Chicago: Friedman and the Development of Monetary-Policy Rules*. Becker Friedman Institute for Research in Economics. BFI Working Paper Series No. 2014-02.

Tobin, J. (1970). Money and Income: Post Hoc Ergo Propter Hoc? *Quarterly Journal of Economics., 84*, 301–317.

Hayek's Overinvestment Theory and the Stability of the Euro Area

Gunther Schnabl

> Without a well-founded trust in this European System of Central Banks the euro will not last in the long-run, the ESCB will in the long run not maintain its ability to act. (Paul Kirchhof (2021, p. 154), translated from German)

I met Jesús first in 2014 in Leipzig, Germany. I had invited him to give two presentations at Leipzig University. They were very well received and Jesús distributed his books and papers to our students. We were inspired by his outstanding thoughts and personality. The topics of the presentations "The Austrian Business Cycle Theory Explanation of the Current Economic Situation" and "The Austrian Defense of the Euro with a Criticism of the Current Antideflationist Paranoia" remain very topical today. I remember that we discussed at dinner the role of the euro for macroeconomic stability in Europe and the possibility of negative interest rates. Jesús argued that the euro could contribute to fiscal discipline in Europe and that negative interest rates were under free market conditions impossible.

G. Schnabl (✉)
Leipzig University, Leipzig, Germany
e-mail: schnabl@wifa.uni-leipzig.de

D. Howden, P. Bagus (eds.), *The Emergence of a Tradition: Essays in Honor of Jesús Huerta de Soto, Volume I*,
https://doi.org/10.1007/978-3-031-17414-8_23

Since 2014, negative interest rates have become increasingly a reality in the euro area, albeit under non-free market conditions. The European Central Bank (ECB) charges negative interest rates on the deposits of commercial banks at the ECB, which are increasingly shifted to the depositors of the commercial banks. The ECB has brought up so-called (Targeted) Longer-term Refinancing Operations with a negative interest rate up to -1.0%. The extensive government bond purchases of the ECB have pushed interest rates of some government bonds into negative territory. The increasing inflation is pushing real interest rates of bank deposits and euro area government bonds in ever deeper negative territory.

The growing degree of financial repression has encouraged—in particular via the extensive government bond purchases of the ECB—debt taking in the euro area, with government debt levels reaching record highs. The institutional arrangements which aimed to contain public debt are hollowed out. We observe the gradual transformation of the ECB from a Deutsche Bundesbank-type central bank, which is strongly focused on price stability, to a central bank, which seems mostly committed to finance government expenditure (Stark et al., 2020).

The coronavirus crisis has paved the way toward higher inflation in the euro area. The EU Next Generation Fund (750 billion euros) has opened the door to a new institutional framework, where the European Commission will issue its own debt, which is purchased by the ECB. Based on the works of Mises (1912), Hayek (1931), Huerta de Soto (2011, 2012), and Schnabl (2019), the past and the future path of the stability and the credibility of the euro is explored.

Reasons for the European Financial and Debt Crisis

Mundell's (1961) theory of optimum currency areas as well as the overinvestment theory of Mises (1912) and Hayek (1931) is crucial for understanding the role of the ECB for regional boom and bust within the European Monetary Union and thereby the growing instability of the euro area.

The Flawed Institutional Framework of the EMU

Prior to the European Monetary Union, two different central bank and growth models in Europe prevailed (De Grauwe, 2020). Germany had an independent central bank with a strong focus on price stability. Low inflation ensured low real interest rates, which constituted the basis for buoyant investment, exports, and growth. The independence of Deutsche Bundesbank ensured fiscal discipline. Government expenditure had to be mainly financed via tax revenues. Some neighboring countries such as Austria and the Netherlands imported the German model by pegging the exchange rates of their currencies to the German mark.

In contrast, in southern and western Europe, the growth models were oriented toward consumption and government expenditure. An important source of public financing were the central banks, which were subject to guidance by the governments. Inflation was high. The resulting depreciations of the currencies against the German mark provided an additional growth stimulus, as the Deutsche Bundesbank did not respond by depreciating the German mark. This promoted the role of the German mark as the leading store of value and stability anchor in Europe.

When the euro was introduced in 1999, the German central bank model with its narrow focus on price stability was embedded in the Treaty on the Functioning of the European Union (Art. 127 TFEU). The ECB was banned from financing government expenditures (Art. 123 TFEU) and the bailout of overindebted countries was prohibited (Art. 125 TFEU). In contrast to the United States, the common monetary policy was not paired with a common fiscal policy, with fiscal policies of the member states of the European Monetary Union (EMU) remaining widely independent. As a tool of fiscal coordination, limits to general government deficits (3% of GDP) and the stock of general government debt (60% of GDP) were established (Art. 126 TFEU).

The high degree of heterogeneity of the member states became the Achilles' heel of the monetary union. Mundell (1961) had argued that an optimum currency area had to consist of countries with a low likelihood of asymmetric shocks, that is, with synchronized business cycles. Asymmetric shocks would necessitate a high degree of wage flexibility and/or labor mobility. As tight labor market regulations in most EU member states prevent wage flexibility, fiscal policies could be seen as the main mechanism to cope with asymmetric shocks and idiosyncratic business cycles.

Yet, since the early years of the euro different parts of the euro area followed different business cycles. After the turn of the millennium structural reforms in Germany, which aimed to ensure the compliance with the Maastricht debt criteria, depressed growth in Germany (Schnabl, 2018). Fiscal and wage austerity combined with a loose monetary policy of the ECB triggered extensive capital outflows, inter alia to several southern euro area countries and Ireland. There, the credit inflows combined with an unprecedented low interest environment stimulated investment, consumption, tax revenues, and government spending. Behaving procyclical, the national fiscal policies in both parts of the euro area failed to counterbalance the idiosyncratic business cycles (De Grauwe, 2020).

After the European financial and debt crisis, the same pattern reemerged, but inversed. Whereas the monetary policy rescue measures of the ECB led to an extraordinary degree of monetary expansion, the southern euro area crisis countries and Ireland were urged into fiscal austerity to contain government debt. At the same time, the loose monetary conditions stimulated growth, tax revenues, and government expenditure in Germany, where stock and real estate prices surged. This put the stage for a potential financial crisis in Germany, which was suppressed in 2020 by the ECB's *Pandemic Emergency Purchase Programme* in course of the coronavirus crisis.

Although the coronavirus crisis hit all parts of the euro area, the heterogenous economic development in the euro area continued (Mayer & Schnabl, 2020). The southern euro area was hit stronger by the lockdown measures and travel restrictions due to the strong dependence on tourism. In contrast, the export industries of the northern part of the euro area profited from the faster recovery of the United States and China. The problem of idiosyncratic business cycles within the euro area remains unresolved, with the monetary policy of the ECB becoming ever more expansionary.

Overinvestment and Crisis in the Euro Area

The overinvestment theory of Mises (1912) and Hayek (1931) helps to explain recurrent and thereby persistent crisis in the euro area. An unsustainable overinvestment boom is triggered, when the central bank sets the central bank interest rate below the natural interest rate, which is defined as the equilibrium interest rate balancing private savings and investment (Huerta de Soto, 2011). Investment rises as low interest rates set by the central bank signal higher savings and thereby higher future consumption. As investment rises beyond private savings, the surplus demand for capital is financed by credit creation of the commercial banks.

As the capital market interest rate has fallen, investment projects with lower expected returns are financed. The average productivity of investment projects declines. The investment boom in the economy can spill over to asset markets, as during the boom stock prices of enterprises and banks rise, while deposit rates remain low (Schnabl, 2019). Low interest rates facilitate purchases of real estate, with—possibly—an unsustainable real estate boom setting in.

After the turn of the millennium (average) interest rates in the southern euro area declined for three reasons. First, as the southern euro area countries joined the EMU, their interest rates converged toward the low level of Germany due to the macroeconomic convergence process. Second, in response to the bursting of the dotcom bubble, the ECB strongly cut interest rates from 4.75% in October 2000 to 2.0% in June 2003. Third, credit inflows from Germany accelerated. An overinvestment boom was triggered, which was accompanied by proliferate consumption, excessive government expenditure, and speculation in real estate markets (Schnabl, 2018).

After the ECB increased interest rates, as in the overinvestment theory of Mises (1912) and Hayek (1931), the boom ended and the southern European countries and Ireland were thrown into severe financial crises. As banks collapsed, rescue measures for banks as well as collapsing tax revenues contributed to fast rising government debt. The financial crisis turned into a debt crisis, also labeled "euro crisis," which was finally resolved by the statement of the ECB president Draghi (2012) to do "*whatever it takes*" to save the euro.

The ECB cut the key interest rate to zero and embarked on growing government bond purchases, which from 2012 onwards now triggered an overinvestment boom in Germany (Schnabl, 2018). Thanks to euro depreciation and unprecedented cheap financing conditions for enterprises, German exports flourished and real estate prices hiked. As the ECB did not tighten monetary policy during the recovery after the crisis, the boom of exports and real estate continued. Even after the outbreak of the coronavirus crisis the boom persists, as a new unprecedented monetary expansion is further inflating the ECB's balance sheet.

The upshot is that the ECB behaved with respect to the monetary overinvestment theory in an asymmetric way (Schnabl, 2018): Whereas the

ECB tended to keep interest rates too low during boom phases, it avoided keeping interest rates too high during recessions. This implies an increasingly and persistently loose monetary policy, which is reflected by the key interest rates remaining at and below zero. The ECB's balance sheet was gradually expanded based on extensive purchases of government bonds and other assets as well as longer-term refinancing operations.

Negative Side Effects of Monetary Crisis Management

Although the crisis management of the ECB could prevent a collapse of the euro area, it has negative side effects in form of paralyzed growth and growing inequality.

Zombification and Low Growth

"To combat the depression by a forced credit expansion is to attempt to cure the evil by the very means which brought it about." Hayek (1933, p. 20). The persistently low interest rates of the ECB and the quasi-unconditional liquidity provision to banks via longer-term refinancing operations can be assumed to paralyze growth, as Schumpeter's (1912) creative destruction is prevented and distorted economic structures are conserved (Huerta de Soto, 2011). As Hayek put it (1931, p. 98): "if voluntary decisions of individuals are distorted by the creation of artificial demand, it must mean that part of the available resources is again led into a wrong direction and a definite and lasting adjustment is again postponed."

The negative impact of the monetary policy crisis management on investment and growth in the crisis countries is transmitted via the banking sectors, which are bailed out by the credit provision of the national central banks at eased collateral requirements. The envelope of the so-called (Targeted) Longer-term Refinancing Operations has reached 3300 billion euros. Additional government expenditure was made possible by extensive government bond purchases of the ECB, with the holdings of government bonds having reached more than 3500 billion euros.

Within the euro area, the TARGET2 payment system has evolved as an implicit credit mechanism (Sinn & Wollmershäuser, 2012). The national central banks of the southern euro area countries have accumulated large TARGET2 liabilities, which are reflected by large assets of Germany. From a balance of payments perspective, the TARGET2 liabilities correspond to an international zero-interest rate credit liability with infinite maturity.

If enterprises can expect that low-cost liquidity provision will persist independent from the profitability, the efforts to strive for innovation and efficiency increases are subdued. For Japan—where the (close to) zero-interest rate period continues since the mid-1990s—Sekine et al. (2003) find forbearance lending: Banks continue to provide irrecoverable loans to keep (potentially) insolvent enterprises and themselves alive. Peek and Rosengren (2005) associate Japan's central bank crisis management with a misallocation of capital, which makes survive companies with poor profit prospects (which they call "*evergreening*"). Caballero et al. (2008) show that—given the central bank's low-cost credit provision via *zombie banks*—*zombie enterprises* become dependent on cheap liquidity provision, with productivity increases declining.

In the monetary overinvestment theory too favorable refinancing conditions during the upswing trigger additional investment projects with comparatively low expected returns. The average efficiency of investments decreases. During a downturn and crisis, investment projects with low efficiency are dismantled. With an increasingly loose monetary policy stance as in the case of the ECB, the average efficiency of investments declines during the boom and remains low during the recovery after the boom. In the euro area productivity growth has gradually declined, becoming negative in many countries during the coronavirus crisis.

Redistribution Effects and Redistribution Conflicts

The increasingly loose monetary policy of the ECB has several redistribution effects (Hoffmann & Schnabl, 2016). As interest rates are gradually depressed by the ECB, high and rising government debt levels are kept sustainable. The institutions which are holding the governments bonds (e.g., pension funds, life insurances, and banks) suffer from shrinking interest rate revenues. The European middle class, which mainly saves in bank deposits, suffers as deposit interest rates were depressed to zero or even become negative. Rising inflation devalues savings and government debt in real terms.

In particular, young people suffer, because—given the low or negative productivity gains—wages of new entrants in the labor market tend to be depressed. Real estate prices and rents increase, in particular absorbing growing shares of the incomes of young people. As asset prices are strongly driven upwards, the older generation, who has acquired assets earlier, profits. Social advancement on the basis of wealth accumulation has become merely impossible, turning the economic perspectives of the young generation gloomy.

Given low or negative productivity growth, distribution conflicts within the EU become more likely. Previous to the euro, high productivity gains were generated particularly in the north, as the continuous appreciation of the German mark forced German enterprises to continuously improve efficiency and push forward innovation (Müller & Schnabl, 2019). This was even more the case as the common market allowed the industrial enterprises in the north to realize substantial economies of scale. The resulting large productivity gains could be partially redistributed to the southern European countries, leaving all countries better off. However, with productivity gains in the northern part of the euro area converging toward zero or even becoming negative, the intra-E(M)U redistribution is becoming a zero-sum game.

The Erosion of Trust

The consequence is an erosion of trust in the ECB and the established political parties.

High Inflation Perceptions and Erosion of Trust in the ECB

ECB president Christine Largarde has launched the campaign "ECB Listens" to make euro area citizens to participate in the ECB's monetary policy review process. The new German ECB board member Schnabel (2019) is trying to convince the German public that growing criticism of the monetary policy of the ECB is misplaced.

Nevertheless, there is growing distrust. Perceived inflation is substantially higher than officially measured inflation (Fig. 1). This can be due to the fact that people tend to perceive increasing prices stronger than falling prices (as ECB representatives put it). Alternatively, official inflation measurement is biased toward low inflation, as policy makers have decided to exclude asset prices from inflation measurement (Israel & Schnabl, 2020).

Also, the trust in the ECB is fading. Net trust in the ECB—that is, the difference between the percentage of interviewed people who tend to trust the ECB minus the percentage of people who tend not to trust the ECB—has substantially deteriorated since euro introduction and has in many countries become negative (Fig. 2). Despite fluctuations linked to

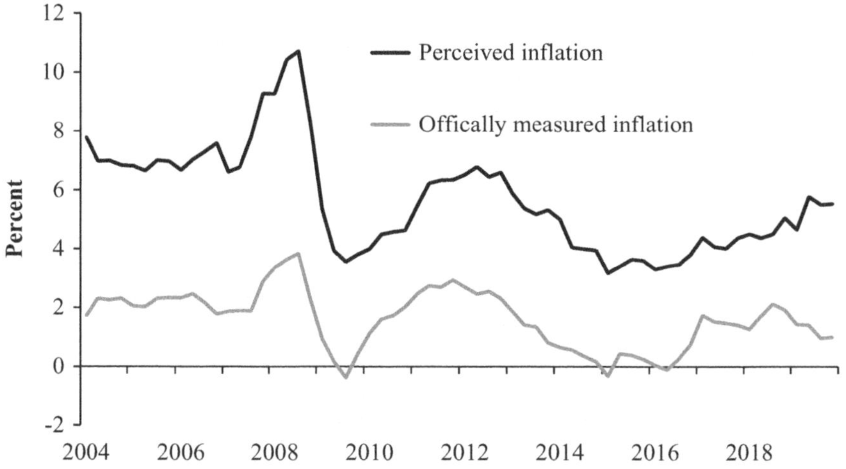

Fig. 1 Officially measured and perceived inflation in the Euro area. Source: European Commission. Perceived inflation as median

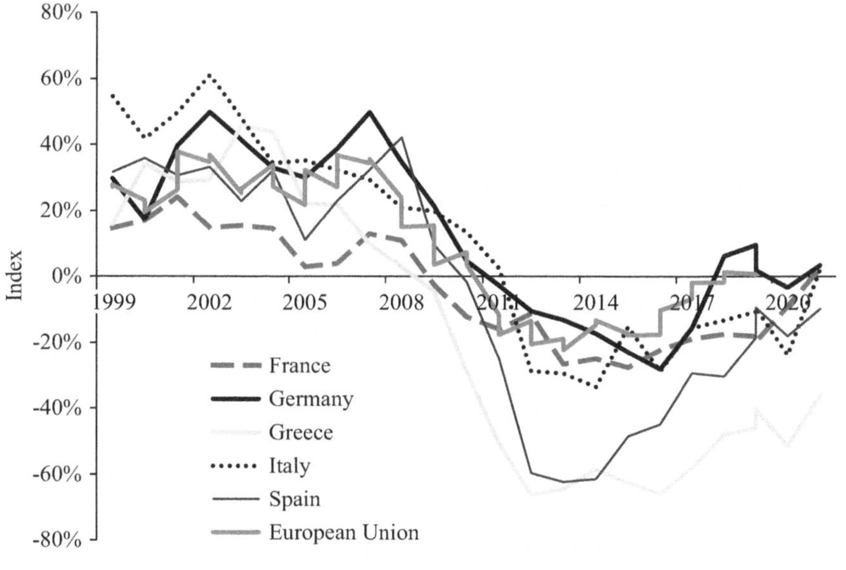

Fig. 2 Trust in the European Central Bank. Source: European Commission, Eurobarometer

the business cycle, there is a clear downward trend. This distrust is even stronger in some southern euro area countries such as Italy, Spain, and Greece, than in Germany. While the trust in the ECB recovered partially after the financial and debt crisis, it may turn negative again as inflationary pressure is currently increasing.

Political Polarization

Perceived inflation in the euro is substantially higher than real growth. This implies a perceived loss of real income, which is likely to contribute to political dissatisfaction. This is reflected in the IWP index of trust, which aims to trace the political polarization process in the European Union (Müller & Schnabl, 2021). The index measures the share of votes in parliamentary elections for political parties at the extreme left and extreme right of the political spectrum.

The spectrum of extreme right parties includes far-right extremism, right-wing populism, and Eurosceptic parties that reject the current European political order. The spectrum of extreme left parties includes old and new parties that have communist and/or Marxist-Leninist positions, as well as parties whose policies are based on an anti-capitalist view and reject the current market-based order. Parties and elections in Europe provide a respective classification scheme for each party which is in line with the classification in the academic literature.

Figure 3 shows the Index of Trust in the EU27 and the United Kingdom, which is compiled based on the share of votes in parliamentary elections given to non-extremist parties. A lower value indicates a stronger political polarization. According to this index, in the early 1990s the political landscape in Europe stabilized, mainly because the communist parties in central and eastern Europe lost votes. Since then, the political polarization is showing—despite some fluctuations—a continuous upward trend. Whereas in the southern European countries support tends to grow more for extreme left-wing parties, in central and eastern European countries extreme right parties tend to gain votes.

Outlook

There are two possible directions of causality between the political polarization process and the monetary stance of the ECB. First, the monetary policy of the ECB is increasing disparities and therefore the inclination to

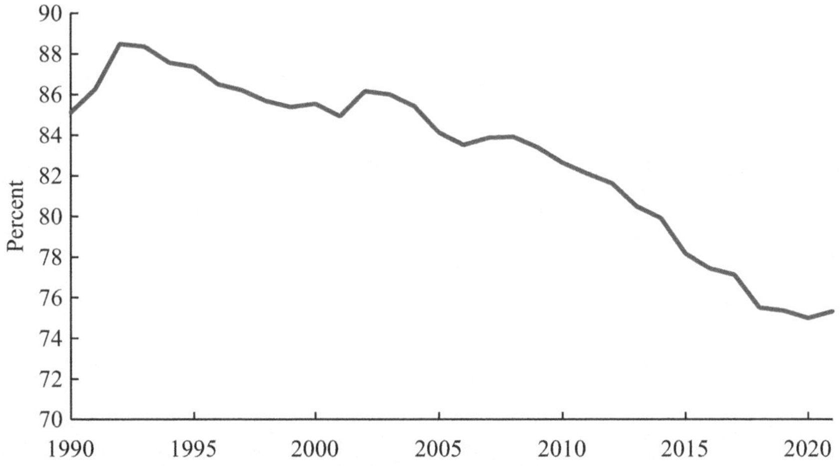

Fig. 3 IWP Index of Trust: EU27 PLUS_SPI United Kingdom. Source: Müller and Schnabl (2021)

vote for extreme parties. Second, the increasing political polarization tempts policy makers to provide social benefits to the population. As—given the paralyzed growth dynamics—tax revenues are not sufficient for financing, the governments have to rely increasingly on ECB government bond purchases.

The €750 billion Next Generation EU Fund, which was announced as "*a magnificent signal of solidarity and willingness to reform*" aims to cure the structural problems of the euro area by even more central bank financed government expenditure, now with debt also raised at the level of the European Union. This process may lead to a gradual centralization of fiscal policy at the European level, which could help to absorb asymmetric shocks via the establishment of a transfer union.

Albeit this approach will help to conserve the euro area in the short term, it is likely to further hinder growth and increase inequality, as higher debt levels will force the ECB into even stronger monetary expansion. This implies that the original Deutsche Bundesbank-type monetary policy has become transformed into a monetary policy, which is close to the pattern as observed in many southern European countries before their entry into the European Monetary Union.

To this end, unfortunately, the pious hope of Jesús Huerta de Soto (2012) that the euro will bring fiscal and monetary discipline to Europe has not been fulfilled. This shows that for all of us, forecasts are subject to a high degree of uncertainty. This does not rule out, however, that the current rise of inflation in the euro area will trigger a recollection of the values of Deutsche Bundesbank, which still remain embedded in the Treaty on the Functioning of the European Union. The overinvestment theory of Mises (1912) and Hayek (1931) and the outstanding works of Huerta de Soto (2012) could provide important insights for a stability-oriented relaunch of the ECB's monetary policy.

References

Caballero, R., Hoshi, T., & Kashyap, A. (2008). Zombie lending and depressed restructuring in Japan. *American Economic Review, 98*(5), 1943–1977.

De Grauwe, P. (2020). *The Economics of Monetary Union* (13th ed.). Oxford University Press.

Draghi, M. (2012). *Verbatim of the remarks made by Mario Draghi*. Speech by Mario Draghi, President of the ECB, Global Investment Conference, London, 26 July 2012.

Hayek, F. A. (1931). *Prices and Production*. August M. Kelly Publishers.

Hayek, F. A. (1933). *Monetary Theory and the Trade Cycle*. Jonathan Cape.

Hoffmann, A., & Schnabl, G. (2016). The Adverse Effects of Unconventional Monetary Policy. *Cato Journal, 36*(3), 449–484.

Huerta de Soto, J. (2011). *Geld, Bankkredit und Konjunkturzyklen*. Lucius & Lucius.

Huerta de Soto, J. (2012). Die Verteidigung des Euro: ein österreichischer Ansatz. *ORDO, 63*, 21–44.

Israel, K., & Schnabl, G. (2020). *Alternative measures of price inflation in Germany since 1999*. CESifo Working Paper 8583.

Kirchhof, P. (2021). *Geld im Sog der Negativzinsen*. C.H.Beck.

Mayer, T., & Schnabl, G. (2020). Post-corona EMU: Economic Distancing by Parallel Currencies. *Intereconomics, 55*(6), 387–391.

Mises, L. v. (1912). *Die Theorie des Geldes und der Umlaufmittel*. Duncker und Humblot.

Müller, S., & Schnabl, G. (2019). The Brexit as a Forerunner: Monetary Policy, Economic Order and Divergence Forces in the European Union. *Economists' Voice, 16*, 1.

Müller, S., & Schnabl, G. (2021). A Database and Index for Political Polarization in the European Union. *Mimeo*.

Mundell, R. (1961). A Theory of Optimum Currency Areas. *American Economic Review, 51*(4), 657–665.

Peek, J., & Rosengren, E. (2005). Unnatural Selection: Perverse Incentives and the Misallocation of Credit in Japan. *American Economic Review, 95*(4), 1144–1166.

Schnabel, I. (2019). *Narratives About the ECB's Monetary Policy—Reality or Fiction?* Speech by Isabel Schnabel, Member of the Executive Board of the ECB at the Juristische Studiengesellschaft, 11 February 2020.

Schnabl, G. (2018). The Failure of ECB Monetary Policy from a Mises/Hayek Perspective. In A. Godart-van der Kroon & P. Vonlanthen (Eds.), *Banking and Monetary Policy from the Perspective of Austrian Economics* (pp. 127–152). Springer.

Schnabl, G. (2019). Central Banking and Crisis Management from the Perspective of Austrian Business Cycle Theory. In D. Mayes, P. Siklos, & J.-E. Sturm (Eds.), *The Oxford Handbook of the Economics of Central Banking* (pp. 551–584). Oxford University Press.

Schumpeter, J. (1912). *The Theory of Economic Development.* Harvard University Press.

Sekine, T., Kobayashi, K., & Saita, Y. (2003). Forbearance Lending: The Case of Japanese Firms. *Bank of Japan Institute for Monetary and Economic Studies, 21*(2), 69–92.

Sinn, H.-W., & Wollmershäuser, T. (2012). Target Loans, Current Account Balances and Capital Flows: The ECB's Rescue Facility. *International Tax and Public Finance, 19*(4), 468–508.

Stark, J., Mayer, T., & Schnabl, G. (2020). The ECB Needs to Rediscover Itself. *The International Economy, Summer*, 36–37, 55–57.

The Two Gresham's Laws: Parallel Currencies in a Small Country

Pedro Schwartz

The superstition that money is an instrument to foster growth in real, not merely nominal, terms is widespread. This mistake is due to the belief that the authorities can trick people into thinking that their income grows when it is nominally multiplied by inflation rather than by increased productivity. Governments hope that individuals thus will redouble their efforts as workers and investors and multiply the demand of goods and services. I am not saying that financial services are not factors of production nor that a

With this contribution I want to celebrate forty-two years of teaching economics of my old friend Jesús Huerta de Soto. He is has become well known as an unremitting champion of social and economic freedom. He is also well known for the conviction and free style with which he proposes and defends his ideas. I well remember how difficult it was to convince him that he should sit down at his appointed place when presenting his doctoral thesis instead of marching up and down while telling the awarding Committee what to think, as Carlos

P. Schwartz (✉)
Universidad Camilo José Cela, Madrid, Spain
e-mail: pschwartz@ucjc.edu

D. Howden, P. Bagus (eds.), *The Emergence of a Tradition: Essays in Honor of Jesús Huerta de Soto, Volume I*,
https://doi.org/10.1007/978-3-031-17414-8_24

reasonable expansion of money and credit will not contribute to the growth of an economy—when I say reasonable I mean real financial services not those that result of inflation or bubbles. This is why in today's financial economies we need methods to avoid excessive issue of high-powered money and bank money. Along the centuries, a great variety of these methods have been used to contain the inclination of governments, central banks, and merchants to create money in excess and grant credit imprudently. Some of these *rules of issue* have been the following:

(a) Linking the creation of *fiat money* to the variation in the precious metal reserves of the issuer. The best known of such systems is the gold standard.
(b) Another solution, akin to the gold standard, is to fix the exchange rate of the national currency to a generally recognized foreign reserve currency such as the dollar, by means of a *currency board.* This system has the disadvantage of the possible misbehavior of the reserve currency. Still, it was adopted by Honk Kong in 1983 (HK$7.80 = US$1 with intervention by the monetary authority when the market exchange rate oversteps maximum and minimum limits). Other outside currencies are sometimes chosen, such as the euro by EU members not in the monetary union. Some French speaking countries in West Africa were at first tied to the French franc and now to the euro. Panama has been dollarized since 1903. It issues only small denomination coins (one balboa cent = one $cent). Ecuador also emits small change in the form of sucres, exchangeable for dollars on sight. The leftist Governments of Ecuador have tried more than once to rid themselves of dollarization in search of seignorage and free spending. But as soon as high valued coins were issued, the public rushed to banks to change them for dollars. Prof. Hanke of the Cato Institute has counted thirty-seven dollarized economies in the world. Dollarization can-

Rodriguez Braun also remembers. I was the supervisor of the thesis and Rodríguez Braun was a member of the judging Committee. That was a foretaste of the gusto with which Jesús Huerta has expounded the doctrines of the Austrian School of Economics. With his publications in many languages and his many years of untiring pedagogy he has helped revive the fortunes of that school against the hostility of many in the profession. He has thus helped transmit the idea that there are different ways of cultivating economics and that the skepticism regarding the free market impoverishes our vision of the world.

not last without a balance of payments surplus and a balanced budget. Domestic prices and wages must be fully flexible, so that exports are kept up to whatever world circumstances demand. Foreign capital must be attracted and put to productive use. This makes anti-cyclical economic policy well-nigh impossible. Argentina tried dollarization from 1900 to 2002 (1 peso = $1) but failed by disobeying the zero public deficit rule.

(c) Monetary unions usually create a new (solid) currency, which members adopt as their national currency. The system is akin to the gold standard, only the union is exposed to the dangers of a possibly unorthodox central bank. Discipline is then imposed by some agreed rule—in the EMU the Maastricht access conditions and the Stability and Growth Pact. The Southern members have had great difficulty in obeying the zero public deficits and public debt rule. COVID-19 has led to the "temporary" suspension of these rules.

(d) Some economists such as Milton Friedman in his later years proposed that the money supply should be increased on the same trend as the supply of goods and services, no attention given to cyclical variations, so that the quantity theory ($P = MV \cdot Y^{-1}$) holds.

(e) Lately central banks have decided that the best rule to maintain the purchasing power of money would be to define an inflation objective and keep to it. In the EU, the ECB has chosen 2% inflation as the aim and so has the Bank of England. The Fed is said to be following an inflation rule implicitly.

(f) Another of those rules has been having traction of late, the Taylor Rule, which ties the central bank discount rate to expected rate of inflation and the output gap.

A Different Monetary Rule

We believe that small developing economies could use a different monetary system resulting in stability with greater capacity to absorb shocks than straight dollarization: the running of parallel currencies with floating exchange rates. I will analyze two examples: Peru in Latin America and Kenya in East Africa.

The first case we examine is that of the parallel currencies system of Peru. A national currency, the *nuevo sol* runs together with a universally accepted currency, the dollar, but is not linked to it by a fixed exchange rate. The US dollar is not legal tender, but this only matters for the payment of taxes. The two currencies are widely used in transactions, valuations, and assets. Any sizeable depreciation of the sol alerts the *Banco de la*

Reserva of Peru that there may have been an excessive issue of the national currency or a disregard of the rule of a balanced budget or simply a shock originating in national politics or in the world economy.

The second case we study is that of Kenya, with a private currency running in parallel with the official shilling. That currency is created by its users, at their cost and through their effort, since it originated as minutes of cell phone use purchased by migrant Kenyan workers in South Africa, transferred to their families through the network with the help of a SIM card. Fundamentally, over-emission of *M-pesa*, the parallel money, is checked by the labor cost of acquiring those telephone minutes. Since the system has evolved into having local branches holding nominal deposits, the check is the limits to the amounts deposited, as set by the issuing telephone company Safaricom, in conjunction with the Kenyan central bank. The incentive for such minimal regulation is care for the good name of the telephone company and the continuation of a remunerative business. Light regulation has helped the extension of the system to neighboring nations, such as Uganda and Tanzania; over-regulation on the other hand has impeded its extension to West Africa.

The cases of Peru and Kenya are different from those of dollarization or euroization and other monetary systems guaranteed by a currency board. What is the basis for confidence in such an anti-intuitive system as that of parallel currencies? None other than a flexible exchange rate, managed by a central bank wedded to monetary stability.

A visit to the Banco Central de Reserva del Perú allowed me to observe the functioning of a parallel currency system in that country; and the Kenyan students of my courses on money at the University of Buckingham allowed me to understand the use of M-pesa. I could see that in both cases it was the choices of firms and individuals that reduce the national central banks to the subsidiary role of reinforcing the confidence in the currency.

As I say, in *fiat* money systems the minimum expected contribution of central banks is to keep the value of the money they issue as stable as possible, though their value is never absolute as that of other measuring rods such as the meter or the kilogram (Friedman, 1967). To that end, they should keep to an issuing rule on which people can rely. Those expectations of good behavior will evaporate if the central bank finances government deficits by lending it money or buying public debt. Monetary stability will also be endangered if the central bank takes economic growth or anti-cyclical policies as one of its goals. Regarding the cycle, the central bank must restrict itself to keeping real money supply stable from year to year. This should be especially so in developing economies where we witness proactive central banks ceaselessly playing with the value of the currency. In those countries and also in advanced economies, money is managed top-down by the authorities, usually with disastrous results. With monetary competition between parallel currencies, the choice is the market's, a bottom-up decision.

Gresham's Laws

A necessary step is to analyze the so-called Gresham's law or rather Gresham's *laws*. I do so with the help of Mundell (1998), which confirmed my intuition that the usual formulation of Gresham's law ("bad money displaces good") was incomplete: that Gresham's law had a direct and an inverse formulation.

The great financier Sir Thomas Gresham (1519?–1579) served three English monarchs, King Edward VI, and the queens Mary I and Elizabeth I. They favored him because of his able management of the currency and the skill he showed in the financial operations in Flanders as Elizabeth's Royal agent in Antwerp. He also amassed a large personal fortune.

The silver shilling, the legal coin of the realm, had been debased by Henry VIII, who was always short of funds. The policy of debasement was continued by his son Edward I. Queen Elizabeth tried to issue coins with original fineness but they soon disappeared from circulation. Gresham advised that the debased coins be withdrawn or marked with a punch, which soon made away with settling debts with nominal but inferior currency. And thus the traditional silver shilling reappeared in the realm's business.

These events are an example of *both Gresham's laws:* direct and inverse. Bad money directly expels good when the law gives them both legal tender status. Inversely, good money expels bad when exchange rates are legally left to the market. We shall see that two currencies can both circulate in a country if local authorities behave, do not abuse their money supply powers, and pay heed to the warning given by a prolonged devaluation of the national currency.

In this chapter, we shall see how a regime of parallel currencies can function as a system of stable money, a blessing for underdeveloped countries or countries having difficulties joining a monetary union. A system of parallel currencies allows an economy in crisis to introduce a soft devaluation at its own pace. Once the crisis abates, the money supply can be maintained at levels compatible with price stability. I shall now detail the conditions under which monetary competition can contribute to price stability and reduce cyclical volatility.

Fixed and Flexible Exchange Rates

Keynes in his *Tract on Monetary Reform* (1923), undoubtedly his best book, presented two possibilities for British exchange policy: to let sterling float or to fix the exchange rate to the dollar. In the first case, the United Kingdom could maintain the internal purchasing power of sterling. In the second case, the external value of the British currency would be guaranteed in terms of a world currency. As he summed up, "stability of prices *versus* stability of exchange" (heading of Ch.4.2). As between these extreme possibilities, Keynes chose floating sterling, since a fixed exchange with the dollar was equivalent to giving up a national monetary policy. A fixed exchange regime with the dollar could have unfortunate consequences because the errors of the Fed would impinge on the currencies linked to it. In fact, the Federal Reserve up to 1933 practiced a contrary policy contrary to the rules of the gold standard. These rules forbade sterilizing the considerable gold entries into the US. The Fed should have allowed that gold to enter monetary circulation and would thus have pushed the price level upwards. This would have led to an increase of imports and a re-equilibrium of the American and the world's balance of payments. The inverse happened again during the presidencies of Johnson and Nixon: the Fed financed the growing budget deficits resulting from the Vietnam War and the War on Poverty, which led to a two-digit rate of inflation. When Paul Volker in 1979 corrected that course by putting his foot on the brake, so to speak, dollarized economies such as Chile suffered a harsh deflation and were forced to return to floating the exchanges. The recessions or inflations of a small, dollarized country due to the ups and downs of the Fed's monetary policy have little back-effect on the world economy though they cause large variations of the local economy. The financial crises of Greece and Cyprus are not a counter-example: they endangered the euro because of the fragile expectations regarding resilience of the EMU.

So, one can understand the decision to let the currency float and aim at more flexible reactions to sudden changes of course by the world currency authorities. However, this means giving up a healthy discipline and tempting local governments to run large budget deficits, "print" money, and cause local runaway inflations.

We must note that, when a national monetary authority moves over to floating, it rarely chooses a clean float. One must however distinguish between a managed float to give a free hand to local populists and a managed float as that of the Peruvian Reserve Bank to preserve a steady exchange rate. As we shall see, Peru manages the exchanges to stabilize the national currency.

Two Monies in Peru: One Legal Tender, the Other *De Facto*

In response to these dangers, the *Banco de la Reserva de Perú* applies a special monetary policy, consisting in the systematic use of two currencies to stabilize the domestic price level. After the shock of the deflationary reforms cum devaluation effected by President Fujimori in 1990, a reform of the Constitution establishing central bank independence ushered a new era of orthodox money management (Martinelli & Vega, 2022). Peru could have chosen to dollarize the economy, as Panama did from 1902 and Ecuador or El Salvador more recently. These last two are countries, for example, with a history of hyperinflation have decided to use the dollar as the national currency to all effects. In a dollarized economy the money supply depends on the surplus of the balance of payments, so that dollarization is made easier by a steady export surplus and recurrent foreign investment, as Panama enjoys with the income of the Canal. Dollarization has two advantages and two disadvantages. The positive effects are that inflation is brought down to the American level overnight, so to speak; and that for all intents and purposes the hands of future populist governments are tied. Despite the harsh consequences of the sudden adoption of a stable currency in an inflationary economy, which may cause popular trouble, once dollarization is established, the public will resist abandoning it. This is what happened in Ecuador when the government of Rafael Correa tried to give up the dollar as a national currency. A similar reaction has been observed in Italy when populist parties proposed to go back to the lira: opinion polls showed that, despite the strict fiscal measures imposed by the EU, the public was decidedly in favor of a stable currency. The two drawbacks are that the national central bank loses the difference between the negligible cost of "printing" the national money and what the government can buy with it, called seignorage; and that the country is exposed to sudden inflationary or deflationary changes of policy by the Fed.

The Peruvian government has chosen a different way than dollarization for its monetary policy: to permit the use of two currencies. In fact, the dollar and the new sol are both legal tender, except that taxes must be paid in soles. It is an advantage that Peru has a recurrent source of dollars through guano, copper, sundry minerals, and oil exports. Nationals, both as individuals and corporations, can hold bank deposits in both currencies, which is a boon for mining companies having to pay dividends and repay loans abroad. The mechanism was set up under Julio Velarde as Governor of Banco de la Reserva del Perú, the central bank. He was kept at the post by six presidents and has recently been confirmed by the new populist President Castillo. Every day at 11:00 am, the central bank, in view of market conditions, official fixed the buy-and-sell exchange rates until the next day. If the demand for *soles* goes uncovered because there is an excess of *soles* seeking dollars, the bank will tighten. Tightening may mean increasing the rate of discount (which can be different for dollars or soles) or better still, by increasing the legal reserve of commercial banks at the central bank.

The Peruvian Reserve Bank has set itself an annual inflation objective between 1% and 3% and is in fact fulfilling it with a rate below 2%, an extraordinary figure in Latin America. Only in August 2021 did it rise to 5% (Banco Central de la Reserva del Perú, 2021, chart 8.3), which is not surprising, given the special finance to help recovery from COVID and the run on the currency following the populist presidential victory. We shall see whether the bank imposes restrictive measures to bring the inflation figure back to trend. As for the rate of exchange, and writing at the end of 2021, the sol has lost 12.7% in the last 12 months: again, it will be a good test of the system to see if the national currency recoups some of this loss in the year 2022.

In sum, the Peruvian system is one of monetary competition, an essential *trait* of the system. We often hear that countries undergoing foreign exchange crises should issue temporary *scrip* money to alleviate the dearth of means of transaction. This expedient was used by the Province of Buenos Aires when the local government issued *patacones* on the failure of the currency board. And The *Economist* of London proposed the issuance of scrip money when German banks refused to go on financing Greece's balance deficit. This misses the point of a permanent two currency system, such as that of Peru. Scrip money would keep people buying and selling until the monetary monopoly of EMU could be restored. The object in this case is more ambitious: to set up a permanent discipline whereby monetary inflations and deflations can be avoided, while shocks originating in the world currency can be avoided.

Telephone Money in Kenya

Individual inventiveness shows itself in all its splendor in Kenya, a country that suffered painful bouts of inflation above 15% between 1998 and 2008 and only sporadically benefits from moderate price rises. My Kenyan students at Buckingham University introduced me to a new currency born there called M-pesa (for Mobile Pesa or money in Swahili). It now is also used in Uganda and Botswana, and ten other countries around the Indian Ocean, where commercial banking services are little used (Mas and Radcliffe, 2010). Kenyan miners in South Africa started to transfer minutes of mobile telephone use to their relatives in their villages. Then, mothers and grandparents started to use those telephone minutes guaranteed by *Sqfaricom,* a subsidiary of Vodafone, to purchase goods locally. A SIM card inserted in the mobile phone permitted money transfers and purchases, with the telephone numbers of both parties acting as account numbers. The Supreme Court, despite complaints from the commercial banks, decided that Safaricom did not need a banking license to transfer funds, accept deposits, and grant microcredits. Though the central bank guarantees the one-to-one shilling value of the M-pesa, regulation is very light. The Kenyan Central Bank only intervenes to limit the deposit amounts to 100,000 M-pesa and daily money transfers to 300,000, to avoid criminal use and this acts as a check on over-issue. According to the central bank in 2016 (the last year for which I have obtained figures), M-pesa transactions amounts to the equivalent of 153 million dollars. In recent years, the use has grown and become almost universal in Kenya, certainly so among the general population. In effect, it is a crypto-currency, not subject to the ups and downs of the value of bitcoin or ethereum. It is used for daily transactions, small deposits, and credit in amounts adequate for the agricultural and service economy of a developing country. From the theoretical point of view, it is an instrument against inflation—in the form of a speeding up of transactions that avoids the loss of value of unmoved deposits. It also opens the wide world of *Fintech* to individuals and small firms unaccustomed to using banking services.

"Gresham" Dynamic Equilibrium of Two Legal Tender Currencies

In *fiat* money systems where money has no intrinsic value, central banks can at most aspire to keep a stable value for the national currency (Friedman, 1967). For that, they must keep to a rule and make the people confide in their maintaining it without fail. That expectation of good behavior will vanish if the central bank finances budget deficits or if the objectives of the central bank include directly fostering the growth of the economy or counteracting the cycle. Rare is the central bank that keeps to the remit of monetary stability. Those policies lead us to examine institutional arrangements that move away from the top-down to the bottom-up management of money. The answer lies in monetary competition, whose essence is the devolution of monetary decisions to individuals and firms.

For a country of average size, running two currencies could afford the twin advantages of monetary flexibility and a modicum of seignorage. However, four conditions must be fulfilled.

1. The rate of exchange between the two currencies must be flexible and not be used as an instrument of commercial policy.
2. The deviation from exchange rate stability must be used by an independent central bank as a sign that appropriate tightening or loosening of the supply of the local currency will be announced and applied.
3. The costs of moving from one currency to the other must be free of prohibitions and special taxes.
4. The fiscal policy of the smaller country must abide by the rules of financial orthodoxy, principally maintaining a balanced budget or even a budget surplus.

If those conditions are not fulfilled and if residents and investors do not trust the authorities to do so, the "good" will displace the "bad" currency. In that case, the efforts of the local authorities to stop the move away from the local currency by regulations and even penalties will be of little avail and simply increase the size of the black market. In any case, the introduction of a world currency in parallel with the local currency will need the previous application of very strict stabilization measures so that the public becomes convinced of the permanence of the new policy.

The case of M-pesa is somewhat different. It is a private money invented by its users, which circulates in parallel with an unstable official currency and is especially attractive because of the low switching costs. Once the parallel currency has become popular, Safaricom will be led to limit excessive new issuances of the money.

Conclusion

This chapter leads to two unfamiliar conclusions. One: that there are two Gresham's laws, direct and inverse; the other, that a small country may find it convenient to have two legal tender currencies. A preliminary version of the mathematical model supporting these conclusions can be found in Castañeda et al. (2020).

The direct Gresham's law indicates that when the authorities try to impose a bad quality official currency at an exchange rate that overvalues it, the good quality money will be displaced at least in its function as a store of value. However, in application of the inverse Gresham's law, the "bad" or local currency will not be displaced by the "good," on condition that the exchange rate is flexible and local monetary policy is orthodox. A permanent arrangement of two currencies in competition will help the smaller country avoid the loss of value of its money due to local inflation, keep part of the seignorage income, and also dampen the shocks originating both in the international currency and from national politics.

The case of M-pesa is similar but not identical. Here the direct Gresham's law will prevail. Since the rate of exchange of M-pesa/Kenyan shilling is one to one, there will be a slow displacement of the official shilling, except of course for large operations. The shilling rate of inflation will fall. If it is not contained, a black market for M-pesa could appear.

References

Banco Central de la Reserva de Perú. (2021). *Reporte de inflación*, September.

Castañeda, J., Damrich, S., & Schwartz, P. (2020). *A Model of Parallel Currencies Under Free Floating Exchange Rates*. The Johns Hopkins Institute for Applied Economics. SAE./.No.160/June.

Friedman, M. (1967). The Role of Monetary Policy. *American Economic Review, 58*(1), 1–17.

Keynes, J. M. (1923). A Tract on Monetary Reform. In *The Collected Writings of John Maynard Keynes* (Vol. IV). The Royal Economic Society.

Martinelli, C., & Vega, M. (2022). The Case of Peru. In T. J. Kehoe, & J. P. Nicolini, (Eds.), A *Monetary and Fiscal History of Latin America, 1960–2017*. University of Minnesota Press.

Mas, E., & Radcliffe, D. (2010). *Mobile Payments Go Viral. M-PESA in Kenya*. Bill and Melinda Gates Foundation.

Mundell, R. (1998). Uses and Abuses of Gresham's Law. *Zagreb Journal of Economics, 2*(2), 1–30.

Dynamic Efficiency in the Process of Desocialization

Josef Šíma

> There is nothing more regrettable than the frequent case of the politician who gets into power with a free market programme supported by the public who, when the crunch comes, due to his lack of tenacity or belief in his own ideas, or to diffidence when putting them into practice, does not come anywhere near the expectations created, losing all his own prestige and, what is worse, the prestige of the libertarian ideals he claims to defend. (Huerta de Soto, 2009, p. 197)

I was very privileged to be responsible for arranging translations of several of Jesús's books into Czech. Also, as the president of the Prague Conference of Political Economy, I was delighted to hand him over the Franz Čuhel Prize for Excellence in Economic Education in 2006. Typically, on those occasions, Jesús would come to Prague and give a great talk in front of hundreds of people. I remember at one of these big events we were making our way through the crowds to the podium as the event was scheduled to start in two minutes and Jesús whispered to my ear: "I forgot the transcript of my talk in the car, what shall we do now?". Luckily for us, the event was to be translated and we were

J. Šíma (✉)
Metropolitan University Prague, Prague, Czech Republic
e-mail: josef.sima@mup.cz

D. Howden, P. Bagus (eds.), *The Emergence of a Tradition: Essays in Honor of Jesús Huerta de Soto, Volume I*,
https://doi.org/10.1007/978-3-031-17414-8_25

Economists have always coped with the problem of explaining the mechanism of the coordination of human activities in large societies. They explained how decentralized decision-making gives rise to exchange and thus to prices that guide all of us as entrepreneurs, in the broadest sense of the term, to find our meaningful place in the process of this complex division of labor. The process is dynamic and messy as a result of the constantly evolving nature of "the data"—such as preferences or knowledge. Therefore, the "miracle" of market coordination needs to be seen as a never-ending process rather than an end-state to be reached. The logic of the processes in question has sometimes been compared to that of dogs chasing—but never catching—a rabbit (Rothbard, 2009, p. 322).

If this process of a constant market drive toward coordination is interfered with by an act of governmental intervention, such as a price control, the miracle of coordination is crippled and unsurprising consequences follow—shortages or surpluses, lines of people in front of stores or factory gates. If this artificial barrier to coordination is removed, the natural mechanism of coordination starts performing its marvels again.

The real world, however, is not a world of preexisting coordination, where we can easily identify the situations of market efficiency before, during, and after the presence of the interventionist, as in our example above. Our world is not just a world of "normal" radical market uncertainty (Kay & King, 2020), disequilibrium, and unpredictable flux. It is a hampered

just passing by the translators' desk who also—fortunately—wanted to have a copy of the transcript prior to the speech. So while walking by we just grabbed the copy of the transcript from their desk, climbed to the podium and Jesús delivered a marvelous talk for some 250 of his Czech fans. My best and unforgettable story with Jesús however is from Madrid when I visited him at his apartment where I not only had a splendid dinner with him but more importantly was able to admire his book treasures which he proudly presented to me along with an interesting story behind each volume. At one point he started reading a lengthy passage in Latin from one of those old books written in Salamanca. Suddenly, he exclaimed in delight: "Have you noticed?! The first use of the term subjective utility!" I realized then more than ever before that he is a man who genuinely cares about ideas, about economics, and freedom – and I could feel that he really loves what he does.

economy, full of big and small government entities, run by power-hungry agents of the state who produce myriads of artificial barriers to smooth market operations daily. They not only commit violent political acts in their attempts to modify the outcome of voluntary market transactions but add new uncertainty to the system as those interventions often interact and clash.

Too often central banks inject new money into the economy via the loans market, which launches new housing construction, resulting in a *greater* number of apartments that would not have existed without this intervention. And at the same time, other branches of government concurrently work in the opposite direction by imposing rent controls that lead to the construction of *fewer* apartments. These two regulations may easily, to a smaller or bigger extent—which we will never be able to quantify—counterbalance each other and, in a way unintentionally limit market distortions. If rent controls are abolished in such a situation and one of the forces disappears, only the effects of an inflationary boom will have an impact on the housing market, causing its artificial boom. More resources might be misallocated and wasted as a result. Is that a good reason for keeping rent control in place? Does efficiency calculus or economic maxim to strive for market coordination require such a conclusion? Should economists, as policy advisors, not recommend the abolition of rent control unless central banks are abolished at the same time so that inflationary booms are eliminated? How can efficiency be achieved in such a world? Moreover, how do we answer those questions once we realize that in our world we face the existence not simply of two possible counter-balancing forces stemming from governmental interventions, but thousands of those forces crippling the market economy at any given moment?

And we can go even further down the road to the unfree world and ask the question again. What advice do economists have for policy-making in countries where market forces were almost completely eliminated by the system of central economic planning, and consequently countries set off on the road from socialism toward a market-based economic system?

Dynamic Efficiency as a Guiding Principle of Desocialization

The debate about returning market efficiency to formerly socialized systems may be very tricky as the economic system is dramatically deformed, and reforming such a system may bring about painful and unpredictable results to many. Yet it is exactly the situation where correct policy decisions need to take place, and where floppy thinking and conceptual confusion can cause a lot of harm. Huerta de Soto's concept of dynamic efficiency is a desirable ingredient in the recipe for desocialization and a wonderful application of his broad and deep understanding of economic and social processes. He suggests that we cannot avoid bridging boundaries of traditional disciplines as we face

> a fascinating field of research that centres precisely on determining which principles of social ethics or distributive justice drive and are compatible with the market processes that characterize dynamic efficiency. (Huerta de Soto, 2009, p. 19)

The economic debate about desocialization obviously cannot be separated from the debate surrounding the underlying questions of social ethics and justice. It is indeed true that one of the most visible manifestations of central planning is a sluggish economy and disincentivized labor force. Yet the goal of desocialization is not about improving efficiency in the narrow sense of encouraging production and avoiding waste of resources in a particular field of production, neither is it about limiting a post-transformation recession or maximizing investments, savings, or GDP growth. Improvement of efficiency has other, deeper, meanings and implications. As Frank Knight correctly pointed out, "…when more than one form of useful output… is involved, the necessity arises for having a measure of usefulness, of value, before efficiency can be discussed" (Knight, 1969, p. 42).

> And here comes Huerta de Soto with his key insight that efficiency is not a free-floating concept, a goal for policy-makers in their role of cognitive supermen to be achieved. It is tied to the concept of property rights and justice. Efficiency is not a policy tool to be used for justification of tweaking and manipulating property rights and legislative fiat. Efficiency is the outcome of the process in which private property owners are allowed to operate and search for entrepreneurial solutions and profits. *[F]rom a dynamic standpoint, efficiency is not compatible with different models of equity or justice…, but instead arises exclusively from one (that based on the respect for private property and entrepreneurship)* (Huerta de Soto, 2009, p. 22, emphasis added).

The narrow conception of efficiency, which focuses only on "resource allocation" and is so often used in general equilibrium framework, is of very limited use for the real world of omnipresent governments in which market reforms or transition strategies are contemplated. As nobody knows where the counterfactual free-market outcome would be, the focus has to be not on some fictitious end-state (such as proper number of apartments built) but rather on the dismantling of all artificial barriers preventing the dynamic operation of entrepreneurs (such as scrapping the laws prohibiting market pricing of apartments). As Huerta de Soto—echoing O'Driscoll and Rizzo and their 1998 classic (O'Driscoll & Rizzo, 1998) —explains:

> To find fault with the market because it fails to reach a limit which no one has knowledge of and which varies continually not only constitutes a serious methodological error, but can also lead to the absurd justification of interventionist economic policies which ultimately hinder the real market process, when this very process is the driving force behind the perpetual quantitative and qualitative increase in the possibilities of the production frontier. (Huerta de Soto, 2009, p. 22)

By linking the economic efficiency argument to the underlying legal structure in his dynamic efficiency concept, Huerta de Soto offers an extremely useful device for desocialization strategies and reforms (as well as a solid building block of Austrian Law and Economics).

Unfortunately, the reality of desocialization in Central Europe is proof that Huerta de Soto's insights and warnings against a too narrow efficiency calculus were in vain. The countries that attempted to liberate their economic systems generally took significant steps away from their socialist past and became "normal countries" (Shleifer & Treisman, 2014)—where the intervention of the state in the economy is "not inevitable but highly probable" (Boettke, 2021, p. 113) given the prevailing ideology of our age—but they failed to do much more. Even if the political pendulum after the fall of communism opened some room to reformers, known for their free-market credentials to engage in privatization and desocialization, these reformers too often exemplify the "paradox of the libertarian social engineer" (Huerta de Soto, 2009, p. 57). Their general appreciation of market operation notwithstanding, these reformers unfortunately deliberately designed and advocated policies "in contradiction with the essential principles of freedom" (ibid.) as a part of their strategies to boost efficiency in the very narrow sense, rather than fully appreciating private property underpinnings of the dynamic efficiency. In my own country of the Czech Republic, state ownership of banks has been thus advocated to encourage loan provisions to local businesses; or monopoly privileges in telecommunication granted to allegedly encourage investments to landlines (Šíma & Šťastný, 2000). Even with the most charitable interpretation and understanding of the operation of real-life politics, these policies were not "political compromises" (bad as they are) neither were they attempt to design policy response to behavioral anomalies in the name of "better-informed" decision-making by market participants (dangerous as they may be for the future of the market system). These policies were nothing but old-fashioned paternalism stemming from a mistaken and confused understanding of what market efficiency is, understanding it to be detached from the underlying private property nexus.

What often (though not always and with differences in individual countries) started as a free-market revolution ("Our choice is a market economy without any complicating and obfuscating adjective added to the word market." Klaus, 1991, p. 12) led to the gradual vanishing of reform ethos in the whole of Central Europe. As former Deputy Governor of the Czech Central Bank, Hampl (in Šíma & Nikodým, 2015, p. 288), trenchantly remarked: "Today we are much further away from Hayek and much closer to [Joseph] Stiglitz, and are thus floating somewhere in the middle of the grey and boring European intellectual mainstream." And as half-baked reforms failed to deliver promised results and undertook "a continual loss of the content of free-market ideology" (Huerta de Soto, 2009, p. 189), the consequence was predictable. The concept of market order was largely discredited, the concept of private property humiliated, and as no other real constraints on democratic action was put in place, nothing was there to prevent "anything goes in politics" behavior and omnipresent cronyism from dominating political life.

For the long-term success of desocialization processes, a combination of several factors is necessary. (1) Governments must step down from the economy's commanding heights and thereby *eliminate artificially created obstacles to dynamic efficiency*. Hence, a legal framework without monopolies (to pay justice to Gustave de Molinari's "one well-established truth in political economy," Molinari, 1977 [1849], p. 3) and without special privileges needs to be instituted. Only then can the law play its role of assuring harmonious and peaceful coexistence of market participants rather than being a source of legal plunder and a tool of politically driven redistribution. (2) In such a legal framework that prevents social predation by protecting private property and freedom of contract, the *entrepreneurial discovery process* of trial and error will not guarantee immediate or automatic success in human betterment but enables the existence of "a procedure for discovering facts which, if the procedure did not exist, would remain unknown (Hayek, 2002, p. 9) and will grant us innovation, which is "the child of freedom" (Ridley, 2020, p. 359). This competition-based process of production of new knowledge and innovations gives us improvements of life in the sphere of consumption, health, science, education, and so on. While growth-compatible rules of the game and active and innovative players are important and necessary, they are not sufficient ingredients to successful desocialization and development. (3) As desocialization and progress, in general, have a cultural component, it is crucial to cultivate the understanding of the process without undermining laissez-faire principles in the long run, while also strengthening and maintaining a guilt-free entrepreneurial spirit. Ludwig von Mises reminded us of the importance of this component when he analyzed the factors needed for lasting free social order in the aftermath of World War II arguing that "Economic prosperity is ...first of all, an intellectual, spiritual and moral problem," (Mises, 2000, p. 42). In line with Mises (and Hayek), Jesús Huerta de Soto also correctly calls for systematic cultivation of founding principles of a free society and emphasizes the critical importance of education of intellectuals and opinion-shapers who "act applying the established principles of the pure theory of freedom to the everyday reality" (Huerta de Soto, 2009, p. 192). Without this effort, any institutional changes will not be robust enough to last.

More Efficiency, More Justice, More Morality

Despite popular criticism, the market system does not undermine morality. After all, economic progress (with its invisible-hand-based mechanism of operation) aroused from Smithian moral sentiments and the modern age owes its existence to McCloskeyan bourgeois virtues. Thanks to the great work of Jesús Huerta de Soto and his elaboration of the concept of dynamic efficiency—which is rooted in the bedrock of a free society: voluntary action in the framework of private property and contract—we can still be much more certain that "the contradiction between efficiency and justice is false. What is just cannot be inefficient, and what is efficient cannot be unjust" (Huerta de Soto, 2009, p. 22). This is a crucial point for all those who cherish freedom and advocate institutional changes as policy-makers and reformers. This is also a point to be taken home by those who want to cultivate policy debates as second-hand dealers in ideas, opinion-makers, or policy-shapers. And it is also something to internalize by those who make their living on the market, by businesspeople and entrepreneurs. Markets are good and just! And there is even more to it. As recent research shows, market dealings not only uphold and are compatible with existing morality, they also "support [our] moral improvements." (Storr-Choi, 2019, p. 235) Simply, markets make us better people. And thanks to dynamically efficient markets, we can simultaneously become more prosperous, uphold private property, keep peace and social harmony, and strengthen those social virtues that are indispensable to a flourishing society.

References

Boettke, P. J. (2021). *The Struggle for a Better World.* Mercatus Center at George Mason University.

Hayek, F. A. (2002). Competition as a Discovery Procedure. *Quarterly Journal of Austrian Economics, 5*(3), 9–23.

Huerta de Soto, J. (2009). *The Theory of Dynamic Efficiency.* Routledge.

Kay, J., & King, M. (2020). *Radical Uncertainty.* The Bridge Street Press.

Klaus, V. (1991). *A Road to Market Economy.* Top Agency.

Knight, F. (1969 [1935]). *The Ethics of Competition.* Books for Libraries Press.

Mises, L. v. (2000). 'Europe's Economic Structure and the Problem of Postwar Reconstruction. In R. M. Ebeling (Ed.), *Selected Writings of Ludwig von Mises – The Political Economy of International Reform and Reconstruction* (pp. 31–42). Liberty Fund.

Molinari, G. (1977 [1849]). *The Production of Security.* The Center for Libertarian Studies.

O'Driscoll, G. P., & Rizzo, M. J. (1998). *The Economics of Time and Ignorance.* Routledge.

Ridley, M. (2020). How Innovation Works And Why It Flourishes in Freedom. Harper.

Rothbard, M. N. (2009). *Man, Economy, and State with Power and Market* (2nd ed.). Ludwig von Mises Institute.

Shleifer, A., & Treisman, D. (2014). Normal Countries: The East 25 Years After Communism. *Foreign Affairs, 93*(6), 92–103.

Šíma, J., & Nidodým, T. (2015). Classical Liberalism in the Czech Republic. *Econ Journal Watch, 12*(2), 274–292.

Šíma, J., & Šťastný, D. (2000). A Laissez-Faire Fable of the Czech Republic. *Journal of Libertarian Studies, 14*(2), 155–178.

Storr, V. H., & Choi, G. S. (2019). *Do Markets Corrupt Our Morals?* Palgrave Macmillan.

The Greatest Economist Who Ever Lived

Mark Skousen

No book since David Ricardo's *Principles* has had such a great influence on the development of economics as the *Grundsätze*.—Knut Wicksell (1958, p. 191)

It was the reading of his book that made an 'economist' out of me.—Ludwig von Mises (1978, p. 33)

It is a privilege and honor to participate in this Festschrift for Jesús Huerta de Soto. I admire him as a scholar and a gentleman, his indefatigable promotion of the Austrian and Spanish Scholastics schools of economics, and his willingness to engage in dialogue and debate even among dissenting colleagues (not all members of the Austrian School are so inclined).

A classic example is Jesús's magnum opus, his 885-page tome, Money, Bank Credit, and Economic Cycles, published by the Mises Institute in 2006. He goes out of his way to credit the works of other scholars, including Mises, Hayek, Rothbard and Kirzner. I was pleased to see that my own works were cited repeatedly on gross output, the business cycle and the gold standard, even when we disagreed on certain topics and policies. (One thing we do agree on—defending the euro as a form of the gold standard.)

M. Skousen (✉)
Chapman University, Orange, CA, USA
e-mail: mskousen@chapman.edu

D. Howden, P. Bagus (eds.), *The Emergence of a Tradition: Essays in Honor of Jesús Huerta de Soto, Volume I*,
https://doi.org/10.1007/978-3-031-17414-8_26

> I really got hooked when I found Menger's *Grundsätze* such a fascinating book, so satisfying.—Friedrich Hayek (1998, p. 48)

> I now rate Walras and Pareto, who were my first loves, so much below Menger.—Sir John Hicks (1979, p. 63)

> The entire theory of capital and cycles we have presented here rests on this concept of Menger's....In short Austrian School theorists have developed the whole theory of capital, money and cycles which is implicit in the subjectivism that revolutionized economics in 1871.—Jesús Huerta de Soto (2009, p. 511)

Given his strict Misesian views, and a skeptical view of Adam Smith, I was surprised that he arranged in 2010 for Unión Editorial, the prestigious Spanish publisher, to translate my Making of Modern Economics into a handsome Spanish edition entitled La Formacion de la Teoria Economica Moderna. In my history of the great economic thinkers, I make Adam Smith and his system of natural liberty the heroic figure in economics. Jesús prefers to give the Austrians top billing, and the Spanish scholastics before them. However, I think it helped that I devote three chapters in my book to the Austrians, who are typically given short shrift in other histories of economic thought.

A year later, in March, 2011, Jesús and his wife Soles hosted me and my wife Jo Ann in Madrid. He invited me to give a lecture on the Austrian vs the Chicago schools of economics, base my latest book, Vienna and Chicago, Friends or Foes?

Before the lecture, they showed us their beautiful apartment and private library, which contains many rare books, including all the editions and translations of Human Action. He has a special section in his library of his favorite books in economics, which he has bound in black leather, such as books by Mises, Hayek, Rothbard, Menger, Kirzner, and other great Austrians, and he has two of mine in black leather: The Structure of Production and Economics of a Pure Gold Standard.

I was also impressed to hear that Jesús is not just an academic economist, but a successful businessman. He runs an insurance company in Madrid, and picked us up in a Bentley. After my lecture, we went out to the most expensive restaurant in Madrid. His ancestors include a famous bull fighter and discoverer Hernando de Soto. He's also a devote husband. He and his wife have six children, all living in the Madrid area. He's built a huge following in Austrian economics in Spain and throughout Europe, and his books are being translated rapidly. He was the Hayek Lecturer at the London School of Economics in 2010, and has received several honorary degrees, including one in Moscow.

My lecture was before 100 students and professors, and after my presentation, we had a spirited debate on the differences between the Austrian and Chicago schools, and the financial crisis in Spain. I found myself defending Milton Friedman, but there was no rancor or ill-feelings.

Both Jesús Huerta de Soto and I are strong advocates of the Austrian School. Jesús considers Ludwig von Mises as the greatest economist ever, and uses the Spanish translation of *Human Action* as the primary textbook in his classes.

But Mises would be the first to give credit to Carl Menger and his revolutionary book, *Grundsätze der Volkswirtschaftslehre*, published in 1871 in Vienna, Austria. It was eventually translated into English with the title *Principles of Economics* by James Dingwall and Bert F. Hoselitz, published by the Free Press 1959, and reprinted in 1976 by New York University Press, with an introduction by Friedrich Hayek.

Carl Menger (1840–1921) and his followers enhanced Adam Smith's positive vision of the capitalist system. He saw himself as a follower of Adam Smith's "system of natural liberty" who strengthened the house that Adam Smith built; as a remodeler rather than a teardown.

In many ways, Menger was a revolutionary discoverer of both macroeconomics (through his time structure of production) and microeconomics (subjective demand and marginal analysis), all in one book, the *Grundsätze*.

Therefore, in honor of the 150th anniversary of the publication of his magnum opus (1871), I am pleased to declare that Carl Menger deserves to be considered the greatest theoretical economist who ever lived.

I dedicated my own book, *The Structure of Production* (Skousen, 1990), to Menger. It was Menger who inspired my development of gross output (GO), a measure of spending at all stages of production that the government adopted in 2014.

With the publication of the *Grundsätze*, the Austrian School was born and made economics a real science.

Menger was born in the city of Neu-Sandez (now Nowy Sacz) in Poland, the son of a lawyer and a mother who came from a wealthy Bohemian merchant. He studied law at the Universities of Prague and Vienna and earned a doctorate in Krakow. In the 1860s, Menger became an economic journalist covering the stock market in Vienna, and it was there that he noticed a discrepancy between what the classical economists taught about price theory and what he observed among stockbrokers and speculators. In 1867, he began a study of political economy, challenging the classical cost-based theories of value with a new theory of marginal subjective pricing. After publishing his magnum opus in 1871, he became an adjunct professor at the University of Vienna, and a year later was appointed a full member of the law faculty teaching finance and political economy both in seminars and lectures. In 1873, he received the university's chair of economic theory at the youthful age of 33.

He quickly became a man of influence. In 1876, he began teaching Archduke Rudolf, the crown prince of Austria, the only son of the emperor Franz Joseph I, and heir to the throne. His lectures incorporated the laissez faire policies of Adam Smith, and together he and the prince co-authored an anonymous pamphlet in 1878 criticizing the higher Austrian aristocracy.

Menger grew increasingly pessimistic about the future of Austrian-Hungarian empire and its authoritarian regime. His pessimism may have contributed to the Archduke's suicide in 1889. Noting that his mentor foresaw the horrors of war in Western Europe in the early twentieth century, Mises commented, "He [Menger] had transmitted this pessimism to his young student and friend, Archduke Rudolf…The Archduke committed suicide because he despaired about the future of his empire and the fate of Western civilization, not because of a woman" (Mises, 1978, p. 34).

By the turn of the century, the Austrians were considered the most dominate school in economics, thanks to Menger's two most influential students, Eugen Böhm-Bawerk and Friedrich Wieser. Menger unexpectedly retired in 1903 at the age of 63, supposedly to spend more time revising his *Grundsätze,* but the real reason was the disclosure that he had a long-term "common law" relationship with his housekeeper Hermine Andermann, who was Jewish. They had a son, Karl, who later became a mathematician at the Illinois Institute of Technology (Skousen, 2016, p. 183).

Menger died in 1921, deeply worried about the future of Europe after World War I. Fortunately, the Austrian School of economics continued into a third generation, led by Ludwig von Mises, Friedrich Hayek, and Joseph Schumpeter, among others, and continues to influence new generations of economists in the United States, the Americas, Europe, and Asia.[1]

[1] A full biography of Carl Menger is soon to be published the Austrian Center in Vienna, Austria. For a summary of his life, see Hayek's Introduction to Menger's *Principles of Economics* (Hayek, 1976), and chapter 7, "Out of the Blue Danube: Menger and the Austrians Reverse the Tide," in Skousen (2016, pp. 171–196).

How I Use Menger in My Classes

I use Menger in a variety of ways in the classroom, in both micro and macro courses.

Example #1: Real Wages vs Goods/Services

In microeconomics, I first talk about his pathbreaking method, "the general theory of the good," as outlined in chapters 1–2 of *Principles*. Instead of focusing on the division of labor (Adam Smith's approach), and the distribution of income (David Ricardo's model), Menger began with a discussion of the character of goods.

Even today, most economists measure economic growth and the standard of living by the level of real per capita GDP, or average real wages.

Average real hourly wages in the US have stagnated since the 1970s. With this fact in mind, one might think that America's standard of living has not changed in 40 years.

Now let's consider another way to measure the standard of living by looking at changes in the goods and services that Americans buy and use over time. This is the approach Menger took.

Menger's model is more complex. He examines the change in the quantity, quality, and variety of goods and services over time, and to what extent individuals and family units enjoy Q, Q, and V. As Erich Streissler notes, "Mengerian goods are three-dimensional. They have *quantity, quality, and variety* as separate dimension of dynamic change" (Black et al., 1973, p. 165). Lionel Robbins adds, "This business of conservation to meet future needs, according to Menger, involves four aspects of behavior: conservation of quantity, conservation of quality, choice between goods, and choice such as to secure the greatest result all around" (Robbins, 1998, p. 272; Menger, 1950, pp. 95–96).

Using Menger's approach, we discover that the standard of living has increased dramatically since 1970s and more and more Americans are using new and better goods and services.

I believe the disaggregate approach by Menger is superior to the aggregate "average wage" model used by most economists. I cite a variety of economic indicators, such as average size of new homes, and households with computers, TVs, microwave, air conditioning, washer and dryer, dishwashers, and so on in both my textbooks, *Economic Logic* (2017) and *The Making of Modern Economics* (2016), depending on the research of

Cox and Alm (1999), and Stanley Lebergott (1976, 1993). They show that since 1900, and even since the early 1970s, the average household enjoys bigger homes, more appliances, and better quality of life across the board. It gives students a more comprehensive and accurate picture of progress.

Example #2: Why Prices Are Determined at the Margin

I also use Menger's insights in teaching price theory. What determines the prices of goods and services?

Most businesses use a "cost plus" approach, as well as going by what competitors are charging, to estimate the right price for their products or services. In reality, prices are not ultimately determined by their cost of production, but what customers are willing to pay. How often do we see businesses unloading unsold merchandise at below cost? Or what about a newly designed automobile comes on the market and car dealers charge a premium for the new hot car, unrelated to its cost of manufacturing?

Thus, we see that pricing is ultimately subjective, based entirely on what customers are willing to pay. Knowing the cost of production is important in business, and can be used to estimate what price you should charge, but there are no guarantees that you can sell the product at a certain percentage above your costs.

In the 1860s, when Menger was a financial reporter covering the stock market in Vienna, he discovered that prices of stocks are based on only a small (marginal) number of buyers and sellers.

There may be a million shareholders of Apple stock, but only several thousand may be buying or selling Apple stock on any given day. These traders determine the daily price of Apple stock—not the entire owners, or what they themselves paid for the stock (their cost basis).

Thus Menger discovered a fundamental error of the classical school, that the cost of production determines prices. He replaced it with subjective marginal analysis that forms the basis of economic science today.

In class, I ask students: What determined the price of your home that you live in or rent? I note that maybe only 1 in 30 homes is for sale at any one time. What determines its price? The answer: Sellers set their price based on appraisals of a few similar homes in the neighborhood that have recently sold.

What if suddenly 1 out of every 10 homes came on the market to sell? There might be a glut of homes, and sellers would have to sharply reduce their sale price. Or what if the neighborhood suddenly became a desirable place to live? Home prices in the area might jump 50% in a year.

Thus, prices are determined by a small marginal number of homeowners who wish to sell at that time.

I also ask students: Is the supply curve for signed Babe Ruth baseballs perfectly inelastic? Afterall, Babe Ruth died in 1948, and there is only a limited supply of signed Ruth balls.

It turns out that the supply of Babe Ruth baseballs is quite elastic, because the collectibles market is determined by the supply of signed baseballs "for sale" at a given time. It's not determined by the total number of signed balls in the universe. If the price of a Babe Ruth ball rises high enough, more collectors will put their prized baseball on the market. The supply is flexible—and so is the demand.

Example #3: Using Tobacco to Demonstrate the Theory of Imputation

In his *Principles*, Menger used the example of tobacco to introduce marginal price and cost theory. He asks, "Suppose that the need for direct human consumption of tobacco should disappear as the result of a change in tastes...?" (Menger, 1950, p. 64). What a modern example!

I hold up a pack of cigarettes and ask, "Suppose people stop smoking. Would the price of a pack of cigarettes fall?" Students know the answer. It would fall to zero, since there is suddenly no demand for cigarettes anymore. As Menger puts it, "it is certain that all tobacco products already on hand…would immediately lose their goods-character" (p. 64).

But what about the value of the factors of production—land, labor, and capital—used in the making of tobacco products? Would they fall to zero? Menger points out that those of exclusive or specialized use, such as tobacco seeds, would lose their entire value, but because farms and machinery have other uses, they do not lose their value entirely. They can be used to produce other agriculture products, such as wheat, corn, or soybeans, or perhaps even be converted into condominiums. Their value falls to the next best *marginal* use (Menger, 1950, pp. 65–66).

Thus, Menger's tobacco example introduces the concepts of marginal utility and opportunity cost. It also demonstrates that even the costs of production are not fixed, but are variable, in the long run.

During the economic recession in the early 1980s, oil prices fell sharply, and so did the cost of producing oil rigs, which often sat idle and did not have other uses.

Thus, Menger developed his theory of imputation. It was a sharp break from the Ricardian cost-of-production theories. As Roger Garrison notes, "The direction of causation was reversed by Menger. A consumption good is not valued because of the labor and other means of production that were used to produce it. Rather, the means of production are valued because of the prospective value of the consumption goods" (Garrison, 1981, p. 19).

Introducing a More Complete Macroeconomic Model

The *Grundsätze* not only introduced us to a more accurate view of the theory of the firm in microeconomics, but it also established the foundation for macroeconomics, the model of the economy as a whole.

He did this by focusing on the "causal connections between goods" (Menger, 1950, p. 56).

In his first chapter, "The General Theory of the Good," Menger rejected the simplistic two-good model (production and consumption goods) of the classical school. Instead of focusing on goods as if they were homogeneous, he envisioned consumer and investment goods as an array of goods—of the first order, the second order, the third order, and so forth.

He defined finished consumer goods as "goods of the first order," because they "serve our needs directly." Goods of a second order are used in the production of goods of the first order. Goods of a second order are used in the production of second-order goods. And so forth. There is a vertical hierarchy, from lower-order goods (close to consumption) to higher-order goods (furthest from consumption).

Production is defined as the process of transforming higher-order goods into successively lower-order goods. Menger viewed economic production as "the process by which goods of higher order are progressively transformed into goods of lower order and by which these are directed finally to the satisfaction of human needs" (Menger, 1950, p. 67).

Sir John Hicks recognized Menger's approach as "the typical business man's viewpoint, nowadays the accountant's viewpoint, in the old days the merchant's viewpoint" (Hicks, 1973, p. 12). The economy consists of a production process over time, as goods go from a raw commodity stage through the production stage, and are finally distributed to their final use.

Menger Provides the Missing Link Between Micro and Macro

To demonstrate the production process, Menger used the simple example of making bread, a consumer good. Starting at the beginning of

> production (the highest order), seed grain is planted in the ground by machines and labor. This stage represents "goods of the fifth order." The "goods of the fourth order" consists of grain mills, wheat, rye and labor services, all used to produce flour. "Goods of a third order" include flour, baking utensils, and the journeyman baker and other workers to produce bread. Then the bread must be distributed to the wholesaler, what we might call "goods of the second order." And finally the bread reaches the consumer, and thus represents a "good of first order" (Menger, 1950, pp. 56–57).

At each stage of production, the process moves toward final use, and value (profit) is added.

We can represent Menger's simple bread-making example below is illustrated in Fig. 1. In this case, we simplified the diagram by combining the second and third orders to represent the production process.

Stanford economist John Taylor has created a more accurate view of a 4-stage production process of a cup of coffee. See Fig. 2 below.

Four-Stage Macro Model of the Economy

Menger (1950) then speaks in terms of a general model of the "goods in the human economy." He refers to "thousands of other things that do not have the capacity to satisfy human needs directly," referring to higher stages of production. Next he refers to four general stages of production in agriculture, from the farmer in the fourth stage, the producer of farm products in the third stage, the wholesaler who transports the produce in the second stage, and lastly the retail consumer whose needs are satisfied in the first stage (Menger, 1950, pp. 56–57).

Fig. 1 Four stages of production of bread. Source: Skousen (2015, p. 34)

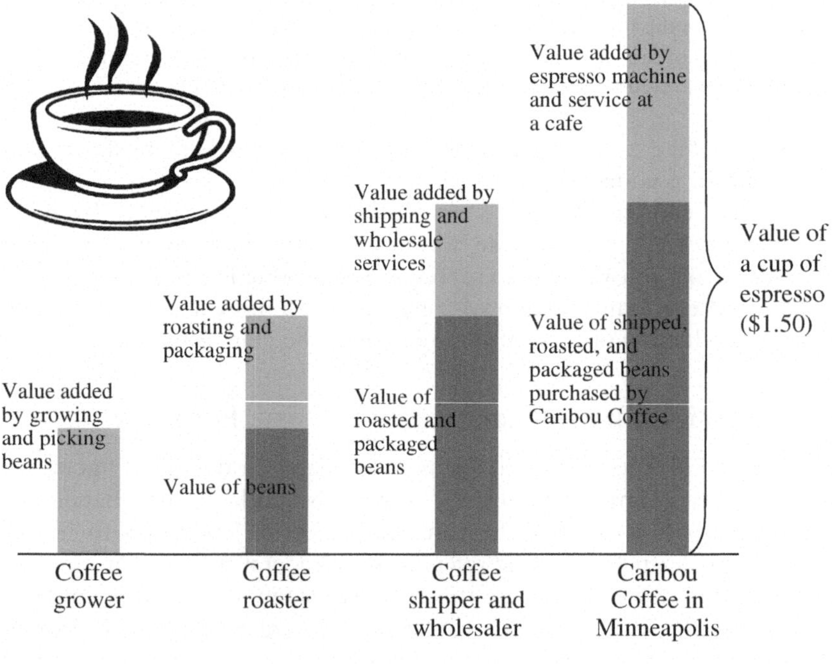

Fig. 2 Taylor's four-stage diagram of the production of a cup of espresso. Source: John B. Taylor Economics (2004, p. 147)

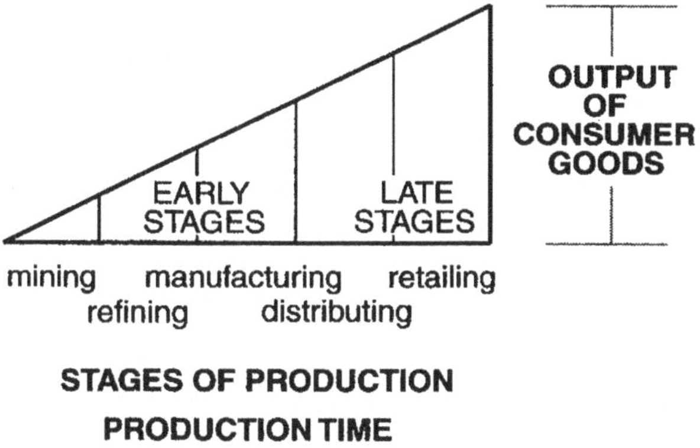

Fig. 3 A 5-stage generalized industrial model of Hayek's triangles. Source: Garrison (2001)

Menger's stages of production macro model was greatly advanced with the introduction of Hayek's triangles in his lectures at the London School of Economics, published as *Prices and Production* (Hayek, 1931). The triangles illustrate Menger's time structure of production with a triangular diagram whose area shows the total value of the successive stages from the highest order (resources) to the middle order (production) down to the lowest order (consumer) goods, adding value at each stage (see especially Hayek, 1931, pp. 44 and 52).

However, Hayek never went beyond high theory, never applied his stages of production to government statistics. Hayek's triangles were purely theoretical and did not conform to modern economic statistics.

It wasn't until a generation later that Austrian economists developed diagrams to reflect Menger's vision of macroeconomics.

Roger Garrison improved Hayek's triangles with five-stage model for an industrial economy (Garrison, 2001). See Fig. 3 above.

Today's economists and accountants recognize this theoretical hierarchy as the stages of production. Drawing from Hayek's triangles (Hayek, 1931), I've generalized into a universal four-stage model for all goods and services in Fig. 4 to better conform to statistical indexes used by the various government agencies, private industries, and Wall Street firms.

Seeking a Complete Macroeconomic Model

The "causal connection between goods" has also had an evolution as economists sought to find the best way to measure annual economic growth, and the various components of the economy. Irving Fisher (1911) devised an "equation of exchange" to measure total spending in the economy.

$$M\ V = P\ Q$$

where M = the money supply, V = velocity of money, P = price level, and Q = total transactions.

For Fisher, PQ represents total sales or revenues at all stages of production, what Menger calls the value in exchange for the production of all goods of the first order (final use) through goods of the last order (raw commodities and all resources) combined.

Hayek's triangle is a diagram that illustrates the total value, expressed in dollars or other currencies, of total revenues at all stages of production. My own Skousen Steps (see Fig. 4) is a general 4-stage model of production at all levels.

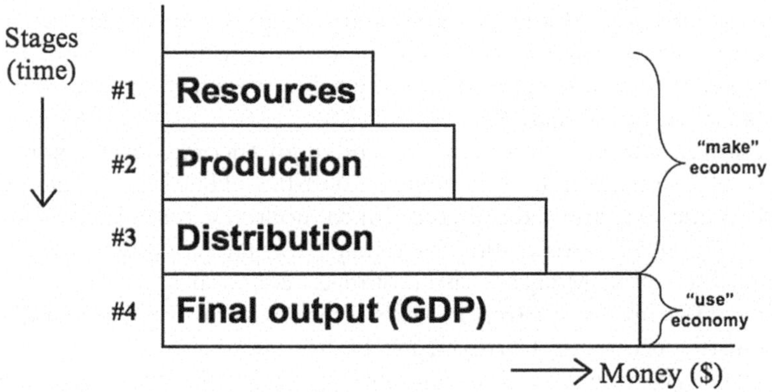

Fig. 4 Universal four-stages of production model. Source: Skousen (2015, p. xviii)

Kuznet's Fatal Mistake in National Income Accounting

Simon Kuznets, the Russian American economist, was the first to measure spending in the economy in his development of gross national product, now gross domestic product (GDP). When creating GDP, he recognized the value of all intermediate stages of production, but focused solely on the "end product" or national income, which meant subtracting "the value of that part of the nation's stock of goods that was expended…in producing the total" (Kuznets, 1934, p. 1).

It was a fatal error. By ignoring the value of the supply chain, or intermediate production, we were left with GDP—spending of *final* goods and services only—as *the* measure of the economy. This has led to much mischief. Since consumption expenditures are by far the largest sector of GDP, the media is constantly promoting an anti-saving mentality and the false notion that "consumer spending drives the economy."

Even though the economics textbooks clearly state that GDP measures "final" spending on finished goods and services only, the media largely ignores the value of the business-to-business (B2B) supply chain, all the intermediate "goods in process" that eventually end up as the final product.

With the publication of my book *The Structure of Production* in 1990, I proposed that it was time to measure the entire production process that Menger originally wrote about in 1871. In chapter 6, I made the case that the Bureau of Economic Analysis (BEA), which published the quarterly GDP statistics, should also account for intermediate production (the supply chain) in the entire production process, to be called gross output (GO).

Surprisingly, in April, 2014, under the leadership of BEA director Stephen Landefeld, the federal government begin measuring GO. I considered it the greatest breakthrough in Austrian economics since Hayek won the Nobel prize in 1974.

Now, in the twenty-first century, we have a "top line" (GO, or total spending) in national income accounting, and a "bottom line" (GDP). The economics profession has finally caught up with the world of accounting and finance.

I won't go into details of all the benefits of GO, but in summary, (1) GO shows that business spending (B2B) is almost twice the size of consumer spending in the US; (2) business spending is far bigger and more important than consumer spending; (3) GO is more consistent with growth theory, that saving, investing, capital formation, technology, and other "supply side" factors are the key to economic growth and a higher standard of living; (4) GO is a much better measure of the business cycle than GDP; the supply chain is much more volatile than GDP; and (5) GO is a leading indicator of where the economy is headed.[2]

I also argue that GO is complementary to GDP and therefore can be integrated into standard economics textbooks. As Dale W. Jorgenson, J. Stephen Landefeld, and William D. Nordhaus state, "Gross output [GO] is the natural measure of the production sector, while net output [GDP] is appropriate as a measure of welfare. Both are required in a complete system of accounts" (2006, p. 6).

My own textbook, *Economic Logic,* now in its 5th edition, shows how it can be done (see Skousen, 2017, chs. 14 and 15).

Conclusion

In his *Principles,* Menger also made another singular contribution to economics by demonstrating the money, the lifeblood of the economy that links microeconomics to macroeconomics, did not develop by government edict but by the natural evolution of trade. Those commodities that are more "marketable" become more and more likely to become a medium of exchange, or money. Gold and silver eventually became the ideal medium of exchange through the "invisible hand" of exchange (Menger, 1950, pp. 257–285; White, 1999, pp. 1–11).

Thus we see how Menger was in the forefront of developing a sound model of microeconomics through the production process; a way of developing macroeconomics by adding up all the transactions of goods and services; and the vital role of money to measure economic performance, all through a "general theory of the good." As Schumpeter concludes, "The whole of the organon of pure economics thus finds itself unified in light of a single principle—in a sense in which it never had been before" (Schumpeter, 1954, p. 913).

[2] For more information, go to www.grossoutput.com. I issue a quarterly press release on GO and B2B spending. The website also includes many of my lectures on GO.

Hayek summarizes the contributions of Menger: "There can be no doubt among competent historians that if…the Austrian School has occupied an almost unique position in the development of economic science, this is entirely due to the foundations laid by one man" (Hayek, 1976, p. 12).

It all started with Carl Menger.

References

Black, R. D. C., Coats, A. W., & Goodwin, C. D. W. (Eds.). (1973). *The Marginal Revolution in Economics.* Duke University Press.

Cox, W. M., & Alm, R. (1999). *Myths of Rich and Poor.* Basic Books.

Fisher, I. (1911). *The Purchasing Power of Money.* Macmillan.

Garrison, R. B. (1981). *The Austrian-Neoclassical Relation: A Study in Monetary Dynamics.* Ph.D. Dissertation, University of Virginia.

Garrison, R. B. (2001). *Time and Money: The Macroeconomics of Capital Structure.* Routledge.

Hayek, F. A. (1931). *Prices and Production.* George Routledge.

Hayek, F. A. (1976). Introduction: Carl Menger. In C. Menger (Ed.), *The Principles of Economics* (pp. 11–36). New York University Press.

Hayek, F. A. (1998). In S. Kresge & L. Wenar (Eds.), *Hayek on Hayek.* University of Chicago Press.

Hicks, J. R. (1973). *Capital and Time: A Neo-Austrian Theory.* Oxford: Oxford University Press.

Hicks, J. (1979). Is Interest the Price of a Factor of Production? In M. Rizzo (Ed.), *Time, Uncertainty, and Disequilibrium: Exploration of Austrian Themes.* Lexington Books.

Huerta de Soto, J. (2009). *Money, Bank Credit, and Economic Cycles* (2nd ed.). Mises Institute.

John B. T. (2004). *Economics* (4th ed.). Boston: Houghton Mifflin.

Jorgenson, D. W., Stephen Landefeld, J., & Nordhaus, W. D. (2006). *A New Architecture for the US National Accounts.* University of Chicago Press and National Bureau of Economic Research.

Kuznets, S. (1934, June 7). *National Income, 1929-32.* Bulletin 49. National Bureau of Economic Analysis.

Lebergott, S. (1976). *The American Economy.* Princeton University Press.

Lebergott, S. (1993). *Pursuing Happiness: American Consumers in the Twentieth Century.* Princeton University Press.

Menger, C. (1976 [1950, 1871]). *Principles of Economics* (J. Dingwall & B. F. Hoselitz, Trans.). New York University Press.

Mises, L. v. (1978). *Notes and Recollections.* Libertarian Press.

Robbins, L. (1998). In S. G. Medema & W. J. Samuels (Eds.), *A History of Economic Thought: The LSE Lectures*. Princeton University Press.
Schumpeter, J. A. (1954). *History of Economic Analysis*. Oxford University Press.
Skousen, M. (2015 [1990]). *The Structure of Production*. New York University Press.
Skousen, M. (2016 [2001]). *The Making of Modern Economics* (3rd ed.). Routledge.
Skousen, M. (2017). *Economic Logic* (5th ed.). Capital Press.
White, L. H. (1999). *The Theory of Monetary Institutions*. Blackwell Publishers.
Wicksell, K. (1958). *Selected Papers on Economic Theory*. London: Allen and Unwin.

The Entrepreneur and Entrepreneurship: A Practical Framework for Firm Analysis

Juan Torras

In many mainstream economic, academic, and business management papers and articles, the role of the entrepreneur is highlighted as an important agent of economic change, as a leader and an innovator. Nevertheless, there continues to be a lack of its full conceptual integration into the economic analysis. The personal or anthropological aspects related to the

---

It has been a pleasure for me to contribute to this Festschrift for my friend Jesús who was introduced to me by my father Dr. Juan Torras-Trias in the late 1970s as a future Austrian School intellectual leader. Our friendship includes our families, including my son Luis as one of his disciples.

From our visit to L'Aiguille du Midi (MPS 86) I remember the always brave Jesús crawling to the lift due to vertigo.

The objective of my contribution is to present a synthetic graphical model that I'm using since the 90's, as senior consultant, to explain the entrepreneurial function.

J. Torras (✉)
Instituto von Mises Barcelona, Barcelona, Spain
e-mail: juan.torras@misesbarcelona.org

D. Howden, P. Bagus (eds.), *The Emergence of a Tradition: Essays in Honor of Jesús Huerta de Soto, Volume I*,
https://doi.org/10.1007/978-3-031-17414-8_27

world "founder" or "promoter" which are easy to spot at the initial stage of any business are confused with the conceptual aspects that must be integrated into the theoretical corpus of economic science and business management models.

We can find some references in some early scholastics and the School of Salamanca about the role of merchants, their moral implications in trade and their contribution to the general welfare. Later, Richard Cantillon (1755) and Jean-Baptiste Say (1803) made the initial formal contributions. In fact, Say was the first to use the word "entrepreneur," not reported in the well-known works of Adam Smith (1776), David Ricardo (1817) and their followers of the "classical school." John Stuart Mill (1948) introduced the word "entrepreneur" to the Anglo-Saxon world. He referred to a persona who assumes both risk and business management, but he did not integrate it into his theoretical economic model.

Furthermore, in the neoclassical economic analysis, based on static models of equilibrium, entrepreneurship has no place either, since the entrepreneur is an economic agent that cannot be integrated into the elegant neoclassic equilibrium paradigm based on mathematical models and perfect information.

In the twentieth century, Joseph A. Schumpeter (1942) must be mentioned; his concept of the entrepreneur is mainly focused on the disruptive innovation process under neoclassical market equilibrium, not integrated into his neoclassical theoretical approach. In the USA, Frank Knight (1921) made an important contribution introducing the lack of information and differentiating risk from uncertainty, but again his attachment to the neoclassical paradigm of equilibrium did not allow him to cover the gap of a full integration of the entrepreneurial concept.

In parallel, in the field of "Business Economy and Administration," the entrepreneur's role has been studied and formalized. It is usually linked to the innovation process and the issues related with founders, start-ups, and the transition of ownership or succession plans. In any case, they are not integrated into economic theory.

Moreover, Keynesian macroeconomics, as a holistic approach based on aggregate concepts, does not contemplate the role of the entrepreneur as an economic agent, even if it serves as a formulation tool for economic policies by governments. The macroeconomic model does not include the market process dynamics inherent to entrepreneurship in its formulation.

It was from the seminal works of the late Ludwig von Mises that the concept of the *entrepreneurial function* was fully integrated into economic science under the paradigm of the Austrian School.

In this chapter, we propose a graphical model to analyze the basic synthetic functions integrating a firm, based on the theoretical propositions of the Austrian School about the *entrepreneurial function*. It is not our intention to elaborate a "Theory of Entrepreneurship," but to introduce the concept of the *entrepreneurial function*, as different from the *managerial function* and capital *ownership* (*corporate function* as we call it in our proposed model).

The Entrepreneur

The *entrepreneur* is a critical concept in our model. We consider him in the conceptual economic sense rather than in the anthropological one related to the founder of a company or start-up or the "Owner-Operator," a classical figure in small- and medium-sized companies.

At this stage, it is important to make a series of preliminary considerations, before we explain how to integrate the *entrepreneurial function* and the *entrepreneur* into our proposed synthetic model to analyze the basic elements of a firm.

A "theory of entrepreneurship" has been developed following different methodological orientations: sociological, economic, psychological, and from the point of view of empirical business management.

It is not our intention in this contribution to go into detail about its theoretical implications and its relation with the "entrepreneur" as a conceptual economic agent and the related "entrepreneurial function."

There have been and still are important contributions by different economic and business economic thinkers, as well as management consultants or practitioners, on the role of the entrepreneur and entrepreneurship theory.

The "Austrian School" is an alternative paradigm to the Keynesian-neoclassical paradigm, which is the "mainstream" in academic and policy-making environments.

The *entrepreneurial function*, inherent to any human action, is considered a key driver to the economic process in a dynamic economy based on private property and free monetary exchange.

It considers the analysis in a system of diffuse knowledge, uncertainty, and lack of information, where the concept of the *pure entrepreneur* is well-defined and fully integrated into the logic of a dynamic market process.

The leading thinkers that developed this paradigm in particular are: Carl Menger, Eugen von Böhm-Bawerk, Ludwig von Mises, Friedrich A. von Hayek, Murray N. Rothbard, and Israel M. Kirzner, among others, and in Spain today, professor Jesús Huerta de Soto.

Joseph Schumpeter cannot be considered a member of the Austrian School, but neither was he a Keynesian. For him, the entrepreneur was focused on the innovation process in an equilibrium static situation as a disruptive force. He failed in his attempt to develop an integrated theory of the entrepreneur, within his Walrasian theoretical approach. However, he has had an impact on the consideration of the entrepreneur in mainstream economic science and academic business management research.

The *entrepreneur* is an essential element in the real market economy. Many empirical researchers have elaborated academic business case studies about the concept of the real entrepreneur and its impact on innovation and the starting of new business. We can quote, aside of many business cases: Juan Rosell et al. (1985–2011), David Kirby (2003), Francesc Casabella (2021), Daniel Gross (2010), and Xavier R. Blanco and Jesús Salgado (2015).

The entrepreneurial spirit only flourishes in a competitive economy. But the *entrepreneur* has incentives under the state's interventionism to obtain regulatory advantages at the consumers' expense.

It is important to differentiate the figure of the *entrepreneur* (as the promoter of business in a firm's real-world activities) from the theoretical concept of the *pure entrepreneur* linked to the exercise of the *entrepreneurial function*.

In this sense, we speak about the *entrepreneur* in economic terms as a conceptual figure not linked to capital ownership. It is related to the exercise of the *entrepreneurial function* in a firm. In colloquial terms, we talk about the person who has promoted and developed a company, through their own means, or with third party financial resources and capital.

That is the reason why we differentiate what we call the *corporate function* (ownership linked to capitalists) from the *entrepreneurial function* exercised by the entrepreneur. There exist on this subject some important papers and discussions about the *pure entrepreneur* as conceptualized by Israel Kirzner (1973) and the *entrepreneur* as the *uncertainty bearing* individual who then must be a property owner as highlighted by Salerno (2008). But in our proposed model we apply the concept of *entrepreneurial function* to both the entrepreneur either as a physical person or as a "function" that is responsible for the business leadership of the firm in an environment of uncertainty. In the modern capital markets, the ownership or capital property may have different legal forms and in each one it can be considered the exercise of the *entrepreneurial function* in the related capital markets.

The *entrepreneur* anticipates what consumers may require in the future, in a permanent state of alertness, given that knowledge is diffuse and uncertainty is inherent to the *entrepreneurial function* related to any human action.

In simple model proposed, we consider the evolution of the firm and its relationship to its institutional governance: the Board of Directors, management organization, and the Shareholders' Assembly.

At the same time, our model highlights the interaction of the *entrepreneurial function* and the *corporate function* (ownership—capital) with the *managerial function*, as considered by the business management theory.

The Entrepreneurial Function and the Analytical Model

The firm is an organization streamlined to formalize the collaboration between different economic agents, more or less hierarchical, subject to management inefficiencies.

At the same time, it could be more or less market-oriented, with different typologies of shareholders (from a family to a private equity or listed on the stock market). Usually it will have a legal structure of limited responsibility, which has allowed firms financing—either from external indebtedness or by equity sale—and its growth.

The firm—as an organization and a structure—reaches its full development in a market economy, though it is not necessarily inherent to it. We can consider well other institutional organizations such as non-profit institutions, public services. or state-owned companies.

We include in our analysis the propositions made by the late Nobel awarded Ronald Coase (1937) who analyzed the emergence of firms as an alternative to the market process system for all related transactions in the market, reducing the impact of transactional costs. We also include Harold Demsetz (1983), and Demsetz and Villalonga (2001), who analyzed the relationship between the management function and the firms' ownership (the "agency problem").

The *entrepreneurial function*, as considered in our proposed model, mainly consists of decision-making in an environment of uncertainty, seeking to anticipate the future situations of a market process, discovering new opportunities and obtaining business profit or loss through its speculative action, depending on the success in the anticipation of market demand.

That implies deciding what employment, management, and coordination must be given to the different resources available in the market—either physical, intangible, organizational, human, or financial—to provide a product or service after a time period that could be valuable in the market at a price that would compensate the anticipated costs.

The possible entrepreneurial profit is not the reward to the shareholders in pure theoretical economic terms. Entrepreneurial profits or losses are signals and bits of knowledge enabling the coordination of the economic process.

The *entrepreneur*—in a pure sense without any capital ownership—is primarily a discoverer of opportunities in a system characterized by a scarcity of resources and information, the spread of knowledge, and the diversity of market processes, which are continuously interrelated. Where others see risk, the *entrepreneur* perceives the profit opportunity, advancing resources to satisfy the uncovered consumers' needs.

The *entrepreneurial function* can be personalized from the aforementioned analytical point of view, while at the same time, it can be delegated formally in terms of leadership competencies by the CEO in their own managerial organization.

To better analyze the *entrepreneurial function*—as we already said—we propose in our synthetic graphical model to differentiate it from the company's resources ownership, defining the *corporate function* that integrates the aspects related to them.

The ownership (*corporate function*) in the wide sense can include institutional investors such as private equity funds, venture capital, listed equity, institutional investors, and a family or a single founder.

The shareholders that develop the *corporate function* at the same time exercise the *entrepreneurial function* in the context of the capital markets.

There is a relationship between the *entrepreneur* who exercises the function without ownership and the shareholders-owners who develop the *corporate function* in the capital markets through the firm's corporate governance institutions, namely the board of directors.

Not only is it proposed in our model to separate the *entrepreneurial function* from its relationship to the capital (corporate function), but also to the concept of entrepreneurship from the exercise of the firm's management and the effective business leadership role in its operative context (what we call the *managerial function*).

Performance in times of uncertainty is the essence of the entrepreneurial action in a process of continuous search for opportunities and the opening of new paths in the market processes. For that purpose, the *entrepreneur* needs to rely on the most qualified management resources, related to their specific business and objectives. Moreover, the management team should act in the most efficient possible way, applying the best managerial practices to achieve the business objectives.

The *entrepreneur* must ensure the legitimate interests of the ownership of the company, coordinating, planning, and managing the resources put at their disposition.

It is not the intention of this chapter to go into further detail about the *managerial function*, which constitutes the focus of academic research and insights of the practical management sciences of business administration and organization, as well the contributions of practitioners and academic specialists in different fields from strategy, general management, finance, business, and leadership development of systems and processes. Our model proposes an equilateral triangle to graphically make this relationship explicit and clear (Fig. 1).

Implications of the Proposed Model

In the first place, we highlight the importance of *entrepreneurial function* empowerment through the leadership competencies model as a structural element of business organization.

The more permeable entrepreneurship is to the firms' management organization, it will be more flexible, dynamic, and oriented to the seizing of market opportunities.

In the second place, the development of business corporations whose property is distributed proportionally in limited liability securities has sometimes led to confusion regarding the role of the *pure entrepreneur* with that of the capitalists or co-owners of the company and its managing director.

The *entrepreneurial function* is critical for the effective coordination of dispersed knowledge in an open, decentralized economic system, based on free monetary exchange, private property, and the division of labor. It is critical for economic calculation as well.

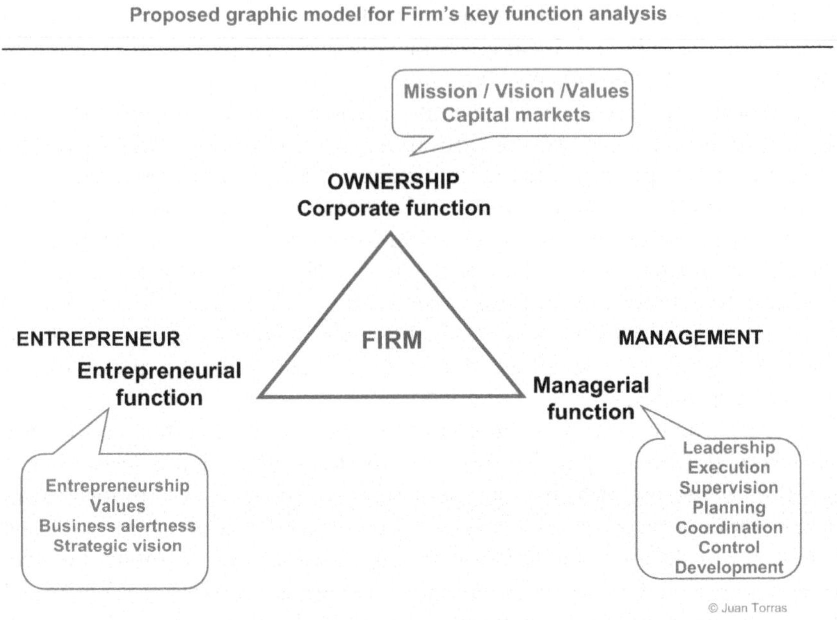

Fig. 1 Our graphical-analytical framework

These propositions have a significant impact on the development of the economic system, because firms—led by the exercise of the entrepreneurial function—can grow, providing effective value to the market. At the same time, it makes possible the economic calculation and the effective coordination of dispersed knowledge.

Finally, M&A transactions development, relying on high external financial leverages (LBO–MBO) that would be supported by the free cash-flow generated, has a consequence for the capital markets in terms of the interaction between the *entrepreneurial function*, the *corporate function*, and *managerial function*.

Our model can be used to explain to CEOs and chairmen or founders, for example, during the executive search of a new CEO or CEO during succession planning.

The Entrepreneurial Function and the Family Business

In many small- and medium-sized companies, usually with a family ownership structure, it is easier to identify the *entrepreneur*. Although, in some cases the same person usually integrates the three functions: the *entrepreneurship*, the *majority owner*, as well as the managing director, who in many cases is the only element that exercises the *managerial function* ("*owner-operator*" model).

Unsurprisingly, there is a family origin in the ownership as well as in the exercising of the managerial function in most companies. In the first place, the family constitutes a source of the initial capital funds. The entrepreneur who founds a company, relies primarily—as source of initial capital—on his savings and that of his family or friends. The family's net-worth then has its own origin in the exercising of the *entrepreneurial function* by some members of the family, what is known as the first generation of the family firm.

However, at the same time, the family can provide management resources, who without entering into their qualifications, will be trustworthy, protecting the exercise of the *entrepreneurial function* and looking out for the interests of the *corporate function*.

The development and growth of family businesses requires a satisfactory response to the professional development needs of the *managerial function*, if there is a real desire for the consolidation of the entrepreneurial organization in a competitive environment.

It also creates obligations for new approaches to the *corporate function* that involves a greater diversification of family net-worth and considers the incorporation of capital outside of ownership, which guarantees long-term financial stability, whether it be through the acquisition of resources in the stock market, or by opening up to institutional investors.

Lastly, an usual case in family firms is the succession of the founder, CEO and at the same time the "*entrepreneur*." In those processes, it is important to ensure that the *entrepreneurial function* will be properly covered—regardless of if the successor is a member of the family, a promoted professional or someone coming in from the external market. In any case it is a recommended practice to reinforce the corporate governance, namely the Board of Directors and disseminate the *entrepreneurial function* throughout the management team structure, delegating and empowering through a leadership competencies model.

I am not going to enter into details about the implications of these three levels of the family business development. The objective has been to exemplify the value of the analytical model which differentiates: *the entrepreneurial function*, the *corporate function* linked to the *ownership*, and the *managerial function* related to the operative management.

Conclusion

In all business organizations it is possible to identify who is ultimately responsible for the exercise of the *entrepreneurial function* either as a specific person ("founder" or CEO), an institution (board of directors) or a combination of them both, related to the following aspects: definition of objectives, vision and corporate strategies aligned with the mission, and the vision and objectives aligned with ownership; alertness to new non-explicit market opportunities; the exercise of business leadership and the opening of new avenues; the selection and coordination of resources, including management, ensuring their adequacy in line with the objectives assumed and the market conditions; a dynamic interaction with the management organization; and an interaction with the ownership of the company usually through the Board of Directors.

Since we have already highlighted a proactive, dynamic, market-oriented business organization, in order to take best advantage of market opportunities for profit, it is recommended for this purpose to disseminate the *entrepreneurial function* into the management organization. For this purpose, an empowered management leadership model—aligned with the corporate objectives—and a firm's market-orientation culture will have a direct impact on its performance and on the development of its human capabilities.

References

Blanco, X. R., & Salgado, J. (2015). *Amancio Ortega de cero a Zara*. Esfera de los Libros.

Cantillon, R. (1755). *Essai sur la nature du commerce en general.*

Casabella, F. (2021). *Bichos Rojos en Navidad*. Circulo Rojo.

Coase, R. (1937). *The Theory of the Firm.*

Demsetz, H. (1983). *The Structure of Ownership and the Theory of the Firm.*

Demsetz, H., & Villalonga, B. (2001). *Ownership Structure and Corporate Performance.*

Gross, D. (2010). *Forbes Greatest Business Stories of All Time*. Wiley.
Kirby, D. (2003). *Entrepreneurship*. McGraw-Hill Education-Europe.
Kirzner, I. (1973). *Competition and Entrepreneurship*. University of Chicago Press.
Knight, F. (1921). *Risk, Uncertainty and Profit*.
Ricardo, D. (1817). *Principles of Economic Theory*.
Rosell, J., Trigo, J., & Torras, J. (1985–2011). *Crear 80.000 Empresarios*. Plaza & Janes.
Salerno, J. T. (2008). The Entrepreneur Real and Imagined. *Quarterly Journal of Austrian Economics, 11*, 188–207.
Say, J. B. (1803). *Treatise on Political Economy*.
Schumpeter, J. (1942). *Capitalism, Socialism and Democracy* (2nd ed.). Martino Fine Books.
Smith, A. (1776). *Wealth of Nations*.
Stuart Mill, J. (1948). *Principles of Political Economy*. Prometheus Books.

Well Rooted Lessons, Odd Offshoots, and the Realization that the Fruit Has Not Fallen Far from the Tree

Leonidas Zelmanovitz

One may say that, as an "institution builder," Huerta de Soto created the Spanish branch of the Austrian School of Economics, a school of thought with now dozens of academics and practitioners all around the globe advancing our knowledge of economics, and having his unique perspectives as their departing point.

As many of his students would say, tongue in cheek, I consider myself, in that way, another one of Jesús' "disciples," spreading a message inspired

Professor Huerta de Soto, who was presiding my dissertation committee, finally closed the comments of the committee on my presentation. He was not happy. Apparently, I had failed to understand everything he tried to teach me over the years. I answered the comments the best I could and left the room saying to myself good-bye to the chance of ever becoming a doctor. When I returned to be informed of the committee's decision on my grade, I was surprised to know that not only had I not failed, but that they also granted

L. Zelmanovitz (✉)
Liberty Fund, Indianapolis, IN, USA
e-mail: lzelmanovitz@libertyfund.org

D. Howden, P. Bagus (eds.), *The Emergence of a Tradition: Essays in Honor of Jesús Huerta de Soto, Volume I*,
https://doi.org/10.1007/978-3-031-17414-8_28

by his teachings. More seriously, teachings, in his case, not aimed at achieving salvation, but aiming at the advancement of our knowledge about the economic order best suited for a free society.

As demonstrated with the anecdote about his verbal onslaught at the end of my doctoral presentation, and the gracious way in which he presided over my grading and celebration, Huerta de Soto has deeply rooted scientific convictions and yet, he is not dogmatic or intransigent. On the contrary, he is inspirational and his teachings offer a solid cornerstone for further academic and professional developments by his students, as other testimonies along this volume demonstrate.

As we all know, one of his strongest convictions is about the deleterious effects of fractional reserve banking on the economy by inducing "Austrian" business cycles. To mitigate that, his proposal for a free banking institutional arrangement with a 100% reserve requirement offers an ideal type background against which existing or proposals for future arrangements may be evaluated (Huerta de Soto, 2006, p. 715).

Another of his most important intellectual contributions is surely his fleshing out of the theory of dynamic efficiency (Huerta de Soto, 2009). There are many insights to be drawn from that exposition of the theory, no need to go there for this readership. For the purposes of this article, I just would like to highlight what follows. Once the concept of static efficiency is deemed insufficient for the understanding of economic activity, and mismatches between inflationary credit creation and the availability of voluntary savings are perceived to be the result of the existing institutional settings, then, a more robust macroeconomics in general and a more fruitful theory of economic development in particular may be proposed (Huerta de Soto, 2009, p. 28).

Based on my dissertation, late in 2015, my book on the philosophy of money was released (Zelmanovitz, 2016). In spite of having only 446 pages, Huerta de Soto read it. So much so, that he honored me with a very kind presentation of its Spanish edition published by Unión Editorial as part of a collection that he is the editor (Zelmanovitz, 2018).

---

me the highest grade possible! We left the campus for a restaurant in the *Recoletos* neighborhood with the other members of the committee, Gabriel Calzada, my dissertation supervisor, joined by my family, his wife, Mrs. Sonsoles, and one of their daughters. We had a pleasant meal with Huerta de Soto presiding the table and delighting us with stories with varied degrees of seriousness, among them the one that he no longer reads books with less than five hundred pages, since those are for intellectual lightweights!

In the book, I argue that considering the main function money performs for human societies, that is, to facilitate the coordination of the many individual economic plans, the most important attribute the monetary system may possess is to provide, to the extent possible, money with a stable purchasing power.

So far so good. However, in any system in which the functions of medium of exchange and unit of account are performed by the same instrument, changes in the demand for the medium of exchange may only be matched automatically by the market if money is endogenous. In any case, there is no guarantee that part of the adjustment of supply and demand will not happen by changes in the price of liquidity (interest rates), but by changes in the purchasing power of the monetary unit. For those reasons, in the search for "ideal" monetary arrangements, I expressed (a) my skepticism with monetary systems that rely entirely on exogenous money, and (b) my sympathy for arrangements that would allow for the separation of monetary functions. No wonder Huerta de Soto considers my ideas "eclectic"...

I assume that for my professor, a redeeming aspect of my monetary musings is that I acknowledged that James Buchanan's argument about the anachronism of fractional reserve banking had convinced me.

One of the topics in my dissertation that led to some discussions with the committee was my treatment of the fiscal prevalence hypothesis. The thesis is simple, even in the most developed nations, in case of emergencies, the fiscal needs trump private property rights, and monetary prerogatives are just one more weapon in the armory of the nation state. Those are the reasons why we cannot hope to get rid of the prerogatives. The best last hope for liberty continues to be constraining abuses of political power, including of the monetary prerogatives, by constitutional rules. One can see why, on one hand, my professor would praise my effort to deal with "unavoidable practical implications" and, on the other hand, he would not be happy with my research.

Nonetheless, it was from my interest in the intersection between monetary and fiscal policy that my decision to start researching capital theory arose. At first glance, that seems odd, since these fields seem to be miles apart. But, you see, my approach was influenced by Huerta de Soto's insights about the effects of mismatches between real savings and investments (Huerta de Soto, 2006, p. 265). The reasoning valid for credit expansion by the banks is also valid for other forms of destruction and misrepresentation of real wealth, such as when financial resources are diverted from productive investment to pay for current expenses (and unproductive investments) by the state.

Eventually, my research on capital matured in my second book (Zelmanovitz, 2021). Again, my thesis is a simple one. In the book, I argue that there is no concept more difficult to understand in economics than that of capital. However, capital is central to economic reasoning, so we must understand it rightly. In order to use this concept, economists tend to identify capital either as "goods" or as "funds." The conception of capital as "goods" considers capital as a collection of heterogeneous things that enhance the productivity of human labor—anything from an ax to a web browser could qualify. The conception of capital as "funds" reduces everything simply to its precise monetary expression. Capital in this sense refers to all the funds accumulated in the past that are available for future production.

Both in current economic debates and in the history of economic thought, scholars usually categorize capital theories as fitting into either or both of those two models. But this is a mistake. Understanding capital correctly requires a much more nuanced understanding of what capital is, and what role it plays in economic life.

In order to understand the nature of capital, we must first consider property. Everything that exists in the world belongs either to someone or to no one. In other words, all the material and immaterial goods that exist in human societies either are represented by property claims of an individual or an entity, or are *res nullius*, "things with no owners." Capital goods, like all other goods, are also represented by property claims. This representational character is key to understanding what capital is. Some property claims are titles so liquid that they are "as good as money," such as bank deposits or shares in a money market fund. Others are not. Capital is not only capital goods, things, processes, and ideas that exist in the real world. The property claims that represent them are also a form of capital, even if they do not have a precise monetary expression.

We need a representational theory of capital (RTC) to move past this false dichotomy. Not only are capital goods represented by property titles, but also those titles form a continuum from the ones with low to high salability. Due to certain characteristics, some capital goods are much harder to sell than others are (say, ocean cargo ships versus trucks). However, even capital goods with the same characteristics may vary in salability depending on the kind of property title.

Considering capital either as the object of property claims (capital goods) or as the most liquid forms of their representation (funds of money) misses two important issues. The first of these is the concept of representation itself. The idea of representation allows us to overcome the fallacy of understanding capital either as things that exist in reality or as a social construct, but it accepts that it is both. The second error is to misunderstand the myriad forms in which capital may be represented, such as property deeds, shares in a partnership, bonds of a corporation, and so on.

Understanding capital rightly creates the possibility for greater economic well-being. The application of this more robust ontology that sees capital not only as "things" or "money" but also as property represented by all sorts of claims—not only the most liquid ones—will allow us to make better-informed decisions.

Let us consider an application of RTC and the monetary theorizing behind it, to some of the monetary innovations brought about by the development of new technologies such as cryptocurrencies. Let us put them in some context first. For more than three hundred years now, starting with the establishment of the Bank of England, the supply of monetary instruments in Western societies has been a partnership between the state, which supplies the monetary base, and financial intermediaries, traditionally, commercial banks. The banks do their part by creating claims on base money, be that the banknotes of old, checking accounts, or more recently, credit card balances. Therefore, it is nothing new that financial intermediaries, by giving credit, are supplying the market with privately created monetary instruments. It goes without saying that those instruments do not enjoy the same trust as the monetary base, be that metal coins in the past, or fiat money today, but still, they are accepted as money substitutes.

The question now is what has changed, if anything, with the recent monetary innovations. The development of cryptocurrencies has led to the creation of at least two different kinds of private digital monies, the volatile kind, such as *Bitcoin* and *Ether*, and the stable-coins, like *USDC*, *Tether*, or the not-yet-launched *Libra*, now called *Diem*. It has also led to the creation of Central Bank Digital Currencies (CBDCs).

The volatile kind of cryptocurrencies as tokens issued by private issuers is better compared to equity titles than to debt obligations, since they are not a claim redeemable in something else. Their value, whichever it is, is a consequence of the utility it provides, notably, as a means of payment for transactions that, for one reason or another, are not more easily liquidated by state currencies, such as transactions with illegal objects, for instance. Their scarcity is generated by their protocols and the costs in terms of real resources of running the network of computers responsible for keeping track of their block-chains in a decentralized way.

The stable-coins, given the fact that they are intended to be substitutes of state currencies tradable in digital spaces, resemble more clearly money substitutes created by regular financial intermediaries. The difference is that their issuers are not (mostly) subject to financial regulations yet. They essentially aim at being more efficient means of payment than their traditional financial competitors and in this way, gaining a share of the market until now served by commercial banks, credit card companies, foreign exchange brokers, and remittance companies.

The CBDCs, on the other hand, are clearly state money and as such, part of the monetary base. Their development is clearly a reaction to some of the private innovations mentioned above. For instance, the e-CNY, the digital currency of the Chinese central bank, ostensibly aims to be an instrument for co-operability between the platforms of Ant and Tencent and possibly an instrument to enhance competition among financial providers. Those fintech companies now dominate the services of digital payments in China and are increasing their share of other financial services through that. Even if we do not attribute more sinister motivations to the PBOC, their aim with the introduction of the digital yuan is to curb the creation of money substitutes by those (until recently) lightly regulated companies.

If we do attribute ulterior motivations to their initiative (and of other central banks as well), the idea of increasing the share of the monetary base in the total money supply comes first to mind. Until now, the private commercial banks have performed a useful service of helping the real economy to clear their transactions by using more convenient means of payment than the monetary base itself, be that substituting for coins in the past, or substituting for paper notes today. In the process of issuing monetary substitutes, the banks have, by proxy, also intermediated real savings and helped the efficient allocation of capital in the economy. The suppliers of cryptocurrencies and digital means of payment platforms like the ones in existence in China today have performed similar roles.

From that, we may conclude that as much as they use new technologies, as much as they are indeed innovations, so far, they have not substantially challenged the existing structure of financial markets. Granted, volatile cryptocurrencies, with their nature of equity and not of debt, are an innovation that have challenged some established assumptions about the nature of money, notably, Mises' regression theorem. However, even that is debatable, since Mises' reasoning may well be understood as an application of the subjective theory of value. That is, the "regression" explaining the value of a new monetary instrument is to the utility it provides to the money holders in general, and not the particular existence of a previous monetary instrument from which the new one evolved (for more on that, see Davidson and Block, 2015). If this interpretation is accepted, the utility provided by, say, avoiding capital controls in Argentina or hyperinflation in Venezuela is the explanation for the current value of those cryptocurrencies, in spite of the fact that they were created with no link to a previous money.

The CBDCs, however, have a potential to be more disruptive to current arrangements. By coupling the features of the monetary base with the easiness of a digital means of payment, it is possible, under certain arrangements, for them to reduce the endogenous supply of money substitutes, and with that, of private allocation of capital.

Even if the economic agents are to keep their accounts with existing financial institutions, if those institutions (or new fintechs for that matter) are forced, in real time, to transfer those funds to the central bank, those branches of government will hold all the liquidity in the economy. Even if the banks are allowed to give credit, they will need first to borrow funds from the central banks, and it will be extremely difficult, if not at all impossible, to avoid political allocation of credit, for example, being forced to give privileged conditions for "green investments."

To conclude, financial repression is an instrument of wealth destruction by the creation of "false rights" (in Rueff's terminology). Such destruction may be done by monetary inflation, inflationary credit expansion, or just by the allocation to less efficient uses of real savings as it would be the case with the centralization of savings in the hand of central banks in most if not all proposals of CBDCs.

I think that anyone familiar with Huerta de Soto *corpus* easily perceives how, in spite of being an odd offshoot, his lessons left deep roots in my thinking, and this particular fruit of my research has not fallen far from the tree which it came from.

References

Davidson, L., & Block, W. E. (2015). Bitcoin, the Regression Theorem, and the Emergence of a New Medium of Exchange. *The Quarterly Review of Austrian Economics, 18*(3), 311–338.

Huerta de Soto, J. (2006). *Money, Bank Credit, and Economic Cycles* (First English Edition). Ludwig von Mises Institute.

Huerta de Soto, J. (2009). *The Theory of Dynamic Efficiency*. Routledge.

Zelmanovitz, L. (2016). *The Ontology and Function of Money: The Philosophical Fundamentals of Monetary Institutions*. Lexington Books.

Zelmanovitz, L. (2018). *La Ontología y Función del Dinero: Los Fundamentos Filosóficos de las Instituciones Monetarias*. Nueva Biblioteca de la Libertad, 55. Union Editorial.

Zelmanovitz, L. (2021). *The Representational Theory of Capital: Property Rights and the Reification of Capital*. Lexington Books.

Index[1]

[1] Note: Page numbers followed by 'n' refer to notes.

D. Howden, P. Bagus (eds.), *The Emergence of a Tradition: Essays in Honor of Jesús Huerta de Soto, Volume I*,
https://doi.org/10.1007/978-3-031-17414-8

The manufacturer's authorised representative in the EU is Springer
Nature Customer Service Centre GmbH, Europaplatz 3, 69115 Heidelberg,
Germany. If you have any concerns regarding our products, please
contact ProductSafety@springernature.com

Printed and bound by CPI Group (UK) Ltd, Croydon, CR0 4YY
01/10/2026
02225908-0001